COLONIAL LIVES

Cassandra
L. Bales

COLONIAL LIVES
Documents on Latin American History, 1550–1850

EDITED BY

RICHARD BOYER
GEOFFREY SPURLING

New York   Oxford
OXFORD UNIVERSITY PRESS
2000

Oxford University Press

Oxford   New York

Athens   Auckland   Bangkok   Bogotá   Buenos Aires   Calcutta
Cape Town   Chennai   Dar es Salaam   Delhi   Florence   Hong Kong   Istanbul
Karachi   Kuala Lumpur   Madrid   Melbourne   Mexico City   Mumbai
Nairobi   Paris   São Paulo   Singapore   Taipei   Tokyo   Toronto   Warsaw

and associated companies in
Berlin   Ibadan

Library of Congress Cataloging-in-Publication Data
Colonial lives : documents on Latin American history, 1550–1850 /
edited by Richard Boyer, Geoffrey Spurling.
p.   cm.
Includes bibliographical references and index.
ISBN 0-19-512512-6 (paper). — ISBN 0-19-512511-8 (cloth)
1. Latin America—History—To 1830—Sources.   2. Latin America–
–History—1830–1898—Sources.   3. Spain—Colonies—America—History–
–Sources.   I. Boyer, Richard E.   II. Spurling, Geoffrey.
F1410.C725   2000
980.3'1—dc21   99-18180
                                                                                      CIP

Printing (last digit): 9 8 7

Printed in the United States of America
on acid-free paper

For our kids
Nicolas, Thomas, and Christophe Boyer
and
Nicolas Spurling

Contents

Maps and Figures

Acknowledgments

Coordinating the submissions of so many collaborators seemed, at times, like organizing and running a marathon. At the start we ran together, then we spread out along the course, facing hills and other obstacles in distinctive ways. A few colleagues had to drop out, others stopped to rest or walk for awhile. Without trying to keep track, we could not help but notice the pauses to get married, to publish books, to complete degrees, to have babies, to change jobs, to teach courses, and to sojourn in Latin America or Europe while consulting (what else?) archives. Eventually twenty-four of us crossed the finish line. Yet our sense of accomplishment was overshadowed by the news that Kim Hanger had died on March 9, 1999. Disheartened and saddened at losing a friend and colleague, we nevertheless take some small consolation that a portion of Kim's work will be available to readers of this volume. All of our collaborators put a great deal of energy into this project, and we thank them for their enthusiasm and good humor in answering uncounted E-mail messages from the editors.

Conversations with many colleagues encouraged us to pursue the project at the outset and as it progressed. We would like to thank in particular Lyman Johnson, Mark Burkholder, Bill Beezley, and Bill French. We are also especially grateful to Francis Dutra, who read the completed manuscript closely and made detailed comments and corrections.

At Simon Fraser University the multiple skills and high energy of Joan MacDonald helped us at every stage to keep track of people, paper, and persiflage. We would also like to thank Amber Pikula, Andy Jaques, and Peter Rogers, whose assistance was particularly important early in the process. Paul DeGrace made the maps, one from a sketch painstakingly drawn by Chris Archer just after he thought the editors would leave him alone for awhile.

It was a pleasure working with everyone at Oxford University Press in the preparation of this book. Gioia Stevens and Stacie Caminos provided encouragement and overall direction, while Christine D'Antonio helped us get over some steep hills as we neared the finish line.

We'd like to thank our families for enduring the *tonterías* and *tumultos* we inflicted on them. They reminded us that *Colonial Lives* was constantly intersecting with *our* lives. Thanks especially to Josette and Joanna for their patience and help throughout the project.

As editors, we enjoyed the conversations and consultations that were an integral part of putting this text together. We look forward to many more as *Colonial Lives* goes out to a wider circle of colleagues and students, whom we now invite to join us, and our collaborators, in discussing these documents.

Document Themes

African/Afro-Latin American Peoples
>   Abercrombie, Few, Hanger, Kraay, Landers, Lipsett-Rivera, Socolow, Spurling

Crime
>   Abercrombie, Boyer, Few, Hanger, Lipsett-Rivera, Restall, Spurling, Twinam, van Deusen

Cultural Contact/Ethnogenesis/Resistance
>   Borah, Few, Francis, Hanger, Horn, Landers, Nazzari, Penry, Powers, Restall, van Deusen

Economy and Work
>   Borah, Büschges, Horn, Kraay, Landers, Nazzari, Powers, Restall, Spurling

Environment
>   Powers

Ethnicity
>   Abercrombie, Borah, Büschges, Few, Francis, Horn, Nazzari, Penry, Powers, Restall, Twinam, van Deusen, Spurling

European-Mestizo Peoples
>   Abercrombie, Büschges, Few, Hanger, Landers, Lipsett-Rivera, Nazzari, Penry, Powers, Restall, Rivera, Schwaller, Spurling, Twinam, van Deusen

Family
>   Abercrombie, Büschges, Hanger, Kraay, Landers, Lipsett-Rivera, Nazzari, van Deusen

Gender
>   Abercrombie, Boyer, Büschges, Few, Hanger, Holler, Lipsett-Rivera, Nazzari, Restall, Rivera, Spurling, Twinam, van Deusen

Gossip and Communication
>   Abercrombie, Boyer, Few, Penry, Socolow, Spurling

Governance, Colonial
>   Archer and del Cid, Francis, Powers, Rivera, Schwaller

Sexuality

Abercrombie, Boyer, Few, Holler, Rivera, Restall, Spurling

Slavery

Kraay, Landers, Socolow, Spurling

Town Life

Abercrombie, Borah, Boyer, Büschges, Few, Hanger, Holler, Kraay, Landers, Lipsett-Rivera, Nazzari, Penry, Rivera

Violence

Abercrombie, Few, Lipsett-Rivera, Penry, Restall, Twinam, van Deusen

Witchcraft

Abercrombie, Few

Women

Abercrombie, Boyer, Büschges, Few, Hanger, Holler, Kraay, Lipsett-Rivera, Nazzari, Restall, Twinam, van Deusen

Document Genres

Civil Litigation
Borah, Büschges, Horn, Socolow, van Deusen

Confession Manual
Schwaller

Criminal Litigation
Abercrombie, Boyer, Hanger, Lipsett-Rivera, Restall, Spurling, Twinam

Dowry
Nazzari

Inquisition Trial
Few, Holler, Restall, Rivera

Inspection/Inquiry (*Visita*)
Francis

Letter
Penry, van Deusen

Manumission Suit
Landers

Town Council Records and Initiatives
Penry, Powers, Restall

Viceregal Report
Archer and del Cid

Will
Kraay, Nazzari

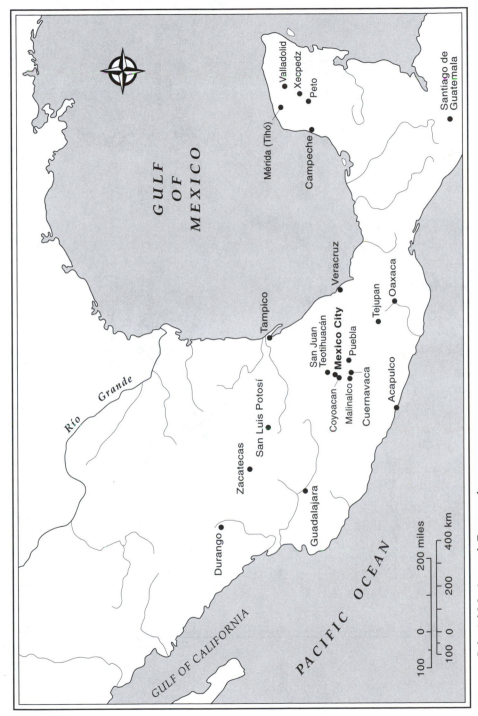

Map 1 Colonial Mexico and Guatemala.

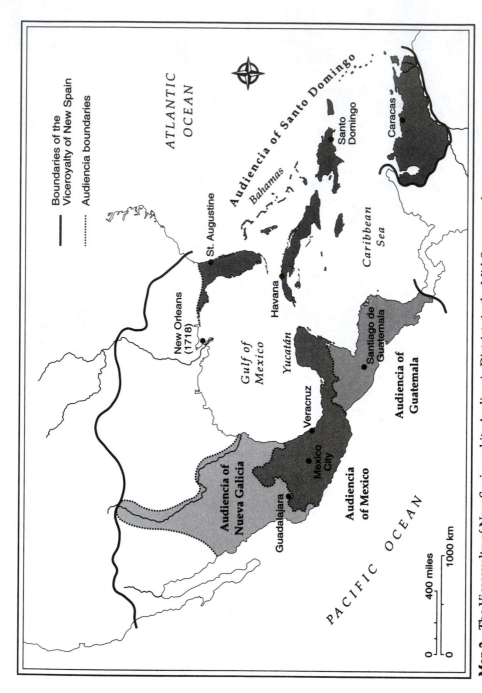

Map 2 The Viceroyalty of New Spain and its Audiencia Districts in the Mid-Seventeenth Century.

Map 3 Colonial South America.

Map 4 Viceroyalties, Audiencias, and Selected Brazilian Captaincies in Mid-Seventeenth-Century South America.

INTRODUCTION

Richard Boyer and Geoffrey Spurling

This book began with the almost daily conversations of two colleagues who share a common campus, similar intellectual interests, and often the same students. It evolved into a project when we decided to co-edit a collective work that would offer a new way of looking at, thinking about, and interpreting colonial Latin American history. The documents we and our contributors have assembled reflect a wide range of current research interests; none have been published in English before. Each is accompanied by an introduction and supplementary notes, providing enough context and commentary to allow you, the student reader, to engage in historical analysis.

We put together *Colonial Lives* for three reasons. First, we noticed that many of the surprising, provocative, and even mundane materials that historians currently work with are simply not available to you. As a result, you rarely get a chance to see how general statements are built up from primary materials, and seldom if ever do you see how particular documents may be read to question received wisdom or to add to it.

Second, we wanted to create ways for you to *do* history, not merely to read it. The analysis of these documents will involve you in the kind of critical reading—the drawing out and making sense of nuance, variation, and specificity of detail and situation—that is so essential to the historian's craft. This kind of interpretive reading will also give you the material and the skills to engage in a critical dialogue with textbooks, which must omit or subsume a good deal of detail in their synthetic summaries.

Third, we wished to expose you to the dramas of ordinary people who lived in the colonial era. These narratives are not only engaging in and of themselves; they also give vivid glimpses of the profound impact of economic, ecological, religious, and cultural processes. However important the abstractions that define political systems, social organization, and economic practice, we can perhaps best engage these broader generalities as they intersect with the lives of individuals. Thus, an apparently simple story of an insult, a seduction, or a homicide can tell us a great deal about the structures of colonial governance and the mentalities of people living in colonial societies. Such sources, then, "document" colonial life, and in so doing they bring into focus the complex dynamics of colonialism itself.

Colonial Lives does not have any of the standard primary documents that are often part of the reading syllabus in Latin American history courses. This collection contains no papal bulls, no diary entries from Columbus, no letters from Cortés, and no excerpts from the chronicles. Though interesting and important, you can already find such sources in most university libraries.[1] Instead, the documents assembled here—civil and criminal court cases, town council records and petitions, administrative and ecclesiastical investigations and decrees, Inquisition trials, wills, letters, and even the irreverent lyrics of a popular street dance—bring to life the concerns, perspectives, and struggles of a wide range of individuals. Indigenous peoples, Africans and Afro-Latin Americans, *mestizos,* and plebeian and noble Spaniards and Portuguese populate these documents. They are all present and they speak, however constrained their voices may have been by the settings and contexts within which they were recorded.

It is crucial to underscore that *Colonial Lives* is a collection of documents in translation,[2] and that all translations are interpretations. In fact all statements that say "X means Y" are interpretations. Each document in this volume, then, already carries in its apparent bedrock of raw material scores of interpretive decisions. These are usually hidden from view, but we have asked the contributors to make the process of translation, and thus of interpretation, as visible as possible.[3] You will see authors doing this in different ways and to different degrees, through their notes and through at least a sampling of their translation decisions. Many of them found the exercise of providing a complete, readable translation—one that underscored, rather than buried, the places where they did not know for sure what a passage meant—a novel and challenging process. We hope that you too will "translate" by assessing for yourselves what are more and what are less probable meanings in the documents. Sometimes you may disagree with the contributors, but then historians disagree with each other all the time. The many voices, meanings, and narratives that can be found in historical sources deserve multiple and distinct critical readings.

In interpreting these archival sources, it is important that you first try to understand the original intention of those who created and expressed themselves in the documents and the overt meanings they carry. Who created the document? Why? How? And when? All are simple but fundamental questions. It is equally important that you seize on the asides, the apparently subsidiary stories and vignettes, and the telling details that illuminate the fabric of everyday life. It is in the mention of a room's layout and furnishings, of a person's clothes, of an afternoon walk, of sleeping patterns, of private intimacies, of allegedly purloined meat stashed in a bed, of a turn of phrase that caused surprise or anger, or of satire and gossip in reported conversation that we catch revealing glimpses of the colonial world.

All of the documents in this collection begin with introductions by the historians who have worked with them in carrying out their research. The introductions place the documents in social and political context (by genre, time period, location, purpose, circumstances), but they do not include detailed analytical commentaries. That we leave to you. The notes that accompany the documents provide

Figure 1 A public scribe drafts a letter or petition for a woman in the Plaza Mayor of Mexico City (Linati [1828] 1956, plate 9).

further contextual information and comment on alternative meanings and difficulties in translation and interpretation. At the end of each chapter a brief list of readings points you to more fully developed analyses of the themes found in the document that you may want to consult to prepare an essay or to pursue a subject in more detail. The bibliography gives full citations to all sources referred to in the text. Finally, the glossary provides definitions of all non-English terms; in some cases there are multiple definitions of the same term if its usage varied or if it had a number of common meanings. Key terms in Spanish and Portuguese, or in an indigenous or African language, have purposefully been left in the documents to help you participate in their translation/interpretation, with the aid of the glossary (and often additional endnote commentary).

In working on their translations, the contributors have followed a set of conventions to give the documents a common look and to make them more readable.

They have dropped most of the "saids" and "aforesaids" that tend to clutter colonial manuscripts.[4] They have sometimes added a few words (always enclosed in square brackets) to clarify unclear referents in passages. They have added punctuation as it is largely absent (or is highly irregular) in the original documents, regularized the spelling (which can vary even within the same document), and shortened dates to a month-day-year format.[5] All document subheadings, numbered for ease of reference, have been added by the authors or the editors. In two chapters (Abercrombie and Borah) contributors more dramatically transformed their documents, shifting the testimony from the third person, as recorded in the original ("the witness said . . ."), to the first person ("I said . . .").

As is evident from the table of contents, the documents are arranged in chronological order. Two cross-referenced lists follow, one of themes, the other of document genres. You may want to use the themes and genres to structure the sequence of your readings and to group documents for specific analyses. In introductory courses, you will likely find *Colonial Lives* paired with a text that provides a comprehensive synthesis; at more senior levels, you might find the reader linked to monographs that focus more specifically on related themes.[6]

At first glance *Colonial Lives* may appear to be a selective and somewhat idiosyncratic grouping of documents. In a way it is, for we did not attempt to achieve encyclopedic coverage. Yet in another way it is not, for the collection reflects issues and themes of current interest to researchers, providing you with a sample of the kinds of material contemporary historians are working with. Moreover, the book's temporal and spatial sweep encompasses much of the diversity characteristic of colonial Latin America, covering more than three centuries and stretching from Florida and Louisiana in the north to São Paulo and Montevideo in the south.

We hope that the text's chapters convey some of the excitement, and even in some cases the sense of discovery, that all of us experience when working in archives. Of one thing we are confident—those of you who read this book will never think of colonial Latin America in quite the same way again. It will be difficult to read the decrees of administrative and ecclesiastical officials, the ponderous statements of colonial intellectuals, or the writings of early explorers and chroniclers without considering the intrigues, struggles, and ambivalencies that characterized their lives and those of the people who lived around them.

NOTES

1. See, for example, Benjamin Keen (ed.), *Latin American Civilization*, Third Edition, 2 vols. (Boston: Houghton Mifflin, 1974); Lewis Hanke and Jane M. Rausch (eds.), *People and Issues in Latin American History. The Colonial Experience—Sources and Interpretations* (New York: M. Wiener, 1993); Marvin Lunenfeld (ed.), *1492: Discovery, Invasion, Encounter—Sources and Interpretations* (Lexington: D.C. Heath and Co., 1991); and the extensive selection amassed in John H. Parry and Robert G. Keith (eds.), *New Iberian World: A Documentary History of the Discovery and Settlement of Latin America to the Early 17th Century*, 5 vols. (New York: Times Books, 1984). For a new, comprehensive reader that nicely combines primary sources and short analytical articles, and that makes very innovative use of visual materials, see Kenneth Mills and William Taylor (eds.), *Colonial Spanish America: A Documentary History* (Wilmington: Scholarly Resources, 1998).
2. In fact portions of them are translations of translations, as when a notary recorded a Spanish translation of testimony originally voiced in, for example, Nahuatl or Yucatec. And even

when the transposition was not from one language to another, typically the notary shifted the testimony into the third person when he wrote it down, sometimes summarizing the "sense" of another person's words, that is, what they "meant" to the notary, rather than recording them more directly.

3. Even the placement of a comma or a period, for example, or the substitution of a personal name for a pronoun when the referent is not clear, are interpretations. Contributors have commented in their endnotes—some more than others—when their intrusions were particularly problematic, or when the translation of a particular phrase or sentence was made even more difficult by vague or indecipherable wording, a tear or a blot on the manuscript, or the illegibility of the handwriting.

4. For example, the Spanish equivalent of "the said witness told the said judge that the aforesaid witness . . ." might be reduced to "the witness told the judge that the previous witness . . ."

5. For example, May 5, 1595, rather than "in five days of the month of May of one thousand five hundred and ninety-five years." Contributors have made other changes as well. The corrections (copying errors) that recording notaries typically listed at the end of each witness's testimony have not been translated, nor, for the most part, have the margin notes that mark document sections or that might flag important testimony for the eyes of a court official.

6. For a thorough and clearly written survey text, see Mark Burkholder and Lyman Johnson, *Colonial Latin America*, Third Edition (New York: Oxford University Press, 1998). For a list of monographs and articles that deal with themes directly connected to the issues raised in the documents, see the suggestions for further reading at the end of each chapter and the bibliography.

CHAPTER

1

The Indians of Tejupan Want
to Raise Silk on Their Own

(Oaxaca, Mexico, 1543)

Woodrow Borah

INTRODUCTION

To engage in a new industry in colonial Mexico required a viceregal license. This meant going to Mexico City, obtaining a formal audience with the viceroy, and receiving a viceregal order signed by the viceroy, and duly prepared and attested to by a court notary. The originals of the orders were given to the petitioners. The following document is the text that was entered in the central viceregal register (at this time the *ramo* of Mercedes, that is grants, in the Archivo General de la Nación, Mexico City). During the colonial period, as business grew, various sections of the grants archive were split off from the original one of Mercedes. But the form of the early orders is that of a petition and the viceroy's decision. Pertinent documents that had been submitted to the courts earlier were usually included in the body of the decision, which very often provides a review of the preceding history.

This document includes an earlier approval of a license granted in 1538 to three Marín brothers to raise silk in the town of Tejupan in the Mixteca Alta region of Mexico for five years.[1] The Indians of the town were to provide the labor and build the houses and appliances; the Marín brothers were to furnish the initial three pounds of silkworm eggs (*simiente de seda*), and direct the Indians who would thus learn the industry. At the end of five years, the Marín brothers would take the original capital of three pounds of silkworm eggs and withdraw from the town, leaving everything else to the Indians.

The initial license was granted with Indian approval. And although the document does not say why, an obvious benefit would have been that the fifth of the silk raised and spun would be used to meet the town's tribute assessment. In the 1530s and 1540s Tejupan had been required to pay tribute in gold dust obtained from the sand and gravel of streambeds by panning. But with deposits becoming exhausted, Tejupaneros were meeting their tribute payments with ever greater difficulty. Accordingly, both Indians and Spaniards were searching for a substitute for gold. The Mixteca region was too far from a Spanish center for easy marketing of foodstuffs or other items, but silk in hanks, ready for weaving, could easily be transported and find a ready market among the Spanish population, which was avid for luxury goods. The Indian towns, whether held by *encomenderos* or directly by the Crown, had a good supply of labor. Raising silk became the answer, and a silk boom was on.

The Dominican missionaries approved and helped spread the industry. Fray Toribio de Motolinía, one of the early Franciscan missionaries, has left us an enthusiastic account of the silk raising in the Mixteca area. In the year 1540 he spent a month traveling there and reported that, despite the short time since the industry had begun, it would produce more than fifteen or twenty thousand pounds of silk yarn. "The silk is so good that the masters claim that the *tonoci* is better than the *joyante* of Granada: the *joyante* of this New Spain is extremely good." In the Mixteca area silkworms could be raised throughout the year and "in quantity twice a year" as against the Spanish yield of one annual crop. Mexico City already had twenty looms for silk.[2] Through sale of the silk, towns could pay their tribute to the king, or to the local *encomendero* who had been granted the tribute in reward for services, and the Indians might hope for a surplus for themselves. Once they learned the industry, their only outside expenditure was for silkworm eggs, which initially had to be bought.

The document of 1543 came at the expiration of the five-year contract with the Marín brothers. The Indians of Tejupan, probably a delegation of elders, came to the viceroy to ask that the Marín brothers be given their three pounds of silkworm eggs and be required to leave the town, and that ownership of all the houses and implements made for silk raising and spinning the thread from the cocoons be transferred to the *pueblo*. The viceroy so orders and grants the town license to raise silk. The *corregidor* is to enforce the terms and, most revealingly, is ordered to reinstate the royal tribute as set forth in the prevailing assessment. Obviously, the assessment had been suspended during the five years of the contract with the Marín brothers, and replaced by the fifth of the silk produced that was paid to the royal treasury.

We have a certain amount of information about the subsequent history of silk raising by the town of Tejupan, because a part of the town records of silk raising and town expenditures survive for the years 1550–64, and were published as the *Códice Sierra* in 1933.[3] They were kept in Nahuatl and in pictographs. The town was then paying a tenth of the silk raised as tithe to the Church in addition to the royal tribute. During the years of the contract with the Marín brothers, the royal tribute was set at fifteen pesos of gold dust every twenty days. This amounted to 270 pesos of gold a year since the *nemontemi*, the five or six extra days of the solar year in the Nahua calendar considered ill-omened by the natives, apparently were not counted. Subsequently, as the population decreased the tribute was reduced by a third. On January 9, 1550, payment in gold dust was finally changed to delivery of silver *reales*, the normal money of the country. The tribute probably was paid from the beginning of silk raising in silver pesos and *reales*, but this order of 1550 formalized the type of payment. On October 7, 1564, after an inspection of the town by Gonzalo de las Casas, the son of Francisco de las Casas and the then *encomendero* of the neighboring town of Yanhuitlán, the *audiencia* assessed the town at the rate of ten silver pesos per tributary for a total of 1,567 and a half silver pesos. To meet the charge the town was to raise eight pounds of silkworm eggs, each pound usually yielding seventy-five or more pounds of silk thread. Whatever remained after paying the royal treasury was to be used for town expenses. The labor would be supplied by the townsfolk.[4]

Community raising of silk by the royal towns in the Mixteca Alta region characterized the economy of those towns until the opening of serious trade with China via the Manila Galleon. Because Chinese silk was cheaper and better than the Mixteca product, the price fell, and by the late 1580s or the 1590s the towns abandoned silk raising.[5]

THE DOCUMENT[6]

At the petition of the Indians of Tejupan that they do not wish to raise silk with the Marín [brothers].

1.1 The Marín Brothers' Petition of 1538

I, don Antonio de Mendoza, viceroy and governor, etc., make known to you Juan Núñez Sedeño, His Majesty's *corregidor* in the town of Tejupan, that on December 4, 1538, a contract was made before me between Juan Marín, Francisco Marín, and Hernando Marín [on the one hand], and the Indians of that town [on the other], to raise silk for five years in the said town as is stated in the contract, the tenor of which follows. Most Illustrious Lord, Juan Marín, Hernando Marín, and Francisco Marín[7] state that it has come to their attention that a town called Tejupan, held by His Majesty, which is in the province of the Mixteca, near Oaxaca, has the means to raise silk because there are many native mulberry trees,[8] and since we know how to raise silk, we beg Your Lordship to approve that for five years we may raise as much silk as we can. Of all the silk we shall raise in the five years, we shall give to His Majesty a fifth, raised, spun into thread and gathered into hanks. The Indians of the town shall build the houses and make other things needed, gather the leaves for the raising of the silkworms and the spinning of the thread during all the time that raising the silkworms and spinning the thread may take. At the end of the five years, we may take [only] the three pounds of silkworm eggs that at present we are making available to the enterprise for raising [silkworms] this first year. So His Majesty is well served since the Indians of the town will become trained in knowing how to raise and spin silk and [they will have] the things and apparatus made and agreed upon for doing so. The *vecinos* of the province will take up the industry.[9] From all of this His Majesty will be well served, the *vecinos* gain, and the natives will be spared worse labors and receive more profit, and thus Your Most Illustrious Lordship will do them good and show favor. [signed by] Juan Marín, Francisco Marín, and Hernando Marín.

In Mexico City on December 4, 1538, the Very Illustrious Lord Viceroy and Governor of this New Spain, having seen the petition presented before His Lordship by Juan Marín, Francisco Marín, and Hernando Marín, stated that in the name of His Majesty he accepts what they offer and ordered the officials of His Majesty to take from the above named the bonds and security that they might deem necessary for carrying out what the petition contains, and after the execution of the bonds, His Lordship ordered the carrying out of what was needed for the raising of the silk in conformity with this petition.[10] [signed by] Don Antonio de Mendoza. By command of His Lordship, Francisco de Lucena.

1.2 The Indians of Tejupan Petition to Raise Silk on Their Own

And now the Indians of that town appeared before me and reported that the time of the contract was finished and that they wished to raise silk on their own for the profit and usefulness that [the industry would] bring them. They asked me to order that they be given a license enabling them to raise silk[11] and that neither the above persons nor any others place obstacles in their way, and that after freely taking the three pounds of silkworm eggs that in accordance with the contract they are to take, all the remaining silkworm eggs and houses and other instruments and apparatus [be left] since they were theirs and made by them for the said purpose. Having reviewed [the case], because the time of the contract has expired and the Indians have declared they are not willing to continue it and wish to raise silk by themselves, I issue this order in accordance with the petition commanding you as soon as you have been shown the order that you provide and order that when Juan Marín, Francisco Marín, and Hernando Marín take merely the three pounds of silkworm eggs, the remainder and all the other things and apparatus made for the purpose [of silk raising] and the houses and huts that were built, to remain with the Indians of that town of Tejupan. You are to allow them and permit them to raise silk and not stop them nor allow any obstacle whatever nor that Juan Marin, Francisco Marín, and Hernando Marín raise silk in the said town since the contract and agreement made with the Indians of the town has expired. You are to take care to collect the tributes in which the natives of the town are assessed, in accordance with the assessment. Dated June 7, 1543.[12] [signed by] Don Antonio de Mendoza/Antonio de Turcios.

NOTES

1. The Mixteca Alta is in northern Oaxaca. Lying on Mexico's central plateau at an elevation of 3,000 to 6,000 feet, the Mixteca has a cool, dry climate. The only work in English on silk in colonial Mexico is Woodrow Borah, *Silk Raising in Colonial Mexico* (Ibero-Americana: 20, Berkeley and Los Angeles, University of California Press, 1943). Information that has come to light since its publication mainly concerns town enterprises, of which that of Tejupan was one. The *Códice Sierra* (ed. Nicolás León; Mexico City: Museo Nacional de Arqueología, Historia y Etnografía, 1933) is noteworthy for its pictographs of silk raising and its detailing of Tejupan expenditures. Its publication was in preparation for so long a time because of economic crisis, the Mexican Revolution, and the death of Dr. León.
2. *Memoriales de Fray Toribio de Motolinía, manuscrito de la colección del Señor Don Joaquin García Icazbalceta. Publícalo por primera vez su hijo Luis García Pimentel* (Mexico City, Paris, Madrid, 1903), pp. 10–11. Editors' note: *Tonoci*, in Motolinía's apposition, may refer to an "ordinary" grade of silk that masters were judging better than the coveted "bright" silk of Granada, or possibly it was a good grade of silk, New Spain's equivalent of "bright" silk, that suppos-

edly was better. Unfortunately Motolinía did not continue with his comparison by noting how New Spain *joyante* compared with *joyante* produced in Granada.

3. See note 1.

4. The history of tribute assessments for the town of Tejupan, probably from about 1529 to October 7, 1564 is recorded in *El libro de las tasaciones de pueblos de la Nueva España. Siglo XVI* (Mexico City, Archivo General de la Nación, 1952), pp. 467–68. Under the prevailing legislation of the Catholic Kings of 1497, the gold peso of 22 $^1/_2$ carats fineness was worth 450 *maravedís*, or twenty *maravedís* a carat. Accordingly, the order of the *audiencia* allowing equivalent payment that the peso of gold dust of nineteen carats fineness was worth 380 *maravedís*, and the tribute of Tejupan of 270 pesos of gold dust could be paid in silver pesos of 272 *maravedís* at 377 pesos, 1 *real*, 8 *granos*. (I thank Dr. Engel Sluiter for this information.) The common money of New Spain ran 12 *granos* = 1 *real*, 8 *reales* = 1 silver peso. The general revision of tribute in 1564 came as part of the reform of the 1550s and 1560s abolishing many exemptions and introducing uniform rates. It vastly increased the burden on the Indian towns.

5. See Borah, *Silk Raising*, pp. 89–91, especially the table of prices on p. 91.

6. AGN Mercedes, Volume 2, fol. 89v–90v.

7. The Marín brothers were from Murcia, a province of Spain well known for its silk.

8. The mulberry trees were native to the region and furnished a coarser leaf than the European mulberry, but they could be used for silk raising.

9. The role of the viceroy is obscure. He may well have sought out the Marín brothers in order to start a silk industry. We know, for example, that he was trying to do so in the neighboring area of Puebla. Note the statement on the *vecinos* of the province.

10. The original petition must have been couched in the first person, but in accordance with notarial custom has been rewritten to third person. In this translation I have changed it back to the first person.

11. A viceregal license was required to raise silk because it was a new rather than a native industry. The latter under the Spanish regime required no special license. The terms of the order bar the *corregidor* and his successors from interfering, as well.

12. The town is returned to paying tribute according to its previous assessment. The date of the document might be mistaken for the date of the tribute assessment since there is no punctuation, but the list of assessments in the *Libro de tasaciones* (pp. 467–68) does not have any for 1543. On the other hand, the date occurs in the customary place for a document.

DOCUMENT THEMES

Cultural Contact/Ethnogenesis/Resistance; Economy and Work; Ethnicity; Governance, Indigenous; Indigenous Peoples; Town Life.

SUGGESTIONS FOR FURTHER READING

Borah 1943.
Códice Sierra 1933.

CHAPTER

2

Land Concentration and Environmental Degradation: Town Council Records on Deforestation in Uyumbicho
(Quito, 1553–96)

Karen Vieira Powers

INTRODUCTION

Located within the Viceroyalty of Peru, the Audiencia of Quito formed an administrative unit consisting of the territory that is today known as Ecuador, although it stretched slightly farther north into southern Colombia and encompassed a larger portion of the Amazon basin than Ecuador does currently. Although the *audiencia* included tropical areas on both the Pacific Ocean and in the Amazon basin, the majority of its indigenous population inhabited its high intermontane valleys and the subtropical slopes of the eastern and western cordilleras. The area's inhabitants derived their subsistence from a vertical economy in which they were able to benefit from a variety of crops and extract a number of items not available in their highland, nuclear communities. At times they established colonies in various ecological zones, up and down the mountain slopes, both toward the coast and toward the Amazon; at others, the desired commodities were obtained through barter with lowland peoples. This required the constant movement and/or extraterritorial residence of large numbers of native peoples. Thus, dispersed settlement patterns and migration were highly characteristic of the pre-Hispanic societies of Quito. In addition, the Inka invasion of the area just decades before the Spanish arrival caused displacement of Quito's native peoples, as some fled their highland communities to live in lowland refuges or were assigned by the Inka to colonies outside their communities of origin. As we shall see later, Spanish colonization exacerbated these displacements and set in motion a number of additional population movements.

Both the *audiencia*'s remote location from Lima, the viceregal capital, and its relative lack of precious minerals made Quito a backwater of empire during the Spanish colonial regime. This meant that Spanish colonists residing in the *audiencia* maintained considerable de facto autonomy, especially in the first half of the sixteenth century, since the *audiencia* itself was not officially established until 1563. One result of the colonists' independence was Spanish monopolization of the best lands. From the time of the Spanish invasion in 1534 until at least the end of the sixteenth cen-

tury, the area surrounding the capital city, San Francisco del Quito, experienced serious land conflicts that led to a major migration of indigenous peoples. In the early
years of the colony the Quito *cabildo* (municipal council) had granted so much land
to the first Spanish *vecinos* that by 1578 the city and towns in the district were completely hemmed in by privately held lands. Since most of these concessions were
made to the municipality's own officers, their descendants monopolized extensive
tracts of land to everyone else's detriment. Consequently, throughout the sixteenth
century both Spaniards and Andeans were forced to encroach on *ejidos* (common
pasturelands) and forests, building houses, planting crops, and raising livestock.

Land-grabbing by early Spanish *vecinos* was facilitated by the temporary absence of displaced Andeans. In the early years of the colony, many indigenous
peoples migrated away from Spanish-occupied territory (mainly in the fertile intermontane basins) and took up temporary residence in subtropical and lowland
areas. As the Spanish invasion expanded to include those areas, however, many
Andeans returned to their nuclear communities in the highlands. In addition, the
sixteenth century also saw a type of migration known as *forasterismo*,[1] in which
many people migrated away from their communities of origin to avoid tribute
and forced labor; their destinations were usually other indigenous communities
where *caciques* managed to hide the *forasteros* from Spanish census takers, assigning them lands and using them as an alternative labor supply. Later, in the
1570s, the Spanish regime embarked on a systematic relocation scheme in which
indigenous peoples were aggregated into Spanish-style towns in order to facilitate tribute collection, labor appropriation, and Christian conversion. This policy,
known as *reducción*, exacerbated the practice of *forasterismo*—that is, out-
migration to avoid state exactions. In sum, returning migrants and the in-
migration of *forasteros* from other areas, combined with the Spanish grantees' monopoly of resources, produced an agrarian crisis, especially in the environs of the
city of Quito. Erosion caused by introduced European livestock (sheep, cattle, etc.)
and further encroachment pushed Andeans on to marginal lands. In 1598, for example, the bishop of Quito, fray Luis López de Solis, commented that land seizure
in some areas had extended to "the doors of the Indians' houses."[2]

By the year 1551, as Spanish migration to the *audiencia* increased, access to
other natural resources, like water and pasturelands, were diminished as well,
and the Indians had already been squeezed out on to the timberlands. The case
of Uyumbicho, a highland Andean community four leagues (about twelve miles)
from the city of Quito, illustrates the pressure on natural resources. The land
squeeze experienced by its inhabitants, and the Spaniards' exasperation over deforestation, are clearly and passionately outlined below in the records of the city
of Quito's *cabildo* sessions, spanning a period of forty-three years. In the process
of selecting and editing these records, I have limited my presentation here to the
cabildo's discussion of the town of Uyumbicho and the problem of deforestation.[3]

THE DOCUMENTS

*[Records related to the inspection and boundary-marking of Uyumbicho's forestlands by
the cabildo of the city of Quito, 1553–96]*[4]

Indians pushed into forested areas b/c Spanish taking over land

2.1 June 23, 1553: The Cabildo of the City of Quito Orders an Investigation into Deforestation in Uyumbicho

I, Diego Méndez, royal scribe of the city of San Francisco del Quito, certify that in this city on Friday, June 23, 1553, the following *cabildo* members met in session: Señor Antonio de Osnayo, *corregidor* and *justicia mayor* of this city, and señores Juan de Padilla, *alcalde ordinario*, and Rodrigo Núñez de Bonilla, Pedro Martín Montanero, Antonio de Rivera, Diego Sandoval, and Francisco de Olmos, *regidores* of this city. These officers stated that cutting timber in the forests of Uyumbicho is causing great harm to this city because everything is being chopped down in a disorderly manner. They agreed that the *alcalde*, Rodrigo de Salazar,[5] and the *regidores*, Francisco de Olmos and Diego de Sandoval, should visit the woodlands to inspect the areas that have been cleared and that the latter should report their findings to the *cabildo* so that its members could decide what needs to be done.

2.2 July 7 and 9, 1553: Inspection of the Forestlands of Uyumbicho by the Cabildo

Members of the *cabildo* were sent by the *corregidor* to inspect the forested slopes of Uyumbicho and to prepare an eyewitness account. Upon arrival, they found huge, newly established farms, the forest slashed, and the mountainside burning . . . a problem they feel needs to be remedied immediately. It is imperative that a solution be found to end this destruction because these timberlands are essential to the welfare of the entire city of Quito. To this end, the *cabildo* ordered that the Indian peasants be forcibly evicted from the forest, their houses burned, and their crops confiscated. If they return they are to be given a public whipping of one hundred lashes.

2.3 February 15, 1563: The Cabildo Imposes Fines

Because there are no monetary fines imposed on the Indians who are chopping down the trees in Uyumbicho, they continue to be the ones who are most responsible for the forest's destruction. To remedy this problem, we order that any Indian caught cutting wood in Uyumbicho, which is four leagues [twelve miles] from this city, have his tools confiscated along with the poncho he is wearing . . . both of which will be given to the person who reports him.

2.4 March 13, 1596: Inspection of the Timberlands of Uyumbicho by the Cabildo[6]

Having come to inspect the forested slopes of Uyumbicho on the outskirts of the city of Quito, we found houses, huts, and corrals where some Indians called the Chuachungos live.[7] They have established farms for cultivating corn. These Indians ordinarily live here on the slopes instead of in their towns, and in this way they escape indoctrination in the Holy Catholic Faith.[8] They are also destroying

Figure 2 A *cabildo* notary (scribe) receives money from an Andean man in payment for legal services (Guaman Poma de Ayala [1615] 1980, f. 521).

the timberlands, and in order to preserve the latter, we order that these Indians leave these lands and return to Panzaleo, the town in which they were resettled.[9]

2.5 March 14, 1596: Testimony of Martín Pérez de Recalde, Spanish Resident of Uyumbicho

I have witnessed that the Indians who have been resettled in this town of Uyumbicho have established numerous agricultural fields on the slopes near the town, and they have cut down and destroyed large expanses of forestland.[10] This is damaging to the woodlands and dangerous to the Indians' own livelihood, since these lands contain firewood as well as construction timber. I have also seen that large numbers of cattle have been introduced into the forestlands by Indians and Spaniards alike, which is very prejudicial not only to the forests, but to the Indians' crops as well. Both the farms and the cattle have destroyed the mountainous slopes as well as any new growth that tries to get established. The only lands I can suggest assigning to these Indians, however, are lands near Panzaleo on slopes that have already been deforested.

2.6 March 14, 1596: Testimony of Friar Joan de Paz, Priest of Uyumbicho

The Indians who are settled in this town of Uyumbicho have established many small farms on the surrounding timberlands where they plant their crops. They use the forest because they do not have sufficient lands for subsistence. Also, because they raise crops on forestlands they can only plant for two years, at which point they make another clearing; all of this is very damaging.[11] They have occupied all the slopes of the mountain, which descends to the town, and the forest, which proceeds toward Panzaleo. They also have large herds of cattle that roam around in the woodlands doing great damage to the Indians' own farms as well as to the forested slopes. The Indians themselves would like to remove their cattle from this area because of the damage they do to the crops, but there is nowhere to take them. I do not know where lands might be found for these Indians, since there are no lands available in the vicinity of the town.

2.7 March 14, 1596: Testimony of Captain Alonso de Cabrera, Lieutenant Corregidor of Quito

I have witnessed that the Indians who have settled in this town of Uyumbicho have established numerous farms on the mountain slopes . . . and each day they destroy more forests in order to put land under cultivation. I have also seen that large herds of cattle belonging to both Indians and Spaniards are grazing freely in the woodlands, which is deforesting and destroying the mountainsides. Everyday more and more forestland is consumed. I have also noticed that the population of Indian *forasteros* from Latacunga, Siccho, Puruaes,[12] and other regions is growing daily, and that they are settling on the wooded slopes and establishing agricultural fields there.

2.8 March 14, 1596: Testimony of Don Francisco de la Vega Zumba, Cacique of Uyumbicho

I have seen that there are many agricultural fields on the mountainous slopes that have been established both by the Indians of the town and by Indian *forasteros*, as well as large numbers of cattle, and the combination of these is very damaging to the forests because the Indians continually cut down trees and destroy the land. And so that the woodlands will be conserved, it will be necessary to forbid cultivation there and to remove the cattle. I also have cattle there. And so it will be necessary to assign new lands to the town's inhabitants . . . and to evict the Indian *forasteros* and *advenedizos*.

2.9 March 14, 1596: Decision of the Cabildo Regarding the Deforestation of Uyumbicho

After receiving the above testimony, the *corregidor*, don Francisco de Mendoza Manrique, and the members of the *cabildo* of Quito met to discuss the damage that the introduction of agriculture and livestock had done to the forested slopes of Uyumbicho. And after deliberation, they ordered that, for the conservation of the timberlands and for the well-being of all concerned, the Indians of Uyumbicho, the Indian *forasteros*, and the Spaniards of the vicinity be barred from cultivating crops or raising livestock on the forested slopes surrounding the town. And so that this would be enforced inviolably, they vowed to assign new lands to the Indians on which they would be permitted to grow crops and raise cattle. To this end, they ordered an inspection of the lands in the vicinity of the town and vowed to reassign some of them, even if they had to assign them other forestlands.

2.10 March 15, 1596: Land Assignment Made by the Cabildo to the Indians of Uyumbicho

We declare that the Indians of Uyumbicho be assigned the following lands: an island of land that is bordered on one side by the supply station (*tambo*)[13] on the main highway, on another by the entrance to the forest, on another by a swamp, and on the last side by a gorge; another island of land that is bordered by a brook, a gorge, the foot of a steep mountain, and don Francisco de la Vega Zumba's farm; the outer ridges of the mountain that looks down on the town; the high *puna* surrounding the town. This land should be measured and distributed to each tribute-paying Indian. And we demand that from here on the *caciques* and Indians of Uyumbicho cease cultivating and raising livestock in the timberlands under penalty of removal from office and perpetual exile to the city of Guayaquil for *caciques*, and one hundred lashes and exile from the town for common Indians.[14]

NOTES

1. From *forastero*, an Andean who had abandoned his/her community of origin.
2. Archivo General de Indias (AGI) Quito 76, doc. 51, Carta de Fray Luis López de Solis, Obispo de Quito, 1598.
3. Parts of this introduction have appeared earlier in Karen Vieira Powers's *Andean Journeys: Migration, Ethnogenesis, and the State in Colonial Quito* (Albuquerque: University of New Mexico Press, 1995), p. 40.

4. Excerpts derived from the *cabildo* sessions of the city of San Francisco del Quito, recorded in *Libro Segundo de Cabildos de Quito* (Quito: Archivo Municipal, 1934), pp. 342–57.

5. There is no explanation in the documentation for Salazar's earlier omission from the list of *cabildo* members who met on June 23, 1553. It may be that he was absent and those present volunteered his services.

6. It is not clear why the Quito *cabildo* acted only intermittently in dealing with the problem of deforestation in Uyumbicho (if we can judge from the *cabildo* records, which show no discussion of the issue from 1553 to 1563, nor from 1563 to 1596, though Spanish and indigenous migration to the area continued to increase). In part, it may have been caused by the founding of the *audiencia* in 1563 and the resulting jurisdictional confusion. Before the establishment of the *audiencia*, the city of Quito had claimed jurisdiction over a much larger area than just the city proper and its immediate environs.

7. The Chuachungos were *mitimaes* (colonists with economic and/or military responsiblities) who had been transplanted from the southern Andes by the Inka and then resettled by the Spaniards in the *reducción* town of Panzaleo.

8. The concern here was that the Chuachungos had fled their resettlement town and were sabotaging one of the Spanish *reducción* policy's most important goals: Christian conversion.

9. Panzaleo was the Chuachungos' *reducción* town.

10. Here the original *cabildo* record was recorded in the first person.

11. Slash and burn agriculture was especially detrimental to the fragile environment of the high forested slopes. After only two years of planting, the soil was useless for further agricultural endeavors. This meant that the subsistence farmers using this area had to leave the land fallow and move on to another area to repeat the same injurious process.

12. Latacunga, Puruaes, and Sicchos were areas to the south of the Quito basin; the first two were intermontane valleys, while the latter was an area on the western slopes adjacent to Latacunga.

13. *Tambos* were supply stations and inns for travelers established along highways by the Inka and used by the Spanish regime.

14. I have not found any other documents regarding this matter. However, since they were relocated to other timberlands, and since indigenous in-migration to the Quito basin proceeded unabated throughout the seventeenth century, we can conjecture that the problem of deforestation was exacerbated.

DOCUMENT THEMES

Cultural Contact/Ethnogenesis/Resistance; Economy and Work; Environment; Ethnicity; European-Mestizo Peoples; Governance, Colonial; Indigenous Peoples; Land; Migration; Rural Life.

SUGGESTIONS FOR FURTHER READING

Alchon 1991.
Crosby 1972.
Dean 1995.
Melville 1994.
Powers 1995.
Salomon 1986.

CHAPTER

3

The Telling of Tales: A Spanish Priest and His Maya Parishioners

(Yucatán, 1573–90)

Matthew Restall

INTRODUCTION

In the late sixteenth century the Spanish colony of Yucatán, a province of the Viceroyalty of New Spain, was populated by a small group of settlers concentrated in one modest city, Mérida. These Europeans and their African slaves were outnumbered many times over by the indigenous Maya population, whose subjugation had taken more than three decades and who had only been "pacified" in this colonial corner of the peninsula since the mid-1540s. Yet by the 1570s, when the story below begins, the bureaucracy of colonial rule was sufficiently established for officers of the Inquisition in Mérida to initiate full investigatory proceedings against Andrés Mexía, a secular parish priest accused of various abuses and misdeeds.[1] The legal proceedings, eventually united into a single, lengthy case file, included three petitions written in Yucatec Maya by Maya notaries and authored by the ruling councils of half a dozen indigenous communities (documents 3.1 to 3.3), as well as witness testimony and defense arguments recorded in Spanish as part of the Inquisition's investigation (of which documents 3.4 and 3.5 are examples).[2]

The Maya World

The existence of texts like documents 3.1 to 3.3 reflects the rapid adoption by late sixteenth-century Maya communities of Spanish legal forms such as the Roman alphabet and Spanish document genres, enabling the Mayas to engage the colonial legal system in their own interests. These samples represent not only dozens of Maya-language petitions written in the colonial period to protest the deeds of individual Spaniards, priests, or officials, but also a larger body of thousands of documents recording the last wills and testaments, land transactions, political elections, and other legal business of Maya community members. This material offers us a window onto the Maya world in colonial Yucatán, revealing aspects of political activity, religious behavior, family interaction, economic endeavor, and cultural adaptation to colonial circumstances.

The focus and locus of most of Maya life during the colonial period was the self-governing municipal community, called a *cah* in Yucatec Maya. There were some two hundred *cahob* (plural of *cah*) in colonial Yucatán, all of which boasted their own ruling councils (*cabildos*) that included a notary empowered to write legal records such as those featured here—records that were by nature corporate products, authored and signed by the prominent Maya men of the *cabildo*.

These men represented not just the *cabildo* or the interests of its officers, but also the extended families that comprised the entire community; this structure of representation might serve the specific needs of the *cah* as a whole (as is apparently the case in document 3.1), of a dominant faction within the *cabildo* (as may be the case in document 3.2), or of a particular group within the community (as in document 3.3). Whatever the circumstances, written records reflected the centrality of the *cah* to Maya identity, as well as to political pursuits, economic subsistence, cultural persistence, and religious practice.

Priests and Parishioners

What was to the Mayas a *cah* was to the Spanish colonists a *pueblo* and a *visita*, a constituent element in the civil and ecclesiastical structure of provincial administration.[3] A collection of *visitas* made up a parish—one of which, at the southeast end of the colony of Yucatán, had as its late sixteenth-century pastor one Andrés Mexía (Mejía in modern orthography). Document 3.5 is one of several statements of defense made by this priest in response to various accusations levied against him by his Maya parishioners.

Mexía's parish included the six communities mentioned in the documents below (Oxtzucon, Tahdziu, Tetzal, Tixmeuac, Xecpedz, and Yalcon), as well as a number of others, all covering an area of well over one hundred square miles. The size of this jurisdiction was not unusual; judging from a letter of 1580 by fray Hernando de Sopuerta, the provincial (the Franciscan in charge of the province) to whom the petitioners appeal in document 3.3 below, there was an average of eight Maya communities in each parish.[4] This figure was higher in the *curatos* (curacies or secular parishes) and on the southern and eastern fringes of the colony, where a year might pass between a priest's visits. As a general rule, Spaniards preferred to live in the cities and towns they founded in the colonies, and priests were seldom the exception; making the rounds along scrub-forest paths must have been arduous work, especially in the high humidity of the Yucatec summer. Although Mexía refers in document 3.5 to "the *pueblo* where I most reside," it is clear from his case records that he primarily lived in the only Spanish city in the colony, Mérida.[5]

The documents presented below show that clerical absenteeism was a concern of the Mayas early in the colonial period. Although we are given no clues as to the meaning they ascribed to Spanish priestly ritual, Maya parishioners certainly appear to have valued it, denied as they were the public religious rituals of their prechristian past; just sixteen years before Mexía's arrest, in the brutal summer of 1562, the provincial fray Diego de Landa (who became bishop in the 1570s) had presided over the arrest and torture of over four thousand Mayas (two hundred to death) in a campaign against "idolatry." The Mayas seem to have had specific notions (albeit not fully articulated here) as to the exercise of Christian ritual, as well as expectations regarding the economic role and moral behavior of Spanish priests. In short, a priest who took (whether it be food, as in the first document, or liberties with local women, as in the third) more than he gave (in religious service and economic usefulness) aroused active resentment.[6]

As much as the Mexía case illuminates many aspects of life in late sixteenth-century Yucatán, it is but a single case that should not be taken as an indictment of the entire colonial clergy. To be sure, Mexía was not unique. The priestly abuse of the sacrament of confession, especially through sexual molestation (see documents 3.3 and 3.4), was something of a problem throughout the Catholic world and helped lead to the creation of the confessional box. Indeed the year before Mexía's 1578 arrest seven Franciscans in Yucatán petitioned the ecclesiastical authorities to ban confession from taking place in clergymen's houses or anywhere else other than a church. Furthermore, there are several dozen recorded cases of accusations against Spanish priests in Yucatán by colonists and Maya communities alike. About three-quarters of Spanish, and all Maya, complaints allege specific sacramental malpractices (almost all to do with mass, last rites, and confession); about a third of all cases include accusations of sexual solicitation of Spanish or Maya women or Maya boys, mostly through the contact of confession, and half of these also include allegations of improper relations between priests and their housekeepers.

Despite this evidence, and the fact that we cannot know how many other cases have not survived or were never reported, we must assume that in a colony such as Yucatán most priests carried out their duties most of the time in good faith, committing crimes no worse than those of mediocrity or modest participation in the colonial system of economic exploitation. For their part, the Mayas did their best to control or circumvent the Spanish monopoly on priesthood and sacramental performance, by campaigning for a priest's removal (see documents 3.1 and 3.3), by seeking to improve relations with a priest (see document 3.2), or by engaging in a variety of other (mostly legal) religious activities such as those of religious brotherhoods. In this sense, the Maya relationship to the colonial church was similar to the broader Maya-Spanish relationship, which was characterized by negotiation and adaptation under circumstances of fundamental inequality and occasional overt hostility. Not surprisingly, Spanish plaintiffs (usually individuals) fared better in the colonial judicial system than Mayas (usually communities), but *cahob* could prevail, even if (as in the Mexía case) it took the influence of a Spanish ally to win mere temporary relief.

A Priest's Story

Although the Mayas who sent complaints against Mexía to the provincial capital of Mérida provide fewer details than we might like, the Inquisition's investigation is lengthy and suggests just how the pastor went about offending his indigenous parishioners, particularly with respect to the sexual accusations of documents 3.3 and 3.4.[7] For example, it was Mexía's sexual abuse of a fifteen-year-old Maya girl in Mérida that first provoked inquisitorial attention. One Sunday early in May 1578 the girl, María May, went to the cathedral with two fifty-year-old Maya women who worked with her as maids for a local Spaniard. Seeking confession, the women encountered Andrés Mexía, who persuaded them to come to his house, where he took María into his bedroom and sat her on his bed beside him. She was halfway through her confession when Mexía "placed his hands upon her breasts," and while "fondling them" he commented on "how pretty she was and how firm and fine were her breasts" (which Mexía said appeared to be "full of milk," according to the version of the story told by María's two friends).[8] The priest also told the girl that he would give her absolution if she returned to his house on other occasions; she would only have to sweep his bedroom and she would be "well fed."

Unfortunately for Mexía, as soon as María left the room she burst into tears and proceeded to tell the story not only to her two friends but also to another Maya woman working in the priest's kitchen; her friends then persuaded her to expose Mexía to their master (*amo*), who denounced him to the bishop's office. Bishop Landa was shocked but probably not surprised; four years earlier he had removed Mexía from office after discovering that he had committed "a very grave crime" and "carnal sin" (in Landa's words) with a woman while confessing her, but the Archbishop in Mexico City had reinstated the pastor. Now Landa immediately and personally initiated an investigation, taking statements from María May and four other witnesses;[9] also notarized were complaints from two Spaniards of the *conquistador* families of Vela and Montejo, who testified not to the María May incident but to Mexía's suspicious behavior and scandalous character. By the end of the month (May 1578) Mexía was incarcerated in a room in the bishop's palace, his legs in irons.[10]

With characteristic zeal, and no doubt motivated in part by personal disappointment,[11] Landa waited until he had built a solid case against the licentious pastor before dispatching in July the file (or *proceso*) to the Tribunal of the Holy Office (the newly founded [1571] Inquisition) in Mexico City, where Mexía himself would be sent later that same month. Working with local Inquisition officials, including the dean of the cathedral, Landa's aim seems to have been to demonstrate a pattern of behavior in order to show that the pastor "was accustomed to committing similar excesses and crimes." He did not have to wait long.

Mexía had been under arrest only three days when Landa received word from a fellow Franciscan of a complaint made five years earlier against Mexía by two Maya women from Yalcon (a *cah* in the Valladolid area to the east), Catalina Hau and her mother, María Tui. Catalina's testimony (see document 3.4) detailed her rape by Mexía in the sacristy of the Yalcon church, a story largely substantiated by her mother and another Maya witness. The women had immediately complained to the *cah* governor (*batab*) and *cabildo*, who took the matter to Valladolid's colonial authorities; whereas Mayas such as María May, who lived as domestic servants in Mérida, depended upon the goodwill of their masters, women such as Catalina Hau, who were members of a *cah*, enjoyed the protection of the community authorities, who had access to the colonial legal system (also see document 3.3).

As Catalina Hau recounted (see document 3.4), just days after the Yalcon complaint was made in Valladolid, she was again raped by Mexía. When her mother (according to her mother's own testimony) protested that "she was appalled by such an indecent thing," the priest "whipped her two or three times with his horse's reins" and threatened to beat her again if she said a word to anyone. These were not idle words of violence between equals, but threats from a male colonial official against a subject female in a society structured by hierarchies of gender and race—and, moreover, threats from an official who had brutally demonstrated his ability to carry out his intentions with impunity.

Although Catalina Hau and her mother may have taken these threats seriously for a while, they cooperated with officials the following year, and again in July 1578 when Landa's investigators toured the parishes where Mexía had worked. Officials not only received confirmation of the Yalcon story, but found dozens of other Maya parishioners willing to testify to Mexía's predilection for sexual violence and his generally scandalous lifestyle. Thus, in addition to recompiling a collection of complaints from 1573 (including documents 3.1 and 3.4), Landa was able to gather extensive evidence that the official reprimand given Mexía that year had done little to alter his behavior. The resulting list of charges consisted of 110 individual items contributed by seventeen communities.

The charges clustered around four central allegations. First, in several *cahob*, Mexía lived with, and slept nightly in the same bed with, a mistress (*manceba*) who was a married woman, and he made no attempt to hide this fact. Second, he behaved in an openly licentious and sexually abusive manner toward his female parishioners, and was often physically abusive toward the councilmen of the *cabildo*. Third, he played cards a great deal more often than he performed his clerical duties, which was almost never. And fourth, he violated the moral economy of the *cah* (what the Mayas perceived as the norms and acceptable limits of economic relations) by demanding excess fees for the performance of sacraments such as marriage, by employing without pay dozens of men and women in each *cah* as his personal servants, by demanding large quantities of candles, maize, honey, fowl, and pigs as fee and tithe payments and grossly underpaying the men he obliged to transport the goods to Mérida, and by taking economic advantage of his position as a Spaniard and a priest in a dozen other ways.

It is significant that these economic matters were the focus of most of the complaints and accusations. Thus, while questions of sexual abuse occupy most of the pages of the seventeen-year series of investigations into Mexía, these offenses may not have been what primarily concerned the all-male community councils; Mexía's abuse of women may have been limited to sporadic and isolated incidents that, however horrific for those involved, lacked the broader impact of his systematic economic exploitation of his parishioners. However, Maya *cabildos* seem to have realized that sexual misconduct was the red flag that caught the attention of senior church officials, and while they were no doubt genuinely outraged by Mexía's sexual abuses, they may have made strategic use of such behavior in their campaign to rid themselves of a priest who took much in worldly goods and gave little in spiritual satisfaction.

One might imagine that in the summer of 1578 Landa was both pleased at having quickly amassed enough evidence to be rid of Mexía and dismayed by the degree to which the pastor had been living for years a life so far from the bishop's vision of clerical propriety. The charges were damning enough to justify sending the captive Mexía to Mexico City to face the Inquisition's judges, who interrogated him within a week of his arrival. The pastor protested his innocence and the conditions of his incarceration; his alleged mistresses were his maids, and his absenteeism was due to illness, aggravated by his treatment at the hands of Yucatán's Franciscans. Mexía's pleas bought him some time, and fate then bought him an even longer reprieve. Having moved the case along swiftly in his own province, Landa found that he had far less influence from afar. Then, shortly afterwards, Landa died, and, once again using his powerful connections in Mexico City,[12] Mexía succeeded in having his file closed and himself released.

Mexía had lost his curacy when Landa had arrested him in 1578, and he had still not regained it by the mid-1580s. But he did return to Yucatán, and, in the late 1580s, to his former parishes. He also returned to his old habits of pastoral practice—judging from testimonies of 1589, when fray Hernando de Sopuerta (Landa's protégé and now provincial of the local Franciscans) revived the Mexía case (see document 3.3). This was at least the fourth high-level inquiry into alleged wrongdoings by Mexía over the previous sixteen years, and yet he remained a priest, continued to abuse his parishioners, and still showed a capacity for effective defense (as demonstrated by Tetzal's attempt earlier in 1589 to avoid Mexía's wrath and make amends; see document 3.2). Nevertheless, drawing upon the records compiled by Landa, as well as a smaller number of more recent testimonies, Sopuerta convinced the Inquisition in Mexico City to again summon Mexía.

Appearing before the tribunal in 1590, the pastor made the same plea as he had in 1579; the case against him, insisted Mexía (see document 3.5), consisted of lies by simple Indians, fabrications by women manipulated by their malicious husbands. He also appealed for sympathy for a fellow clergyman, claiming that the past year of travelling from Yucatán and awaiting inquisitorial verdict in Mexico City had left him sickly and destitute, having narrowly escaped death at sea. One cannot easily judge the impact of Mexía's appeal. It seems weak beside the stack of detailed accusations. But when later that month (July 1590) Inquisition officials in Mexico City voted to condemn Mexía, he was neither imprisoned nor expelled from the church, but merely exiled for two years from Yucatán, fined two hundred pesos to defray Inquisition expenses, and banned for good from hearing the confessions of women. When his sentence of exile was completed in 1592, Mexía returned to his curacy once again, also being appointed to the bishop's staff in Mérida. He held both positions until at least 1594. And there his story ends.

Reading the Documents

In reading the documents presented below, note in particular the differences in terminology, style, genre, authorship, and argumentative strategy between the three texts translated from Yucatec Maya (documents 3.1 to 3.3) and the two translated from Spanish (documents 3.4 and 3.5). For example, reverential speech, a central component of formal discourse in Mesoamerica before and after the Spanish Conquest, can be seen in all three Maya texts (most obviously in document 3.3). Consider too the contrasts between a Maya statement of complaint and one of reconciliation, between Maya testimony expressed via *cah* channels and that given in the format of inquisitorial interrogation, between individual and corporate communication, between formulaic phrases and personal expression, and between the text (what is apparently said) and subtext (what may be the underlying meaning, concern, or intent). Each genre in its own way allowed for the presentation of particular perspectives while also circumscribing open expression, just as opportunities and limitations were rooted in the relationships of the authors to the colony's political and social structures and cultures.

THE DOCUMENTS[13]

3.1 Petition by the Cabildo of Xecpedz, Yucatán, 1573

I who am the governor (*batab*),[14] don Gaspar Cupul, with the *ah cuch cab*[15] Canche and the *ah cuch cab* Poot and the *ah cuch cab* Tzuc, and the principal men, make our declaration regarding our lord (*yum*)[16] the padre Andrés Mexía: He is not in the habit of giving us what is owed;[17] neither have we sold to him here in Xecpedz; nor does he send a man from Tihó.[18] Why? We ask nothing of him. As our lord the padre is good so he does well by us; yet because he says mass here in a twisted fashion,[19] once again his children are left high and dry.[20] What do you say to that? As to the question of eating: he also doesn't come because of that. In other words, there's nobody here in the *cah* because there's no food.[21] This is the reason why the priest[22] does not come here; it is because we have no food, nor will we give him any. Our father the padre, he doesn't remember us, although we lead good lives. This is the reason that I, along with the principal men, have written, so that the goodness of our hearts regarding our father the padre be known. That's all. Here we write on the day of Saint Lawrence the tenth day of August.

    This is my statement, I, don Gaspar Cupul.

> Don Gaspar Cupul;[23] Gonzalo Uayu;
> Francisco Poot; Francisco Hol, notary;
> Martin Tzuc; Alonso Cupul; Juan
> Canche; Francisco Nahuat, *maestro*.[24]

3.2 Statement Made by the Cabildo of Tetzal, Yucatán, 1589

Here on the 9th of March of the year '89, we are gathered together in the *cah* of Tetzal, I who am don Pedro Pol, the governor, with the *alcalde* Juan Hau, and the *regidores* Juan Ek and Pedro Cach.[25] We assert the truth of the word of all our elders and their names. We truly declare our hearts. Our lord, padre Andrés Mexía, we reconcile ourselves to him and he likewise reconciles himself to us. For there was formerly bad feeling on our part because of women's talk[26] and the telling of tales, for which reason he reprimanded us. For this reason we wrote a letter to the governor (*halach uinic*)[27] in Tihó. Through a messenger we explained that telling tales about priests is a bad thing, when their truthfulness is not clear. It is because of the telling of tales that previously we went to Tihó and returned here to the *cah*, and that our lord the principal official (*kuluinicil*)[28] spoke of it with the padre, and we attested to it. But because of our Christianity we gave up our anger with the padre and that which we had said earlier about him. We neither request anything of him, nor do we have anything else to say about it, because it's all in the past. We are telling the truth. Nothing is going to be remembered by us a second time, because we know nothing about it—just tale-telling and women's talk. All our elders affirm that this is true. Thus we write our names together, our lord the *kuluinicil* and the other principal men and witnesses:

> Don Pedro Pol, governor; Juan Hau, *alcalde*; Juan Ek, Pedro Cach, *regidores*; Diego Mo, notary.

3.3 Petition by the Cabildos of Oxtzucon, Peto, Tahdziu, Tetzal, and Tixmeuac, Yucatán, 1589

God keep you on this the last day [of the month]. You, our father, know we come to Tixmeuac with the nobles. When don Pedro Xiu, governor here in the *cah*, told us of your greetings, of the happy tidings you gave him, we were persuaded that your words were good. God be blessed,[29] you know how you protect us. Regarding the statement you made to the nobleman [don Pedro Xiu]: He told us all that you arranged for him here. We are asking you, for God's sake, will you protect us, as you say you will, so that we can carry out our desire to tell the truth about the deeds of the padre Mexía and what he does in the *cah*. So that you will thus hear the story of it, we write this letter to the lord padre, fray Hernando de Sopuerta.[30] If he takes into account what we now say about this padre, extracting all that is true, then, as you said in your letter, a judge, who is a friar,[31] should come to investigate. For here is our statement to you, lord. As you write in your letter to us, when those of Tixmeuac first heard mass here, it was you who first received us into Christianity.[32] This is the reason that we place ourselves before you, so that you, lord, will satisfy our wish. We who are here in Tixmeuac, we are coming from Oxtzucon, Peto, Tahdziu and Tetzal, we who are here with our principal men. Thus we wrote to you at dusk on Sunday. Give us your written word, lord, to the men we are sending there to Tihó. We will wait here. You write the truth. We will hear your word.

This is the truth. When he hears the confession of women, he then says, "If you don't give yourself to me, I won't confess you." This is how he abuses the women: he does not hear a woman's confession unless she comes to him; until they recompense him with their sins,[33] he does not hear the women's confession.

That is the whole truth of how the women are made to prostitute themselves. May God Eternal[34] keep you, our lord.

We who are your children:

> Don Juan Cool, governor of Peto; don Francisco Utz, governor of Tahdziu; all the *alcaldes*.

3.4 Testimony of Catalina Hau Given to Inquisition Officials, Valladolid, Yucatán, 1573

Then there appeared in the town of Valladolid on December 2, [1573], Catalina Hau, native and resident of the *pueblo* of Yalcon, married to Cristóbal May, resident of the *pueblo*, before the lord inspectors (*señores visitadores*), having been sworn in before God and Holy Mary his mother by making the sign of the cross with her hand and by promising to say the truth and by saying "I swear" and "Amen." And questioned in her language by fray Gaspar de Naxera with respect to each item,[35] she said the following:

To the first item the witness said that she knows padre Andrés Mexía as pastor in town, and she has seen him performing his duties and visiting her native *pueblo* of Yalcon; and thus the witness responded to the item.

To the fourth item she[36] declared that one day in April this year padre Andrés Mexía was visiting her *pueblo*, and that after attending mass she was waiting among the congregation to see if anyone came to confess, and that being moved by the pain of her sins the witness herself came to confess to the padre, and that she came with her mother, María Tui. And the witness asked the padre Andrés Mexía to hear her confession for the love of God, and he told her to sit on a seat by the main altar of the church where the gospel is said, and that having importuned her to get down on her knees, the padre ordered her to say the first part of the catechism and the Ave María. And after the witness said the Ave María, he put his hand on her stomach and asked her if she was pregnant and she replied "no," and the padre said, "Tell me the truth! I know that you have slept (*as hechado*) with three Spaniards," and she replied that such a thing did not occur, that it was not true. And then he told the witness to go into the school room, and she refused to go into the room, and he threatened her in a loud voice, and in fear she sat at the door to the room. And meanwhile he called to her mother to confess, and while her mother was confessing, the witness heard the padre say to her mother, "I must speak to your daughter to explain to her how to be obedient." And after confessing her mother, he left her where she had been confessing and called the witness to come with him, and she went with him out of fear and not wishing to cause a scene. And he forcibly pushed her into the sacristy of the church, and he had carnal relations (*acceso carnal*) with her against her will in the sacristy, and the witness did not fight back out of fear of the padre. And after this happened she left the sacristy in tears and went straight to her house with her mother, and the witness told the *cacique*[37] what had happened, and the *cacique* told her to come and complain to the magistrates of this town [i.e., to the Spanish officials in Valladolid], and this the witness did. And a few days after the witness appeared [to complain]—this was in the month of July—she and her mother were going to their *pueblo*, having heard mass in this town, and on the road they encountered the padre, coming with his servants before him from the *fiesta* of Saint Peter in the *pueblo* of Tikuch. And he said to the witness's mother, "Old woman, why have you accused me of sleeping (*que me heche*) with your daughter?" And she replied that she had not accused him but that it was true what she had said to the *batab*. And the padre ordered them to return to this town so that he could deal with them; and having gone a little way, he dismounted from his horse and ordered the witness's mother to hold the horse's reins, and the padre Andrés Mexía took the witness by the arm and pulled her into the bushes, saying he wanted to talk to her. And there he had carnal relations with her, and this was against her will. And before the lord officials she lamented and expressed her outrage (*se querella e agravia*) over the brutalities and offenses (*las fuerças e agravios*) committed by the padre Andrés Mexía; and thus the witness responded to the item.

And she said that she knew nothing with respect to all the other items. And she said that it was true that she was twenty years old, more or less, and that her testimony was made in the language of the land [Yucatec], and that it was a true statement of what had happened. And having [her statement] read back to her, she affirmed and ratified it. And she was not able to sign, [but] the lord officials signed:

> Alonso Muñoz Çapata;
> fray Gaspar de Naxera; before me,
> Diego Cansino, notary.

3.5 Petition by the Priest Andrés Mexía to the Inquisitor Judging His Case, Mexico City, 1590

Presented in Mexico on July 7, 1590, before the Lord Inquisitor *licenciado* Sanctos Garçía.[38]

I, Andrés Mexía, clergyman and ordained priest (*clerigo presbítero*), state that at the order of Your Most Illustrious Lordship, I have come to this court from over three hundred leagues from here;[39] and that on the journey I endured much hardship from roads, rivers, and marshes, and from the sea—for the ship in which I came overturned and was lost, and I escaped half drowned. I also lost the meager possessions I was carrying, leaving me with no more than the clothes on my back. And in this city I have suffered much illness and poverty and privation; after the year that has passed since I left home, I have had many expenses and losses, having another just the other day, when a *negro* that I had left in my benefice died on me. Due to all of which:

I entreat Your Most Illustrious Lordship, for God's sake, may it please you to look upon my case with eyes of compassion and mercy, as the Holy Office is always accustomed to doing, taking into consideration the aforementioned hardships which I have endured. All of these, together with the suspension of my orders[40] and my lengthy imprisonment, are surely applicable to my punishment for the guilt that may now result against me. Furthermore, the people who have testified against me are Indians induced by my enemies[41] and moved more by passion and vengeance than by Christianity. This is clearly evident from the fact that, after making accusations against me, they gave me an apology, in writing, before four Spaniards, saying that they had made the complaint against me in anger; and they excused themselves more profusely than in the apology, whose testimony is in my case file (*el proçeso de mi causa*).[42] Thus Your Lordship will find in the case proceedings (*proçesso*) my presentation of sufficient grounds for the enmity in which I am held by the three Indians[43] whose wives, sisters-in-law, and women friends have sworn against me; for only those three Indians from one *pueblo* are involved in this business, and the other six *pueblos* that I have in my benefice have never acted thus against me, not even in the *pueblo* where I most reside. And while Bishop Montalvo visited me three times, the aforementioned three Indians never then petitioned against me, although what they say now leads one to understand that the malice and enmity with which they view me goes back three or four years.[44] Due to all of this, as well as to the rest of my defense and the favorable arguments I have made, I entreat Your Lordship, for God's sake, to be merciful towards me, and I make this request in humility.

I also acknowledge notice of the final conclusion of these proceedings (*autos*).

Andrés Mexía

Notes

Acknowledgments   I am grateful to Geoffrey Spurling, John Chuchiak, and Francis Dutra for their comments on this chapter.

1. Priests in Yucatán were either Franciscan friars or secular clergy such as Mexía; there was a certain amount of rivalry between the two groups.
2. Matthew Restall's *The Maya World: Yucatec Culture and Society, 1550–1850* (Stanford, 1997) and "'He Wished It in Vain': Subordination and Resistance among Maya Women in Post-Conquest Yucatan," *Ethnohistory* 42: 4 (1995) provide the most immediate context to the documents presented here, as they not only analyze colonial-era Maya society using a variety of indigenous-language sources but specifically discuss the above documents. A complementary study using different sources and placing far more emphasis on religion is *Maya Society under Colonial Rule: The Collective Enterprise of Survival* (Princeton, 1984) by Nancy M. Farriss.
3. In Yucatán and the rest of New Spain, the term *visita* could refer both to an inspection and to the district subject to it.
4. At the time of Mexía's arrest by the Inquisition, Yucatán was divided into twenty-two *doctrinas* (groups of parishes or *visitas* under the control of the Franciscans, who had thirty-eight friars in the colony) and four *curatos* (manned by seventeen secular priests, most of whom, like Mexía, were attached to the cathedral in Mérida).
5. While periodically occupying various rural curacies from the late 1560s to the 1590s, Mexía also held a number of positions on the staff of the cathedral and bishop in Mérida. I am grateful to John Chuchiak for providing biographical information on Mexía based on sources in the Archivo General de Indias, in Seville, Spain.
6. Inga Clendinnen's *Ambivalent Conquests: Maya and Spaniard in Yucatan, 1517–1570* (Cambridge, 1987) and Matthew Restall's *Maya Conquistador* (Boston, 1998) offer contextual material on both the Spanish Conquest and early inquisitional activity in the colony. John Chuchiak focuses on Yucatán's Christianization campaigns in "The Indian Inquisition and the Extirpation of Idolatry: The Process of Punishment in the Ecclesiastical Courts of the *Provisorato de Indios* in Yucatán, 1563–1812" (Ph.D. dissertation, Tulane, 1999). The relationship between Spanish priests and their indigenous parishioners in central Mexico is dis-

cussed by William Taylor (*Magistrates of the Sacred: Priests and Parishioners in Eighteenth-Century Mexico* [Stanford, 1996]) and by Robert Haskett ("'Not a Pastor, But a Wolf': Indigenous-Clergy Relations in Early Cuernavaca and Taxco," *The Americas* 50: 3 [1994]).

7. Richard Boyer's *Lives of the Bigamists: Marriage, Family, and Community in Colonial Mexico* (Albuquerque, 1995) provides a fine introduction to how the Inquisition functioned in colonial Mexico.

8. The previous quotes are from María's own testimony but are corroborated in the statements made by her two friends.

9. The format was similar to that of document 3.4, only in this case the translation and writing down was done by the interpreter general and Maya nobleman Gaspar Antonio Chi, best known for working with Landa during the 1562 "idolatry" trials and for being one of the Maya informants for Landa's pioneering ethnography, the *Relación de las cosas de Yucatán*.

10. There is a further twist to the personal politics at work here. María May's master was Francisco Hernández, the son or nephew of a *conquistador* of the same name who had been relentlessly persecuted and ruined by Diego de Landa twenty years earlier, when Landa was custodian of the Franciscans in Yucatán; the elder Hernández had confessed his crimes and blasphemies, which amounted to strong criticisms of clerical activities in the colony, shortly before a premature death caused in part by the stress of the conflict and prison conditions. No doubt this helps to explain why the younger Hernández was so quick to denounce an abusive priest, but it is certainly ironic that it was Landa himself, now bishop, who zealously took up the case (the key to the irony lies in Landa's character; his campaign against Hernández the elder was motivated not by personal vindictiveness but by a fanatical devotion to the authority and reputation of the church).

11. Since Mexía's reinstatement four years earlier, Landa had appointed him to several positions, including the privileged one of the bishop's own confessor.

12. Mexía was born in Mexico City around 1540 and lived there until he was twelve; his father, Alonso de Castro, was one of Yucatán's conquistadors.

13. The 350 pages of the Mexía case file are preserved in Mexico City's Archivo General de la Nación, under *Inquisición, legajo* 69, *expediente* 5, folios 154–329. The three documents that I have translated from Yucatec Maya (3.1 to 3.3) are folios 199, 275, and 277; the two translated from Spanish (3.4 and 3.5) are folios 170–72, and 324.

14. The *batab* was the ruler of the *cah* both before and during the colonial period (he was not technically a *cabildo* member, but in effect he presided over it). Indigenous rulers in colonial Mexico were supposed to be elected annually, but in fact local variants were practiced throughout New Spain; in Yucatán, some *batabob* ruled as long as factional politics allowed, some held twenty-year terms of office, and some sat in the *batab*-ship for life, even passing the position on to a son. Similarly, although the *cabildo* was an institution imposed by the Spaniards, indigenous communities in colonial Mexico interpreted its structure and function according to local political traditions.

15. The *ah cuch cab* was, like the *batab*, an office that was carried over from preconquest times, with the difference that the Spanish authorities recognized the *batab* as the community governor (referring to him as *gobernador* or *cacique*), whereas *ah cuch cab* became an "unofficial" position which some communities used as a post outside the *cabildo*, while others (as seems to be the case here) treated it as equivalent to the *cabildo* positions of *alcalde* or *regidor*.

16. The Maya term *yum* means both "father" and "lord," the two often being mutually inclusive, as is the case here.

17. The phrase "what is owed" could also be glossed as "our music" (the Maya text does not clearly indicate whether *pax* or *p'ax* is meant), which would make sense as the petitioners later object to the way Mexía says mass. The immediate context, however, appears to be economic. In early colonial times communities like Xecpedz that were far from Mérida (referred to here with its precolonial and colonial Maya name, Tihó) seldom saw Spaniards and thus viewed visiting priests as useful economic contacts; priests in turn engaged in economic enterprise to supplement income through tithes, fees, and tribute in the form of local produce (to which the petition also refers). Priests sometimes abused this relationship; in the list of charges made by seventeen *cahob* later in the year (discussed in the introduction above), Xecpedz asserted that Mexía visited them only twice, each time demanding goods for which he failed to pay.

18. That is, Mexía has not sent a subordinate priest to give the Mayas of Xecpedz what they feel they are owed, either in payment for goods provided or in sacramental performance.

19. This is presumably a reference to language: Mexía probably said mass in Latin, and/or his grasp of Yucatec was inadequate from the Mayas' viewpoint. Although we know from elsewhere in the case file that he spoke some Maya (and also, supposedly, Nahuatl), there were also complaints from other *cahob* that this pastor would neither preach nor hear confession in the tongue of his parishioners. Furthermore, in September 1573 (forty days after Xecpedz wrote up their complaint), Mexía was reprimanded by the civil authorities in Valladolid for not preaching or hearing confession in Maya (and thereby interfering with colonial relations by upsetting the subject peoples). Maya communities continued to complain, even as late as the 1830s, that the priests assigned to their parishes spoke Maya poorly. The colonial Church, of course, very rarely ordained non-Spaniards.

20. The literal translation of this phrase would be "a second time, dry (or cold), his children." The Maya petitioners refer to themselves as Mexía's children not only because he is their "father" (*yum* and *padre*), but also in accordance with the stylistic devices of Mesoamerican reverential speech.

21. The Maya population suffered greatly in a series of famines and epidemics in the 1560s and 1570s that contributed to a demographic decline of up to 50 percent between the censuses of 1549 and 1580–86. In stating "there's nobody here" the petitioners are probably referring to population loss through flight as well as mortality; there is evidence that in times of crisis the unconquered parts of the peninsula to the south and east offered refuge and alternative sources of food for Mayas from the colony.

22. I have taken the Maya term *u tibon* as a variant on *tibol* or *tibob*, a relatively rare term for "priest"; note, however, that an alternative reading might simply be "to us," rendering the sentence "This is the reason why he does not come to us here."

23. This and the following names are written as signatures, as are the names at the feet of the other two documents.

24. The *maestro* was a Spanish-imposed position, whose various duties included schoolmaster and choirmaster, to which the Mayas gave considerable importance, as reflected here in the placing of the Xecpedz *maestro* among the senior *cabildo* members.

25. The core *cabildo* posts of *alcalde* and *regidor*, which we might translate as "judge" and "councilman," were treated by the Maya as rungs on the career ladder to which community notables might aspire. Unlike Spanish *cabildos*, the numbers of *alcaldes* and *regidores* varied from *cah* to *cah*.

26. Indicative of the nature of ethnic and gender structures in colonial Mexico is the fact that the Spanish version replaces "women's talk and the telling of tales (*canxectzil y[etel] chupulchi*)" with "Indian gossip (*algunos chismes de indios*)" (this is the only one of the three documents that was translated at the time—by Gaspar Antonio Chi on April 12, 1589).

27. Before the Conquest the *halach uinic* was the supreme political officer, or territorial ruler, of a province; as Tihó (Mérida) was the colonial provincial capital, the reference here is to the Spanish governor of Yucatán.

28. *Kuluinicil* is a Maya title meaning "principal man" (i.e., the *batab* or governor of the *cah*); it is also used below in the plural, *kuluinicob*, to mean "the principal men" (i.e., the *cabildo* officers and other community notables).

29. The literal sense of this phrase is "good words will be said about God (*dios*)."

30. Sopuerta was in charge of this second phase of the Inquisition investigation into Mexía; the addressee of the petition appears to be the head Franciscan in the nearby *cabecera* [regional head-town] of Tekax, clearly a friar perceived by the Maya notables of the region as sympathetic to them.

31. In early colonial Yucatán, this means a Franciscan friar. The relative unpopularity among the Mayas of secular priests, as opposed to Franciscans, as reflected in the disproportionate number of Maya complaints against seculars, played into secular Franciscan politics. The Maya nobles authoring this petition realized that because Sopuerta was a Franciscan and Mexía was not, they stood a much better chance with a judge who was a friar.

32. I have added some emphasis to clarify what I take to be the meaning; the literal sense is "that those of Tixmeuac (*tixmiuace*) here heard mass you received us (*uahmaatex*) we first enter into Christianity here."

33. An alternative (or, rather, parallel) translation is, "fornicate with him"; the matter hinges on how one pronounces the phrase *pak keban*, an ambiguity made possible by the diacritics of written colonial Maya.

34. Literally, "no end of his days" (*ma xul u kinil*).

35. According to Spanish practice, a set of items or questions (here termed *capítulos*) were drawn up in advance by the investigators and put to each witness. The opening questions were typically formulas on such matters as the witness's identity, age, understanding of the procedure, and acquaintance with the accused; note that here either the interrogator or the notary skipped the formulaic second and third items. In translating the testimony under the fourth item I have reduced some of the repetition while still preserving the orality of the text; Catalina Hau is of course speaking in Maya, while fray Gaspar de Naxera dictates his translation of her words to the notary, who writes them down in the third person.
36. "esta que declara" in the document.
37. A term of Arawak origin brought by the Spaniards from the Caribbean and used by them to refer to the chief or governor of any indigenous community; "cacique" would have been Naxera's translation of "batab."
38. This heading is written in abbreviated form by a notary; the rest of the document is written and signed by Mexía himself.
39. Mexía is referring to his trip from Yucatán to Mexico City, which would have required journeying by land to the Yucatec port of Campeche, then by sea across the Gulf of Mexico to Veracruz, and finally by land again up to the Valley of Mexico.
40. His rights as an ordained priest to perform the sacraments.
41. This appears to be a reference to Spanish enemies, who remain unnamed in Mexía's records of defense; note, however, that the claim to being a victim of one's enemies was a common element in the Spanish legal discourse of defense.
42. This apology is presumably the statement included here as document 3.2.
43. These "sufficient grounds" consist of statements similar to this one (document 3.5), with Mexía denouncing his accusers as malicious liars.
44. The phrase "malice and enmity" is intended to cast aspersions on the motives of Mexía's accusers and the veracity of their allegations; the "Indians" failed to complain three or four years ago, Mexía is suggesting, because they only recently invented their accusations. In fact, more than three Mayas and more than one *cah* testified against the priest, while the Maya willingness to express resentment towards him went back at least seventeen years in at least one community—as evidenced by documents 3.1 and 3.3, and in the many other pages of testimony in the Mexía case files.

DOCUMENT THEMES

Crime; Cultural Contact/Ethnogenesis/Resistance; Economy and Work; Ethnicity; European-Mestizo Peoples; Gender; Governance, Indigenous; Indigenous Peoples; Inquisition; Religion; Rural Life; Sexuality; Violence; Women.

SUGGESTIONS FOR FURTHER READING

Boyer 1995.
Chuchiak 1999.
Clendinnen 1987.
Farriss 1984.
Haskett 1994.
Restall 1995.
Restall 1997.
Restall 1998.
Taylor 1996.

CHAPTER
4

Directorio Para Confesores: "Lords Who Hold Temporal Government Over Vassals"
(Mexico, 1585)

John F. Schwaller

INTRODUCTION

One of the important motivations for the Spanish conquest and colonization of the Americas was the desire to spread Christianity to the New World. Many friars and priests[1] who accompanied the *conquistadores* became important figures in colonial life. As missionaries worked to convert the native peoples they quickly realized that it was more feasible for them to learn the native languages than for the millions of indigenous people to learn Spanish. Consequently the friars and priests set about learning the native tongues and then translating Christian didactic works into the native languages. The early arrival of the printing press in Mexico, circa 1533, assisted in the spread of Christianity by allowing for the relatively inexpensive publication of books to assist the missionaries in their work. The first work published in Mexico, for example, was a brief statement of Christian doctrine for use in the evangelization process.

Nearly all such works composed and printed in Mexico for use in the Christianization of the natives were written as aids to the parish priest. One of the most common of these, often written in bilingual format, were confessional guides that provided the priest with possible responses to questions commonly asked in confession. Newly arrived friars with as yet little grasp of the native languages found the guides especially useful, for questions cast in the native tongue together with a range of responses to them allowed them to proselytize and minister to their charges with a minimum of delay. Yet, as noted, these works were mostly developed to assist the priest in the confessional itself.[2] The example considered here is somewhat different in that it was developed as a training exercise that both instructed priests in the underlying principles of moral theology and in the application of them to specific cases.

The larger document from which this passage is taken was written at the command of the Third Provincial Council of Mexico.[3] In accordance with church law, such councils consisted of the archbishop and bishops of a territory known as an ecclesiastical province, which were to hold regular meetings in order to apply church law to local conditions. The Third Mexican Council, held in 1585, was especially important since it had as one of its main purposes the implementation of the decrees of the Council of Trent.[4] Trent was the response of the Catholic Church to the Protestant Reformation. Consequently, the Third Mexican Council seems all the more significant in Mexican Church history because another council was not held for two centuries.

In the selection found here, several important themes of the Catholic Church's response to the Reformation are clearly seen. The Protestants in general discounted the necessity of individual confession to a priest. Rather they felt that confession was a matter best left to the believer and God. They abandoned personal confession through a priest, in favor of general confession in the context of the church service or liturgy. The Catholic Church continued to argue in favor of individual confession to a priest as the best means to assure true contrition and to change behaviors. The issues raised in this document are merely a starting point in detailing the Church's attempt to change the hearts of the people.

The section on temporal lords begins with the premise that the role of the secular governor is to allow his subjects to live in peace and tranquillity. Moreover the ruler has the personal responsibility to see that justice is done among his subjects regardless of their wealth or station. The poor are to be accorded the same level of justice and protection as the rich. The ruler must make himself available to hear the complaints of his subjects, but most importantly he must be careful to appoint honest and qualified individuals to positions of authority under him. These are presented not as political ideals, but as theological imperatives; the ruler is morally responsible before God for the fair and equitable government of his subjects.

The greater part of this section lists the numerous ways in which the secular ruler can enter into sin. All of these in one way or another have to do with injustices that the ruler might visit on his subjects. Readers of this document will therefore have the chance to see what theologians of the sixteenth century believed were the most common, and most serious, infractions committed by rulers against the people they ruled. The final section clarifies much of what came before by explicitly stating that *encomenderos* should be considered secular lords. The bishops responsible for drawing up this guide to moral theology wanted to protect the natives from exploitation. They wished to accomplish this by making absolutely clear that priests understand that they were responsible for vigilantly assisting Spaniards with authority over Indians in making a good confession. In so doing the bishops felt that the Spaniards would eventually change their attitudes and behaviors.

In addition to the listing of common abuses, it is possible that bishops were also leveling veiled criticisms at royal government. At one point they indicate that the ruler sins by selling public offices such as that of scribe or sheriff. (By 1585, these and other offices were routinely sold by the royal government.)[5] The bishops also enlist the secular rulers into the effort to improve the moral tone of the territory, and readers will want to note how.

Unfortunately, while the Church could use moral persuasion, there was very little that it could actually do to enforce its moral order. If a ruler were found to

have sinned, the priest could impose a penance,[6] but that required the cooperation of the penitent. If the sinner refused to cooperate—to confess to a priest, to
receive formal forgiveness (absolution), and submit to a satisfaction (usually the
recital of specified prayers over a set period of time)—and to change his or her
ways, the only response of the Church was excommunication.[7] In the sixteenth
century this powerful weapon also prohibited others from having contact with
the excommunicated person. Yet excommunication was relatively rare, for in general the faithful tried to comply with Church teachings. Readers will want to think
about whether Spanish "temporal lords" likely accepted Church teachings in carrying out their duties as colonial governors and may wonder even if Spanish
"spiritual lords" lived up to them.

THE DOCUMENT

Temporal lords have to consider that their occupation is the governing with care
of their vassals and subjects,[8] so that they may live in peace and tranquillity. Lords
must judge the great and the lesser equally, and see that the poor and those in
need of human favor are more particularly cared for, because generally they are
the more aggrieved and those who can less be defended and who can less find
favor and find help from their lord. Even worse, only with difficulty can they gain
an audience with the lord to recount the ways they were aggrieved and to request that the lord defend and free them from those who mistreat their persons
and estates.

Thus the first and principal obligation of temporal lords is to appoint officials in the community[9] who are God-fearing men of good habits who are capable of doing well the work they have been given. The lord needs to ensure that
they do their job well, to listen to complaints against them, and to quickly provide a remedy.

The principal and most prejudicial sin against the community that a temporal lord can commit is to appoint officials who are unqualified by filling positions
through requests, affection, or kinship. When the lord fails to punish or remove
[officials] after hearing of the damage that has befallen the community because
they failed to serve their office well; or because they commit injuries against the
village,[10] its people, or its estates; or because they do not enforce the laws and or-
dinances that are issued; or because they are individuals who scandalize the community with their bad habits: in these cases, the lords sin gravely in appointing
such officials or in not removing them when they realize that they do not serve
their offices well.

The lord is also obligated to see that satisfaction is made for damages and
assaults committed [by officials] against the community, and if satisfaction is not
forthcoming, the lord is obligated to make restitution.

The lord also sins if he abandons residency in, and oversight of, his district,
unless it be due to some pressing need such as the demands of some office or
other in the territory, or by being forced through obedience to one who can command him.[11] In such a case he will be required to leave someone to appropriately
govern his estates. If he fails to do so he will sin gravely.

Lords commit a sin when they levy tribute requirements or taxes for public works in the community—for example, bringing water springs to the city, building bridges to pass safely over rivers, or fixing roads—without having given orders that such be done as part of the tribute levies.

They also sin if they take advantage of the service and labor of their subjects by making them work in their own homes [or] lands, by using them as servants, by taking advantage of them by purchasing their possessions or estates or by forcing them to sell them, and by usurping their service and labor for themselves without giving just satisfaction after they have received or taken it;

They sin if they take for themselves the common goods of the community or village or if they usurp the pasture, rivers, or ponds that are held in common;

They sin if they sell public offices such as scribe or sheriff, etc.;

They sin if they do not comply with the laws that govern all or if they enforce them only against the poor but not the rich;

They sin if they do not fully comply with the wills and testaments of their predecessors; if they do not pay what they owe, especially to their servants for that which they have done for them;

They sin if they have forests that are protected solely for their hunting (which only the King can allow, paying damages to the workers) and yet not permit to others even though they pay damages.

They also sin if they force anyone to marry, or if they disturb the marriage of those who wish to wed through free will.[12] They also sin if they condemn someone without hearing him or without sufficient proof. They also sin if in having the right to present candidates to ecclesiastical benefices[13] they present persons who are unsuitable for them, or if presenting suitable candidates they deny the worthier one. They are obliged to make restitution just as prelates[14] are, in accordance with what was decreed at the Council of Trent.

The lords also sin . . . if they are not careful and diligent in eliminating public sinfulness in the community, such as concubinage,[15] gambling, playing prohibited games; and in eliminating usury[16] and usurious contracts made even in public, unjust and harmful to one's neighbor by forcing individuals to serve in ways not legally required, or unjustly making them sell their own things for less than their cost. They also sin if they consent to false measurements, because as it is said: "the error which one does not resist, one accepts," for being negligent in correcting those who are sinful is no different from favoring them. He who does not oppose the public villain does not lack the scruples to keep hidden company with him.

Because drunkenness is something so public, so ordinary, and so harmful to the public health of the Indians and so much of an impediment to their becoming good Christians and even *being* good Christians, governors in this land have particular obligation to be diligent to diminish the drunkenness of the Indians and to remove the occasions for the same from them. The governor sins gravely in [policing drunkenness] if he is not careful or if he pardons offenders too easily because the principal intent and obligation of those who govern in the Indies is to secure the conversion of the heathens[17] and help them to live in a Christian manner once converted.

The lords need to comply with the instructions, decrees, and provisions of His Majesty that were issued for the good treatment of these natives. They sin mortally[18] especially if they order or permit that [the natives] be distributed or sent to the mines to dig or engage in other tasks there. Work in the mines leads to their destruction and to their abhorrence of the gospel, leading them to reject indoctrination and conversion. Moreover it leads to other offenses such as robbery, violence, and injuries that occur when they are forced to be absent from their wives, children, and lands. This violence is so much greater because the natives are poor and cowardly. They have less protection from the insolent power of the miners and their slaves with their greed to extract silver with the blood of these downtrodden ones whose conversion and spiritual and temporal maintenance, and the prevention of scandal and infamy against our sacred religion, is the obligation of His Majesty and his ministers.

From labor distributions of natives to estates, houses, and farms and from those who are subjected to violence and force in cloth mills and smitheries and other occupations also follow offenses as will be noted more extensively below in the declarations and responses of this Holy Council.

Lords also sin if they spend excessively on frivolous things, leaving their estates and incomes indebted, resulting in great anguish to themselves and to their heirs. It makes an extreme situation in which they oppress and trouble their subjects in order to maintain their estates. It also prevents them from giving alms, which their state and occupation particularly obligates them.

The *encomenderos* of this territory must examine their consciences in light of what has been stated here, confess, and correct in themselves all of their shortcomings. The confessors should be informed of the state [of the soul of the *encomendero*] and their means of dealing with the Indians as a result of what is noted here, and inquire if they attempt to secure the doctrine, conversion, and spiritual benefit of the Indians on their *encomienda*, entrusted to their charge. If they do not comply with this, the confessor will seek to [have them] avoid [their shortcomings] and make them recall it, aspiring with great care and vigilance that there be competent spiritual ministers, to educate the natives and administer the holy sacraments to them. As the natives cease to sin and our Holy Christian Faith grows in them, they might be succored and treated as Christians, and poor and frail folk, preventing that they be wronged or scandalized.

NOTES

ACKNOWLEDGMENTS   I would like to thank Stafford Poole, C.M., for his friendship over the years and his continued enthusiasm for the Directorio project on which he and I have worked for nearly twenty years.

1. The clergy of the Catholic Church consists of two main groups, the secular and regular clergy. The latter were clerics who lived under a "rule" that they have vowed to obey in communities symbolically or physically set apart from the rest of the world. The secular clergy lived in the world and ministered to ordinary people in parishes. The most important religious orders in New Spain were the Franciscan, Dominican, Augustinian, and Jesuit orders. Not all clerics were ordained to the priesthood, especially among the regular clergy. Certain orders, such as the Dominicans and Franciscans, refer to their members as friars (brothers).

2. In the Catholic Church there are seven acts known as sacraments. One of these is the act of confession, whereby one tells a priest about the sins that one has committed. In the medieval church the priest and church member would just sit down in the church and engage in a dialogue. By the sixteenth century it became the practice to enter into a small booth, with a grille between the priest and penitent. That booth became known as the confessional.

3. Entitled "Directorio para confesores," or "Guide for confessors," it can be found in the Archivo de la Catedral Metropolitana de México (Mexico City), vol. 120, Directorio del Santo Concilio Provincial, 1585. This impressive and substantial work of 327 folios deals both with issues of canon law governing the training and selection of priests to be confessors and with issues of moral theology that priests might encounter in their ministry. The Directorio was not published, because it quickly ran afoul of royal officials in search of greater control over the church, and because of squabbles between the secular clergy and the religious orders. Yet it clearly circulated as a manuscript and points extracted from it were published in letters bishops sent to parishes in their dioceses. The Council of 1585, therefore, had some influence in reducing the amount of variation in matters relating to confession.

4. The Council of Trent, 1545–63, was convened by the papacy in order to reform the Catholic Church in the face of the Protestant Reformation.

5. The Crown had sold the offices of notary and alderman in municipal councils since the beginning of the century. The demand for these appointments far outstripped their availability, and nearly all those who sought the offices fulfilled the minimum criteria. Consequently the Crown provided that those who were willing to pay the highest price, in a public auction, could gain the office. Members of the local colonial elite prized these offices as a means of demonstrating both their wealth and their willingness to serve the Crown.

6. Penance consists of those acts that the priest imposes on persons who confess their sin. The penance serves both in a spiritual economy whereby an evil act is absolved through a good deed, and as a means of further inculcating the penitent in the values of Christianity. Penance normally consisted in the saying of prayers, the giving of alms to charity, and in private penitential acts.

7. Excommunication is the ritual cutting off of an individual from the body of the faithful. The person who was excommunicated was not to engage in any activity with the faithful. He or she was also prohibited from partaking in any Church ritual until penance had been performed.

8. In this passage a distinction is being drawn between those residents of a region who enjoyed certain freedoms, subjects, and those who were restricted in some way, vassals. In the Middle Ages subjects were free to travel and work where they wished. Vassals were generally restricted to the manor of their lord. Here Spanish residents are considered subjects and native peoples vassals.

9. The Spanish term that I have translated as community is *república* or "republic." The Spanish Crown envisioned society as consisting of two sociopolitical entities occupying the same physical space, a *república* of Spaniards and a *república* of natives.

10. While *república* here refers to a large territory as well as a people who occupy it, the village, or *pueblo* was a legally defined term. It consisted of a group of peoples who dwelled together in proximity to one another and who exercised corporate control over their mutual resources of pasture, forage, and water.

11. This passage is dealing both with Spanish *encomenderos* who leave the district of their *encomienda* and with local magistrates who abandon their posts.

12. Free will is a important aspect of Christian thinking. For the Catholic Church the sacraments were valid only if all parties entered into them without coercion. Thus a person could not be forced to marry another.

13. An ecclesiastical benefice is a position within the Church that carries a guaranteed income. They were normally positions as parish priests.

14. A prelate is a high official of the Church. For the religious orders these included abbots or priors of monasteries and friaries, provincials, and generals; for the secular clergy, bishops and archbishops.

15. Concubinage is the cohabitation of persons not legally married.

16. Usury is the loaning of money at excessive interest. For the Church in the sixteenth century any interest was considered usury. What is important in this passage is that selling goods at less than cost and forcing people to work for free are also considered usury.

17. The actual term here is a "gentile," which means pagan or heathen, a non-Christian, especially a native, who has not formally embraced Christianity.
18. Catholic moral theology envisions sin as being of one of two types: mortal and venial. Mortal sin is sufficiently grave as to prohibit one from entering heaven if it is not absolved before death.

DOCUMENT THEMES

European-Mestizo Peoples; Governance, Colonial; Religion.

SUGGESTIONS FOR FURTHER READING

Burkhart 1989.
Poole 1987.
Schwaller 1987.
Taylor 1996.

CHAPTER
5

"In the Service of God, I Order These Temples of Idolatrous Worship Razed to the Ground": Extirpation of Idolatry and the Search for the *Santuario Grande* of Iguaque

(Colombia, 1595)

J. Michael Francis

INTRODUCTION

In 1595, the Audiencia of New Granada (modern-day Colombia) launched a brief campaign aimed to extirpate Indian idolatry in the province of Tunja. It appointed one of its own judges (*oidores*), Egas de Guzmán, to inspect the province (a region roughly the size of the State of Maryland) inhabited by a group of Indians known as the Muisca.[1] Among his many responsibilities, Guzmán received instructions to assess the status of the spiritual conversion of the Indians to Catholicism and to eradicate all physical remnants of Muisca religion.

The following document, housed in Colombia's National Archive, is part of the material Guzmán gathered during a nine-day inspection of the *pueblo* of Iguaque (located in Colombia's Eastern Highlands). Iguaque was one of the province's largest *encomiendas*, with a tributary population of 157 Indians.[2] Guzmán's inspection of the province was brief, and he rarely spent more than a few days in a given town. Iguaque, however, was an exception. Rumors had reached the *visitador* that the *pueblo* was the site of an important Muisca shrine, the *santuario grande*, and Guzmán hoped to discover its location. The proceedings open with the confessions of seven Indian nobles from Iguaque, six of whom confessed that they possessed *cucas*, or holy houses. However, when the *cucas* yielded no great treasure, Guzmán began his inquisition of the *pueblo*'s inhabitants. Dozens of Iguaque's Indians were then arrested, questioned, and tortured, as Guzmán attempted to determine the nature of local religious practices and the location of the *pueblo*'s hidden shrines. In the end, two dozen Indians from Iguaque were found guilty and sentenced for the possession of pagan sanctuaries and for practicing idolatry. The *santuario grande* of Iguaque was never found.

It is worth noting that the looting of Muisca sanctuaries was a common occurrence throughout the early colonial period. In fact, in 1569 such practices were officially condoned by the *audiencia* which, in 1577, launched its own crusade against Indian idolatry. It too was a brief campaign, but it proved remarkably profitable. In only ten *pueblos*, an estimated 44,129 pesos (a conservative estimate since most of this loot was never officially declared) were confiscated from Muisca sanctuaries.[3]

THE DOCUMENT[4]

5.1 The Campaign Begins

On October 25, 1595, in the *pueblo* and *repartimiento* of Iguaque of the *encomienda* of Juan de Otalora, señor Egas de Guzmán, counsel to our Lord the King, his senior judge on the *audiencia* of this kingdom and *visitador-general* of the province of the city of Tunja, addressed the assembled Indian men, women, *principales*, and *caciques*. Speaking through the interpreter Cristóbal de Sanabria, his honor told the Indians that he came on a visit of inspection, to procure that they be good Christians, and to see that they did not keep old shrines and idols. To this effect and to extirpate all idolatrous practices, he commanded that anyone among them who maintained such shrines or temples dedicated to the devil declare it openly. In the name of His Majesty the King he promised to forgive those who told the truth, but vowed that all who concealed such practices would be dealt with and brought to justice in accord with the will of God and His Majesty.

There immediately appeared before the judge an Indian *principal* named Pedro Conba, who stated that he possessed a shrine known as a *cuca* or holy house. Don Juan, the *cacique* of this *repartimiento*, promptly declared that he too had a house referred to as a *cuca* that was left to him by an uncle. The *principal* don Fernando then declared that he had no such house. Don Diego Unbayan stated that he had a house known as a *cuca*, meaning a holy house, left to him by his forebears. Juan Ribe declared that he possessed a house called a *cuca*, bequeathed to him by his forebears, but that he did not know what was inside. An Indian named Ventura said that he had a house called a *cuca* that he inherited from his father but that he did not know what was inside. Sebastián Sepaquen then declared that he had a house known as a *cuca* left to him by his forebears but did not know what was inside. No further Indians testified in the opening proceedings and these were closed and the record signed by the judge, the notary, and the interpreter.

5.2 Interrogations, Confessions, the Collection of Evidence

Accompanied by me [the notary], as well as the interpreter and others, the judge and *visitador-general* went directly to inspect the houses and huts referred to by the Indians and searched each one thoroughly in order to see if they contained idols or shrines. He discovered none, and given that there were no shrines in any of these huts, he ordered that one of the Indians be threatened. Producing a rope, on the orders of Judge Guzmán, Alonso de Molina began to tie the hands of the Indian Ventura, who begged them do him no harm and said that he wanted to declare what he knew. Through the interpreter Cristóbal de Sanabria the Indian stated that the *principal* Pedro Conba was the one who knew who possessed shrines, after which no further questioning was undertaken with the Indian.

Thereupon the judge ordered that the Indian Pedro Conba be stripped of his clothing and asked him to state and declare if he or other Indians have any such shrines. Conba said that he knew nothing, and in light of the Indian's reticence and previous declaration, the judge, to intimidate and frighten him, ordered Alonso de Molina to tie the man's arms with a rope, telling the Indian through the interpreter that he should speak the truth, because if he did not he would have to be tortured. In order to strike fear in Conba, his arms were tied and the rope thrown over a beam in the hut and pulled slightly, in a manner such that it did him no physical harm. He said that an Indian woman named Clara kept a cotton idol but that he did not know what was inside it.

The judge ordered the woman to appear before him and through the interpreter ordered her to reveal this shrine, which she said was hidden in a distant field and which she would show him. The judge ordered me [the notary] and the interpreter to go with her to see what was there. We were led by the Indian woman to a field some five hundred strides from the village, where she pointed to some stones under which there was a small clay pot containing two hollow figurines made of unrefined gold wrapped in a bit of cotton and colored cloth and filled with earth. Beneath other stones shown us by the Indian woman was found a piece of white cloth the width of the palm of the hand and a bit of cotton, within which was wrapped a figurine of unrefined gold filled with earth and six tiny emerald-like gems of no value. Apart from myself [the notary], the witnesses to these proceedings—the interpreter Cristóbal de Sanabria, the *alguacil* Diego Gómez, and Antonio de Porras—removed the figurines. As notary I hereby attest that no other things were found or removed.

The judge, noting the clear proof of the *principal* Pedro Conba's dissembling, ordered the Indian brought to his lodgings to be able to deal with him as he saw fit and to learn the truth regarding the whereabouts of the great shrine reputed to exist in this *repartimiento*. At the hour of evening prayers, the judge had Pedro Conba formally detained as a prisoner under the custody of the interpreter Cristóbal de Sanabria, who led him away. The next morning, Sanabria announced that Pedro Conba had fled in the night, escaping by way of a hole in the roof of the hut where he was being held. Despite a thorough search for Pedro Conba, the Indian has not appeared.

Following the events described above, on October 27 of the same year in the aforementioned *repartimiento* of Iguaque, an Indian called Aguicha, speaking through the interpreter Cristóbal de Sanabria, voluntarily testified before the judge that he had a shrine in his house that had been left to him by his forebears. The judge went in person to the Indian's hut, and in my presence as notary, García produced two figurines of unrefined gold wrapped in a small cloth that also contained a few tiny emeralds. These were of such low quality that they were worthless.

The same day, the *alguacil* Bartolomé de Ospino brought to the judge two small figurines of unrefined gold wrapped in a cloth, given him by an Indian named Juan Pirasaque on behalf of the *capitán* don Fernando.

Also on October 27, there appeared before the judge an Indian named Diego Sipaquencha, who voluntarily testified through the interpreter Cristóbal de Sanabria that he had in his house two figurines of unrefined gold. The figurines were found in the Indian's house, wrapped in a cotton cloth along with several tiny, worthless emerald-like stones, to which fact I attest as notary.

In the *repartimiento* of Iguaque on October 27 of the same year, an Indian named Juan Neaquenchia voluntarily appeared before the judge and through the interpreter Cristóbal de Sanabria said that on a hill outside this pueblo there is a shrine that was bequeathed to him by an uncle and that he would reveal to them if they would accompany him. After reading the testimony of the Indian, the judge ordered me as notary, along with the *alguacil* Bartolomé de Ospino, the interpreter Cristóbal de Sanabria, Alonso de Molina and the *corregidor* don Pedro de Orellano, to investigate. We went with the Indian to the place he indicated, [which was located] on the former site of the *pueblo*, on a hill nearly a league and a half away. The final third of the way, given the steep and uneven terrain, we went on foot. Among some stones at the top of the hill the Indian showed us a white pouch, within which there was found a gold figurine and two eagles of thin gold leaf, the beaks of which appeared to be made of fine quality gold. There was also a small figurine and another figurine of unrefined gold designed as a clasp, as well as five moldy cotton blankets, which were of no value. The gold and blankets were brought to the judge, who found that the metal was worth seventy pesos. The Indian stated that the shrine referred to also belonged in part to Pedro Conba.

In the *pueblo* of Iguaque on October 27, 1595, the judge and *visitador*, his honor Egas de Guzmán, in order to discover and verify the truth relating to the shrines, rites, and ceremonies of the Indians of this *pueblo*, ordered to come before him a certain Hernán Sánchez, resident of this district. The judge administered the witness with the legal oath, which he took and by which he swore on his life to speak the truth, and being asked by his honor, he said that about a year and a half ago he had been appointed by the former *corregidor* as *teniente de corregidor* for this *pueblo* and that of Chiquisa. The witness, having been in this *pueblo* at that time, saw the Indian Juan Cacaria, who was then *gobernador*, exchange heated words with the *capitán* Pedro Conba. Having separated the two, the witness overheard Cacaria speaking with other Indians from this *pueblo*, saying that Pedro Conba possessed too much gold in his shrine and that it would be good to inform the *corregidor* of this fact, in order to take the gold from Conba, who made no good use of it. In this regard the witness to the statements made by Cacaria (who is now in custody) adds that the same day as the events described above he heard a Spanish-speaking Indian named Juan Saisipa say that the principal shrine in this *pueblo* contained a great quantity of gold, a fact he had learned from an Indian named Neaquenchia, who claimed to be *jeque* of the shrine. The witness states that this is the truth and is all he knows regarding what he has been asked.

The same day, following the testimony of Hernán Sánchez in which he claimed that Juan Cacaria—who is now being held in custody—knew the location of the shrine, the judge called the Indian prisoner before him. The Indian was asked to state and declare what had happened. Cacaria replied that it was true that some two years ago, when a certain Luis was *corregidor*, the present witness had fought with Pedro Conba and other *principales* of this *repartimiento*, and for this reason had threatened to expose [the location of] the shrine. But afterwards they became friends, and for this reason he had not revealed the shrine, nor does he know anything about it, not even its location. The judge therefore ordered the Indian, who seemed to be about forty years old, to be taken back to jail.

On the same day the judge had the Indian again brought from the jail in order to learn the truth from him. As soon as the Indian appeared, and as he seemed to be a strong and robust man, the judge ordered him stripped of his clothes and had his upper arms tied with a rope. Thus bound he was hoisted to a height of more than two *palmos* off the floor and was then commanded to declare the truth and to reveal the whereabouts of the great shrine and the bones of the old *cacique*. The Indian promised that if they let him down he would tell the truth, and having been lowered to the ground stated that an Indian named Diego Raga knew where the shrine was and said that they should call him to testify.

The judge summoned the Indian Diego Raga to appear before him, and once he had appeared and had been informed through the interpreter that Juan Cacaria alleged that he had the bones of the old *cacique* and the shrine, the Indian Diego stated that that was a lie and that he knew nothing. After this refutation the order was given to again hoist the Indian Juan Cacaria with the rope, and again he was raised two *palmos* above the floor and warned that he was to speak the truth. He immediately said that they should let him down and call for his mother, because she and Diego knew where the bones of the old *cacique* were. The Indian woman was promptly summoned, and once all three were together, with Juan Cacaria on the floor bound only by the arms, they—and in particular Diego—said he [Diego] knew where the bones of the old *cacique* lay and that he would take them there and give them the bones. Asked where they were, he stated that they were in this *repartimiento* on a hill some two leagues away. As it was now nearly vespers and too late to depart, the judge ordered the *alguacil* Bartolomé de Ospino to take Juan Cacaria, Diego, and the Indian woman into custody and to go to look for the bones of the old *cacique* early the next morning. The *alguacil* then led the Indians away.

After the events described above, on the same day of October 27, 1595, the judge, in the use of his faculties to discover the truth and in view of the evidence against the *capitán* don Alvaro, who is now in custody, ordered the man brought before him. Once in his honor's presence, don Alvaro was commanded to speak and declare the truth regarding the shrine that he possessed or whether he knew of another person who had one. He said that he knew nothing about any shrine nor about people who might have one. The judge ordered his shirt removed and had him laid on his back, naked and tied firmly to two benches. Without further tightening the cords, the judge then ordered water poured into his mouth and nostrils. After one jug of water had been poured on him, he was warned to tell the truth and immediately said that he had no shrine but that an Indian named Pirama had six figurines and should be called to testify.

The judge then summoned the Indian Pirama, who declared without being pressed that he had in his house six gold figurines and that he would surrender them, adding that don Alvaro was innocent. I as notary, and in the company of several others, went immediately to the house of the Indian Pirama, who removed from his hut seven figurines of unrefined gold and a few small emeralds of no value. After further proceedings involving don Alvaro, the Indian Pirama testified that in another of his fields he had two other figurines of gold and four of cloth, which he will produce in the morning because at this hour it was already dark. With this the judge ordered the *alguacil* Bartolomé de Ospino to take don Alvaro and the Indian Pirama into custody and to keep them closely confined.

In this *repartimiento* on October 27 of the same year, the judge, using his powers to discover the truth and in the light of the evidence against don Fernando, the *principal* of this *repartimiento*, ordered the latter brought before him. Through the interpreter Cristóbal de Sanabria, don Fernando was commanded many times to testify regarding the shrine that he possessed as well as any idols of gold or cloth or of any other form, and to reveal whether he knew of any other Indians who may have such things. Fernando replied that he had no shrine, nor knew of any Indians who did. In view of this denial the judge ordered him stripped of his clothing and bound by the thighs to two benches; the cords were then tightened [in the manner of a tourniquet] by two and a half turns and a jug of water was poured into his mouth and nostrils. Since after all of these measures and other procedures and threats the Indian refused to confess to anything, the judge ordered him untied and sent back to jail, noting that if it seemed worthwhile or necessary, the judge, as was his customary right, would have him tortured again.

On October 28 of the same year, and obeying the orders of the judge, I as notary, along with the *alguacil* Bartolomé de Ospino, the interpreter Cristóbal de Sanabria, and Alonso de Molina, left this *repartimiento* for the site of the old *pueblo*[5] in the company of the Indian man and woman Diego Raga and Francisca Fusgay, those named by Juan Cacaria. There, more or less one league from this *repartimiento*, in some stone caves facing a hill and impossible to reach on horseback, Diego indicated a cave inside which there was found a large *tunjo* of cotton cloth. Wrapped within it were bones and a skull that Diego Raga said were those of the old *cacique* named Unbaguya, who was not a Christian and whose remains were kept for veneration. When it was untied no gold was found, and there were only a few small, worthless emeralds and five or six moldy and torn cotton blankets. The Indian then revealed a small gold clasp hidden beneath a stone and that seemed to be worth about two pesos. Despite a search of all the caves and under all the stones around the cave referred to, nothing else was found.

Immediately thereafter, I as notary, and accompanied by those mentioned above, left the cave where the corpse of the old *cacique* was found and departed in the company of an elderly Indian named Pirama, to whom the *capitán* don Alvaro had referred. The Indian led us along the road that runs from this *repartimiento* to Villa de Leiva, and as the road he took us on was rough, I [the notary] stayed behind. The *alguacil* Bartolomé de Ospino and Alonso de Molina went with the Indian and later explained that Pirama had led them high into the hills where he showed them a chest and six cotton *tunjos* which they brought before me. They stated that no gold had been found, and we thereupon returned to the *repartimiento* at approximately three o'clock in the afternoon.

When we arrived back at Iguaque we exhibited to the judge the body and bones of the *cacique* and the six small cloth *tunjos* referred to, as well as a few blankets in which the bones of the old *cacique* were wrapped and the little gold clasp. The six small *tunjos* were cut open with a knife and within were found some tiny emeralds of no value, rotten corn, cotton seeds, beans, and other rubbish. The judge ordered that all of this be burned along with the bones and blankets in the small square in front of the church, and in accord with his orders fires were lit and these things were burned. The witnesses to this act and to the opening of the *tunjos* were señor Arroyo de Guevara, don Andrés Patiño, and many others, to which I as notary hereby attest.

In this *repartimiento*, at approximately seven o'clock in the evening of the same day, further proceedings were undertaken with the *capitán* Ventura to make him declare whether he possessed any shrines either of gold or of cloth. He stated that he had two figurines of unrefined gold, both of which he then exhibited and handed over to the officials.

Thereafter, at the same hour of seven o'clock in the evening, interrogations were begun involving the Indian woman Francisca Fusgay. Her arms were tied with a rope and she was ordered to speak the truth. Just before being hoisted off the floor with the rope, she begged that this not be done and said that she would deliver the two gold figurines that she used in her shrine. The *corregidor* Pedro de Arellano went in the company of the Indian woman and returned with the two figurines, which were of unrefined gold.

Further questioning was then undertaken with the Indian named Pirama, and he was commanded to state and declare what sort of shrine he possessed and its whereabouts. Having been warned that he would be tied with the rope and raised off the floor, he said that he had four gold figurines at his shrine and pleaded not to be bound. The Indian said that he would fetch them immediately, and the *alguacil* Bartolomé de Ospino went with him and returned with the four figurines of unrefined gold and handed them in.

The proceedings then continued with Juan Pirasuca, who of his own free will and without being pressed, declared that he had in a clay pot in his house two gold figurines that comprised his shrine, and that they should go with him and he would hand in the figurines. Bartolomé de Ospino went with the Indian and brought back the two figurines of unrefined gold and delivered them over.

Following the above, on October 29 of the same year, there appeared before the judge the aforementioned Cristóbal de Sanabria and Luis Sasmia, an Indian from the *pueblo* of Iguaque. The former said that Luis Sasmia came to his house the night before and gave him four figurines of very poor quality gold and a few worthless emeralds, all of which were then handed over to the judge.

Following the above, in the *pueblo* of Iguaque on October 30, 1595, the judge and *visitador* said that as he had been given word that an elderly Indian man and woman of this *repartimiento* possessed the bones of an Indian *cacique* that they keep hidden and worship as a shrine according to their pagan customs, he ordered them to appear before him in order to discover the truth. Speaking through Cristóbal de Sanabria, the Indian man stated that his name was Pedro Unbarique and that the name of the Indian woman was Elena Pine. Judging by their appearance, the man appeared to be about ninety years old and the woman looked more than fifty-five years old. As both were *chontales* and of such advanced age they were not made to swear an oath, giving their testimony in the spirit of the proceedings and in the presence of Leandro Sánchez, the defender appointed for these Indians and for the others mentioned in these proceedings.

They stated that some seven years ago an Indian named Domingo—now very ill—removed from the church in this *repartimiento* the bones of don Juan, former *capitán* of this *repartimiento*. To remove them, Domingo had been given the key to the church by a young Indian *sacristán*, a native of Santa Fe and an assistant to Father Alonso, who was then the local priest. The bones were buried in a field near the pueblo, but the two Indians testified that they did not know why the bones were removed from the church and added that they knew nothing more about this matter. Asked if they worshipped the bones of the dead man like a shrine, they responded that they did not bury them for that purpose nor did the bones serve as a shrine. The Indian woman said that Unbagoche, who is now deceased, showed her the location of this Indian's bones, but that she knew nothing about them nor had she seen them until today, when by order of the judge she went with three Christian men, showed them the place where they lay, and they were then dug up and brought back to this *repartimiento*. Those who went on the orders of the judge to remove the bones of this Indian were the *alguacil* Bartolomé de Ospino, Alonso de Molina, and Alonso López. They declared that only the bones of the old *capitán* were found and that no gold was discovered with the bones or in the vicinity, and that this is the truth of what took place.

Following the above, in the *pueblo* of Iguaque on October 30, the *alguacil* Bartolomé de Ospino addressed the judge and produced the two small figurines of fine gold that he said Elena Pine had given him and that she had had in her shrine. The Indian woman had freely declared this fact and handed over the figurines.

Thereafter, on the same day, the *alguacil* Bartolomé de Ospino came before the judge and *visitador-general* and brought with him an Indian from this *pueblo* who calls himself Pedro. The Indian showed the *visitador* two figurines of unrefined gold that he said he had as a shrine left to him by his forebears and that he handed over voluntarily.

The same day there came before the judge an Indian named Lucas Cuyteque, who of his own will handed over a burned figurine of unrefined gold that he said was left to him by his forebears. The judge, in order to make [Lucas] reveal the whereabouts of his shrine and to identify other persons who have them, ordered him bound. To this end and to frighten him, for a brief moment the Indian was hoisted off the floor with his arms tied behind him. He stated that he had no other shrine nor did he know of anyone else who had.

In the *pueblo* of Iguaque on this same day, of October 30, the judge and *visitador-general* called before him Luis Aguaquen, an Indian from this *pueblo*, having received word that the latter had a shrine inherited from his forebears. Through the interpreter Cristóbal de Sanabria, he was commanded to speak and declare the truth and was warned that he would be tied and raised off the floor with the rope, which he was shown. He said that he knew nothing, and the judge then ordered his hands tied behind his back and that he be hoisted off the floor. He was bound and hoisted about one *palmo*, and being thus suspended, Luis Aguaquen declared that they should untie him and he would tell them the truth. On the orders of the judge he was lowered to the floor and still bound as described stated that it was true that an uncle had left him a shrine in which there were two gold figurines and two *tejuelos* of fine gold. He said he had been told to make a shrine with these but had not done so, and these objects were being kept by an Indian named Pirateque. In light of this testimony, the judge ordered the Indian brought before him. The Indian was brought and produced the two figurines of unrefined gold. Luis Aguaquen said that if they set him free he would fetch the *tejuelos*. On the orders of the judge he was freed and then brought the two *tejuelos* of fine gold and handed them over to the judge.

In the *pueblo* of Iguaque on the same day, the judge and *visitador-general* stated that in order for this case to proceed in accordance with legal and juridical form— and due to the absence of Francisco García de Frutos, defender-general of the natives—he was appointing and appointed Leandro Sánchez, resident of this *pueblo,* as defender of all the Indian men and women implicated and held in custody in these proceedings. The judge ordered the latter to accept and to swear the obligatory solemn oath.

Leandro Sánchez was immediately notified of this act and accepted the post of defender of the Indians. He then took the oath on the sign of the cross, according to the forms of law, and swore to carry out his duty well and faithfully, to gather their statements and protect them, and that he would do all that was required of a good defender. In view of this acceptance and oath, the judge granted him formal powers to defend the Indians and to undertake whatever measures might assist in their defense.

5.3 The Guilty Are Charged

Following the above, in the *pueblo* of Iguaque on October 31, 1595, the judge and *visitador-general,* having approved these acts, stated that he intended and hereby did charge the Indians now in custody: the *cacique* don Juan, don Fernando, don Diego Unbayan, Juan Riba, Ventura, Sebastián, Juan Pitasique, don Diego Sipaguancha, Juan Neaquenchia, Juan Cacaria, Diego Raga, Piramaca, Francisca Fusgay, Juan Pirasuca, Luis Sasmia, Antonico, who provided the key [to the church], Domingo, who is not present, Elena Pine, Pedro Pacacura, and Luis Aguaquen as guilty as a result of these proceedings and their own confessions. The judge ordered them brought to face the charges and respond as they see fit and stated that, without regard to what they might say, in the light of the evidence in this case the charges shall stand for two years from the conclusion and publication of these proceedings. In this *repartimiento* at the close of the month of October at approximately seven o'clock in the morning, I as notary read the above charges and evidence to Leandro Sánchez, defender of the Indians.

In the *pueblo* of Iguaque on October 31, 1595, Pedro Ganbasicha, a native of this *pueblo,* came before the judge and showed his grace two figurines of unrefined gold that he had kept as a shrine and that he then handed in.

In the *pueblo* of Iguaque on the same day, there came before the judge an Indian who stated his name as Gonzalo Conbaria who produced the corpses of two Indians he said were from the old times before the arrival of the Spaniards and that had been buried in some nearby fields. The Indian said that in the *pueblo* the bodies were treated as a shrine, and he exhibited them before the judge along with a belt sheathed in gold leaf that he said had belonged to the dead men. Having seen the above, the judge ordered the two bodies brought by this Conbaria,

Figure 3 Campaigns against idolatry also occurred in the central Andean region in the sixteenth century. This drawing depicts the *visitador-general* Cristóbal de Albornoz, his Andean assistant, and a person accused of worshipping local shrines (Guaman Poma de Ayala [1615] 1980, f. 675).

the bones of pagan Indians as Conbaria had stated, burned in the square of the *pueblo*. The judge thereupon ordered that measures be used upon Conbaria to force him to reveal the location of the gold contained in this shrine, and to this effect he was bound with the rope and raised two *palmos* off the floor. Thus suspended he was commanded to speak the truth, and said that he possessed nothing more than two gold figurines that serve as his shrine and that he will hand over. As he would not declare anything more, he was ordered set loose and was freed from the rope.

5.4 Statement by Defender of the Indians

I, Leandro Sánchez, appointed by your grace to respond on behalf of all the Indians involved in these proceedings and implicated and imprisoned on the charges made against them as idolators and for having kept small figurines and other idols, say that the aforementioned Indians should be absolved of the guilt attributed to them. Although it is true that they have kept certain figurines, they have not used them for idolatrous worship and for this reason have so readily shown them to your grace. And if these Indians have also surrendered a number of other idols, *tunjos*, and bones found outside this *pueblo*, they do not bear the guilt. Rather it is the old Indians, their ancestors, who are to blame, since they were not Christians and it was they who left these things. It is because the Indians I represent are not idolators as they are imputed to be, but rather baptized Christians that they have revealed the location of such things. If they have had some few figurines in their possession, these they inherited from their forebears and they have kept them until now without paying them much attention. And if the Indians do bear some small guilt for having kept these things in their possession, the eight days that they have already spent in custody is a more than adequate punishment.

I thus ask and plead that your grace dismiss the charges made against these Indians. For the reasons stated and argued on their behalf, and since the imprisonment and trouble they have been given and suffered has taught them their lesson and is a sufficient penalty for these wretched Indians, I ask for justice.

5.5 The Judgment of Visitador-General Guzmán

In the *pueblo* and *repartimiento* of Iguaque, on the final day of the month of October of 1595, his honor señor Egas de Guzmán—counsel to our lord the king, his senior judge on the royal *audiencia* of this kingdom and *visitador-general* of the province of Tunja—said that from the proceedings on the shrines in this *repartimiento* it is evident that the remains of the *capitán* don Juan were removed from the church where they were buried and reinterred in a field. On the order of his grace they were exhumed, and because this Indian was a Christian and had been buried in the church the judge intended and did order that his body be reburied in the Church, both because it was befitting for a Christian and because it would serve as a good example to the natives. Friar Juan Gutiérrez, the priest of this *pueblo* and member of the Order of Saint Francis, was respectfully requested to see to the interment of the Indian's remains in the church.

I the notary notified the priest Father fray Juan Gutiérrez of this act, in order that he bury the bones of the aforementioned *capitán* and I, in compliance with the wishes of the judge, certify that the bones that had been brought, and that were said to be those of the *capitán* don Juan, were buried in the church by the priest, Father fray Juan Gutiérrez.

In the *pueblo* of Iguaque in the aforementioned *encomienda* on November 1, his honor Egas de Guzmán made note of the statements made by the *gobernador* don Pedro Conba, the *cacique* don Juan, don Fernando, don Diego Unbayan, Juan Ruiz, Ventura and Sebastián Cipaquen, in which they voluntarily confessed that each had a *cuca* which in the Indian tongue means temple of adoration left to each by their respective forebears. Although it is recorded in these proceedings that his grace the judge inspected these houses and found no idols, there is reason to believe that since these Indians kept them that they retain some memory of the old rites and ceremonies and that it is right in the service of the Lord our God to extirpate all idolatrous abuses and to see that no trace or memory of them remains among the Indians. To make an example the judge intended and did order that the seven houses and temples of idolatry in which the Indians used to perform their ceremonies and idolatrous rites, be immediately burned and demolished, reserving as his grace does the right to impose upon these Indians whatever punishment he sees fit.

In compliance with the above act, immediately thereafter on the same day, month and year, the houses and huts known as *cucas*, which in the Indian tongue means temple of idolatry, were burned.

On the same day there were also burned three other huts known as *cucas*, and the Indians who testified that these were *cucas* did so of their own free will.

In the *repartimiento* of Iguaque in the *encomienda* of Juan de Otalora on November 1, 1595, Juan de Otalora came before his honor señor Egas de Guzmán, and before me, the notary. Without swearing an oath, he stated and declared that he had heard and it was public knowledge in this *repartimiento* that when the old local *capitán* and *principal* don Martín died, he left a shrine that was inherited by his nephew, the *capitán* and *principal* don Fernando, who at present lives in this *repartimiento* and who it is presumed has and possesses this shrine. Juan de Otalora has also heard and been informed that another Indian *principal* from this *repartimiento*—who died many years ago and likewise served as *capitán*—left another shrine, in which he practiced idolatry, which they say contained a quantity of gold, and that was inherited by the *capitán* don Alonso, nephew of a dead Indian. According to what Otalora states, he has been informed that these Indians have and possess these shrines, and the judge ordered him to make this same testimony under oath and to sign it. The latter said that he did not dare to do so because the Indians, on knowing that he testified against them, might then rise up or flee his *encomienda*.

In the *repartimiento* of Iguaque in the *encomienda* of Juan de Otalora on November 2, 1595, his honor señor Egas de Guzmán, speaking through the interpreter Cristóbal de Sanabria and in the light of the last statement made by Otalora (to the effect that don Fernando, *capitán* of this *repartimiento*, possesses the shrine left by his uncle don Martín), ordered don Fernando, who was present, to state and declare the true location of the shrine left by don Martín. He was warned that if he did not, he would be tortured. Don Fernando said that he knew nothing about this shrine since he is neither a relative nor an heir of don Martín, and that the person who will know and be able to reveal this is an Indian woman named Leonor China, daughter of don Martín. The judge immediately called the Indian woman to come before him and through the interpreter ordered her to state and declare the truth regarding the whereabouts of the shrine belonging to her father don Martín, as she admitted to being his daughter. She said that she knew nothing of this shrine or its location, or whether her father possessed any such shrine. Neither don Fernando nor the Indian woman declared anything further.

Faced with the denials of don Fernando and Leonor China, and in order to discover the truth as this case requires, the judge immediately ordered the Indian man and woman subjected to a form of torture with a rope and, according to his instructions, prepared cords and bonds he keeps for this purpose, as well as the water that would be used on them in this torture.

The judge then immediately ordered that don Fernando be stripped of his clothing, and once the Indian was naked, his arms were bound and tied to another rope so that he could be hoisted into the air. On the direction of the judge, the interpreter Cristóbal de Sanabria told him to state and declare the true whereabouts of the shrine, and that if he did not he would be raised off the floor and that this torture would be inflicted and if he died or if his arms broke it would be his own fault and responsibility. The Indian said that he knows nothing about the questions they ask, and on the instructions of the judge they hoisted him off the floor where he was suspended for the length of time it takes to recite two *credos*.[6] Since he denied all knowledge of this matter and declared nothing, the judge ordered the ropes untied and the man set loose.

Immediately thereafter, the judge ordered that Leonor China have her arms tied behind her back and that she be commanded to state and declare the truth. This was done, but she said that she knew nothing. The judge then ordered the rope pulled and she was hoisted about a yard off the floor,[7] where she remained suspended for the time it takes to recite one Hail Mary. She denied any knowledge regarding the questions put to her, and the judge therefore ordered that she be let down and untied.

The judge then ordered the interrogation of the *capitán* don Ventura against whom evidence of guilt had been given in previous declarations and gave instructions for his arms to be bound behind him and that he be hoisted off the floor with the rope slung over the beam. Through the interpreter the Indian was warned that he should speak the truth, but he said he knew nothing. On the signal of the judge, Ventura was hoisted some two *palmos* into the air, where he remained for the time it takes to recite one *credo*. Seeing that the Indian denied everything and refused to make any declaration, the judge ordered him freed and he was immediately let down and untied.

5.6 Final Determinations

In the light of this trial and of the evidence rendered here in the name of the royal high court with regard to the absent Pedro Conba, the *cacique* don Juan, don Fernando, don Diego Unbayan, Juan Riba, don Ventura and Sebastián, all of whom are *capitanes* and *principales* of this *repartimiento* of Iguaque, and against Juan Pitasique, don Diego Sipaquencha, Juan Neaquenchia, Juan Cacaria, Diego Raga, Piramaca, Francisca Fusgay, Juan Pirasuca, Luis Sasmia, Antonio Aguaquen, and

Gonzalo Conbaria for being idolators and for keeping shrines for the practice of their old pagan customs as is evident from these proceedings:

There is guilt established in this trial against the aforementioned don Pedro Conba, the *cacique* don Juan, don Fernando, don Diego Unbayan, Juan Riba, don Ventura and Sebastián, all of them *capitanes* and *principales* of this *repartimiento*, and against Juan Pitasaque, don Diego Sipaquencha, Juan Neaquenchia, Juan Cacaria, Diego Raga, Piramaca, Francisca Fusgay, Juan Pirasuca, Luis Sasmia, Antonio Aguaquen, and Gonzalo Conbaria for keeping old temples, idols, figurines, and Indian bones.

Therefore I the judge must and hereby do find the above guilty and sentence them to the following: I must and do order the absent Pedro Conba arrested wherever he is found and brought before me in order to deal with him as is fit and necessary. The *cacique* don Juan shall have his hair cut off and be exiled from this *repartimiento* for six months.[8] The *capitán* don Fernando is hereby fined twelve pesos in gold—one third of which shall be reserved for the court of our Lord the king and the other two thirds applied in equal parts to defray the expenses of this court and of the present visit of inspection—and if this fine is not paid immediately he shall serve four months' hard labor in the construction of the church of Chiquinquirá. Don Ventura shall serve four months' hard labor at Chiquinquirá under penalty that if he abandons this service he shall serve twice this sentence, receive fifty lashes, and have his hair cut off. Diego Raga is likewise sentenced to serve four months' uninterrupted hard labor in the same works on pain of the same punishment: that if he leaves he shall serve twice the sentence, receive fifty lashes, and have his hair cut off. Domingo, for having removed the bones of don Juan from the church where they were buried, I sentence to fifty lashes, order that his hair be cut off, and that he be exiled from this *repartimiento* for exactly one year, which time he shall serve laboring in the construction works at Chiquinquirá, and if he flees he shall serve twice this time; in regard to this Indian, who is ill, the sentence shall be carried out as soon as he recovers his health. In regard to the absent Indian Antonio from Santa Fe, for having provided the keys to the church in order to remove the bones of the Indian don Juan, I must and do order his arrest, and that he be taken from jail and in the name of justice given one hundred lashes, that he serve one year's labor in Chiquinquirá and two years' exile from this *repartimiento*; should he fail to serve either punishment fully, the sentence shall be doubled. I sentence each of don Diego Unbayan, Juan Riba, Sebastián, Juan Pitasaque, don Diego Sipaquencha, Juan Neaquenchia, Juan Cacaria, Piramaca, Francisca Fusgay, Juan Pirasuca, Luis Sasmia, Elena Pine, Pedro Patacuca, Luis Aguaquen, and Gonzalo Conbaria to have their hair cut off and to receive thirty lashes. As regards the lashes to be given to Piramaca, who is very ill, they are to be reserved until he recovers his health.

The Indians named above are hereby commanded that from this day forward they are to live as good Christians, not to be idolators nor to keep pagan shrines as they have in the past, and are warned that if they do not obey, they shall be punished with great rigor. Fray Father Juan Gutiérrez of the Order of Saint Francis and priest of this *pueblo* was entrusted with this task and was asked to endeavor with particular care to instruct the Indians in the matters of our Holy Catholic Faith. The *corregidor* was then ordered to carry out the sentences I have passed and set down herein.

NOTES

ACKNOWLEDGMENTS   I would like to thank Edward M. Farmer, Trinity College, Cambridge, for co-translating the document.

1. Unfortunately, there is little published material in English on the Muisca Indians of Colombia. My dissertation, currently in preparation for publication, will help fill that gap (J. Michael Francis, "The Muisca Indians Under Spanish Rule, 1537–1636" (Unpublished Ph.D. dissertatation, Cambridge University, 1998). With the exception of the above work, the suggestions for further reading that follow this document therefore refer readers to material from other regions of Spanish America that will help to shed some light on the nature of the proceedings at Iguaque.
2. This would translate into perhaps six hundred people for in general tribute was assessed against adult male heads of households.
3. For example, in 1580 it had been estimated that the illegal theft of native sanctuaries had cost the royal treasury more than 200,000 pesos in unpaid taxes.
4. The proceedings from Iguaque can be found in Archivo General de la Nación (Colombia), Caciques e Indios 58, no. 2, ff. 1–37 (1595). Editors' note: In this chapter the author has retained the original and often variant spelling of Muisca names (e.g., Diego Sipaguancha/Diego Sipaquencha).
5. This would be a reference to a *congregación* or forced resettlement having taken place at some earlier point.
6. The *credo*, of course, was a brief statement of the articles of Christian belief that every Christian would have memorized and repeated countless times. The phrase "en un credo" (in a creed) was a common expression meaning "in a short time." The sense here seems to be that don Fernando was suspended in the air for a brief period but for more than the proverbial "one creed."
7. Note that in this case the notary uses the *vara*, or yard, as a measure, rather than the *palmo*.
8. The decision to cut the hair of those individuals found guilty of idolatry was a deliberate attempt to humiliate and discredit the accused. Although we have no record of Muisca responses or attitudes to having their long hair cropped, colonial officials often remarked that Muisca men considered such a punishment more harsh than the physical torment of the lashes that followed. We do know that during Muisca rites of passage, which involved long periods of seclusion, fasting, and sexual abstention, men allowed their hair to grow long.

DOCUMENT THEMES

Cultural Contact/Ethnogenesis/Resistance; Ethnicity; Governance, colonial; Indigenous Peoples; Religion; Rural Life.

SUGGESTIONS FOR FURTHER READING

Arriaga 1968.
Clendinnen 1987.
Francis 1998.
Griffiths 1996.
Haliczer 1987.
Mills 1997.
Perry and Cruz, eds. 1991.
Reichel-Dolmatoff 1965.
Ricard 1966.

CHAPTER
6

~~~~~~✦~~~~~~

Affairs of the Courtroom: Fernando de Medina Confesses to Killing His Wife
(Charcas, 1595)

Thomas A. Abercrombie

> *El hombre es fuego y la mujer estopa, y llega el diablo y sopla.*
> "Man is flame, woman, tow; along comes the devil and
> blows."
>
> (SPANISH REFRAIN; JUAN RODRÍGUEZ FREYLE, *EL CARNERO*,
> CARACAS: BIBLIOTECA AYACUCHO, 1979, P. 330.)

INTRODUCTION

At about supper time on the 28th of November, 1595, the *oidor* Gaspar de Peralta, judge of the Royal Audiencia of Charcas, located in the city of La Plata (modern Sucre, Bolivia), answered a raucous hue and cry from his next-door neighbor's house to find a scene of domestic horror. Having entered the house and gone into an upstairs bedroom, the judge found his own chief scribe and secretary of the *audiencia*, Fernando de Medina, standing over the bloody corpse of his wife, Beatriz González. The secretary confessed to murdering his wife then and there. Peralta immediately initiated an investigation, hearing (and recording) Medina's detailed story of his wife's long-term adulterous affair with the *audiencia*'s prosecutor, Dr. don Gerónimo de Tovar y Montalvo (hereafter Tovar). Peralta also heard Medina's account of his wife's attempts to bewitch and poison him. From the secretary, as well as from several members of Medina's household, Peralta learned of the amorous couple's schemes to meet when the secretary was out, of visions of their steamy couplings reported by peeping slaves and servants, and of the "common knowledge" of their affair that gossips had spread about town.

As a veteran jurist, Peralta was of course familiar with cases like this, which were relatively common in life and the theme of some of the most widely known literature and drama of the period. Indeed, when Peralta heard this story of cuckoldry and violent revenge, and Medina's defense that he had killed his wife to recover his lost honor, the judge must have experienced déjà vu. For Peralta had arrived in Charcas only a few years earlier, after a ten-year hiatus in his career during which he had been forced to defend himself in Crown courts in Spain after admitting to killing his own wife (and her lover) in Quito in the year 1581, when he was prosecutor of that *audiencia*.

Peralta's own case, later immortalized in the parodic chronicle of errors known as *El Carnero*[1] (written by Peralta's acquaintance Juan Rodríguez Freyle in the early seventeenth century), makes for good historical analysis on its own. Rodríguez Freyle's "fictionalized" account of Peralta's case actually follows the latter's confession quite closely,[2] with some interpolated commentary taken from the early modern classic *La Celestina* (including the opening epigram).[3] During a recreational outing at which powerful men bragged of their sexual exploits, a young gallant named Francisco Ontanera (Diego Montanero in true life) joined in with his own boast: "That's nothing. Why not two nights ago when I was with a very beautiful lady, at the moment of our greatest pleasure we broke one of the balusters of the bed."[4] Not long after Peralta had returned home, his wife asked him to call for a carpenter, so as to repair a broken baluster of their marriage bed. "At the moment he heard this, he remembered what Ontanera had said during their outing. His blood froze in his veins, sadness covered his heart, jealousy embraced his soul, and he went altogether out of his senses, . . . and although driven out of his mind by pain, he held onto himself, so that time would bring the occasion to his hands."[5] And so it did when Peralta laid a trap with the help of his trusted slave, pretending to leave town on business but secretly returning after dark. He caught the lovers together, killing his wife's lover in the bedroom, and after chasing his wife into the garden, killed her in the latrine.

Rodríguez Freyle relates Peralta's story as a morality tale, one that illustrates the dangers of feminine beauty, and the evils of "the tongue of the backbiting murmurer, which being a sharp arrow, burns the wound with fiery coals." To sum up his story he turns to literature, this time quoting (without attribution, as was common in those days) the final passage of *La Celestina*.

> Love is a hidden fire, a pleasant wound, a tasty venom, a sweet bitterness, a delectable pain, a happy torment, a pleasureful and fiery injury, and an easy death. Love, led by lewd and sensual appetite, leads man to his wretched end, as was seen with these lovers.[6]

As Peralta explained to the king in a letter defending his acts, he had "committed a legitimate and permitted act."[7] Indeed, the law allowed a man to kill his wife with impunity when honor was at stake, in particular when cuckolding[8] parties were caught "in flagrante delicto."[9] Charging Peralta with murder, the dead man's mother offered a different story, alleging that the wife-beating, womanizing Peralta had killed his wife over trifles, and had then lured Montanero to his death by writing a note in his wife's hand begging him to come to her aid.[10] The Council of the Indies ruled that Montanero's nighttime visit to a married woman was sufficient proof of his adulterous intent. Peralta was exonerated and then promoted, and sent back to Peru to take up his new post as judge in the Audiencia of Charcas.[11]

And so, on the night of November 28, 1595, Peralta found himself investigating Medina for murdering his wife. Perhaps because he wanted to avoid calling attention to his own prior case, perhaps to avoid the complications of proceeding against friends, neighbors, and colleagues, or possibly because Tovar quickly accused him of partiality, being Medina's intimate friend and advisor, Peralta withdrew from the case, leaving the lengthy proceedings to other judges of the *audiencia*.[12]

Whether or not we can believe Medina's story about his middle-aged wife's affair with the young prosecutor Tovar,[13] Medina did not have the cool head or foresight to wait for revenge until catching the lovers together. He thus failed to prepare the kind of airtight defense that Peralta had used. Instead, he had to prove to the court that the crime against his honor had actually taken place. The burden of proof now depended on making public what prying eyes had secretly spied, and on who had heard what from whom. As usual in colonial Spanish America, the outcome of the trial also depended on the relative power and connections of the principals of the case. Just as important was the configuration of intrigue swirling about the *audiencia*, during a moment when Antonio Gutiérrez de Ulloa, a Crown *visitador* (a "visitor" with special prosecutorial powers to root out corruption) was present, threatening to take over the case as he proceeded against these and other members of the *audiencia*. As Medina was also a scribe of the Inquisition and a *familiar* (a kind of unpaid but official snitch whose job it was to denounce to his superiors whatever heretics, judaizers, and blasphemers he might encounter), his trial also became part of a struggle between the competing jurisdictions of civil and ecclesiastical courts. And there were also personal ties involved. As Tovar was to claim in his defense and his counteraccusations against Medina, most of Medina's witnesses were his slaves, servants, family members, friends, and other persons indebted to him in some way.[14] Yet Medina said the same thing about the witnesses Tovar called to testify in his defense. What is more, Medina later argued that the powerful prosecutor was in league with the *visitador*, and that *audiencia* judges were willing to hear Tovar's defense (amounting to the counteraccusation that Medina had falsely raised the issue of adultery to justify a murder he had committed for other reasons), only to avoid being implicated in the *visitador*'s other investigations.[15]

The document that follows, then, belongs to the seamy underside of some of the great imperial institutions of colonial Peru, but provides only a partial view of those institutions. Instead it opens a window that reveals the private and illicit passions of Crown officials, as well as the bloodless language of obligation and honor used by powerful men in order to get away with murder.[16] Not a story of young love, this is an account of (what may have been) an adulterous May-December affair between powerful people. With more background on Beatriz González, it might also illustrate the ways in which a wealthy married woman could take control of her own life, as well as the risks involved in doing so. What the document's testimony reveals most fully, however, are the intimate details of domestic life in a colonial household, with its large and curious staff, and the knowledge of life in that household bandied about by neighborhood gossips who kept track of the comings and goings and secret affairs of their neighbors.

Trials involving murder, witchcraft, adultery, and the besmirching of honor are not uncommon in the archives of colonial Latin America, but the document from which the following extract comes is more than a little out of the ordinary.

Figure 4   The president and judges of the royal *audiencia*, seated in hierarchical order (Guaman Poma de Ayala [1615] 1980, f. 474).

It is unusual first of all because so many of these matters come together here in a single case. Moreover, it stands out for the high rank of the principals involved, individuals who held high Crown posts within the Audiencia of Charcas. It was no doubt an infrequent occurrence for a judge to be the next-door neighbor and colleague of the man he would investigate for killing his adulterous wife, or for the philandering adulterer to be prosecutor and colleague of both men. High officials, of course, committed and were prosecuted for crimes often enough in colonial Peru, but it is not common for their most private and quotidian dealings to be laid bare in the colloquial speech of their own children, slaves, servants, friends, and neighbors. Medina's confession and the testimony of the initial hearing are also unusual for their immediacy. I do not know of another murder case where testimony was taken at the very scene of the crime, during nighttime hours and in the presence of the corpse. Even so, Medina's confession is unusually (and perhaps suspiciously) well composed considering the circumstances, and rhetorically effective as well, given the moral and legal standards of the day. In sum, this is anything but a typical case, and of course it is only a single case.

Nonetheless I hazard a few preliminary interpretations. The first proceeds from comparison with like crimes from our own age. If nowadays in Latin America or Spain a wronged husband (or wife) may flee the scene of the crime and plead temporary insanity once caught, Medina was eager to confess, and sought to exculpate himself not by reference to "the heat of passion," but by proving the adultery and witchcraft that justified his act.[17] Unlike trial testimony in, say, a Los Angeles courtroom, where reported gossip is the lowest form of hearsay, witnesses in Medina's hearing repeatedly draw upon the murmurings of gossips. We cannot be surprised by this, since in the sixteenth century one's public repute rose or fell according to the public wagging of tongues. He justifies killing his wife as a public act of retribution, necessary to take back his stolen honor. Honor, a product of public knowledge, could be repaired only by violently repudiating the public shame to which a wronged party had been subjected. That is, it was not so much his wife's adultery that had damaged his honor, but public knowledge of that adultery. So, ironically, proving himself to be an infamous cuckhold served Medina's defense very well.[18] By recounting how he had learned of what everyone else already knew, he ceased to be a laughing-stock, and rallied public tongues to join him in accusing the adulterers, go-betweens, and witches, so then to demand their punishment. Just so did Medina have the last laugh, changing the murder of his wife into a well-earned post-facto execution. Asking the court to seize her lover's property and turn it over to him, he sought to complete his revenge, and to recover his honor. Had he stealthily killed his wife and her lover, he might have gotten away with murder, but he could not thereby have repaired his reputation. A public murder, and a public trial, gave Medina a new hearing in the court of public opinion. Only by washing his dirty linen in public could he hope to get it clean.

A public accusation, as opposed to a murmured one, is not gossip but slander. As one might expect given the importance of honor, sixteenth-century courts in the Spanish colonies heard a great many slander cases. Slander, indeed, was the counteraccusation against Medina made by Tovar, who argued that the tale of adultery was fabricated by Medina as a defensive ploy after killing Beatriz in a fit of pique. The reader who notices that the shouting overheard on the night he killed her was about an insult to Medina's brother,[19] rather than about the adultery, or who reflects on the fact that the scribe Medina would have known precisely how to formulate a defense for killing his wife, might be swayed by Tovar's counteraccusations. But many people testified to having conspired in his love affair, and to having seen his amorous adventures with Beatriz González first hand. Could Medina have suborned them all to perjury?

Once the initial proceedings were concluded, Medina was freed by the *audiencia*, only to be transferred to an Inquisition jail, where his status as scribe and *familiar* of the Inquisition no doubt afforded him good treatment. In the viceregal capital of Lima he was tried by an Inquisition court, and given a light punishment. He was stripped of his Inquisition posts, fined 2,000 pesos, and temporarily suspended from his job as secretary while he served out five years of exile in Lima. While there, he continued to press his charges against Tovar. At the same time, he sought to transfer his post as scribe of the *audiencia* to his elder son, Juan Bautista de la Gasca, who was dispatched to Spain bearing fifteen silver bars for that purpose.[20] In the meantime the *audiencia* proceeded against Tovar. The Indian witches and the go-betweens (called *alcahuetes* or sometimes *Celestinas*, recalling the procuress and witch made famous in the eponymous drama), were also prosecuted, though the record of the trial is incomplete. Tovar was suspended from his post, and his property seized at Medina's request, to serve as partial payment in satisfaction of his lost honor. That, at least, was how things stood between November 1595 and January 1598.

For two years (a short time to spend in the colonial justice mill), things seemed to go Medina's way. Yet in spite of the small fortune he had spent to keep the wheels of justice turning, so as to preserve for himself and his heirs both his post and the rest of his wealth, his luck did not hold out. For the well-connected Tovar gained the ear of the Crown *visitador*, and the latter released him, returned his property, and gave him back his post as prosecutor. The *visitador* immediately sought to reopen the civil case against Medina in the *audiencia*, now accusing him of perjury, and of suborning others to give false testimony on his behalf. Moreover, Tovar now insisted that Medina's younger son, Pedro López de la Gasca, was also guilty of the murder, having provided Medina with the dagger. Murder, of course, was a serious charge. But giving false and libelous testimony against a Crown representative was itself a capital crime. So Tovar insisted that father and son alike deserved the death penalty, and that one-half of the family estate be confiscated by the Crown.[21] Released from the Inquisition jail in Lima in 1597, Medina fled with his remaining silver to the sanctuary of Lima's Dominican monastery when, in mid-1598, word reached him that the king (responding to one of Tovar's letters) had ordered the *audiencia* to proceed against him.[22]

But while the *audiencia* considered renewing its case, and the Inquisition prepared to defend its legal jurisdiction by blocking the *audiencia*, the case took yet another turn. While in hiding, Medina fell gravely ill, and called for a priest to hear his confession. What happened next is open to question. Just before he died in late May 1599 (of what cause remains unclear),[23] Tovar produced the sworn testimony of a priest who reported what had transpired between Medina and his confessor.

According to Tovar's witness, Medina's priest had gone to him for advice on how to proceed with a difficult confessional issue. In the normal course of events, the priest would have listened to Medina's confession, assigned him penance, and then given him absolution for his sins, a prerequisite for entering heaven. Instead, the priest had withheld absolution and sought the advice of his own confessor, the priest who gave testimony on Tovar's behalf. According to that testimony, Medina, fearing death was near, had revealed to his confessor that his accusation against Beatriz and Tovar had been a lie. Acting alone, without any help from his son Pedro, he had killed his wife because he had been enraged by her insults against his brother. He had then invented the story of adultery, witchcraft, and poison to justify the act. He had pressured his slaves, servants, and kinsmen to lie for him. Shortly after hearing the confession and reporting it to the second priest, Medina's confessor had died. Medina, however, was hardier than Tovar had imagined, staying alive just long enough to hear of Tovar's new ploy, and to swear out a deposition denying that the reported confession had ever taken place.[24]

What can we make of such testimony? It is not difficult to imagine that Tovar was telling the truth, and that coached by Peralta, Medina had conspired with his slaves and children and *criados* to construct a perjured defense for killing his wife. But since Tovar's new information came exclusively from secondhand sources where the firsthand witnesses were dead, it is equally plausible that Medina and his allies were telling the truth. With both Tovar and Medina dead, and no living witnesses to give further evidence, the *audiencia* then dropped the case, in part due to fear that the Inquisition would intervene yet again.[25]

No evidence remains of further proceedings against those who had lied on Medina's behalf. If, indeed, they had lied. Can it be that the detailed descriptions provided by slaves and servants of Beatriz's couplings with Tovar, and all the stories of secret nocturnal meetings, cross-dressing, gifts of clothes, and dinner deliveries, were lies concocted on short notice, at the scene of the crime or within days of the murder?[26] Did Medina accuse Tovar, as the latter tells it, only to prevent a zealous prosecutor from trying him for murder? Or is it just as possible that Medina's deathbed confession was false? Could it be that his recantation, if it took place, was a bargain with the devil, by which he hoped to persuade Tovar and the *audiencia* not to persecute his family? Would Medina have risked his eternal soul to save his earthly legacy?[27]

As happens all too often in historical inquiry, this document and the story it tells leaves us with more questions than it answers. Medina's compelling confession at the scene of the crime, and the vivid testimony provided by witnesses on his behalf, are certainly more convincing than his reported deathbed retraction. Ultimately the stories that passed the tongues of the inhabitants of late sixteenth-century La Plata,[28] truth or lies, nonetheless polished or tarnished the public repute of men and women, and the *audiencia* remained arbiter of that repute, pronouncing on who deserved respect and who did not, and on what could be said publicly about them, and what had to be whispered. Whether or not it is possible to discover "what really happened" or to fully sort out truth from fiction, we can learn something about what mattered to these sixteenth-century people, and something about the tortured relationship among truth, justice, and power.

Read differently, this kind of court testimony can also instruct us on an issue of more fundamental importance to the historian, an issue that is at the core of our very humanity: how it is that in order to understand our experiences, including the most terrible of events, we shape them into stories, crafting narratives so that others, and we ourselves, can find meaning in them, and perhaps forgiveness.[29] As historians, we must be mindful of such things as we question the verisimilitude of testimonies found in archives, query "fictional" or "factual" chronicles, and as we write our own narratives.

The document that follows includes merely the opening scenes of the extended courtroom drama (totaling 676 folios or 1,352 handwritten pages), the subject of my ongoing research. More investigation of the social context and characters of the story is in progress, including attention to the context of other contemporaneous cases, and other narratives such as *El Carnero*. In selecting passages for inclusion, I have omitted repetitive material (the formal swearing in and the like). Scribes routinely reported the speech of witnesses in the third person rather than first person (as in "the witness said that she heard shouts"). I have changed testimony directly into the first person to render it more immediate, while leaving introductory and concluding comments added by the scribes in the original third person.

THE DOCUMENT[30]

Copy of the summary proceedings and information carried out on the death of Beatriz González, wife of Fernando de Medina, house scribe of the Royal Audiencia of La Plata, before its lords president and judges (*oidores*), and forwarded to the Very Illustrious Licentiate Antonio Gutiérrez de Ulloa, inquisitor and visitor general (*visitador general*).

[signed by] Fernando de Zúñiga.

6.1 The Indictment/Initial Hearing

In La Plata, November 28, 1595, the Lord Licentiate Gaspar de Peralta, of the council of His Majesty and his judge in the Royal Audiencia of La Plata, said that while His Mercy was now in his house he received news from the house of the secretary Fernando de Medina that there had occurred a serious matter. Seeing to it, His Mercy went to that house, and in the bedroom found Beatriz González, wife of the secretary Fernando de Medina, dead on the floor. She appeared to have died as a result of wounds to the body and throat. In order to discover how and why she had died, and who killed her, the Licentiate Peralta carried out the following investigation.

Before me, Lucas de Ribera [scribe].

6.2 Confession of the Secretary Fernando de Medina

Without delay the Lord Licentiate Gaspar de Peralta . . . swore in the secretary Fernando de Medina . . . who promised to tell the truth. . . . Asked if he killed his wife Beatriz González and for what reason, and asked to relate the facts of the case, the witness said:[31]

Although I am a minister of the Holy Office of the Inquisition, and as such should enjoy the privileges conceded to me, I give this declaration so that the truth should be known, without prejudice to these privileges.

What happened is that twenty-seven years ago, more or less, I married Beatriz González according to the dictates of the Holy Mother Church in the Villa de Llerena [in Extremadura, Spain]. And I held her in great honor, treating and feeding her very honorably and providing her with all that was necessary. I did so by carrying out my craft of scribe in the government of the Villa de Llerena, which is an office of great authority, until in the year of seventy-two I passed to this kingdom [the Indies] with my wife and two children. I landed in the Villa de Tolú where I served as public scribe and scribe of the town council, there too holding my wife in great honor, sustaining and feeding her for the two and a half years that I was there. Then I passed to Panama City where I carried out the duties of secretary of that royal *audiencia* for about a year, keeping my wife in great honor and providing her with all necessities. Later I took her with me to the city of Cuzco, where I was scribe for almost a year, sustaining her in the same manner. Afterwards I took her to the Villa de Potosí where I was public and council scribe and general procurer of that Villa, and where I also honored and provided for Beatriz González. Finally I took her to this city where I have in the same way sustained and provided for her.

Last Friday, the tenth of this present month, in company with don Pedro Ozores de Ulloa and the dean of the holy church of this city, the secretary Joan de Losa, Father Pizarro, and other persons, I went to the fields (*chácaras*) of the valley of Coy, where we remained that day and the following Saturday, until on Sunday we returned to this city. It was then that I was informed by my son, Pedro López de la Gasca, and my daughter Joana Leonarda, and by Gracia and the other people of my house, that my wife Beatriz González was in the garden that we have in Guayopacha,[32] accompanied by her children and servants, and by doña Mencia, wife of Joanes de Oñate. And while there on that Friday night, my wife dressed in men's clothing,[33] and went out of the house and garden in the company of Bartolomé Gonzáles, the servant of doña Mencia, and he took her to the house of Dr. don Gerónimo de Tovar y Montalvo, the prosecutor of this royal *audiencia*. She remained with him all night long until the early hours, having carnal access with him and committing the sin of adultery.

Everyone of my house, and other persons outside of it, have told me about this relationship, and that for over a year Dr. don Gerónimo de Tovar y Montalvo [hereafter Tovar] has had carnal relations with Beatriz González, my wife, sometimes in my own house, bed, and rooms, and in my daughter's bed, and in the stable and the salon of my house. And other times [they met] in Tovar's house, to which Beatriz González sometimes went dressed in men's clothing, and sometimes in her own clothing. There she stayed many nights with Tovar, commiting with him the crime of adultery. Many people have testified to this, including Miguel de la Juz, Joan de Olasco, my children, Joana Leonarda, and our slaves Gracia, Isabel, Isabelilla, and Magdalena, and so too will Luisa the Indian and María Ximénez, wife of Joan de Contreras. The latter was persuaded by Beatriz González and the prosecutor [Tovar] to accompany Beatriz, dressed in men's clothing, to the prosecutor's house, where she committed the crime of adultery. And she took to him many shirts and meals and other gifts, thereby depleting my wealth, and tried to kill me by putting many powders into the flask in which wine was brought to me. All the people of my house saw these things and will testify to it.

Moreover, Beatriz González, bending to the will of the prosecutor, went about dealing with Indian witches, striving to kill me or make me lose my mind, as all the above mentioned people know. To this effect, about ten days ago Joana de Tapia, the wife of Sancho Antón, shoemaker, brought some powders to my wife Beatriz González, and gave them to her in the presence of doña Mencia. And the instruments of sorcery (*hechizos*) were found in a chest belonging to Beatriz González, who has many times said she was going to kill me and our children and Alonso Ximénez, my brother.[34] And most recently she said it this very day, as my son Pedro López de la Gasca, and doña Mencia, and María de León, widow of Joan de Balmaseda, will tell you. And so too, certain Indian women are witches, as the black women (*negras*) and people of my house will testify.

What is more, Tovar has lacked the faithfulness he owes to His Catholic Majesty, who gave him the office [of prosecutor], and has failed in his obligation to me as his friend and fellow minister and official of this royal *audiencia*, wherein everyday we had dealings and communicated with one another.

When I finally learned about all of this approximately eight or ten days ago, I endeavored to catch the prosecutor and my wife together. But because they were warned by the rector of the Company of the Name of Jesus [the Jesuits],[35] I did not catch him with her. Today I heard that Beatriz González wanted to kill me with those powders, and she would have succeeded had I not prevented it, with the help of my children and people of the house and servants, by frequently washing and rinsing my wine flasks.

Finally I saw how my honor, and that of my children and kinsmen and relatives, was lost, stolen by one of His Majesty's ministers. He should rather have served as a defensive wall against the commission of crimes; his obligation was to maintain decorum and defend my honor, not to offend it. So unable to get satisfaction with the prosecutor, I killed Beatriz González, my wife. Now I formally accuse her, and the doctor don Gerónimo de Tovar y Montalvo, as guilty of the crime of adultery. I also charge the prosecutor with seeking to take advantage of my wealth and property, by receiving shirts and other things from Beatriz González, and [I charge him] with trying to take, and in effect taking, my honor from me and from my children. And I beseech the lords president and judges to order his arrest and imprisonment, putting him under careful custody and guard, so that I can accuse him and satisfy my honor on his person and property. I would also reserve the right to express many other complaints, which at present have passed from my memory because of the acceleration of events, so that in the future I might make whatever further or better demands I see fit to make.

And the witness, over fifty-two years of age, signed his name, and asked the court, for the proof of what he said, to look for the spells and powders that he had found in a chest belonging to Beatriz González. And he signed his name, Fernando de Medina, and the Lord Judge [Gaspar de Peralta] also signed.

Before me, Lucas de Ribera.

After the above, in the city of La Plata on November 28, 1595, the Lord Licentiate Gaspar de Peralta, His Majesty's judge in this royal *audiencia*, having seen the confession of the secretary Fernando de Medina, arrested him. And although the secretary asked His Mercy to give him the jail of his choice, since he had but returned [the insult] for his honor,[36] the Lord Judge found that since imprisonment could not be excused, that he should be held prisoner until the investigations he had ordered were carried out.

Before me, Lucas de Ribera.

6.3 Complaint Against Ribadeneyra

In the city of La Plata on November 28, 1595, before the Lord Judge, the secretary Fernando de Medina likewise accused Joan de Bastidas Ribadeneyra of being a minister and third person (tercera persona), or go-between (alcahuete), between the prosecutor and Beatriz González.

6.4 Delivery of Witchcraft

In the city of La Plata, on November 28, 1595, during the investigation of the matter, the black woman Gracia handed over and exhibited before the Lord Licentiate Gaspar de Peralta, His Majesty's judge, certain powders, wrapped in rags, that were the witchcraft (hechizos) that Beatriz González kept in her trunk, which were said to have been placed in the flask used to bring wine to the secretary Fernando de Medina. And she also showed the court, wrapped in a piece of paper, some hairs that she said were from the secretary's beard. These were used to keep on killing him.[37] And the Lord Judge ordered all of the packages and papers with their powders and hairs given over to Lucas de Ribera Ynfante, His Majesty's scribe, who received them and wrapped them all in a handkerchief. Then the black woman Gracia said that she had taken some of these things from Beatriz González's trunk, and the rest from her bag, and that these things had been brought to the house by certain old Indian women, whose names she did not know, except for one called Isabel, who lives in the ranchería[38] of Lord Saint Sebastian of this city. She did not sign because she did not know how, so the Lord Judge signed it.

Before me, Lucas de Ribera.

6.5 Testimony of Alonso de Cáceres Alvarado

In the city of La Plata, November 28, 1595, the Lord Licenciate Gaspar de Peralta . . . swore in . . . Alonso de Cáceres Alvarado, resident in this city . . . who said the following:

Since I arrived in this city about a year and a half ago, I have regularly gone in and out of the house of the secretary Fernando de Medina. Many times I have seen coming to that house Joan de Bastidas Ribadeneyra, bailiff (alguacil) of the court and protégé of Dr. don Gerónimo de Tovar y Montalvo, His Majesty's prosecutor in this royal audiencia. Many times there he spoke in secret with Beatriz

González, the secretary's wife, leading me to suspect that he brought messages from the prosecutor. Living with that suspicion, I sometimes saw the prosecutor enter the houses of the secretary, especially into the house where, at present, the Lord Licentiate Gaspar de Peralta now lives. And one day in particular I saw the prosecutor enter into the interior room (*quadra*) where the secretary Fernando de Medina usually slept, while I was in the dining room writing a letter for the mail.[39] María Ximénez, niece of Beatriz González, came to me, and said: "Leave from here, Your Mercy, because Beatriz González is furious with you for being here," so I went out of the dining room and went to finish writing and sealing the letter at the secretary's desk. Afterwards I went out into the patio and looked up, like this,[40] at the inner-room window where the prosecutor and Beatriz González were, but I did not see them where I had left them, but only saw that María Ximénez was peeking through the grate in the window (*celogía*). From that I drew the conclusion that the prosecutor and Beatriz González were commiting adultery against the secretary Fernando de Medina. And I recall that that day I asked María Ximénez why Beatriz González had been angry with me when I was writing in the dining room, and she answered with suggestive words.[41] When I pressed her to answer more clearly, María Ximénez said: "To the devil with them, there they are closeted together in the inner bedroom."

Many times I have seen the prosecutor, Dr. don Gerónimo de Tovar y Montalvo, enter into the rooms of the secretary Fernando de Medina when he was away from the house. María Ximénez would spy through the grate of the window of the room where they slept. Then Gracia and Isabel, the secretary's slaves, told me about Beatriz González's dealings with the prosecutor, so prejudicial to the secretary's honor, when the prosecutor and Beatriz González laid down carnally (*echandose carnalmente*) together. And many times at all hours of the day and night I saw Gracia and Isabel go to the prosecutor's house. By carefully spying on them, I saw her enter and leave that house, carrying to him lunch and dinner and white clothing. . . .[42]

The adultery that the prosecutor and Beatriz González commited against the secretary Fernando de Medina is so public and notorious among the people, that I believe there is no one who does not know about it, given the great boldness by which they dealt with one another in public.

I also saw entering into her house the old Indian women who the black women Gracia and Isabel told me were the witches that Beatriz González made use of for her dealings with the prosecutor,[43] and so that the secretary would not realize what was going on, and to kill him. In these meetings I saw that María Ximénez served as interpreter between Beatriz González and the Indian women. I had a low opinion of all this, and I am certain of its truth for the foregoing, and because Beatriz González many times said bad things about one or two married women of this town. By speaking ill of them like this, she led me to understand that she was jealous of their relationship with the prosecutor.[44] And Beatriz González held in special esteem and affection all the people of the prosecutor's house, such as Ribadeneyra, Diego de la Pila, and Gonzalo de Matos, with all of whom she spoke very familiarly and in secret.

As a person who judged as evil so much dissolution between the prosecutor and Beatriz González, I often reprehended her for it, to which she would answer, that whatever she did, she was not the first person in the world to err. By this I concluded that Beatriz González held some hatred for me, because I had reprehended her, and I knew about the mistreatment to which she and the prosecutor had subjected the secretary, in such great prejudice and damage to his honor and that of his family. This was especially so given how well loved she was, so well cared for and kindly treated and served by the secretary and her family and friends.

Indeed, I hold that it was just this excess of kindness and generosity that the secretary bestowed on her that led her to commit adultery, as a libertine.[45] It seems to me that the death the secretary gave her was just what she deserved, and owed as a debt to the secretary Fernando de Medina. Given how greatly the secretary suffered at the hands of his wife, the whole town was amazed that he did not kill her many days earlier. This is what I know, and it is the pure truth according to my oath.

The witness is about thirty-six years old; the general questions do not apply to him.[46] And he ratified his testimony and signed his name to it, and so too did the Lord Judge Licentiate Peralta sign, and Alonso de Lacergo.

Before me, Lucas de Ribera.

[In the next entry, Miguel de la Juz, an assistant to Fernando de Medina, corroborates the foregoing testimony, adding few further details on the intimacy between the adulterers and the watchfulness and spying they engaged in to preserve their "secret."]

6.6 Testimony of Simón de Ledesma

In the city of La Plata, on November 28, 1595, . . . the Lord Licentiate Joan Díaz de Lopidana[47]. . . swore in Simón de Ledesma, resident of this city . . . who said that:[48]

. . . What I know of the adultery is that over a year ago, in the month of August or September, when the secretary had gone to the Villa de Potosí by commission of the royal *audiencia*, I knew and understood it to be very public and notorious that the prosecutor had committed adultery against the secretary. Knowing this, and to find out the truth, as I was coming down the street from my house, which is just above the houses of Gaspar de Saldaña, walking toward the plaza, whereas the secretary's house is across the street from the monastery of Saint Dominic, I saw two shapes at the door of the secretary's house at about nine or ten at night. They called at the door, and I heard a black woman answer, saying, "Who's there?" And Joan de Bastidas Ribadeneyra, lieutenant bailiff (*teniente de alguacil mayor*) of this court, and the prosecutor's protégé (*criado*)[49] said, "It's me, tell my lady Beatriz González that I am here, and that I bring letters from the Lord Secretary from Potosí."[50] Continuing further down the street, I heard the doors open, and I went with another friend of mine—I don't remember if it was Joan de Villoldo or who it was—and my friend told me, "Do not wonder who those men were at the secretary's door, because they were the prosecutor and Ribadeneyra. Look what pretexts they engage in to cover their villanies, saying that they're bringing letters from the secretary in order to enter his house." Turning around to watch more carefully, I saw that what my friend said was true.

Figure 5 Two Spanish noblewomen in late eighteenth- century Peru, one wearing a veiled head covering similar to the one Beatriz González may have used to disguise herself (see note 52) (Martínez Compañón [1790] 1936, plate 18).

But I did not observe whether the door closed behind the prosecutor and Ribadeneyra, although I suspect that they stayed there for their business, and I imagine that they went in to commit the adultery that was so notorious. . . .[51]

On certain nights I saw Beatriz González go out of her house to the prosecutor's house, and I saw her go there at nine or ten at night, covered in a cape, with a scarf covering most of her face.[52] I was shocked at such carelessness and shamelessness . . . and I hold it for certain that the prosecutor committed adultery with her against the secretary Fernando de Medina. . . .[53]

The witness said he was twenty-five years old, and signed his name. And none of the general questions apply, except that he is an official in the office of the secretary Fernando de Medina, where he is a scribe.

Simón de Ledesma, Licentiate Lopidana.
Before me, Lucas de Ribera.

[The next entry in the document is the testimony of Juan de Olaso Montanes, another "hanger on" of the Medina-González household; it essentially corroborates the foregoing.]

6.7 Testimony of the Black Woman Gracia

In the city of La Plata, November 28, 1595, in the murder investigation, the Lord Licentiate Bernardino de Albornóz,[54] judge of this royal *audiencia*, ordered before him a black woman who said she was called Gracia, a slave, who said she belonged to the secretary Fernando de Medina . . . Having been sworn in . . . she said the following:

What I know about this case is that tonight, after the *ánimas*[55] bell had rung, while I was preparing my masters' supper in the kitchen, I heard the noise of a fight between the secretary Fernando de Medina and Beatriz González, his wife. I went out of the kitchen to see what they were fighting about, and saw that her husband was telling her to shut up and not to shout, because people were gathering in the street. To this Beatriz González said that Alonso Ximénez, the secretary's brother, was a con man (*embustero*), and then she threw herself at the secretary and grabbed hold of his beard,[56] and I thought she would pull it to pieces, and the secretary told her to shut up, for the love of God. But she did not want to be quiet. She was frantic to get out of the house, to complain to the justices. But he would not let her out of the room. Then I went back into the kitchen. Later I heard shouting again, this time by the couple's daughters, and then I saw that Beatriz González was lying dead next to the bed, but I did not see the wounds, though I saw her blood.

When this witness was asked to declare what she knows about the cause of the ill will and anger between Fernando de Medina and his wife, she said the following:

What I know is this: One night, I don't remember what day it was, when the secretary Fernando de Medina was out of the city, when he had gone to the fields of the Teatinos, Beatriz González went out from the house of the garden (*huerta*) of Guayapacha at about eight or nine, through the garden window. She was dressed in men's clothing, wearing some black velvet leggings (*callones*) that belonged to Fernando de Medina, and black shoes and a black hat, a cape belonging to the Licentiate Juan Baptista, her son, the color of the tunic (*sayo*) he is now wearing. I did not see where she went, but she came back to the house and garden after dawn. A boy of doña Mencia's went with her, by the name of Bartolomé González, a young man who that morning carried and gave to me a *toca* [a woman's veil or scarf; also a head-covering worn by men at night]. And I suspect that they had gone to the house of Dr. don Gerónimo de Tovar y Montalvo, prosecutor of this royal *audiencia*, because I had gone there sometimes with messages from Beatriz González, and took to him capons and chickens and both big and little biscuits. I also took him the gift of three new shirts, two of roan with red embroidery (*de ruan de cofre rrandadas*) and another of roan with its handkerchiefs [or cuffs] (*ruan con sus pañisuelos*). And she sent them with the message that she kissed his hands, and that he should dress himself in those shirts. He responded that he kissed her hands many times for this gift. And when I did not return quickly Beatriz González let me have it with a switch. . . .[57]

I also remember that many times they brought the prosecutor's clothes for me to wash, and when I did not finish it my mistress scolded me. I don't remember more right now, but I will say it when I do.

Again I remember that, a good long time ago, when they lived in the other house . . .[58] when Fernando de Medina had gone to Moxotoro to get those pear trees, I saw the prosecutor come into Fernando de Medina's house. He was there a while talking with Beatriz González in the salon, and then they went into the water [storage] room, where I saw them together, one on top of the other. They went in there in the dark, but I could see them by the light of the candle in the salon. So although there was no candle in the water room I could see what they were doing there, one on top of the other. He was in there for two hours before he left. In the morning, Beatriz González climbed up to the attic to see whether from there one could hear anything in the room below, the one with the water jars. I remember nothing more, and I tell the truth.

The witness did not sign because she does not know how. She said she did not know her age, but appears to be about thirty-five years old. Asked the additional questions,[59] she answered that she is a slave, and that she has not been induced.[60]

Bernardino de Albornóz.
Before me, Francisco de Zúñiga.

6.8 Testimony of Magdalena María, the Secretary's Slave

In the city of La Plata, November 28, 1595, at about ten o'clock at night, the above-said Lord Judge ordered brought before him a young girl who said her name was Magdalena, a *mulata* slave who said she belonged to Fernando de Medina. She was sworn in . . . and said the following:

What I know and saw is that this night, while I was setting the table for supper, and while I was in the dressing room with doña Juana, the daughter of Fernando de Medina and Beatriz González, I heard my masters arguing, and I went out and saw them going at one another (*estar asidos*). Beatriz González had hold of her husband by the beard and shirt. Fernando de Medina grabbed her by the hair and took out a dagger, and I saw him stab Beatriz González, his wife, many times, while she cried out "kill me." Then from her wounds she fell dead on the floor, and I saw her lying there dead just as she is now. Then they went out to report what had happened to the Lord Licentiate Gaspar de Peralta, who lives here very near to this house.

What I heard them saying to one another during their argument is this: Beatriz González told her husband, Fernando de Medina, that his brother Alonso Ximénez was a con man, to which he responded that it was a lie. I heard nothing else this night. But what I do know, is that during the afternoon of the day this year when they took out the pendant[61] in this city, I saw the doctor don Gerónimo de Tovar y Montalvo, prosecutor of this royal *audiencia*, enter this house. He came in and went upstairs here (*subió aca arriba*).[62] When I came out of the bedroom I saw Beatriz González with the prosecutor in the big salon, and saw them on a chair. The prosecutor was disarrayed, and was having carnal access with Beatriz González, whose skirts were pulled up. I saw them because I walked in suddenly—the salon door was open—and a black woman named Isabelilla was guarding the door. That was the only time I saw the prosecutor next to Beatriz González. . . .[63] So too did I see Beatriz González sprinkling the prosecutor's shirts with musk (*almizque*) and cologne (*agua de olor*). And a few times I saw her put some white powders into her husband's silver wine flask, although I do not know what those powders were. I do not know or remember anything else right now. That is the truth as I have sworn to tell it.

The witness did not sign, because she did not know how, and said she was sixteen years old, more or less, and that nothing in the general questions asked her is pertinent.

[signed by]
Licentiate Bernardino de Albornóz.

Before me, Francisco de Zúñiga.

NOTES

ACKNOWLEDGMENTS   I ran across this recently catalogued document in the Archivo Nacional de Bolivia in 1995. Thanks are due to archive director Lic. Rene D. Arze for permission to photocopy and publish portions of the document, and to helpful archive staff (especially doña Ana Forenza) for aid in finding allied material. I have benefitted from discussions of the case with many individuals, including graduate students in my seminar on urban Latin America in the department of anthropology at New York University. I thank Juan Pablo Lombana of the University of Miami for urging me to read *El Carnero* in connection with the Medina case. Thanks are also due to James C. Scott and the Program in Agrarian Studies at Yale University (as well as to the Rockefeller Foundation) whose generosity supported writing of a first draft, and to my fellows at the Program, whose comments on presentation of that draft were most helpful. Discussions with Nathan Wachtel and Gilles Riviere, and members of their seminar at the Ecole des Hautes Etudes en Sciences Sociales in May 1997 were also important. A presentation in the anthropology colloquium at the New School for Social Research helped to further clarify my thoughts on honor and gossip (thanks especially to Steven Caton and William Roseberry). Thanks for their insights, queries, and suggestions are due to William A. Christian, Guido Ruggiero, and Gary Urton. I am especially indebted for discussion of the case and for helpful insights to Sarah Elizabeth Penry. Research in Seville during the summer of 1997 and Quito during the summer of 1998 was supported by New York University. Geoffrey Spurling deserves particular thanks for his insights in discussion of the case, and for his helpful editorial suggestions and queries.

1. Juan Rodríguez Freyle, *El Carnero* (Caracas: Biblioteca Ayacucho, 1979). Considered one of the founding texts of Latin American literature, the work contains numerous narratives of passion and crime, some of which, including the case of Peralta, have been classified as fictional. But if the story of Peralta's deeds is a fiction, it is of Peralta's making; Rodríguez Freyle closely follows Peralta's version of events. The two crossed the Atlantic together on the same ship when they went to Spain in the early 1580s to defend themselves before the Council of the Indies. For more on *El Carnero*, see Roberto González Echevarría, *Myth and Archive: A Theory of Latin American Narrative* (Cambridge: Cambridge University Press, 1990).
2. Peralta's account is in: Archivo General de Indias (hereafter AGI), Santa Fe, 16, r. 27, no. 191. Cartagena, 1 April 1583. Peralta to Philip II.
3. In spite of being repeatedly banned, *La Celestina* was widely read in the Indies, although the older romances of chivalry were perhaps even more well known. When the Third Provincial Council of Lima of 1583 ordered the confiscation of vain books, *La Celestina* was the only title specifically named: "One of the things which most damages the Christian Republic is the reading of obscene books and *caballerías* (romances of chivalry), which serve no good effect but to make the imagination boil with obscene and lascivious desires and vain and false fables. Young people are especially swayed by such vanities, to the great detriment of their souls. Such books corrupt them and light libidinal fires, and because of them they begin to try out things of which they had never known about or heard of otherwise. Thus we com-

mand all people, men and women . . . to bring to us . . . books titled *Dianas* no matter who is the author, and the book titled *Celestina*, and books of *caballerías*. Also satires and impertinent books, and immodest and obscene poetry" (AGI, Charcas 48. 1599 Constituciones of the Bishop of Tucumán, following the Tercer Concilio Limense). The following item in the *constitución* sought to prevent men from reading or distributing books about, or acting in accordance with, codes of dueling.

   La Celestina, a dramatized novel about star-crossed lovers and the woman whose love magic and go-between skills (as *alcahuete*) leads them to a bad end, is a founding work of the Spanish Golden Age, published in 1499 by the *converso* author Fernando de Rojas and available in many modern editions. Similar themes pervade Early Modern Spanish literature, from *Lazarillo de Tormes* to Cervantes and the so-called honor plays of Calderón and Lope de Vega (see Matthew D. Stroud, *Fatal Union: A Pluralistic Approach to the Spanish Wife-Murder Comedias* [Lewisburg, Penn.: Bucknell University Press, 1990]). The classic source on colonial reading habits is Irving Leonard, *Books of the Brave* (Berkeley: University of California Press, 1992).

4. Rodríguez Freyle, *El Carnero*, p. 289.
5. Ibid.
6. Ibid., p. 290. If Rodríguez Freyle had known Fernando de Medina's case, he would have had still better reason to quote from *La Celestina*, since the book concerns illicit passion provoked by love magic and curried by go-betweens. Medina rues the theft of his honor, but also Indian witchcraft and not just one but several *Celestinas* (a term that by Medina's day had become synonymous with *alcahuete*). Sometimes the twists and turns of authentic criminal proceedings outreach even the literary imagination.
7. AGI, Santa Fe 16, r. 27, n. 191. Cartagena, 1 April 1583. Peralta to Philip II, f. 1r.
8. The modern Spanish equivalent of cuckold, *cornudo* (horned), derives from the early modern phrase *poner cuernos a* (put horns on). Indeed, Rodríguez Freyle recounts how one jealous man ran home and killed his wife after a crazy person in the plaza had held up two fingers behind his head, in an act familiar to any adolescent.
9. Tovar cited the law to argue that Medina deserved punishment, since he denied committing adultery with Beatriz. In Tovar's words, the law was as follows: "The husband who kills his wife without finding her with anyone should be punished. But he who kills her finding her *in fragrante delicto* [sic], as the law says, can kill them as one, without any punishment. [The same is true when the husband], having three times warned the man who he believes to be offending his honor, then finds him with his wife in a prohibited or secret place" (AGI, Charcas 17, r. 9, n. 56. La Plata, 1 March 1598. Tovar to king, f. 2v.). More on such questions of law can be found in: Mary Elizabeth Perry. *Gender and Disorder in Early Modern Seville* (Princeton: Princeton University Press, 1990), 120.
10. Diego Montanero's parents, Alonso de Paz and doña María Jaramillo, filed murder charges against Peralta in the Audiencia of Quito (AGI, Santa Fe, r. 26, no. 182. Cartas de Audiencia, 1582. Memorial de la querella criminal de Gaspar de Peralta . . .). According to them, Peralta's wife was a chaste and respectable woman who was whipped, bewitched, poisoned (with the help of his mistress, using *bebedizos* and herbs called *ballesteros* and *ponzona*), and otherwise mistreated by Peralta. Peralta, they argued, was a vice-laden, notorious womanizer, who habitually wandered through seedy parts of town seeking women of ill repute, and who entered the houses of honorable married men to defame their wives, disguising himself by dressing in Indian clothes (*en hábito de indio*), carrying a bundle of firewood on his back (ibid., fol. 3v–4r). A few days after killing his wife in her bed over trifles, they say, he threw her corpse into the latrine. Then he plotted with his slave to lure their son to his back garden one night, by writing a note in his wife's hand, begging for help. Peralta then had Montanero killed in the street, dragging his body into his house (ibid., fol. 4v). The couple call on the *audiencia* to interrogate witnesses; Peralta's slave was questioned under torture, but answered that he would speak ill of him [his master] only at the foot of the gallows (ibid., fol. 4r). Peralta replied that these were libelous falsehoods, cooked up by the powerful Jaramillo family and his enemies among the *audiencia's* judges to be rid of a zealous prosecutor and thus free to pursue their usual corrupt ways (ibid., 1r.–2r.). Yet shortly after he was questioned, Peralta emancipated his slave, without taking the usual payment (Archivo Histórico del Banco Central de Ecuador, Protocolos Notariales vol. 194 [escribano Gaspar de Aguilar]. Carta de emancipación, 20 July 1581, f. 446r.–47r.).

Subsequently, while traveling through the territory of the Audiencia of Santa Fe (now Colombia), Peralta was accused of multiple rapes, and of keeping numerous Indian mistresses and a *morisca* for his "obscene desires" (AGI, Escribanía 822A. 1586. Contra los Oydores don Luis Pérez de Salazar y Gaspar de Peralta). He was later exonerated of all charges, including the murder (AGI, Escribania, 953. 1583. Doña María Jaramillo con Gaspar de Peralta . . .); his accusers were ordered to keep perpetual silence on the matter.

11. Joining him was Bernardino de Albornóz, former prosecutor in Santa Fe. The same document appointed a recent law graduate, Tovar, to the post of prosecutor in Charcas (AGI, Charcas 1, n. 50. Real Provisión. 14 August 1591).

12. Tovar goes so far as to imply that Peralta, the first official to arrive on the scene of the crime, had advised Medina on how to proceed (Archivo Nacional de Bolivia [hereafter ANB], EC 1597, no. 2, f. 475r). Possibly, Tovar was hinting at a deeper complicity, that Peralta had helped Medina to plan the murder. At any rate, Peralta did not live to see the case concluded; Tovar reported to the king on Peralta's sudden death from an unspecified illness (AGI, Charcas 17, r. 9, n. 56. La Plata, 1 March 1598. Tovar to king, f. 1r.).

13. In his defense when formal charges were filed against him, Tovar insisted that Beatriz's age made any suggestion of an affair between them unbelievable (AGI, Charcas 17, r.8, n.55. Potosí, 1 November 1597. Expediente de Jerónimo Tovar y Montalvo . . .).

14. See note 26. Tovar also might have pointed out that the protections enjoyed by a *familiar* also extended to his family, slaves, and servants, perhaps making them more willing to lie on Medina's behalf. A detailed account of the legal exemptions enjoyed by Inquisition officials can be found in Paulino Castañeda Delgado and Pilar Hernández Aparicio, *La Inquisición de Lima*, Tomo. 1 (Madrid: Editorial Deimos, 1989), 87–111.

15. Tovar's letter reports his return to duty as prosecutor and the return of his goods, ordered by the *visitador*, and the latter's reinitiation of charges against Medina (AGI, Charcas 17, r. 9, n. 56. La Plata, 1 March 1598. Tovar to king, f. 2v.). The same letter reports (and backs) the *visitador's* accusations against several *oidores*, including Bernardino de Albornóz, in part for conspiring to foster a riot in protest of the *visitador's* actions in La Plata (ibid., f. 3r.). Medina's charges against the *visitador* (and the *corregidor* of Potosí, Pedro Ozores de Ulloa) are in AGI, Escribanía 846A, no. 4. 1598. Hernando de Medina . . . con el fiscal y Pedro Ozores de Ulloa . . .). Medina appears to have been correct about the collusion between Tovar and the *visitador*.

16. More on the matter of honor among elites of the period can be found in: José Antonio Maravall, *Poder, honor y élites en el siglo XVII* (Madrid: Siglo Veintiuno de España, 3rd ed., 1989) and Lyman Johnson and Sonya Lipsett-Rivera (eds.), *The Faces of Honor: Sex, Shame, and Violence in Colonial Latin America* (Albuquerque: University of New Mexico Press, 1998).

17. In Spain, men accused of such "crimes of passion" invoke testosterone as a mitigating factor. Several twentieth-century cases of defense by "me salió de los cojones" ("my balls made me do it") are described in Stanley H. Brandes, *Metaphors of Masculinity: Sex and Status in Andalusian Folklore* (Philadelphia: University of Pennsylvania Press, 1980).

18. There was a risk to Medina's repute in admitting that he was a long-time cuckhold. If he had long known about it without acting, his honor was forever lost; nor was there much honor in being blind to the obvious (as was the protagonist of *Lazarillo de Tormes*). This may explain why Medina accused his wife of making him "dumb" with powders.

19. Medina's slaves Gracia and Magdalena María say (see text) that Beatriz had shouted that Medina's brother, Alonso Ximénez, was an *embustero*, a con artist or cheat. Tovar points out in his defense that Beatriz had uttered "palabras afrentosas," that is offensive or fighting words, indicating the impact of *embustero* as an insult. Tovar went on to detail the nature of Beatriz's complaint against Alonso Ximénez, and further details of the dispute between the couple. According to Tovar, Alonso Ximénez was openly maintaining a sexual relationship (*publicamente amancebado*) with María Ximénez, his own niece. Beatriz would allow neither into her house (AGI, Charcas 17, r. 9, n. 56. La Plata, 1 March 1598. Tovar to king, f. 2r.–2v.). Moreover, Tovar asks that the Crown confiscate one-half of Medina's property, since not doing so would result in a loss to the Crown purse of more than 70,000 assayed pesos, implying that Medina's net worth was 140,000 pesos, quite a princely sum (ibid., f. 2v.).

20. Back in the Medina-González hometown, the Villa de Llerena, Juan Bautista now had to defend his money against a lawsuit brought by the sister of a former priest of Potosí (Juan Gallegos de Espinoza, a chaplain of the Inquisition who had been Viceroy Toledo's confes-

sor) who had once loaned money to Medina (AGI, Contrataciones 741, no. 17. Villa de Llerena, 1596. Autos del Licenciado Ramos de Valencia . . .).

21. AGI, Charcas 17, r. 9, n. 56. La Plata, 1 March 1598. Tovar to king, f. 2r.–2v.

22. Paulino Castañeda Delgado and Pilar Hernández Aparicio. *La Inquisición de Lima*, Tomo I
(Madrid: Editorial Deimos, 1989), 113. They cite José Toribio Medina, O.c., II, 389-390 (sic).
The latter did not publish the provenance of his source.

23. Tovar's will led to further complications. Tovar left 2,000 *patacones* (lumps of silver) to the
Jesuit *colegio*. (Recall Medina's claim that he had been unable to catch his wife with Tovar
because the latter had been warned by the *colegio*'s rector.) The money was also claimed in
1613 by a young woman of Seville, who said she was Tovar's *hija natural*, a daughter born
to the mistress he had taken in Seville while he was a law student there (AGI, Contratación
513B, n.4, r.9. 1613. Autos sobre los bienes del Doctor Jerónimo de Tovar y Montalvo . . .).

24. Reported in: AGI, Charcas 17, R8, N55. Rounding out his new accusations, Tovar also produced testimony of a cloistered nun, who reported another, now dead, nun's story that Medina's slaves had told her they had lied for him (ibid).

25. Ibid., p. 114, citing: AGI, Lima 33. 2 May 1599. Viceroy don Luis de Velasco to the king.

26. Tovar insisted that Medina must have prepared his witnesses before the crime (ANB, EC
1597, no. 2, Traslado de la información sumaria y autos fechos sobre la muerte de Beatriz
González . . ., f. 440v). Tovar also claimed that Medina had promised to free his slaves to
convince them to lie for him (ibid., f. 398r.). Alonso and María Ximénez and others, said Tovar, sought their own vengeance against Beatriz for her stern rectitude and coleric person-
ality, and because she would not tolerate their moral turpitude (ibid., f. 397v). Faced with
an abundance of pro-Medina witnesses, including the children who lamented being dragged
down into *putería* (whoredom) by their mother's behavior, he accused Beatriz of carrying
on affairs with at least two of Medina's witnesses (ibid., f. 398v). Finally, he added that Beatriz had publicly called Medina a *perro judío* (Jew dog), and that Medina had killed her for
this insult (ibid., f. 440r). These were, indeed, the classic fighting words of the period. The
Inquisition did not permit descendants of Jews to serve in its offices. Responding to Tovar,
Medina felt compelled to produce witnesses to affirm his Old Christian background, and to
attest that his father, Pedro López, had also been a *familiar* back in the Villa de Llerena (ibid.,
f. 531r.–37r).

27. The document containing Tovar's evidence of the confession and Medina's denial also refers
to intermediaries sent by Medina seeking Tovar's forgiveness and asking him to drop his
countersuit against Medina. Tovar refused. Yet Tovar did not ultimately prevail. Medina's
first son, Juan Baptista de la Gasca, was appointed *oidor* of the Audiencia of Panama in the
early seventeenth century. I have not located Medina's will, another means through which
he certainly would have sought eternal life for his soul and, through his estate, perpetua-
tion of social status. For more on the contradiction between these two goals in the sixteenth
century, and for an example of an indigenous person's will written by Medina when he was
a scribe in the city of Potosí, see Thomas A. Abercrombie, "Tributes to Bad Conscience: Charity, Restitution, and Inheritance in Cacique and Encomendero Testaments of Sixteenth-
Century Charcas." In *Dead Giveaways*, Susan Kellogg and Matthew Restall, eds. (Salt Lake
City: University of Utah Press, 1998).

28. La Plata, the City of Silver, was a small town at the end of the sixteenth century, and it remains so today as Sucre, official capital of the Republic of Bolivia, and home to the nation's
Supreme Court. As in small towns everywhere, repute still runs a gauntlet of gossips'
tongues in plazas, streets, and marketplaces. Much has changed over the centuries, but some
things remain the same: many of the buildings lived in by people like Peralta, Tovar, Medina, and the unfortunate Beatriz González still stand, curious eyes still peer through window grates, and picturesque tales still travel from one end of town to the other in no time
at all.

29. For an extended discussion of the craft of narrative deployed in early modern judicial testimony, see Natalie Zemon Davis, *Fiction in the Archives: Pardon Tales and Their Tellers in
Sixteenth-Century France* (Stanford: Stanford University Press, 1987).

30. The document is from the Archivo Nacional de Bolivia (ANB), Expedientes Coloniales 1597,
no. 2 (676 folios), "Traslado de la información sumaria y autos fechos sobre la muerte de
Beatriz González muger de Fernando de Medina escribano de cámara de la Real Audiencia
de la ciudad de La Plata. Ante los Señores Presidente y Oidores della. Remitida al muy
Illustre Señor Licenciado Antonio Gutiérrez de Ulloa Inquisidor y Visitador General. Fer-

nando de Zúñiga." All translations herein are mine. In translating I have relied on the 1611 dictionary of Sebastián de Covarrubias Orozco, *Tesoro de la Lengua Castellana o Española* (1611). Modernized edition by Felipe C. R. Maldonado, as revised by Manuel Camarero. (Madrid: Editorial Castalia, 1995).

31. I have deleted Peralta's full formal title, the formalities of the swearing-in ceremony, and repetition of the question here and in subsequent testimonies. At this point I switch to first person, though the text continues in the third person: "the witness said that although he is a minister of the Holy Office of the Inquisition, and as such should enjoy the privileges conceded to him," etc.

32. Guayopacha, which the city of Sucre has expanded to encompass, was once a favored weekend garden spot for well-to-do colonials. See Ana María Presta, *Encomienda, Family, and Business in Colonial Charcas (Modern Bolivia). The Encomenderos of La Plata, 1550-1600* (Ph.D. dissertation, Ohio State University, 1997), 262.

33. More permanent acts of transvestism, or more properly, male impersonation, were not unknown in the period. The celebrated case of Catalina de Erauso, *la monja alférez*, who in the end won social esteem for acting like a man and exemplifying male honor, can be read in her picaresque confessional autobiography: Catalina de Erauso, *Lieutenant Nun: Memoir of a Basque Transvestite in the New World* (Boston: Beacon Press, 1996).

34. The use of herbs (and, as later appears, hair) for witchcraft or as poison was common both to Andeans and to Spaniards, though certainly in the Indies, Spaniards feared Indians as practitioners of the black arts. For, among other things, an account of a priest of the region who a decade earlier had denounced rural Indian witchcraft and idolatry, see Thomas A. Abercrombie, *Pathways of Memory and Power: Ethnography and History Among an Andean People* (Madison: University of Wisconsin Press, 1998), 267–69.

35. It is intriguing that Medina accuses the Jesuit rector of warning Tovar (and another Jesuit of serving as *alcahuete*), perhaps indicating tensions between the Jesuits and the functionaries of the Inquisition. See also note 23.

36. Medina used the phrase "vuelta por mi honor." He means that he had merely replied in kind to an insult to his honor; Peralta used the same words to excuse himself to the king. This appears to be a stock phrase, perhaps from traditions of dueling or *pundonor* (point of honor), a response to an insult required to maintain honor. It is the antithesis of "turning the other cheek."

37. The original reads: "para continuar en matarle," conveying that using beard hairs in connection with powders, the effect was, like the growth of hair, gradual and constant. Use of hair in witchcraft was known in the ancient world as in early modern Europe, and is culturally widespread. Modern Andeans continue to take great care to save and hide cut hair and fingernail clippings, precisely to prevent them from being used in witchcraft. The beard was also strongly associated with a man's honor; see note 56.

38. *Rancherías* were neighborhoods and parishes established for Indians, on the outskirts of the Spanish city center. Each had its own church and patron saint.

39. In the original the phrase is "para el chasque." The colonial mail service made use of the Inka system of roads, rest houses, and runners posted to them (*chasques* in colonial Quechua) who carried messages from one rest house (or *tambo*) to another.

40. Here we see evidence of the immediacy of the testimony, taken, as it were, on location and with a gesture noted along with the words.

41. Recall here that María Ximénez, niece not only of Medina and Beatriz but of Medina's brother Alonso Ximénez, is said by Tovar to have been openly the lover of her uncle Alonso, and to have been banned from the house, explaining Beatriz's harsh words to María and the argument between Medina and Beatriz.

42. Here Alonso de Cáceres relates several examples of secret meetings between Tovar and Beatriz, aided by Pedro López de la Gasca, Luis de Moya, the *alcahuete* Ribadeneyra, and (against her will) by María Ximénez and her husband, Joan de Contreras. The latter two were countrymen of Cáceres, and he had known them in the Audiencia of Santa Fe. Had he known Peralta too?

43. This is one hint that what Beatriz González obtained from Indian witches was not only powder to "dummy up" her husband, but love magic to bind the prosecutor to her. Compare cases of love magic in Ruth Behar, "Sexual Witchcraft, Colonialism, and Women's Powers: Views from the Mexican Inquisition," in Asunción Lavrin, ed., *Sexuality and Marriage in Colonial Latin America* (Lincoln: University of Nebraska Press, 1989), 178–206, and in Guido Rug-

giero, *Binding Passions: Tales of Magic, Marriage, and Power at the End of the Renaissance* (New York: Oxford University Press, 1993).

44. According to Tovar, one of the women Beatriz spoke ill of was María Ximénez.
45. I translate "muger libre en su bibir," as libertine. More literally, it might be translated as "a woman who lived freely." This was a forceful slur against her decency, which was the feminine counterpart to masculine honor.
46. These were questions aimed at revealing any interested relationship, such as kinship or patron-client ties, between the witness and the accused or accuser.
47. At this point, Peralta has stepped aside (not to reappear in the case), replaced by the *oidor* Díaz de Lopidana.
48. Ledesma begins by describing how he had heard of the murder while on the street the very same night as his testimony is given. He does not add significant details.
49. Ribadeneyra was Tovar's *criado* (a term that can mean servant but also retainer, protégé, or client, as in a patron-client relationship) and appears to have lived in Tovar's house. As lieutenant bailiff, he was responsible for carrying out arrests and sequestering property on the prosecutor's behalf.
50. Here Ledesma reports others' speech directly. The scribe presents the reported speech in the first person, embedded within the third person presentation of Ledesma's voice: "oyo que respondio una negra diziendo quien esta ay, e joan de bastidas ribadeneyra teniente de alguazil mayor desta corte e criado del dicho fiscal, dixo yo soy, dezil le a mi señora Beatriz González que estoy aqui. . . ." More literally rendered, this would be: "He [Ledesma] heard a black woman answering, saying who is there? And Joan de Bastidas Ribadeneyra, lieutenant bailiff and protégé of the said prosecutor, said, It's me, tell my lady Beatriz González that I'm here. . . ."
51. Ledesma goes on to report other visits between Tovar and Beatriz.
52. Beatriz González's disguise recalls the veiled look of eighteenth-century *tapadas* of Lima. See Deborah A. Poole, "A One-Eyed Gaze: Gender in 19th Century Illustration of Peru," *Dialectical Anthropology* 13 (1988): 333–64.
53. Here Ledesma reports having heard that Beatriz had jealously fought with an un-named woman she thought was involved with Tovar, and reports that Ribadeneyra was certainly the *medianero* (intermediary) between the lovers.
54. Yet another judge enters the scene, this time the Licentiate Bernardino de Albornóz. Lopidana, perhaps, had left to get supper or go to bed. By this time it is likely that a number of judges and scribes had gathered in the Medina-González house, and that they relieved one another in turns.
55. The *ánimas* (souls) bell was one of several rung out to mark time and announce the moment for certain prayers. The last bell of the night, called the *toque de queda* (a term that has come to mean the curfew enforced during states of siege), announced the nightly curfew.
56. Recall that Medina had accused Beatriz of using his beard hairs in her witchcraft. Pulling, or even touching, a man's beard was a major affront to his personal honor. In the thirteenth-century legal code, the *Siete Partidas* of Alfonso The Wise, the act merited the death penalty, and justified the murder of the puller by the pulled as a remedy for the injury to his honor. The affront still stung in the sixteenth century. On beard-pulling and the importance of hair in general, see Sonya Lipsett-Rivera, "*De Obra y Palabra*: Patterns of Insults in Mexico, 1750–1856" *The Americas* 54(4): 516, 1998.
57. Here Gracia reports another meeting between Tovar and Beatriz, for two hours in the water storage room.
58. Gracia reports here another visit by Beatriz to Tovar's house, dressed as a man.
59. Another reference to the questions meant to elicit the witnesses' interest in the case.
60. It was assumed that slaves or servants could be induced to lie by threat or bribe.
61. The pendant or standard (*pendón*), bearing the royal coat of arms, was carried in procession during solemn religious holidays, such as Corpus Christi, and during secular ones, such as festivals marking a birth or death within the royal household. The precise reference here, and hence the date, is unclear.
62. Once again, we see evidence of the immediacy of the testimony, taken in the house where the crime took place and on the very same night.
63. Magdalena here reports an all-night visit by Beatriz to Tovar, wearing the clothes of one of doña Mencia's male servants, during which Mencia stayed the night in Beatriz's house to let her in before dawn.

DOCUMENT THEMES

African/Afro-Latin American Peoples; Crime; Ethnicity;
European-Mestizo Peoples; Family; Gender; Gossip and Communication; Honor;
Illness/Disease/Injury/Medicine; Inquisition; Insults; Marriage; Popular Culture;
Religion; Sexuality; Town Life; Violence; Witchcraft; Women.

SUGGESTIONS FOR FURTHER READING

Cook and Cook 1991.
Gilmore 1987.
Johnson and Rivera 1998.
Lavrin 1989.
Perry 1990.
Ruggiero 1993.

CHAPTER
7

~~~~~~

The Spiritual and Physical Ecstasies of a Sixteenth-Century *Beata*: Marina de San Miguel Confesses Before the Mexican Inquisition

(Mexico, 1598)

Jacqueline Holler

INTRODUCTION

By 1521, when Hernán Cortés conquered the Aztec Empire, the Inquisition was already well established in Spain. It was transferred to the newly colonized land as an ad hoc institution under the guidance of missionary friars and, later, Mexico's archbishop. This rather informal arrangement was replaced, in 1571, by an officially constituted Tribunal of the Holy Office of the Inquisition, based in Mexico City and with ostensible authority over the whole of New Spain.[1]

The document presented here is taken from one of the less common types of Mexican Inquisition trials, a major heresy case.[2] The Mexican tribunal spent much more time enforcing socioreligious norms than attacking heresy and crypto-Judaism. About 11 percent of trials dealt with heresy; the remainder investigated less serious crimes such as bigamy, witchcraft, superstition, and blasphemy. In 1598, however, the Holy Office of Mexico received information about an alleged group of *alumbrados*, heretics whose religious beliefs emphasized mental prayer and denigrated the authority of the Church. The Mexican group apparently believed that the Day of Judgment would soon come and that the group's members would be selected to found a New Jerusalem on earth. Among the group denounced was a religious woman called Marina de San Miguel, apparently of some importance within the group because of her mystical visions, which others believed to be revelations from God. Marina was imprisoned in November 1598. Her confessions, presented here, were taken between that date and January 1599.[3]

Although the Inquisition functioned as a sort of police force, the confessions were not taken in the same way that a modern statement might be taken from the accused in a criminal case. A person was imprisoned and investigated in response to a denunciation. In contrast to modern police arrests, those arrested were not informed of the charges against them. Rather, the suspect was urged to confess whatever he or she might have done that was worthy of punishment by the Holy Office. The inquisitor's questions, the confessant's testimony, and any other events that transpired were recorded by a notary, who was instructed to record testimony in a complete and accurate manner.

Notaries were professionals who carried out their task carefully and, for the most part, conscientiously. Readers will note, however, that these are not verbatim transcripts as are modern court transcripts. Notaries transcribed testimony in the third person ("she said that . . ."). They very occasionally summarized rather than transcribed, particularly in the sections of the case that followed set formulas. For example, when a suspect was asked to recite the catechism, the notary did not record the words the suspect said, but simply said that the suspect had said it well, or poorly, or had said sections of it, or could not recite it. Within these limitations, however, the documents followed the suspect's testimony very closely, and are remarkably personal and reminiscent of speech. Moreover, such records are detailed. Every attempt was made to elicit a truthful, complete, and remorseful confession from the individual, for such a confession would "discharge the conscience" and bring the suspect to penitence, and thus to God's forgiveness. Questions were often open-ended, and suspects were usually allowed to speak without interruption and at great length. Only after the confession(s) of the suspect were judged complete was an actual accusation created. This would contain the charges alleged by those who denounced the suspect as well as any information the suspect had willingly confessed. At this point, the actual trial began, and the suspect responded to the particular charges contained in the accusation with the assistance of legal counsel appointed by the court.

Historians now use Inquisition documents as a way to access the experience of individuals who might otherwise be absent from documentation. In the case of Mexico, the Inquisition section of the National Archive offers one of the most complete bodies of documentation for the sixteenth century. The information contained in this case provides a very rare glimpse into the life of a sixteenth-century woman whose life deviated dramatically, in many ways, from the standard picture of Spanish American women in colonial times. I have rendered the original text of Marina's confessions into English as faithfully as possible. However, because the document is almost totally unpunctuated, I have added a certain amount of punctuation. In addition, I have removed the repetitive use of the term *said*, as in "the said witness said that the said man accompanied her to the said house." Though the literal translation conveys very well the legalistic character of this document, the accretion of so many *saids* impairs readability.

Marina de San Miguel confessed nine times. Because of the length and detail of her confessions, I have found it necessary to edit some material. The confessions still yield a great deal of information about Marina's life, particularly in regard to her spiritual and sexual activities. Readers will want to consider the circumstances of the document's production and how they affect its usefulness; the strategies used by both Marina and her interlocutor in their unequal encounter; the credibility of Marina's testimony; and how that testimony changes over time.

Readers will also no doubt want to know Marina's fate. In the auto de fe of March 25, 1601, a gagged and haltered Marina was paraded naked to the waist upon a mule. After abjuring her errors, Marina received one hundred lashes. She was also sentenced to a fine of 100 pesos and to ten years' reclusion in the plague hospital, where, evidently, she became very ill. The remainder of her story eludes us.

THE DOCUMENT

7.1 First Confession

In the city of Mexico, Friday, November 20, 1598. The Lord Inquisitor *licenciado* don Alonso de Peralta in his morning audience ordered that a woman be brought before him from one of the secret prisons of this Holy Office. Being present, she swore an oath *en forma devida de derecho* under which she promised to tell the truth here in this audience and in all the others that might be held until the determination of her case, and to keep secret everything that she might see or believe or that might be talked about with her or that might happen concerning this her case.

She was asked what her name is, where she was born, how old she is, what her profession is,[4] and when she was arrested.

She answered that she is Marina de San Miguel, a *natural* of the city of Córdoba in the kingdoms of Castile; that she is fifty-three years old and is a *beata*[5] of the Order of Saint Dominic; and that she occupies herself in needlework[6] and in teaching girls to do the same. She was arrested last Saturday, which was the fourteenth of the present month, and placed in one of the secret prisons of this Holy Office. And she declared her genealogy in the following form:

Parents

- **Gonzalo Abril,** *natural* of La Granja, next to Fuente Ovejuna in the diocese of Córdoba, blacksmith (*herrador*), who died in Puebla de los Ángeles.
- **María González de Escalorán,** from Córdoba, who died in this city of Mexico and who had no profession.

Paternal Grandparents

- **Juan Abril,** resident and *natural* of La Granja, farmer (*labrador*), deceased.
- **Marina Atín,** his wife, resident of the said place, deceased.

Maternal Grandparents

- **Hernán Gil,** resident and *natural* of Córdoba, saddler (*albardero*), deceased.
- **Catalina Rodríguez de Escalona,** his wife, resident and *natural* [of Córdoba], already dead, who had no profession, other than raising her children.

Father's Siblings[7]

- **Sebastián Abril,** who was an army officer (*alférez*) in Italy and got married in Fuente Ovejuna to doña Mayor de Castillejos, and who has children; one is called Pedro Alonso Romero and the daughter doña Lucrecia Romero, and the others she doesn't remember, nor their ages, and they were rich farming people, and she doesn't know whether they are dead.

- **Bartolomé Abril,** resident of La Granja, farmer, married, and she doesn't know whom he married nor whether he has children, only that he lived in La Granja, and she does not know whether he might be dead.

- **Pedro Abril,** who went to Italy, and they said that he was a military field officer (*maese de campo*), and she does not know what became of him, nor whether he got married, and she has no other uncles or aunts on her father's side.

Mother's Siblings

- **Doctor Hernando de Escalona,** physician, resident of the city of Lerida in Catalonia, where he married doña Thomasia, and she knows that he had children, one of whom was called doña Catalina, and she does not know whether they are dead.

- **Martín de Córdoba,** merchant (*mercader*) in Medina del Campo, where he got married, and she does not know to whom; and she heard that he had a daughter, whose name she does not remember, nor does she know whether they're dead.

- **Victoria Gil,** married in Córdoba to Juan de Baratorno, and they have children, whose names she does not remember, nor [does she know] whether they are dead.

- **Ana de los Ángeles,** *doncella*, who went to Lerida with the said Doctor Hernando de Escalona.

- **Isabel de Escalona,** *doncella*, who left with the said, her sister.

And she has no more uncles and aunts on her mother's side.

Siblings

- **Juan Abril,** who died in Peru, single, blacksmith, who left no children.
- **Luisa de Los Ángeles,** *doncella*, who died in Mexico in the house of this woman. And she had no more siblings.

Husband and Children

This confessant has never been married nor had children and is a *doncella* and has taken a vow of chastity.

She was asked what caste and parentage are her parents and grandparents and the others, transverse and collateral, whom she has named, and if they or any one of them or this confessant have been imprisoned, given penitence, reconciled, or condemned by the Holy Office of the Inquisition.

She said that they are *cristianos viejos*, and that none of them has ever been imprisoned, given penitence, reconciled, or condemned by the Holy Office, and that this is the first time that she has been imprisoned by it.

She was asked whether she is a Christian, baptized and confirmed, and if she hears mass, confesses, and receives communion at the times ordered by the Holy Mother Church.[8]

She said that she is a Christian baptized and confirmed by the grace of God, and that she was confirmed in this city by a bishop, friar of the Order of Saint Dominic, called Diego de San Francisco. She said that she confesses and receives communion at all the times ordered by the Holy Mother Church, and that the last time she confessed was Sunday the eighth in the church of Saint Dominic with fray Honorato Navarro, and she received communion.

She made the sign of the cross and said the Our Father, Hail Mary, *Credo*, Salve Regina, the Ten Commandments, and Fourteen Articles well in Spanish.[9]

She was asked whether she knows how to read and write and whether she has studied any subjects.

She said that she knows how to read and write and she has not studied any subject, and that her brother taught her the alphabet and how to make letters; and she learned writing from a book that her brother gave her, and without more teaching, by her own work and industry, she learned to read and write.

She was asked for the story of her life.

She said that she was born in the city of Córdoba [in Spain] in the house of her parents, where she was raised until they died,[10] and she was left at nineteen years, and while they lived she occupied her time in working for and serving them. And at the age of three, she came with her parents to this land in a fleet whose commander she cannot remember, as she was so young. Once arrived in this city of Mexico, they lived in the street of San Agustín for nine years. And having made some money[11] they returned to the city of Córdoba where her father spent lavishly, in such a way that they came to poverty, and [so] returned to this city of Mexico in the fleet of General Pedro Meléndez. When her mother died here, her father married again to a widow, Leonor Arías, and because her father wanted to get married the confessant went to the *colegio de las niñas* (girl's residential school), where she spent four years. After her father got married, he found his wife with a man and killed him, though his wife recovered from her wounds. For this reason her father went away to Peru.[12] And so she left the school and went to live at the school, "I mean at San Pablo,"[13] with Mariá de Acosta, wife of Diego Rodríguez, a tanner (*curtidor*). And she lived there two years, and after that she took her sister out of the said school and together they took a little house in the street of San Agustín. There they lived for seven or ten years on their sewing and from teaching girls. While they were living there their father came back and surrendered to the *cárcel de corte*. He was exiled and went to Puebla, where he died, leaving the confessant with her sister. And later the confessant went to the house of Juan Núñez, accountant, *vecino* of this city,[14] where she was for ten months. After that she rented a house across from his until she bought the house where she currently lives, which she bought from some Indians for 200 pesos. After that she spent 300 pesos on it, using 200 pesos she inherited from her father and what she earned by the needle and from teaching girls. And for thirteen years she has lived there, until she was brought before this Holy Office. And she has associated all this time with very honored, good-living people, both religious and secular.

She was asked what goods she has in order that they may be sequestered, so that she will not lose them.[15]

She said that the house is hers, and the white clothing that she has in it, and that she has no other treasures as can be seen in her strongboxes. And then she said that she remembered that she has a nephew in her house. He is Alonso Gutiérrez de Castro who is a tailor of jackets (*jubetero*) and son of her first cousin on her mother's side, who is a native of Córdoba where her nephew was born. He lives in her house, and anything he claims to be his is his, because she takes him for a man of good conscience. And she remembers that Alonso Gutiérrez de Castro made some repairs in the house at his expense, making a gift of it as her nephew. Then she said that she did not spend 300 pesos repairing her house, but only 100. And she does not really know how much it was because money comes and goes. And her nephew made the other repairs, making her a gift of the money that he spent, as she has said. He has lived in her house for two years and four months.[16]

She was asked if she knows, presumes, or suspects the cause for her arrest and imprisonment in the prisons of this Holy Office.

She said that she presumes and suspects that the cause of her imprisonment must be that four years ago a secular youth called Luis de Zárate came to visit her. And she does not know where he lives, only that he was sent to her by Gregorio López,[17] who died in the Holy Faith, and who was her spiritual brother. . . . She was with Luis, talking about spiritual things, and about hell, and he said that there was no hell and no devils, and that men[18] were the devils and hell. And she, feeling uncomfortable about this, said to him, "What are you saying, that there is no hell?" Luis de Zárate said that men through their sins were hell. Another day she fell ill in her bed, and lost her senses. This illness lasted three months, and then she came to her senses and, being well, sent to speak with the Lord Inquisitor Doctor Loboguerrero and with fray Gonzalo de Illescas of the Order of Saint Dominic, telling all that had passed with Luis de Zárate, and how she had been sick with this illness. The inquisitor said that with her illness she must have imagined it. And she says that she wants to go over her memory so that she can tell the truth about everything that she might remember.

With this the audience ceased, because it was past eleven. The above was read and she approved it and signed it. And she was ordered to return to her cell, very admonished to examine her memory as she has offered to do.

[signed] Marina de San Miguel
Pedro de Manozca, *escribano*

7.2 Second Confession

In the city of Mexico, Monday, November 23, 1598, the Lord Inquisitor *licenciado* don Alonso de Peralta in his afternoon audience ordered that Marina de San Miguel, *beata*, be brought before him. And when she was present, she was told to say anything she had remembered in her case, and the truth, by the oath that she made [in her first audience].

She said that she has remembered that Juan López de Zárate, "I mean Luis de Zárate," said to her that on the day of justice the flesh will be renewed, and that there will be a New Jerusalem on earth, which was an opinion that Gregorio López held. And [Luis] wanted to know when the day [of justice] would be. And he asked the confessant to entrust it to God, so that [the date] would be revealed [to her]. And this is what she has remembered.

She was told that in this Holy Office it is not customary to seize any person without sufficient evidence of having done, said, or committed, or seen done, said, or committed by others, any thing that may be or appear to be against our Holy Catholic Faith; against the evangelical law that the Holy Mother Roman Catholic Church holds, preaches, follows, and teaches; or against the lawful and free exercise of the Holy Office. Therefore, if she has been imprisoned, she must believe that evidence of a fault of this nature has been presented against her. So for reverence of God our Lord and of his blessed and glorious mother our Lady the Virgin Mary, she is admonished and charged to examine her memory and say and confess the whole truth of anything about which she feels guilty or knows of other people, whoever they are, without covering up things about herself or about others, and without giving false testimony about herself or about others. Because if she does this [tells the truth] she will discharge her conscience as a Catholic Christian, and she will save her soul, and her case will be dispatched with all the brevity and mercy possible, as the Holy Office is accustomed to use with good and truthful confessants.[19]

And being given to understand this admonition she said that she doesn't remember anything else about what she has said. And with that the audience ceased and this was read to her, which she approved and signed. And heavily admonished that she examine her memory she was ordered to return to her cell.

[signed] Marina de San Miguel

It passed before me Pedro de Manozca

7.3 Third Confession

In the city of Mexico, Tuesday, November 24, 1598. The Lord Inquisitor *licenciado* don Alonso de Peralta in his afternoon audience ordered Marina de San Miguel to be brought from her cell.

And when she was present she was told that if she has remembered anything in her case to say it, and the truth, under the oath she made.

She said that what she has remembered is that in the course of her life some spiritual things have happened to her, which she has talked about to some people. And she believes that they have been the cause of her imprisonment, because they were scandalized by what she told them. And the things that happened are these. Well, since her childhood she has had an exercise of mental prayer, in which she always felt great gifts from our Lord. And eight years ago on Palm Sunday, during the night, when she was sleeping (because she goes to bed with a desire to love and serve God) she was awakened and felt and then said she saw with her interior eyes[20] Christ crucified. And he came so close to her that it seemed to her that the body of Christ our Redeemer and her body were united, and appeared not two bodies but one. And at the same moment she felt in her hands and in her feet the burning of fire.[21] In her feet it began in the soles and moved to the other part, and in the hands, on the contrary, the fire began on top of the hand and then passed to the palm. And in her heart, in the same manner as happened with the said burning, she felt an intense interior pain that reached down into her bones. The pain lasted from midnight, when she saw (as she has said) the figure of our Redeemer Jesus Christ, until the dawn. And she could not sleep because the pain was so great that she wanted to cry out, but did not because she did not want to reveal the cause. And two whole years she had the pain from time to time, some days more than others. And the fire and pain in her heart have lasted until today, so that her heart seems wounded. Thus every time she remembers the vision her heart and her left arm tremble.

And thus while I was writing this she began to shake, and raised her hands and lifted her eyes to heaven and then lowered them, smiling and saying many loving words to our Lord Jesus Christ. . . . She remained in a trance, hands down, inclining her head to the left side. . . . And in the same trance she tried with great force to free her hands, and she could not, even though she used much force. Once her hands were untied she opened them and said, "My sweet Jesus, stretch out thy hand; because thou art so good everyone loves thee."[22] And she returned to being in a trance, with her arms open and raised and her eyes and face lifted to heaven, and her mouth a little open as though laughing, and her body inclined toward the right side. Later she put her hands together again with her fingers crossed and seemed as though sleeping.

And the Lord Inquisitor ordered that until the trance stopped no one speak nor say anything, and that I the secretary be on the lookout and write down whatever might succeed.

And then she opened her eyes and began to shake and get up from the bench on which she was seated, saying, "My love, help me God, how strongly you have given me this."[23] And among these words she said to the Lord Inquisitor that when she is given these trances, she should be shaken vigorously to awaken her from her deep dream. Then she returned to being as though sleeping. The inquisitor called her by her name and she did not respond, nor the second time. And the third time she opened her eyes and made faces, and made signs with her hands to her mouth. And then she returned again to being as though asleep. And with a tremble she moaned to herself, without saying anything other than seeming to mumble.[24] And the Lord Inquisitor ordered me, the secretary, to call her, because she was next to me, but she did not respond. The trance lasted for near a half hour, and having called her and pulled her right arm two or three times, she woke up with much happiness, saying that we should pull hard so that she could stretch her senses and pull them away from God. Then she asked God license, to permit that, "this little body return to earth," and that her imagination not be so uplifted. And then, beginning to say, "Sweet Jesus, love of my soul," she returned to being transported, and then asked again that we pull on her arm. She said she would try to pay attention but that she wanted to show the gifts that our Lord has given her even after she was imprisoned.

And returning to full presence in herself, she said that on Palm Saturday shortly after dark she lay down on her bed. Being awake adoring God, she heard an interior voice that said, "Make the betrothals." And then she saw, internally, our Redeemer Jesus Christ in the form of a youth dressed in white. He grasped her hand, and then the vision disappeared. And she understood that this had been a betrothal, which the wisdom of God had given her to understand. And she was left with an interior rapture, and did not return to herself until the morning of Easter Sunday. . . .

And with this it appeared that she might go into another trance, and the Lord Inquisitor ordered her to be attentive. . . . And because it was already close to six, the audience ceased, and having been read the above, she approved it and signed it.

And heavily admonished that she go and reexamine her memory, she was ordered to be taken to her cell. . . .

[signatures]

7.4 Fourth Confession

In the city of Mexico, Wednesday, November 25, 1598, the Lord Inquisitor *licenciado* don Alonso de Peralta in his morning audience ordered that Marina de San Miguel be brought before him from her cell. And when she was present she was told that if she had remembered anything, she should say it, and the truth, under the oath that she swore. . . .

She said that four years ago her interior body was enraptured another time, and she found herself in a place which was purgatory, which was told to her by the youth to whom she was betrothed. . . . In that place she saw many people walking, like human bodies, because God shows things in accordance with the understanding of man. And some of the bodies were in the middle of fires, and others were in holes like wells, which were full of something black which seemed to be boiling tar. Some of them were in it up to their waists, others up to their chests, and others so far that only the tops of their heads could be seen. And others she saw in a lake of bubbling, boiling water, in the same way, and they were quiet and peaceful. And what astonished her most was that they did not take up space, which she didn't understand. And in the same place she saw streets, and in them some priests in vestments, and others with their dalmatics (*dalmáticas*), and these were the priests who say masses for souls. And the holy water that they throw in churches reaches the souls. And the youth dressed in white, whom she takes for Christ our Redeemer, told her that the souls feel very refreshed by masses and holy water. And he wanted to give her some grace, allowing her to bless the souls; and so she did it, and the souls that were already ready to be freed from their pains went to heaven. And there were many saved, because she was carried through all the streets three times, and afterward she found herself very tired. And she heard, internally, that in very clear voices the souls said these words: "Maiden of God, have mercy,"[25] asking her to hurry and bless them, and at the same time they cried out to her, "Our Redemptress." This gave her pain, because she did not like that they called her by the name that belongs to our Redeemer Jesus Christ. And she told this to Friar Andrés de la Cruz, a discalced brother of the Order of Lord Saint Francis, who went to *la China*. He told her that this could be understood as God's using her as the means for removing souls from the pains of purgatory. . . .

She said that about a week before she saw purgatory, she was enraptured by our Redeemer Jesus Christ in the form of the youth, except that instead of being dressed in white he was dressed in purple. And he took her "interior man" to a place in which she saw three large jars, all the same, made out of white and gold metal. And Christ our Redeemer said to her, daughter, this is the inn where they say the bride was taken and made drunk with the wine of love. . . . And she remembers that the drink left her so drunk with the love of God, and the strength of her "interior man" was so great that it seemed he flew to heaven.

She says that after she was imprisoned in this Inquisition God gave her many mercies, and gave her in her cell so much company that she sees internally in her presence many circles of angels and saints, who appear as if in a sketch, in such a way that in one moment she sees them clearly and resplendently; and then they cover themselves, so that she sees only some things, as if they are in shadow. . . .

She said that yesterday she was very afflicted because she could not discover what to say, nor how to begin.[26] Between eleven and twelve in the morning our Redeemer Jesus Christ appeared to her in her cell, glorious as they paint him in the resurrection, and seated on the sun with much brilliance. . . .

She was told that she already knows how she was admonished in the last audience. . . . Therefore now for the second time she is admonished in the same way. . . .

She said that with all her heart and her will, if she knew what was against her she would say it; and she said that she will reexamine her memory.

And with this, because it was close to twelve, the audience ceased. And having been read it, she approved it and signed it. And admonished to reexamine her memory she was ordered to returned to her cell.

[signatures]

7.5 Fifth Confession

In the city of Mexico, Friday, November 27, 1598, the Lord Inquisitor *licenciado* don Alonso de Peralta in his morning audience ordered that Marina de San Miguel be brought from her cell. And when she was present she was told that the *alcaide* said that she was asking for an audience; and that she should say why she asked for it, and tell the truth under the oath that she has already sworn.

She said that she asked for the audience to tell and declare something of which it seems the Mother of God has reminded her. That is that for nine years she has eaten meat on all prohibited days, with license of a physician and of the *provisor*. And she has reexamined her memory about the things she was told to reexamine, and the Lord did not enlighten her about them.

She was told that she already knows how she was admonished . . . and with this she was admonished for the third and final time.

She said that she asks for the love of God that the accusation be delayed so that she may reexamine her memory.

With this the audience ceased and having been read it she approved and signed. And admonished to reexamine her memory as she has offered to do, she was ordered to return to her cell.

[signatures]

7.6a Sixth Confession

In the city of Mexico, Monday, January 25, 1599, the Lord Inquisitor *licenciado* don Alonso de Peralta in his morning audience ordered that Marina de San Miguel be brought from her cell. And when she was present she was told that the *alcaide* said that she asks for an audience, and that she should declare why she wanted it, and tell the truth under the oath she has made.

She said that it's like this. . . . She has been condemned to hell, because for fifteen years she has had a sensual temptation of the flesh, which makes her perform dishonest acts with her own hands on her shameful parts. She came to pollution[27] saying dishonest words that provoke lust, calling by their dishonest names many dirty and lascivious things. She was tempted to this by the devil, who appeared to her internally in the form of an Angel of Light, who told her that she should do these things, because they were no sin. This was to make her abandon her scruples. And the devil appeared to her in the form of Christ our Redeemer, in such a way that she might uncover her breasts and have carnal union with him. And thus, for fifteen years, she has had carnal union occasionally from month to month, or every two months. And if it had been more she would accuse herself of that too, because she is only trying to save her soul, with no regard to honor or the world. And the carnal act that the devil as Angel of Light and in the form of Christ had with her was the same as if she had had it with a man. And he kissed her, and she enjoyed it, and she felt a great ardor in her whole body, with particular delight and pleasure. And the contact with herself, and the pollutions, were more frequent than what she had with the devil. And the devil told her when she resisted him, "This will make you abandon your scruples" . . . and he wouldn't let her confess. And thus for fifteen years she received communion twice each week and sometimes three times, on Wednesdays, Fridays, and Sundays, and on Easter. And she felt a great hunger for the holy sacrament, and wanted to receive it, though she had not confessed the said sins. And she did not confess them because the demon told her not to have scruples, and that she should not confess because of them. And also, because sometimes she imagined that this was the work of the devil and did not want her confessor to know that she treated with the devil.

She said that for about twenty years she had a relationship with Juan Núñez, accountant (*balanzario*), as a spiritual brother. And this relationship lasted until about six years ago. And he talked to her about God, and about loving him, and about resignation to his will. And while they were talking like this he kissed and hugged her, and put his tongue in her mouth, and felt her breasts and shameful parts, say-ing, "All of this is earth." And once he put his finger in her shameful parts, and he said it was just to see whether she was a *doncella*. And now she remembers that this happened twice. And three times Juan Núñez showed her his shameful parts and made her touch them, and she touching them came to pollution. And she doesn't know whether he did. And he told her that all of these things were earth, and could be done if they were not done with an evil intention or will. And about twelve or thirteen years ago, she was dressed and lying on her bed when Juan Núñez arrived and hugged her. And after hugging her he threw himself upon her. She resisted and got up from the bed and said to him, "Brother, what you did makes me afraid." And he said, "Sister, you resisted strongly. I did it only to tempt you." And he never again made this demonstration. And in the twenty years that she knew Juan Núñez she saw him once each week. Kissing her and putting his tongue in her mouth, and hugging her and touching her breasts he did commonly; but touching her shame-ful parts was not ordinary. And about ten years ago Juan Núñez asked her to show him her shameful parts, and she consented, believing that he wanted to see whether she was a *doncella*. And thus she took a candle in her hands and raised her chemise, being seated on a cushion. And he saw her shameful parts, and did nothing but smile. And later, they talked about spiritual things, talking about the love of God, with the will to always love him and one's neighbour. And she had a bad suspi-cion about Juan Núñez, because he told her that he did not esteem penances, like fasts, disciplines, and hair shirts. Because he esteemed loving God more; and thus he told her not to believe in penances, but only in love, because penance without love is worth nothing, and for now this is what she remembers happened with Juan Núñez.

She said that from her relationship with Juan Núñez she learned the custom of kissing and hugging, and thus she kissed and hugged Alonso Gutiérrez whom she has said is her nephew. She has no family relation with him, other than that he is her spiritual son. And he hugged and kissed her with purity of conscience as when two children kiss. And he said to her, "Mother, I love you very much in the Lord." And she responded to him, "God make you holy and pure of heart." And she never had any sensual delight with him; and she does not know whether Alonso Gutiérrez had with her.

And because the hour was over, the audience ceased, and having been read this, she approved it and signed it. And admonished to go on reexamining her memory for the afternoon audience, she was taken to her cell.

[signatures]

7.6b Sixth Confession (continued)

In the city of Mexico, Monday, January 25, 1599, the Lord Inquisitor *licenciado* don Alonso de Peralta in his afternoon audience ordered that Marina de San Miguel be brought from her cell. And when she was present she was told to continue with whatever else she had to say, and to tell the truth under the oath that she had already sworn.

She said that as a weak and miserable woman, she allowed herself to be tricked by the devil for the whole time that she had the dishonest relationship with him. And thus from shame she did not confess. And she received communion in a state of sin. And she has nothing else to say.

And later she asked that the interview end until tomorrow, as she wishes to reexamine her memory to say what she knows and to discharge her conscience. With this the audience ceased and having been read this she approved it and signed. And admonished to reexamine her memory, as she has offered, in order to proceed with all purity and truth, she was ordered to return to her cell.

[signatures]

7.7a Seventh Confession

In the city of Mexico, Tuesday, January 26, 1599, the Lord Inquisitor *licenciado* don Alonso de Peralta in his morning audience ordered that Marina de San Miguel be brought before him. And when she was present she was told that if she has remembered anything in her case she should declare it, and the truth, under the oath she has sworn.

She said that she believed that the devil was our Redeemer Jesus Christ when he appeared to her in that form, and he offered her his heart and soul, saying that they should trade hearts and souls so that she could become more perfect in her heart. And afterward it became clear that this offering had been made to the devil. And she saw this clearly fifteen days ago, because he showed himself to her in his demonic figure. She saw him with her bodily eyes, and with him many demons with snouts and ugly bodies and *guirnaldas*[28] with silver and brilliance, sticking out their tongues and breathing fire, though only a little. And they lifted her with her bed three or four times each day, and she was very afflicted and asked the *alcaide* to send her a confessor because the demons were taking her. And being lifted by these evil spirits, she heard a proclamation that said, "This is the justice that is ordered to be given to Marina de San Miguel, *beata*: That she be taken to hell for hiding her sins from her confessor and treating with the devil and receiving the holy sacrament so many times as she has said in such a bad state." And wanting to defend herself she said that she was not sure that it was the devil, nor that she was receiving communion in mortal sin; and that as an evil one he had tricked her. And they [the demons] responded that they had won her in fair battle and that there was no remedy for it, because the sentence had been handed down in the tribunal of God. And that even should she confess in the Holy Office, it was already too late and the confession would not be valid. And she did not confess these things when she first came before this tribunal because she did not know as she does now that they were all illusions of the devil, and she has nothing more to say.

She was asked who was the demon with whom she had a relationship for fifteen years, and of what legion.

She said that he was called Satan, and that he was of the legion of seraphim. . . . The other two they called Barrabus and Beelzebub pursued and tricked her. But the one with whom she had carnal contact was Satan.

She was asked how—having said in yesterday's afternoon audience that as a weak and miserable woman she allowed herself to be tricked by the devil for the whole time that she has said she had the dishonest relationship with him, and having said that out of shame she didn't confess it, and received communion in a state of sin—now she says that she did not know for certain that it was the devil, nor that she was receiving communion with any fear of mortal sin. See the contradiction there and assent in the truth.

She said that she neither wanted to lie in discharging her conscience nor to avoid telling the truth. And thus she asks and begs our Lady the Virgin Mary to light up her understanding. And the truth is, that she, as a bad woman, wanted to appear holy without being so, and she received communion to appear so. And she has no more to say.

She was told to satisfy the question, and if she knew for fifteen years that the love and relationship she had was with the devil, and whether she knew that she received communion in a bad state.

She said that she did not know until she came to the Holy Office, as she has said, but that she felt certain scruples and suspicions about whether it was the devil or not, and shame made her too uncomfortable to confess it, and also [she avoided confessing] so her confessor would not know that she treated with the devil. . . . And she spoke badly in saying that she clearly knew that she had been tricked by the devil and that she had received communion in a bad state.

She was asked how she could ignore that the things she has declared, being so dirty, obscene, and dishonest, could be anything but from the devil. And thus it can be clearly seen that she is hiding from the path of truth, and that after she determined to confess these things, later she regretted it, and this gives birth to her contradictions. Such that when she lived with the intent of appearing holy, without being so, and having a suspicion that these things were demonic, and not confessing them out of shame, she could not possibly fail to believe that she was receiving communion in mortal sin. Nor can one presume that she did not clearly know that her own acts and dishonest touchings, which brought her so many times to pollution, were very grave sins, which must be confessed if one is to avoid knowingly receiving communion in a bad state.

She said that it is true that she knew that all the carnal and obscene things she has confessed, the union with the devil and having carnal copulation with him as well as her own dishonest acts with which she came to pollution, were bad and grave sins. But as a weak and miserable woman she fell into them, and for discomfort and shame she did not confess them. Because as she was held holy, she wanted to hide her weaknesses. And thus she received communion knowing that she was in mortal sin. And she ratifies this now, and it is the truth, and the devil made her wander into these contradictions.

She was asked what other things happened with Juan Núñez, *balanzario*, and Alonso Gutiérrez. And that as she has decided to proceed with purity, she should tell the whole truth, because as she had no shame in offending our Redeemer Jesus Christ, she should not have it in confessing her sins, which is the principal remedy for the salvation of her soul. And moreover, from today on she should abandon raptures and illusions, as the devil cannot counsel any good thing. And thus in no way should she give him credit, nor should she despair of the mercy of God, because as grave and enormous as her sins are, his mercy is much greater. And thus if he is served to not take her in such a bad state, and to bring her before this holy tribunal, she should have great confidence that it is so she might come to know her misery and misfortunes and beg him with a true heart to use with her his accustomed mercy, giving her strength to defend herself from the snares of the enemy in whose trap[29] she was for so long.

She said that she has said what happened with Juan Núñez and Alonso Gutiérrez, and that if any other thing had happened she would say it, because she must give account to God.

She was asked if she knew that the kisses and hugs that she gave to Juan Núñez and Alonso Gutiérrez could not be given without sinning mortally, because she gave them delighting in them, and because with her contacts with Juan Núñez she came to pollution the times that she has declared.

She said that she didn't believe that she sinned mortally in these things, because she had no intention of doing them to enjoy them, but rather did them because she was melancholy. She did them with pure love and clean intention, because as Saint Augustine says, the sin is in the bad intention and will. And once Juan Núñez told her this, and that the things that he did were earth, and that he did not do them with the intention of sinning with her, but for mortification; and she took this to heart and believed it until now . . . and he embraced her and gave her so many kisses and hugs with a fire so spiritual that he seemed like an angel. And when he came to her shameful parts and to her breasts and legs he said, "Unless you become as children you shall not enter the kingdom of heaven," and, "To the pure all things are pure." He said this to mean that as children with purity of heart and sincerity kiss each other and touch their shameful parts, he with the same sincerity did these things without dirty or obscene words. And later he returned to talking about very beautiful affairs of God, like a man drunk with his love, so inflamed that his ears and face were the color of *grana*.

She was asked how she could have good intentions when she enjoyed the touching, hugging, and kissing and came to pollution. Because even if the first time she thought it good, it cannot be excused because of the danger it put her in. And her own touchings of her shameful parts are sin; and seeing that she came to an act so abominable, one must punish it severely and believe that even the first time she sinned mortally, because of what followed, when she returned to the pollutions and enjoyed them, not only with the kisses which under some pretext can be reduced to good intention without attributing them to evil; but with an act as lascivious as putting the tongue in the mouth, which cannot appear anything but carnality. And even more, having contacts so dishonest in the shameful parts, and having so little shame, born of the greatest misery that has ever been seen or heard or come to human understanding, as to take a candle to look at them [her genitals]. From which it is clearly seen that things went farther and that she went along with similar things, acts, and occasions. It is impossible that things went no farther than what she has declared, and thus she is admonished to tell the truth so that it may be seen that she is telling the truth and repents her past life.

She said that she has told the truth and that nothing more happened with Juan Núñez, and that she did not know at the time that it was a sin, because the relationship[30] was holy and good. And she never had the goal of offending God with her will and intention. Neither did anything more happen with Alonso Gutiérrez, and she remembers now that twice when she kissed Alonso Gutiérrez it gave her the desire to have him touch her breasts, but she did not tell him, nor did he do it. And last night the demons told her that she is condemned for having spoken against Juan Núñez and defaming him; because the things that she told about him here in the tribunal of the Inquisition should have been [told] in a confessional.

And because it was very close to twelve the audience ceased, and having been read she approved it and signed. And admonished to go reexamining her memory, she was taken to her cell.

[signatures]

7.7b Seventh Confession (continued)

In the city of Mexico, Tuesday, January 26, 1599, the Lord Inquisitor *licenciado* don Alonso de Peralta in his afternoon audience ordered that Marina de San Miguel be brought from her cell. And when she was present she was told that the *alcaide* said she had asked for an audience, and that she should declare the reason, and the truth, under the oath she swore.

She said that she asked for [the audience] to say that at the age of sixteen she took a vow of chastity in the Mercedarian monastery in the city of Seville, on our Lady's day in September;[31] and thus she has broken her vow with all her obscene, carnal, and dishonest acts, and at the same time she has concealed the existence of the vow in her sacramental confessions. And she doesn't remember anything else, and for this reason she asked for this audience.

She was asked if she has felt bad about anything related to our Holy Catholic Faith or if she has had any doubts about it.

She said that she has never felt bad about the faith, although she has had certain temptations about it, wondering if there is a heaven, and if it is true that there was a Mother of God and Jesus Christ her son; but she never consented with her deliberate reason in thinking that they did not exist, although she had some lukewarmness in believing it, which she attributed to the devil and confessed to her confessor. And what she [also] thought was that God could remove those condemned to hell from there, and lift them to glory; and she received much comfort in not seeing souls condemned. This lasted until she learned that the church holds the contrary, because in hell there is no redemption, and with this she was sure. But from time to time temptations came to her about whether or not condemned souls could be saved, even though she did not allow herself to believe the contrary of what the Holy Mother Roman Catholic Church holds.

She was asked what she felt about the sacraments of penance and communion.

She said that she felt very good about them.

She was asked if she knew that to receive the sacrament of penance, one must feel pain for and repent one's sins, and have a firm purpose of not returning to them; and that confession must be complete, without hiding any sin or circumstance which might aggravate or change their substance and kind.

She said that she knew this and she knows that all the requisites contained in the question are necessary to achieve the sacrament of penance.

She was asked if she knew that the consecrated host was the true body of our Redeemer Jesus Christ; and that to receive such a high sacrament great purity and cleanness of conscience are necessary.

She said that she knew this and she knows very clearly the contents of the question.

She was asked if she knew all the above-said, how has she used the sacraments so poorly, using them when she was in mortal sin, and adding sin to sin, hiding them so as not to lose her reputation with her confessors; coming to eat the bread of the angels so many and diverse times that it seems she could not commit sins so entrenched[32] if she had the beliefs that she says she has and had about the sacraments.

She said that she firmly believed and believes that the body of our Redeemer Jesus Christ is in the consecrated Host, but as a sinner and a weak woman she dared to take the sacraments with a bad conscience, and not because she doubted them.

She was asked if she has believed that our redeemer and saviour Jesus Christ could do anything that might be evil or imperfect.

She said no.

She was asked what moved her to say that when she had carnal copulation with the devil who appeared as an angel of light and as our Redeemer, she believed that it was with His Divine Majesty, a thing which shocks and offends the ears even to think about it.

She said that when the devil had carnal copulation with her in the form of Christ, later she imagined that it was Christ, and then when she came to her senses she realized that as such a friend of virgins and of purity, Christ our Redeemer would find impossible a dishonest act or any imperfect thing, and thus she believes that it was the devil. And from shame she did not confess it to her confessors (as she has said) so they would not know that she had been involved with the devil, and every time that the devil came to her, evilly putting himself in the form of Christ, she had doubts about whether it was Christ or the devil. But considering that Christ could not sin, she saw clearly that it was the devil, from which she received much pain and affliction; and when the said vision took a long time to come and have carnal copulation with her, she was happy and said to herself, "It is not coming," and gave thanks to God.

She was asked if she saw the devil with her bodily eyes the times that he appeared to her in the form that she has declared, and what they talked about, aside from having copulation.

She said that she did not see him with her exterior eyes, but rather that she was enraptured in such a way that she saw him in the form that she has declared, stuck to and united with her performing the carnal act, in such a way that she felt it in the way she has said, as if she were with a man. And she came to pollution as she could come with him [a man], without feeling on top of her any corporeal thing, other than that without being [corporeal] he [the devil] used force to have carnal copulation with her. And thus she had it, without being able to resist it. And at the same time she remembers that when (as she has said) she touched herself dishonestly, the same devil forced her to do it; and thus she did it many times against her will.

She said she has not lied in all that she has said about lights that she has seen and things that have happened to her, but that the devil made them appear to her to trick her, even though he never told her he was Christ our Redeemer, other than that she saw his figure and the other lights that she has declared. And she only stretched her story in saying that when she woke up with Christ she saw his form, because she did not see it, but rather, enraptured, internally heard an interior speech which said, "Make the betrothal," without seeing who spoke. And at the same time she stretched the truth when she said that when she saw purgatory she saw the figure of Christ, because she did not, only a body in the form of a youth, without being able to make out his face perfectly. And the trances that she has had have been with the aid of the devil. And she faked much of what happened, and thus she faked here in the tribunal, and made a demonstration of how she was enraptured, doing the same thing that she is accustomed to do in her house. For this she begs mercy, and subjects herself to the correction of this Holy Office.

She was asked which things in particular concerning the love of God Juan Núñez talked about with her, and who was the person who taught him these things, and which persons other than Juan Núñez and Alonso Gutiérrez have spoken with her about prayer and the love of God.

She said that Juan Núñez talked to her about mystical theology and God's Union,[33] and gave her a book. . . . And because Juan Núñez is so well read, he knows many things about prayer and contemplation, and he gave her account of them, which in particular she does not remember. And Juan Núñez was the first who taught her the road of love of God and his union. And she has talked about these things, about devotion to the love of God and his union, with friars of all orders except the Mercedarian. And with Alonso Gutiérrez she has not spoken anything other than what she has declared.

She was asked if, with any of the persons with whom she talked of the union and love of God, she had hugs, kisses, dishonest touches, and pollutions, of the type that she has declared having with Juan Núñez, saying that because he had no intent and will to offend God, it was no sin.

She said that the contents of the question never happened with anyone but Juan Núñez.

She was asked to say whether she truly saw the things she has declared, lights and visions, because it appears to be her fabrication, especially because she said that she was enraptured and taken to purgatory where she was taken through many streets, and that when she returned to herself she was very tired from so much walking, but she did not walk corporeally, but only in spirit, as she has said and declared.

She said that she felt much fatigue when she returned to herself, and she does not know what occasioned it, only that God must have permitted it. With this the audience ceased and having read it she approved and signed.

[signatures]

7.8 Eighth Confession

In the city of Mexico, Wednesday, January 27, 1599, the Lord Inquisitor in his afternoon audience ordered Marina de San Miguel to be brought from her cell. And when she was present she was told that if she has remembered anything she should say it, and the truth, under the oath she made.

She said that what she has remembered is that when she was talking about devotion to the love and union of God with a friar of the Order of the blessed Saint Dominic called fray Juan Baptista Gazete, who is now in *la China*, they hugged and kissed the times that he came to her house, for the two years that they knew each other. She does not remember the times, other than that it wasn't ordinary but only every fifteen days, about eight years ago. And although he brought a companion, he didn't see the kisses, because they gave them cautiously. And she does not remember if there were any alterations,[34] but she remembers well that there were no dishonest words, only the hugs and kisses. And if the said friar had alterations, they were not apparent.

She was asked whether fray Juan Baptista Gazete told her that they could kiss and hug in the manner that she was taught by Juan Núñez, having good intentions.

She said he did not tell her whether it was good or bad.

She was asked if when she thought about whether heaven existed, and whether it was true that the Mother of God and her precious son existed, if she ever came to the point of doubting it, or whether she believed it, even in a lukewarm fashion.

She said that she did not doubt the said things, other than that it was a temptation she had, and some lukewarmness in belief, until she came to her senses, and afterward she believed it firmly.

She was asked how many times she had the lukewarmness in believing, and how she could avoid having doubts.

She said that it befell her only once, and that if she had any doubt, [it was when] she was enraptured by this temptation without being in her senses, but coming back to her senses she believed firmly in all the said things.

She was asked to say and declare if she believed that it was Christ our Redeemer the times that she had carnal copulation with the devil appearing in the form of Christ, because—aside from having said that she believed it (although later she said no)—considering that our Redeemer is the highest good and such a friend of cleanness and of virgins, she must have known clearly that it was the devil. But all the times she had the copulation with the devil in the form of Christ she doubted whether it was the devil or not, from which doubts one can infer that she did not believe as firmly as she ought to have that such things could not possibly be from Christ. In this she should urgently discharge her conscience.

She said that the thought whether it was Christ or the devil came to her memory without her wanting it; and thus she was tempted in this by the devil, but when she returned to her senses she firmly believed that it was his work, and not Christ's, because he is the highest good and a friend of cleanliness and chastity.

She was asked whether when she believed that God could take someone out of hell, she thought it was with his absolute potency, or his ordinary.

She said that she thought that he could do it with his absolute potency, because for God nothing is impossible. And afterward she learned that the Church says that in hell there is no redemption; and thus for this reason she stopped believing that God would take anyone out [of hell], not because he could not, but because of what the Church says, and the Catholic faith, and because she knows that if a seraph comes and says things against what the Church says, one must not believe it but rather throw him out as a bad spirit.

She was told that she answers very well. . . .

And with this the audience ended, and having been read it she approved and signed. And admonished to reexamine her memory she was ordered taken to her cell.

[signatures]

7.9 Ninth Confession

In the city of Mexico, Friday, January 28, 1599, the Lord Inquisitor *licenciado* don Alonso de Peralta in his morning audience ordered Marina de San Miguel to be brought before him. And when she was present she was told that the *alcaide* said she had asked for an audience, and that she should declare why she wanted it, and the truth, under the oath that she swore.

She said that she asked for it to say and manifest that the other day for shame she did not say that she had a friendship with a certain *beata*, who died two years ago, who also had made a vow of chastity. And commonly when they would see one another they would kiss and hug, and put their hands on their breasts. And she remembers that with the kisses, hugs, and touching on the breasts she came to pollution ten or twelve times. And she doesn't know whether the *beata* felt it, nor what effect these things had on her. And she [Marina] knowing these things were sins, determined to confess them, although later she did not confess them to her confessors because it seemed to her that she had not sinned mortally because she had no intention of doing so. And although sometimes she had a scruple, shame made her not confess [the sins], and at the same time receive the Holy Sacrament.

She was asked if in the hugs, kisses, and touches any amorous or dishonest words were said.

She said that amorous words were said, and that she said to the other woman, "Mother of my soul and of my life," but no dishonest ones.

She was asked, if she didn't take these things for sins, as she had no desire and will to come to pollution, why she had a scruple.

She said that because she felt that this was a weakness, it gave her a scruple about whether it was a sin or not. And afterward she looked on the bright side[35] and decided to believe that it was no sin; and this removed all her scruples, and she lived in great peace with herself.

She was asked how she could quiet her conscience, not having talked about her scruples with anyone who might enlighten her, especially as she had formed them, and knowing clearly that what obliged her not to confess them was shame; and not confessing them was not looking on the bright side, but rather on the dark side, because in doubt one must incline to the more secure side. From which one infers that she did not sin out of ignorance, but out of malice. And thus she is admonished on behalf of God our Lord to discharge her conscience, making a clear and pure confession so that one sees that she proceeds with purity and procures the remedy of her soul.

She said that she refers to what she has confessed, and that she remembers that the devil, about fifteen or sixteen years ago, incited her to take a mirror, being alone, and to look at her shameful parts, which she did eight or ten times, six with interior touchings, and two times she had pollution, and the other times there was no touching. And she did not confess these things because she did not do them with the motive of offending God, but rather before she gave thanks for having created the said things, and putting them in order for the increase of creatures. And thus the lewd things she sees in little animals serve to remind her of God and to give him thanks for having put everything in such order.

She was asked how she could ignore sinning in the said things when she says she did them incited by the devil, *by the devil*,[36] aside from which she knows that in such things one sins mortally by seeing them; even without touches so lewd and dishonest, with which she came to pollution voluntarily. Because at the point when she determined to have the said touches, she decided also to have the pollutions which followed from them.

She said that she says clearly that she believed she did not offend God in these things, although she knew that she sinned with her sight and with all the other things that she did (as she has confessed), but as she had no intention of offending God nor did she consent to it, and she spoke poorly in saying that the devil tempted her, because she didn't know whether it was he, or nature itself.

She was asked if she knew that she offended God in the said things, that she say and declare how she could have good intentions and not give consent; when she delighted in her shameful parts she put it in execution, taking a mirror to look at them, from which came the temptation of the flesh and the putting into execution. Things so abominable and lewd, that even the devil himself would be offended by them. . . .

She said that it is true that she consented in these things and put them into execution, but she did not believe that she offended God because she did not have the intention of offending him.

She was asked if these things of hers are evil and offend God, and she put them in execution, how could she believe that she did not offend him because she had no will to offend him. Well, it is an impossible case. On one hand she consents in a sin and put it into action, offending our Lord gravely; and on the other hand she had no intention of offending him.

She said that she always based herself on the interior will, with which she determined not to consent to the said things even though she put them into play.

She was asked, if she were to go to bed with a man and have carnal union with him, if she would sin mortally, even though she might not consent with her interior will.

She said that she would sin, because she clearly sees the danger in something declared to be against God.

She was asked, if thus she would sin, what difference is there in the case between the proposed case, and what she has done, which one cannot deny is a thing against what God has ordered; rather the sin she has committed is worse, because it is against nature, and the danger [in it] can be seen clearly as with the touches, kisses, and hugs [with which] she came so many times to pollution.

She said that then she was in bestiality, and now through the questions that have been put to her it is clear how blind she has been.

And admonished that she still go reexamining her memory and discharge her conscience, she was ordered taken to her cell.

[signatures]

In the city of Mexico, Tuesday, Day of the Purification of our Lady, February 2, 1599, the Lord Inquisitor in his afternoon audience ordered Marina de San Miguel brought before him. And once present she was told that if she has remembered anything in her case she should say it, and the truth, under the oath that she has made.

She said no.

She was told that she should understand that the *promotor fiscal* of this Holy Office wants to pose the accusation, and that before it is posed she would be best off to say and confess the whole truth as she has been admonished, because thus there will be more room to use with her mercy . . .

She said she had no more to say.

NOTES

ACKNOWLEDGMENTS   The research for and translation of this document were completed with the generous support of the Social Sciences and Humanities Research Council of Canada.

1. New Spain included modern-day Mexico, large parts of Central America, parts of what is now the southwestern United States, and the Philippines. I say "ostensible" authority because it was virtually impossible to police such a large and diverse area.
2. This document can be found in Mexico City in the Archivo General de la Nación, Ramo Inquisición, Vol. 210, Exp. 3, ff. 307–430. The confessions translated here are found in folios 347r–72v.
3. There are few studies in English of colonial Spanish American women's encounters with the Inquisition. The suggestions for further reading I have listed at the end of the document will provide an introduction to the Inquisition in colonial Mexico and to inquisitorial investigations of religious women in Europe for those interested in pursuing this subject further.
4. Literally, "que oficio tiene," or "what office she holds," the standard formulation, in the sixteenth century, for the question "What does she do?"
5. A *beata* was a semireligious woman who devoted her life to God. *Beatas* generally wore habits and lived chastely, either in communities or in private homes. Unlike nuns, *beatas* were not obliged to take solemn vows of poverty, chastity, and obedience; nor were they

obliged to follow a rule. Many did take simple vows, allying themselves with one of the religious orders. Marina allied herself with the Order of Saint Dominic, an important order in Spanish America.

6. Literally, in "working" (*labrar*), which when used by women refers to work with the needle.
7. Literally, uncles and aunts, siblings of father.
8. In the sixteenth century, Catholics were to attend mass on Sundays and holy days. Though holy days varied from region to region, there generally were about fifty. Confession and communion were obligatory only at Easter; but many people, particularly women, received communion much more frequently than that.
9. Literally, in "romance," as opposed to Latin.
10. That is, in the house of her parents, not in Córdoba. As we will see, they changed their house several times.
11. Literally, having gained something to eat (*ganado de comer*).
12. Marina's testimony does not make clear whether her father and his wife remained together after the adultery and murder.
13. Here the notary has transcribed the testimony verbatim as Marina corrected herself.
14. Juan Núñez de León was accountant of the Royal Treasury, a wealthy and important man. He too was tried and disciplined by the Inquisition (AGN 210, Exp. 2).
15. A suspect's goods were often sequestered for the duration of the trial; any fines levied could be taken from the sale of the sequestered goods.
16. This apparently rambling and irrelevant information shows that Marina was clearly thinking forward to what might occur when bailiffs went to her home to seize her property. She was anticipating that Gutiérrez would be able to keep his property—and perhaps some of hers, if he claimed it—out of the hands of the Holy Office. By detailing his spending on her house, she was presumably attempting to cast it as an encumbered asset that the bailiffs could not with impunity seize.
17. Gregorio López was arguably sixteenth-century Mexico's most famous mystic and was regarded by many contemporaries as a saint.
18. Literally men (*hombres*), but here used in its "universal" sense to include all people.
19. This was a standard admonition given to overcome confessants' reticence.
20. That is, not physically, but in a vision.
21. Literally, "cauterios de fuego", or "cauterization."
22. Here Marina was using the familiar form of address, expressing intimacy.
23. "Que fuertemente me ha dado esto."
24. Literally, to speak through her teeth (*hablar entre dientes*).
25. Literally, give alms (*hazed limosna*).
26. Literally, to have light where to begin (*tener lumbre por donde empeçar*).
27. That is, experienced orgasm.
28. *Guirnaldas* were flowers and fragrant herbs woven into a garland to adorn the head. The sense here is that "with silver and brilliance" they dramatize the grotesqueness of the demons.
29. Literally, lasso (*lazo*).
30. "Trato", which could mean either the relationship or the discussion.
31. The Catholic Church classified vows as either solemn or simple. The former was public and made with formal clerical intervention and ceremony, the latter was private and sometimes unwitnessed and unrecorded. Marina's vow of chastity would have been a "simple" vow but nevertheless seems to have been publicly made. She claimed that she made the vow in the convent of La Merced in Sevilla, which suggests that it was witnessed and "accepted" by a superior. This vow, therefore, went beyond a personal promise; it was a binding obligation to God that she had clearly breached.
32. Literally, so germinated (*tan germinados*).
33. Presumably Marina and Juan were discussing the union of God in the Trinity, a favorite theme of mystical devotion, rather than their own mystical union with God, also a topic of interest to mystics.
34. That is, arousal.
35. Literally, at the better part (*a la mayor parte*).
36. Emphasis and repetition in original.

DOCUMENT THEMES

Gender; Inquisition; Religion; Sexuality; Town Life; Women.

SUGGESTIONS FOR FURTHER READING

Behar 1989.
Bilinkoff 1992.
Boyer 1995.
Ciamitti 1990.
Curcio-Nagy 1999.
Greenleaf 1969.
Holler 1999.
Holler 1993.
McKnight 1999.
Monter 1986.
Myers 1999.
Perry 1987.
Traslosheros H. 1998.

8

Spaniards in the Nahua Countryside: Dr. Diego de León Plaza and Nahuatl Land Sale Documents

(Mexico, Early Seventeenth Century)

Rebecca Horn

INTRODUCTION

Mexico City, built atop the ruins of the Aztec imperial capital of Tenochtitlan, was the center of Spanish life in colonial Mexico. Here Spaniards met Nahuatl-speaking peoples, or Nahuas, in both institutional and informal settings. Although Spaniards initially congregated in the urban center, they moved into the surrounding Nahua countryside to grow wheat or raise pigs for an expanding Spanish market. Attracted by fertile soils and abundant supplies of fresh water, Spaniards first turned to areas to the west and southwest of the city. In this zone lay Coyoacan, a Nahua *altepetl* earlier granted to Hernando Cortés and his heirs as part of a vast *encomienda* called the Marquesado del Valle given to reward him for his part in the conquest. By the late sixteenth century Spanish land acquisition accelerated in the region following a series of epidemics that devastated the indigenous population and cut deeply into agricultural production. Spaniards acquired land in various ways, ranging from royal grants to outright usurpation. But purchase from individual Nahuas was common too and—perhaps because Coyoacan was located so close to Mexico City, perhaps because Coyoacan enjoyed a special jurisdictional status as part of the Marquesado—Coyoacan boasts an unusually large number of extant documents written by Nahuas in Nahuatl to record land sales to Spaniards.

Our selection of documents, dating from the early seventeenth century, concerns the purchases made by a Spanish clergyman, Dr. Diego de León Plaza, in Santo Domingo Mixcoac, a subdistrict of the Coyoacan *altepetl*. León Plaza and others followed a common strategy of land acquisition: they purchased many separate, small pieces of land from individual Nahuas, nobles and commoners alike.[1] They also worked with and were aided by a local official, the *teniente*—in this case the Spaniard Antonio de Fuentes—who typically witnessed land sales or granted possession of the land. Some Nahuas were unhappy with Antonio de Fuentes's role in land sales and they complained to the Spanish *corregidor* and members of the local Nahua town council. Other Nahuas came to his defense, arguing, as we see in the petition included with the land sale documents, that since Antonio de Fuentes's arrival in Coyoacan he had upheld justice and had protected them against mistreatment by the blacks and *mestizos* who lived and worked on the Spanish estates in the region. Together the land sale documents and petition illustrate the close day-to-day contact between Nahuas and the Spaniards, blacks, and *mestizos* resident in the central Mexican countryside in the early seventeenth century.

Nahuatl land sale documents also tell us a great deal about other aspects of postconquest Nahua society that tend not to appear in Spanish documents. The Nahuatl terms *altepetl* and *tlaxilacalli* (subdistrict of an *altepetl*) refer to forms of Nahua sociopolitical organization largely ignored or unrecognized by Spaniards. And the terms *tequitlalli* (tribute land) and *tlalcohualli* (purchased land) reflect a complex land tenure system functioning at the local level. But Spanish practices also had a profound effect, especially in such central areas as Coyoacan. Nahuatl land sale documents were modeled on the Spanish *carta de venta* (bill of sale) and *posesión* (grant of possession) and Nahua notaries often used these Spanish loan words in land sale documents, as seen in some of the examples presented here. Readers will want to note other Spanish loan words (retained in the translation) that reflect the introduction of Spanish material culture, the adaptation of Spanish forms of municipal government, and the integration of Nahuas into the commercial economy. As illustrated by the Nahuatl land sale documents from Coyoacan, Nahua society was a complex mix of Spanish and Nahua practices refashioned in the postconquest setting.

THE DOCUMENT[2]

8.1 Joaquín de San Francisco and Juana Feliciana Sell Land to Dr. Diego de León Plaza

Here in the *altepetl* Santo Domingo Mixcoac,[3] Marquesado del Valle, on the first day of July of the year 1612, I, Joaquín de San Francisco, and my wife, Juana Feliciana, citizens[4] here in the *altepetl* of Santa María Purificación Tlilhuacan, sell to Dr. Diego de León Plaza, *teopixqui*, one field and house that we have in the *tlaxilacalli* Tlilhuacan next to the house of our lord the doctor [León Plaza]. And on the other side it is next to the house of Juan Bautista, Spaniard. Where we are is right in the middle of [in between] their houses. And now we receive [the money] in person.[5] The reason we sell it is that we have no children to whom it might belong. For there is another land and house, but [the land] here we can no longer [work] because it is really in the middle of [land belonging to] Spaniards. [The land] is not *tributario*, for my father, named Juan Altamirano, and my mother, María Catalina, really left it to me. And now I give it to [the doctor] very voluntarily. And now he is personally giving me 130 pesos. Both my wife and I receive it in person before the witnesses. And the tribute will be remedied with [the price]; it will pay it. The land [upon which tribute is owed] is at Colonanco. It is adjacent to the land of Miguel de Santiago and Lucas Pérez. And the witnesses [are] Antonio de Fuentes and señora Inés de Vera and Juana de Vera, Spanish women (and the Nahuas) Juan Josef, Gabriel Francisco, María, Mariana, and Sebastián Juan. And because we do not know how to write, I, Joaquín [de San] Francisco, and my wife asked a witness to set down [a signature] on our behalf [along with the notary?] Juan Vázquez, Spaniard.[6] Witnesses, Antonio de Fuentes, Joaquín [de San] Francisco, Juana Feliciana, Juana Vázquez, Sebastián Juan, [and] Juan Josef. Before me, Matías Valeriano, notary. And both of them, he and his wife, [Joaquín de San Francisco and Juana Feliciana] received the 140 pesos each three months,[7] *?why* before the witnesses who were mentioned. Before me, Matías Valeriano, notary.

In the *altepetl* of Santo Domingo Mixcoac on the second day of July, of the year 1612, before Antonio de Fuentes, *teniente*, here in the *altepetl* our precious father[8] Dr. Diego de León Plaza requested that they give him *posesión* because he already paid the money, and Joaquín de San Francisco and his wife, Juana Feliciana, had received the 140 pesos in person. And then our precious father entered inside the house. [The house] faces toward the great mountain [that is, south]. And then with his hand [the official] brought our precious father inside [the house]. And then Joaquín de San Francisco came out at the exit so that it was confirmed that never again will [he and his wife] enter the house. They made it the property of our precious father. And then [León Plaza] inspected the boundaries where the land ends in various places. He threw stones several times by which his *posesión* was realized.[9] Before the *teniente* and before the witnesses, Sebastián Juan, Juan Josef, and Nicolás. And it was done on the day and month mentioned above, and it was done before two Spanish women, Inés de Vera and Juana de Vera. It was done before Juan Vázquez, Antonio de Fuentes, and Juan Vázquez, notary public.[10] Before me, Matías Valeriano.

8.2 Tomás Lázaro Sells Land to Dr. Diego de León Plaza

In the *altepetl* Santo Domingo Mixcoac *tlaxilacalli* of Tlilhuacan on the tenth day of March, of the year 1612, I, Tomás Lázaro, tribute collector here in the *altepetl*, and my wife are selling [a piece of land] to our precious father Dr. Diego de León Plaza. Our land, which is two *tlalquahuitl*, is next to the fence [or boundary of the land] of Juan Bautista, a Spaniard, and it is also next to the land of our precious father [Dr. Diego de León Plaza]. It is at the edge of a ravine and next to [the land of] Juan Leonardo. And a separate part reaches as far as the land of Diego Sánchez; this land reaches to the *membrillos* which form the boundary with [the land of] Juan Mateo. But [the *membrillos*] are not included, only three cherry trees. And [León Plaza] buys the land on which the trees are [located]. [The land] is not *tequitlalli*, because it is far away and we cannot reach it to cultivate it. Witnesses, Antonio [de] Fuentes, Spaniard, and León de Plaza, Spaniard. And I am Matías Valeriano.

On the day and month mentioned above, our precious father came and took *posesión* of the land. I, Tomás Lázaro and my wife, Francisca, gave it to him personally. Before all the witnesses, and before me, Matías Valeriano, and Juan de [San Francisco?], notary. Juan de León Plaza Portillo, witness.

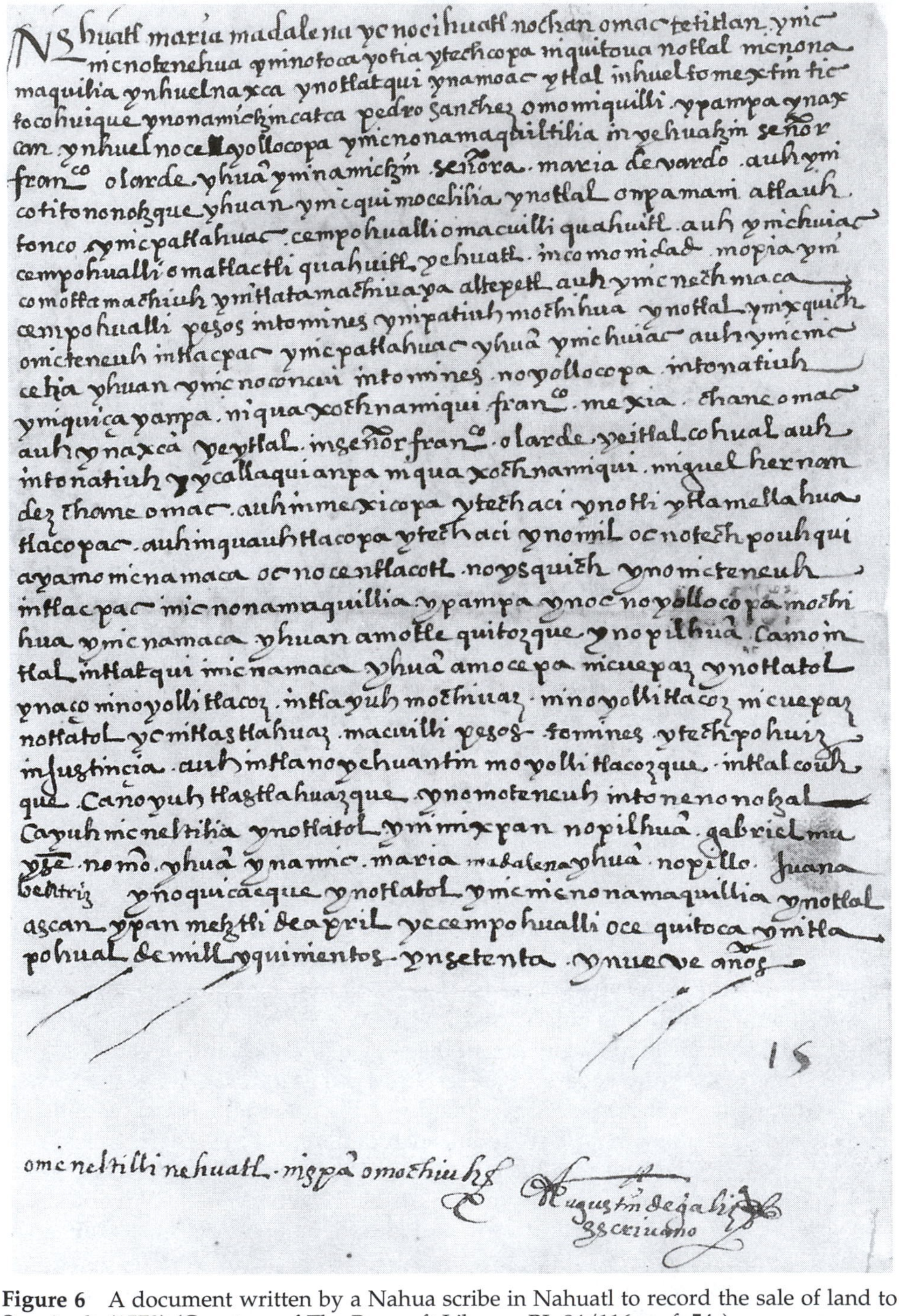
Ns huatl maria madalena ye nocihuatl nochan omac tetitlan ymic
micnotenehua yninotocayotia ytechcopa niquitoua notlal menona
maquilia ynhuel naxca ynotlatqui ynamoac ytlal inhuel tomextin tic
tocohuique ynonamictzin catca pedro sanchez omomiquilli . ypampa ynax
can ynhuel nocel yollocopa ymicnonamaquiltilia in yehuatzin señor
franco olarde yhuã ynnamictzin señora maria de vardo . auh ym
cotitononotzque yhuan ymiquimocelilia ynotlal ompamani atlauh
tonco ymicpatlahuac cempohualli omacuilli quahuitl . auh ymichuiac
cempohualli omatlactli quahuitl yehuatl incomomidad mopia ym
comotlamachiuh ynitlatamachiuaya altepetl auh ymic nechmaca
cempohualli pesos intomines ynipatiuh mochihua ynotlal ymixquich
omicteneuh intlacpac ymicpatlahuac yhuã ymichuiac auh ymicmo
cehia yhuan ymicnocencui intomines noyollocopa intonatiuh
ymiquiça yampa niqua xothnamiqui franco mexia . chane omac
auh ynaxcã yeytlal ingeñor franco olarde yeitlalcohual auh
intonatiuh ycallaqui anpa niqua xothnamiqui miguel hernan
dez thome omac . auh inmexicopa ytechaci ynothi ytlamellahua
tlacopac auh inquauhtlacopa ytechaci ynomil ocnotech pouhqui
ayamo micnamaca ocnocentlacotl noysquich ynomicteneuh
intlacpac micnonamaquillia ypampa ynoc noyollocopa mochi
hua ymicnamaca yhuan amotle quitozque ynopilhuã camo in
tlal intlatqui micnamaca yhuã amocepa micuepaz ynotlatol
ynaco minoyolli tlacoz intlayuh mochiuaz minoyollitlacoz micuepaz
notlatol yemitlastlahuaz macuilli pesos tomines ytechpohuiz
injustincia . auh intlanoyehuantin moyolli tlacozque intlalcouh
que camoyuh tlastlahuazque ynomoteneuh intonenonotzal
cayuh micneltilia ynotlatol ymixpan nopilhuã gabriel mu
ñoz nomo yhuã ynamic maria madalena yhuã nopillo juana
beatriz ynoquicaque ynotlatol ymicmicnonamaquillia ynotlal
ascan ypan meztli de april yccempohualli oce quitoca ymitla
pohual de mill yquimientos ynsetenta ynueve años

15

omicneltilli nehuatl . mixpã omochiuh
Augustin de galis
escriuano

Figure 6 A document written by a Nahua scribe in Nahuatl to record the sale of land to Spaniards (1579) (Courtesy of The Bancroft Library, BL 84/116 m, f. 54r).

8.3 Juan Bautista and María Salomé Sell Land to Dr. Diego de León Plaza

I, Juan Bautista, and my wife María Salomé; our *tlaxilacalli* is Santo Domingo Mixcoac Tlilhuacan. We have a little piece of land; it is not big. We sell it to our precious father Dr. Diego de León Plaza. He gives us three pesos and four *tomines*. And the land abuts his land. The reason why we abandon it and both my wife and I willingly sell it, is because the maize can no longer be grown [on it]; the *caballos* eat all [the crops]. And I mentioned this land abuts the land of our precious father and [the land of] Juan Mateo and Miguel Sánchez. It ends where all the avocado trees stand. [I sell it] because I have other land and houses, because this land I am selling is not *tributario*. Before the witnesses, Andrés Matías, Juan Mateo, and Fernando de Fuentes. To verify my statement, I set down my name, [and], with my name, my *firma*.[11] The document was made on the tenth day of May of the year 1611. [signed] Juan Bautista. Before me, Matías Valeriano.

8.4 Juana Ursula and Juana Francisca Sell Land to Dr. Diego de León Plaza

I, Juana Ursula, and my daughter Juana Francisca are citizens here at Santo Domingo Mixcoac, which belongs with this *altepetl villa* of Coyoacan. And our *tlaxilacalli* is our precious mother Purificación Tlilhuacan. We sell to our precious father Dr. Diego de León Plaza our land and the house on it. And in the same place are twenty-two *higos*. Now my daughter and I together receive ninety pesos in cash. He personally gives it to us before the witnesses Juan de Toval, Spaniard, and Antonio de Fuentes, Spaniard, and before my husband, Lorenzo; I receive the money with which I will repay the money of Tomás Hernández. And I have land and a house in another place. For this reason I sell all the water that stands [on the land we are selling].[12] We abandon it very voluntarily. We personally give it to our precious father. He gives us ninety *pesos* in cash. Before the witnesses, Juan de León Plaza, Bartolomé Quiñones and the above mentioned and named. To verify our statement, one witness puts down our names, our *firmas*.[13] It was done on the twenty-ninth of August of the year 1619. Witnesses, Bartolomé Quiñones, and Juan de León Plaza, witness, and Antonio de Fuentes, witness. Before me, Matías Valeriano.

8.5 Executors for Domingo Matías and Paula Sell Land to Dr. Diego de León Plaza

I, don Juan Jacobo, am *fiscal* and *juez* here in the *altepetl* Santo Domingo Mixcoac. Joaquín Francisco, his wife, Juana Feliciana, Magdalena María, and the relatives of Domingo Matías and Paula, his late wife, [who] have already died, [are present?]. We the *albaceas* [for the estate of Domingo Matías and Paula] sell to our precious father Dr. Diego de León Plaza a piece of land next to the land of Juan Bautista, a Spaniard. And on another side it is next to the land of one named Juan Leonardo, and it goes as far as the ravine and the boundary [of the land] [or fence] where there is a great rock [or rocks].[14] [The doctor] gave me [the *fiscal*] its [purchase] price of thirty-one pesos. The *fiscal* received it. And [Domingo Matías] left this irrigated land for masses with which it will be done.[15] It is *tlalcohualli* and all persons know that it is not *tributario*. And from [the sale] came eight pesos and two *tomines* that [León Plaza] had given him when he was confined [in jail] when the *fiscal* received it; it was when a person died at his house.[16] And as to how [the sale] was carried out, today the *fiscal* received the money before the above-mentioned relatives. They truly put down *firmas*, don Juan Jacobo and don Joaquín Flores, *alcalde*, and the witnesses, Antonio [de] Fuentes, Spaniard, and Josef Pedro Zamorano, on the fourth day of the month of April of the year 1612. Witnesses, Antonio [de] Fuentes, and don Juan Jacobo *fiscal*, Joaquín Francisco, don Joaquín Flores, *alcalde*. Before me, Matías Valeriano, notary.

Here in the *altepetl* Santo Domingo Mixcoac in the *tlaxilacalli* Tlilhuacan, Marquesado del Valle, on the fourth day of the month of April of the year 1612, I, don Juan Jacobo *fiscal* and *juez*, and Joaquín Francisco, and the dead person's relatives, gave the land to our precious father. I received the eleven pesos that Dr. Diego de León Plaza gave to me in person, with which it amounts to, first, the eight pesos and two *tomines* he gave me. Before the witnesses, Antonio de Fuentes, Spaniard, Pedro Zamorano, Spaniard, Juan Josef, don Juan Jacobo *fiscal*, Joaquín Francisco, Antonio de Fuentes, Juan Josef, witnesses. Before me, Matías Valeriano, notary.

8.6 Anastacia Salomé and Her Grandchildren Sell Land to Dr. Diego de León Plaza

Here in the great *altepetl* Santo Domingo Mixcoac in the *tlaxilacalli* Tlilhuacan, Marquesado [del Valle], on the tenth day of February in the year 1612, we, Anastacia Salomé, and my grandchildren, Mariana, Francisca Verónica, and Andrés Lázaro, and Lucas, citizens here in [the *tlaxilacalli* of San Juan Evangelista Malinaltonco sell our land. We sell it to our precious father Dr. Diego de León Plaza. It is there in the *tlaxilacalli* Tlilhuacan next to his house and his land. It is one *mecatl*. It ends at the land of Catalina. Below it is the road that goes straight to Coyoacan. The reason we sell it is we have much land there in San Juan. We will no longer say it is our home. He gives us four pesos and four *tomines*. And the land is not *tributario*. It is *patrimonio*. And [Anastacia Salomé and her grandchildren] received the money. Before the witnesses, Antonio de Fuentes, Spaniard, and Juan Josef, and Diego Hernández, and Diego Jacobo, and I, Matías Valeriano, notary. Because the witnesses do not know how to write, I put down their *firmas* on their behalf. Antonio de Fuentes put down his [own] name. Diego Hernández. Lucas Baltasar, witnesses. Before me, Matías Valeriano, notary.

On the day and month mentioned above, on which our precious father, Dr. Diego de León Plaza, took possession, Anastacia Salomé and Lucas Baltasar and

Mariana and Francisca Verónica gave it to him personally. No one objected, for everyone attested to it and said: let it be done. Witnesses, Antonio de Fuentes, Spaniard, and Juan Josef, Diego Hernández, and Martín Jacobo, and I, Matías Valeriano, notary. Antonio Josef, and Antonio [de] Fuentes, and Diego Hernández, witnesses. Before me, Matías Valeriano.

8.7 Miguel Gerónimo Sells Land to Dr. Diego de León Plaza

I, Miguel Gerónimo, am a citizen here in the *altepetl* Santo Domingo Mixcoac; my *tlaxilacalli* is Atepotzco. I give my land to our precious father Dr. Diego de León Plaza. He gives me four pesos. My land is next to the land of Lucas Juan, and it reaches next to the land of Hernando Ixpopoyotl[17] and it ends next to the road that goes straight to the church at Santo Domingo. Now I give this land very willingly. It is not *tributario,* for it is my *tlalcohualli.* I leave it for I have a lot of land, with all the maguey on it. Now before the witnesses I receive the money. This land is just a little [plot]; it is not big. And I leave all of the water with which I used to irrigate, with which the land is to be watered. And my daughter, Luisa, and I receive the money. And I personally place my cross next to my name. Before the witnesses, Antonio de Fuentes, Spaniard, Bernardo Fuentes, Pedro Tetzotzonqui.[18] The *escritura de venta*[19] was issued in the month of March on the tenth day of the year 1610. Witnesses, Antonio de Fuentes, Miguel Gerónimo. Before me, Matías Valeriano.

8.8 Vicente Juan Sells Land to Dr. Diego de León Plaza

I, Vicente Juan, state today is the sixteenth of November, 1610. I, Vicente Juan, declare my home is here in the *altepetl* Santo Domingo Mixcoac, in my *tlaxilacalli* Santa María Purificación Tlilhuacan. I sell to Dr. Diego de León Plaza my little house and a little land that lies facing it. It is attached to the house, orchard, and land of our father [León Plaza]. It reaches as far as the cross which is at the road,[20] so that it ends at the corner of the house where the road bends and where the foundation [of the house] begins.[21] It is really my *patrimonio* and not *tributario,* for my father gave it to me when [my mother and father] died. And now I relinquish it all. He is giving me forty pesos and two *tomines.* Our precious father Dr. Diego de León Plaza is personally giving [the money] to me. And our precious father is giving thirty pesos of it to someone else; he is giving it to a Spaniard, Sebastián Ruiz, to whom I owed it. And I am receiving the [remaining] ten pesos and two *tomines* in person before the witnesses, so that no one else will ever make objections, so that now I relinquish it forever, so that never again will I make objections [to] the people of the *tlaxilacalli.*[22] And as to how I sell it, it is not in vain (that is, without purpose), for I owe people money that I am paying back. And in order to verify my statement, I set down my *firma,* because I can write. And [it was done] before the witnesses, Sebastián Ruiz, Spaniard, Antonio de Fuentes, Spaniard, and [two Nahua] citizens here, Miguel de San Pedro and Francisco Juan. And all the witnesses declare that it is really his property. To confirm it he puts down his name and *firma*. I, Juan Vicente, declare that I sold my land and my house very voluntarily. It was done before the witnesses Antonio de Fuentes and Miguel de San Pedro. I, Matías Valeriano, notary.

And on the above-mentioned day and month, right then he entered the house, because I received the money, forty pesos and two *tomines*, in person. And now our precious father Dr. Diego de León Plaza took possession of it before the witnesses, Sebastián Ruiz, Spaniard, and Antonio de Fuentes, Spaniard, and before those of the *tlaxilacalli*[23] Tlilhuacan, Miguel de San Pedro, Miguel Juan, and Francisco Juan. And to verify my word, I place here my name, and next to my name my *firma*. I make full statement about how possession was taken before the witnesses, *etc*.[24] And the statement was verified on the nineteenth day of the month of November, in the year 1610. I, Juan Vicente, am selling the land. Witnesses, Miguel de San Pedro and Antonio [de] Fuentes, Spaniard. Matías Valeriano, notary.

And María Marta, the wife of Juan Vicente, came to confirm that they are selling his house very voluntarily. For it is really their property, their possession. Our precious father, Dr. Diego de León Plaza, also buys it very voluntarily. They receive the money, forty pesos and two *tomines*, in person. It is very voluntary on the part of both him and his wife, because the land they have is not large, so that they are giving it to our father. They owe thirty pesos in cash; they are returning the money to the Spaniard Sebastián Ruiz. But it was not sold in the presence of Juan Vicente's wife; she was sick. Afterwards she came to verify that it was really his property, his possession, when she married him.[25] It was formerly the property, the possession, of Juan Vicente. His late grandfather, Francisco Martín, and his grandmother, Ana, bequeathed it to him. And in order that he verify their statement, they set down their names next to their *firmas* on the twentieth day of November of the year 1610. And the witnesses [were] Antonio de Fuentes, Spaniard, and Juan Lorenzo, witnesses. The seller [is] Juan Vicente. Matías Valeriano, notary.

8.9 A Group of Nahuas from Santo Domingo Mixcoac Complain to the Authorities (Early Seventeenth Century)[26]

We are citizens here in Santo Domingo Mixcoac. We state that we found out that Paula and Juana and María and Catalina and Inés and Anastacia complain about the *teniente* before you [the *corregidor, gobernador, regidores*, etc.]. It is Antonio de Fuentes whom they are accusing because they say he mistreats them. [They say] he robs [people's land].

[We say that] since [Antonio de Fuentes] arrived here he is a good person. He helps us and respects us a great deal and many blacks and *mestizos* [used to] come here. [The blacks and *mestizos*] come here and take all the chickens [or turkeys] and they mistreat us about all the orchards.[27] And they are not married. They go about taking concubines. They take people's spouses away from them by which they mistreat us [afflict us]. And [Antonio de Fuentes] made them stop. And now [the people] are very happy. He helps us very well [in a good manner]. But [blacks and *mestizos*] didn't esteem [Antonio de Fuentes] because he arrested them. They always go around with concubines for which he punishes them. And for this reason [the punished ones] don't want there to be justice because [without justice] he would not see [how great] their badness is because they take concubines. And they go around asking for money from us and they are demanding that he be gotten rid of. They complain about the *teniente*. And we [the petitioners] tell [the blacks and *mestizos*]: Why should we give you money? It is already three years that [Antonio de Fuentes] is here now and he treats us very well. That is how we answered them.

And now [the] Spaniard Napolles disputes with the *teniente*. And Napolles goes around to each house exerting pressure on, forcing many people [to say "get rid of the *teniente*"]. [He says:] "Let there be no officer of the justice. I will help you expel the *teniente* because we will be happy if there is no officer of the law on your land." Napolles, Spaniard, keeps a woman at his house and he is forcing her. For this reason [the authorities] arrested him for concubinage. They gave him a fine about which he became very angry and they arrested him. He stole four pigs, the property of a person named Francisco Hernández, Spaniard, and because of that they arrested him. He was scorched [burned] for their relatives accuse them.[28]

And now with great bowing down we ask you [the *corregidor, gobernador, regidores*, etc.] to punish whoever lives in this manner. And if you should take the judge (that is, the *teniente*) away from us we will really be mistreated. For [the blacks and *mestizos*] will take away all of our orchards from which we get [the] tribute that we pay. And they do not live well. They will go about in concubinage and if there should be no officer of justice they [will] beat [kill] everyone. And they do not go to confession. [But now] they are a little afraid [because of the *teniente's* actions and] already live in a better fashion. And so now with great concern and with bowing down we implore you [the *corregidor, gobernador*, and *regidores*, etc.] and we ask for justice. Everyone knows how [the blacks and *mestizos*] mistreat us. They don't go to confession. They are already a little afraid and are already living a little better. And we ask for justice. Let them be punished. We who ask it are Juan Joseph, Francisco de San Juan, and Francisco Juan.

NOTES

1. Spaniards also purchased land from Nahua officials who, acting in an official capacity (for example, to raise revenue for municipal coffers), sold land under their control. Land sales by *altepetl* officials occurred in Coyoacan, but far more common were sales made by individuals who, acting in no official capacity, sold lands that they claimed were worked by and closely associated with their own households. Such sales reflect the complexity of the Nahua land tenure system, especially the importance of types of land (purchased and patrimonial, for example) over which individual households might exercise considerable discretion, even their sale.
2. Archivo General de la Nación, México, Bienes Naciónales leg. 1453, exp. 12, ff. 181r–84r, 189r-v. Square brackets indicate text that is not in the original but that is implied and parentheses provide futher explanation or clarification.
3. Some central Mexican *altepetl* were organizationally complex, themselves made up of constituent *altepetl*. Coyoacan was a complex *altepetl*, made up of four constituent parts, one of which was Santo Domingo Mixcoac.

4. The Nahuatl term *chane*, "householder," or "citizen," is used here to refer to local Nahua residents, as was common in Nahuatl documents throughout central Mexico.

5. Nahuatl forms such as *nomatica* ("with my hands"), *tomatica* ("with our hands"), and *ymaticatzinco* ("with his hands"), all based on *matl* (hand/arm), essentially mean "in person" or "personally," and I have translated them as such throughout the document.

6. The phrasing suggests that Juan Vázquez was asked to sign along with the witness but it is not entirely clear.

7. The meaning of "each three months" is not clear, in part because the preceding few words are not easily translated; perhaps the purchase price was paid in installments. In addition, there is a discrepancy between the purchase price of 130 pesos mentioned above and the 140 pesos mentioned here (though note that below it appears again as 140 pesos).

8. The phrase "our precious father," used here to refer to the Spanish clergyman Dr. Diego de León Plaza, employs the Nahuatl element *tlaço-* "precious, dear." *Tlaço-* "was routinely added to the description of almost any benevolent Christian supernatural," (Lockhart 1992, p. 252) as in, for example, "our precious mother" (*totlaçonantzin*) in reference to the Virgin Mary and "our precious father" (*totlaçotatzin*) in reference to God. Lockhart (1992, p. 552 n. 208) tends to think that "the function of *tlaço-* with religious concepts is to put them in a specifically Christian context."

9. The Nahuas adopted the main features of a Spanish ritual act of possession, in which the seller or the *teniente* leads the buyer around the boundaries of the land parcel. The buyer then goes about the property pulling twigs and tufts of grass and throwing stones in symbolic gestures of ownership. If a house were included in the sale, a buyer might shove a seller (and others) out of the house. The *posesión* presented here beautifully illustrates a variant of this ritual in which the *teniente* leads the purchaser by the hand through the door, after which the seller ceremoniously leaves the house.

10. Apparently the notary who wrote the document repeated Juan Vázquez's name.

11. Nahuas understood the importance of signing and signatures to Spanish legal procedure and the Spanish term *firma* (signature) was an early loanword into Nahuatl.

12. Literally, "inside it" [the land].

13. If a seller is unable to sign, he or she either places a cross on the document or, as in this case, requests that a witness sign for him/her. Whether a seller could sign is at times stated explicitly, as seen in some of the examples below.

14. Whether the boundary of the land is marked by a great rock or a fence made of rocks is not known; the exact meaning of the Nahuatl passage is unclear. Stone boundary markers were known in the preconquest period, though none have been documented with certainty in postconquest Coyoacan.

15. That is, to be sold, the receipts to be used to pay for masses said on behalf of his soul.

16. It is not clear why Domingo Matías had been put in jail or whether it was related to the person who died at his house. León Plaza apparently paid the purchase price of thirty-one pesos in installments, the initial eight pesos and two *tomines* when Domingo Matías had been jailed and the additional eleven pesos mentioned below.

17. Literally "blind person."

18. Literally "stone mason."

19. A variant of *carta de venta*.

20. Or "where I am next to the edge of the road."

21. The Spanish loanword *simiento*, "foundation," appears in this passage.

22. Or "leaders of the *tlaxilacalli*."

23. Or "leaders of the *tlaxilacalli*."

24. At times notaries referred to the body of witnesses by various shorthands, in this case, the abbreviation for the Latin word etcetera, that was as common in sixteenth-century Spanish as it is in twentieth-century English.

25. This part of the document confirms that Juan Vicente's wife, who was sick and therefore not present when he executed the sale (see below), not only agrees to the sale itself but also attests to the fact that—in terms of Nahua land tenure—the land was legitimately alienable in the first place. In particular, she emphasizes that the land had been closely associated with Juan Vicente's family for a very long time, Juan Vicente himself having inherited it from his grandparents.

26. This petition is not dated but it must originate in the early seventeenth century at the same time as the land sale documents that accompany it.

27. Coyoacan was a rich agricultural area known for the cultivation of fruit trees; orchards would not have been an unlikely meeting place between Nahuas and the blacks and *mestizos* who either passed through the region or lived and worked on local estates. At the larger orchards blacks and *mestizos* supervised Nahua laborers. But many Nahuas also cultivated a few fruit trees on their own land plots to sell the surplus in the markets, either locally or in Mexico City, and they were easy prey to thieves and unscrupulous middlemen along the way.
28. It is not clear exactly whose relatives are referred to in this passage.

DOCUMENT THEMES

Cultural Contact/Ethnogenesis/Resistance; Economy and Work; Ethnicity; Governance, Indigenous; Indigenous Peoples; Land; Rural Life.

SUGGESTIONS FOR FURTHER READING

Cline 1984.
Horn 1997.
Horn 1998.
Karttunen 1982.
Kellogg 1995.
Lockhart 1992.

CHAPTER
9

Under Investigation for the Abominable Sin: Damián de Morales Stands Accused of Attempting to Seduce Antón de Tierra de Congo
(Charcas, 1611)

Geoffrey Spurling

INTRODUCTION

In colonial Latin America, sexual relations between men were considered an offense against God and a capital crime.[1] The *pecado nefando* (abominable sin) challenged the basis of the gendered hierarchical order, undermining the reproductive
function of sex and the formation of the core social unit, the family; it was "against
nature," and placed men sexually and metaphorically in the position of women
(as "passives" in intercourse), thus subverting their power and taking their honor.
Punishment of those found guilty could be severe and brutal, ranging from exile
to service in the galleys to death by strangulation (after which the accused's body
was burned at the stake). In the era following the Council of Trent (1545–63), when
instilling sexual discipline became an important part of the Catholic world's response to the threat posed by the Protestant Reformation, the *pecado nefando* and
the other sins of lust took on a particular importance for secular and ecclesiastical
authorities. Yet given the gravity of the offense and the nature of the crime, the
abominable sin could also be used to serve distinct, more local and often inter-
personal political ends—a well-placed accusation could defame an adversary and
ensnare him in a lengthy and potentially deadly legal process.[2]

In the case I have partly translated below, the *corregidor* (provincial governor), *contador* (accountant), and *justicia mayor* (chief judge) Francisco Roco de Villagutierre undertook, in 1611, a judicial inquiry into allegations that Damián de
Morales, the local *protector de los naturales* (protector of indigenous peoples),[3] had
committed the abominable sin. The key accusation was that Morales had attempted to seduce Antón de Tierra de Congo, an African slave.[4] Typical of the
judicial process that characterized colonial criminal proceedings, the *corregidor*
acted as an investigating magistrate, examining a series of witnesses both to accumulate and to assess relevant evidence. The court transcripts reveal this inves-

tigatory process, with each witness adding to the story while inevitably impli-
cating others, who were then brought in for questioning. Hearsay and gossip were
not only admissible as evidence but were in fact integral to the inquiry.[5]

The major events referred to in the document took place immediately north
of Lake Titicaca, in an ecologically diverse area that stretched from the *altiplano*
(the high altitude plain that extends from what is now central Bolivia to encompass the northern reaches of the Titicaca Basin), down the steep eastern escarp-
ment of the Andes to the forested, humid Amazonian lowlands. According to witnesses, Morales's failed seduction of Tierra de Congo occurred on an *estancia*
(ranch) in the Nequeneque valley, located at just over four thousand meters above
sea level and some sixty kilometers from the *reducción* (resettlement) town of
Huancané.[6] From other documentation we know that the *estancia* owner, Diego
Ortiz de Bolunbiscar, who was Antón's master at the time, also held two other
estancias in the valley, with a combined herd of six hundred cows and one thousand sheep.[7] By the early seventeenth century, a number of Spaniards had established *estancias* in the region, introducing European livestock onto pasture
lands that for centuries had supported huge flocks of llamas and alpacas.

The court case itself unfolded at somewhat lower elevations. The *corregidor*
opened his inquiry in Santiago de Sandia, the principal town of the province of
Carabaya, nestled midway down a steep, eastern-sloping valley. To further his
investigation, Roco de Villagutierre had to drop much lower still, traveling
through hot, humid forests to the small gold mining settlements of Aporoma and
Santiago de Buena Vista. The province of Carabaya had been a source of gold in
Inka times; hearing of the region's mineral resources, the Spanish had moved in
very quickly, establishing their first mines there in the 1540s, worked by African
and Andean laborers. Though Carabaya retained a certain importance given the
relative scarcity of colonial Andean gold mines, it paled in comparison to the
wealth generated by the major silver producers to the south, especially Potosí,
and its population remained low.[8]

Roco de Villagutierre's inquiry, which you will read here, takes up just under one-half of the surviving court records.[9] In March 1611, he interviewed Antón de Tierra de Congo, who provided a remarkable description of the events in
the Nequeneque valley, and to seek corroborative evidence, he questioned Martín
de Texada, a *mestizo* boy who was present at the *estancia*. As well, the *corregidor*
heard the testimony of several others, all of whom told what they had learned
about the case (elaborating the story in the process), either through well-devel-
oped gossip networks or from conversing with Tierra de Congo himself. While
the witnesses commented on Damián de Morales's behavior, they also revealed
a set of animosities that characterized relations between some of the major pro-
tagonists. Though the exact circumstances remain unclear, at the heart of this parallel dispute was an unpaid debt, owed by one Juan Bichaco to Alonso Fernández de Córdoba, a key figure in the *pecado nefando* investigation. When Fernández
de Córdoba had traveled to the mining region to collect the money he was owed,
he was blocked from doing so by Francisco de Aguirre, the brother-in-law of
Diego Ortiz de Bolunbiscar, who had been Antón de Tierra de Congo's master
and who was a close friend of Damián de Morales. As you will see, Fernández
de Córdoba apparently did not take this imposition lightly.

Roco de Villagutierre completed his inquiry on May 12, 1611; finding that there was enough evidence to proceed, he ordered that Damián de Morales be arrested and taken to the jail in Sandia. There is no further record of Roco de Villagutierre's investigation, and it is at this point in the court transcripts that I have ended my translation. The case did continue, however, but more than a year later and under a different presiding magistrate. On July 30, 1612, Francisco Gil Negrete, a judge dispatched by the *audiencia*, arrived in Sandia to proceed with the inquiry. He ordered that Antón de Tierra de Congo be brought up from the mining region to testify and that the *corregidor's teniente* (deputy) in Aporoma, Cristóbal Osorio de Quiñones, also appear in court as the judge had heard that the *teniente* had carried out his own inquiry into the *pecado nefando* accusation. Gil Negrete also declared that he would deal separately with a parallel case brought by *corregidor* Roco de Villagutierre against Juan Bichaco (possibly concerning the unpaid debt), who was at the time incarcerated in Sandia. After a few weeks' delay, Tierra de Congo finally arrived, under escort; Gil Negrete interviewed him about whom he may have talked to on the trip and then ordered that in the interim (while the case was being decided) he be shackled and imprisoned. Osorio de Quiñones did not show up for another two weeks, having been immobilized with a fever. On August 30, 1612, he gave his testimony under oath. He told the judge what he knew of the case against Damián de Morales, reiterating much of the detail and hearsay recorded in Roco de Villagutierre's investigation, and he denied having carried out a separate inquiry into the abominable sin allegations. Osorio de Quiñones did allude to underlying disputes and enmities. Apparently he had told the *contador* Francisco Solórzano de Gobantes that it would have been more appropriate for the *contador* to settle a dispute he had with Morales with sword in hand rather than resort to spreading the word about his abominable sin;[10] Solórzano de Gobantes reportedly replied that he was not the first to raise the allegations and that he had merely heard the news from others. As well, when the judge pointedly asked Osorio de Quiñones why Tierra de Congo's present owner, Pedro Ximénez, had requested that he keep Antón from conversing with anyone during their trip to Sandia, the *teniente* answered that Ximénez had told him Antón was *fácil* (simple, malleable) and that "to damage his rivals he shouldn't say anything other than what he had testified before the *corregidor*."[11] Gil Negrete then concluded his examination of the witness, charging Osorio de Quiñones to keep his testimony secret.

And there the surviving court records enigmatically end. At no point in either inquiry do the presiding judges hear the testimony of the accused, Damián de Morales. By chance I came across a document in another archive, completed in 1631, in which Morales listed the offices and commissions he carried out for the Crown in his thirty years of service.[12] After successfully completing his term as *protector* in Carabaya, Morales was commissioned to fill the Huancavelica *mita* (forced labor draft) in the province of Cotabambas and Omasuyos.[13] He was then named to the more prestigious position of judge, water magistrate, and *protector* for the desert coastal port of San Marcos de Arica, the critically important transshipment point for silver bound from Potosí to Lima and eventually to Spain. He took up the post on March 8, 1612. He served in that office for several years, carrying out a number of specialized commissions and even acting as a soldier in preparing the defense of Arica from five English ships that had sailed up the coast. In 1616 Morales was named *juez de residencia* (judge charged with reviewing the performance of a colonial official, in this case the *corregidor*) for the province of Atacama;[14] three years later Morales was commissioned to investigate the possible construction of a large-scale irrigation system. In 1621 Damián de Morales was again named *juez de residencia* for Atacama; ironically, the incoming *corregidor* was Captain Francisco Gil Negrete, the same individual who had investigated him for the abominable sin less than a decade before. Morales appears to have been less active in the following years, though in 1628 he was charged with marshaling people to defend Arica from eleven "enemy ships" that had been sighted off the coast; to carry out the task he was made a captain.[15] Though perhaps not stellar, Damián de Morales's solid colonial career appears to have been unaffected by the *pecado nefando* allegations.

It is not uncommon to encounter only fragmentary materials when working with archival sources like the Morales file, which ends so abruptly; typically, though, their inconclusiveness raises a number of questions. Morales's career path indicates that he was never found guilty; there is no break that would suggest incarceration, exile, or any other form of expected punishment. What might explain this? Was the evidence itself too weak for conviction, given that all the testimony alleged only a failed seduction (and, as you will see in reading the document, possible transvestism) and that the one eyewitness was an African slave, already denigrated before the court as *fácil*? Did the revealed enmities that pitted Morales and his friends against many of his accusers weaken the case? Was Damián de Morales guilty of the abominable sin?

There are a number of other issues and themes to analyze in working with this short document excerpt. Consider, for example, what the court records tell us about notions of sexuality, masculinity, gender, honor, and ethnic/racial identity, or what they reveal regarding the complex, and perhaps somewhat unexpected, relations of power between individuals. You might look closely too at the intricate networks and mechanisms whereby people passed on information from one to the other[16]—in this case even through a satirical rhyming couplet—or examine, in the recorded witness testimony, the telling details on *estancia*, and slave, life. And though difficult to translate, much of the language used is itself fascinating. The notary's shift from third person to direct quotation—unusually extensive in this document—captures colloquial expressions and grammatical idiosyncracies, as well as terms of endearment and insults.

I first read this document in 1985, when I was working in the National Archive of Bolivia (Archivo Nacional de Bolivia) in Sucre. I was carrying out research on Inka economic and political organization in the northern Titicaca Basin for my doctoral thesis, working my way through a wide range of different manuscript sources in part trying to build a regional historical context by reading anything from the area. When I requested the Morales case file I had little idea what it was about; from the catalogued title I knew the date, that it took place in Sandia, and that it had to do with the *pecado nefando*, which sounded intriguing. I was amazed when I started reading. In part what hit me was the subject matter; I had never read anything remotely like it, and certainly nothing—published or unpublished—on the *pecado nefando* in colonial Latin America.[17] But I was also struck by the nature and content of the recorded testimony, the immediacy of the witnesses' speech, even if caught only in fragments. In working on this translation, I have tried to capture some of that colloquial feel, while retaining the contrasting, more legalistic and bureaucratic language in which the "direct quotes" are embedded.[18]

THE DOCUMENT[19]

9.1 Corregidor *Francisco Roco de Villagutierre Issues the Order Beginning the Investigation*

In the town of Santiago de Sandia, province of Carabaya, March 18, 1611, the *contador* Francisco Roco de Villagutierre, *corregidor* and *justicia mayor* of this province for Your Majesty, said that it has come to his notice that about four months ago, when the *corregidor* was absent from this province, a *negro*, who is now [owned by] Juan Fernández Fraysancho [and was] in the hills and mines of Aporoma in this jurisdiction, said that a man named Damián de Morales had assaulted him, to offend God our Lord, with the *pecado nefando*. And in order to know the truth and to punish the guilty, the *corregidor* ordered—and executed—the following investigations and legal proceedings. And he signed.

Francisco Roco de Villagutierre

Before me, Jorge López de Lira, notary.

9.2 *Testimony of Pedro de Bibero*

And forthwith, on the same day, month, and year, the *corregidor*, for the investigation, ordered to appear before him Pedro de Bibero, who resides in the province of the Collao[20] and at present in the town of Sandia. And from him the *corregidor* received the oath by God our Lord and by a sign of the cross that he made with the fingers of his right hand, and having done it well and completely, in conformity with the law, he promised to tell the truth.

And being questioned in accordance with the intent of the judicial edict, he said that about eight days ago, more or less, he was in the province of the Collao in doña Mariana de Rojas's house in the Villa de Betanzos,[21] when Hernando de Llamas arrived at the house from the Huancané area. [Llamas] asked [him] where he was going, and [Bibero] responded that he was coming from the province of Carabaya. Hernando de Llamas then told him that in Huancané, Alonso Fernández de Córdoba, who had come from the mines of Aporoma, was telling [people] that there were *putos*[22] in the mines and that Damián de Morales was one. Morales had told a *negro*, who is now [owned by] Juan Fernández Fraysancho, that he should get ready as that night a *moça* (young, unmarried woman) was going to sleep with the *negro*. And he said that Damián de Morales had put on Indian women's clothing, with his sword under his arm, and had gone to the *negro's* house and had entered into his room where [he] was living, and [the *negro*] then began to lift up Morales's skirt. And Hernando de Llamas said that Damián de Morales went accompanied by others, but he did not name them. And when the *negro* lifted Damián de Morales's skirt, [Morales] struck him with the sword he carried under his arm. And likewise, Hernando de Llamas told [Bibero] how Alonso Fernández de Córdoba said that Damián de Morales went quickly from one place to another in this province and outside of it, and that Diego Ortiz de Bolunbiscar also frequently moved about, searching for Damián de Morales, both of whom offended God our Lord with the *pecado nefando*.[23] And [Bibero] heard what he has said from a man named Olivera,[24] a carpenter who is in Putina,[25] and who himself had heard from Alonso Fernández de Córdoba all of the details and the same circumstances stated here. And Alonso Fernández de Córdoba had told the carpenter how he had gone to the mines of Aporoma to collect a little gold that Juan Bichaco owed him, and how Francisco de Aguirre, the brother-in-law of Diego Ortiz de Bolunbiscar, had not wanted to let him collect [the gold], for which reason Alonso Fernández de Córdoba said that [Francisco de Aguirre] had to pay it to him and all of his things [expenses].[26]

And all that he has said here and heard is true, and nothing else, under the oath that he has taken, and having read this word-for-word he said that he affirms and ratifies it and, if necessary, would say it again under the oath he has taken.

And he said that he is twenty-seven years old, and he signed his name with the *corregidor*.

Francisco Roco de Villagutierre
Pedro de Bibero

Before me, Jorge López de Lira, notary.

9.3 Testimony of Antón de Tierra de Congo

This same month, day, and year the *corregidor*, for this investigation, ordered to appear before him a *negro, ladino* in the Spanish language,[27] named Antón de Tierra de Congo, slave of Juan Fernández Fraysancho. And from him the *corregidor* received the oath by God our Lord and by a sign of the cross that he made with the fingers of his right hand, and having done it well and completely, in conformity with the law, he promised to tell the truth.

And being questioned in accordance with the intent of the judicial edict of this other party, he said that he has known Damián de Morales for more than two years in the province of Sangabán, Morales being *protector* of this province and [he] the slave of Esteban Ramírez de Ayala, *teniente* of the province of Sangabán.[28] And a little more than four months ago, when [he] was in the mines of Aporoma, he said to Antonio de la Rocha, the son-in-law of his master, "Señor, Damián de Morales has come, and he is a *puto*," and Antonio de la Rocha said to him, "*Pues*, how is he a *puto*?"[29] And [he] told [Antonio de la Rocha] how, about one year ago in the Nequeneque valley in the *estancia* of Diego Ortiz de Bolunbiscar, who was at that time [his] master, Diego Ortiz de Bolunbiscar had left for a nearby *estancia* in the same valley. Damián de Morales called this witness and gave him a jug of wine, and [Morales] said to him that he should drink it, that he liked him very much,[30] and that he was his friend and was very plump. And [he] took the jug and threw out the wine because it seemed to him that the wine had some potion[31] in it to make him drunk, and so he did not drink it. And when Damián de Morales had given him the jug of wine he left the house; a little later he returned and said to [him], "Have you drunk it Antón?"[32] And [he] answered, "Yes, I have drunk it," at which Damián de Morales said to him, "*Pues*, as you have drunk it, go inside there to the pantry where there is an *yndia* (Indian woman), and, since you know the Indian language,[33] speak to her." And [he] went into the pantry and began to look for the *yndia* and called for her, and seeing that there was no one there he left to go outside, passing through a room that was next to the pantry where Damián de Morales had his bed and where he was in bed. And when [he] was leaving, Damián de Morales called to him and said, "Antón, you are my friend. I like you very much, and you are very plump; come over here and we can talk a little." Not wanting to speak to him any more, [he] went through the door to the outside to prepare a meal for his master, leaving Damián de Morales lying on his bed. And in the afternoon his master returned with his father, Pedro de Bolunbiscar; at night [he] gave his master, his master's father, Damián de Morales, and another Spaniard, named Antonio de Andrada, their dinner. [He] went to the kitchen to eat, and his masters went to bed. And after a good while, when he was eating his dinner with a *mulato* named Francisco and a *mestizillo* named Martín, an *yndio* of Damián de Morales, whose name and whereabouts [he] does not know, came to tell him that the *yndio*'s master had called for him. And [he] went and found Damián de Morales lying, clothed, in his bed. He said to this witness, "Antón, since you are my friend and you know the Indian language, go to a house that is up over there on that rise where you will find an *yndia*. Talk to her and bring her here to my bed." And [he] went to the house and arrived at the door, where he began to call for the *yndia*, when a female dog with puppies that was in the house ran out and bit him in the leg.[34] He then went into the house and began to call out for the *yndia*, and while he was there looking for her, Damián de Morales entered the house where [he] was searching and said, "Wait a little and the *yndia* will come soon." And [he] responded, "Señor, there is no *yndia* here." And Damián de Morales said to him, "Antón, let's be friends," and he put his hand through his breeches, pocket, saying, "You are plump Antón," and he moved his hand over his buttocks, feeling him, and then he moved [his hands] to the front to touch what was his (*lo suyo*). And this witness said, "I am a man like you. [35] Why do you search me out and assault me in this way?" And Damián de Morales said to [him], "Be quiet Antón, don't say anything; take some money and we will go to Ayapata."[36] And this witness said, "I don't want money nor do I want to go to Ayapata; I have a good master." And he left the house and returned to the kitchen where Antonio de Andrada was sleeping; [he] told him how Damián de Morales had wanted to fornicate with him, and Andrada replied, saying, "Go Antón, and tell your master." And [he] did not say anything to his master, but did tell Francisco Mulato and Martinillo Mestizo. And Andrada asked this witness why he hadn't killed Damián de Morales, and [he] answered that he hadn't done that because he was a friend of his master. And [he] told the *yndio* who served Damián de Morales, whose name and whereabouts [he] does not know, and the boy said, "I want to leave and not serve my master, since you say he is a *puto*." And when [he] was in Aporoma a little more than four months ago, Damián de Morales scolded him and wanted to hit him with a stick because he had ordered him to wash some clothes and [he] did not want to do it. And he then said, "Don't hit me because I'll tell the Spaniards that you are a very big *puto*," and Damián de Morales said nothing and left.

Asked if Damián de Morales on any other day or night, apart from what has been stated here, called [him] and with promises or other things spoke with him and provoked him to offend against God our Lord in the *pecado nefando* or in any other thing, [he] said that one day in Aporoma Damián de Morales called [him] and said, "Let's be friends Antón; wait awhile." And [he] replied that he didn't want to, but that he wanted to go and prepare food for his master at the time, Pedro Ximénez, and so nothing happened.

Asked if he has heard, seen, or understood that Damián de Morales or any other person may have offended God our Lord in the *pecado nefando*, he said that he doesn't know anything about what the question asks other than what he has already said about Damián de Morales.

Asked if one day Damián de Morales said to [him], "Antón, tonight an *yndia* is coming to sleep with you," and that the same night Damián de Morales, or some other person, was dressed in Indian women's clothing and went to the room where [he] was staying and entered into it, and this witness got out of bed to lift the skirt of the person who entered in the room, he said that he denies what the question asks, and nothing else happened beyond what he has said and affirms and ratifies, and if it is necessary, he will state it all again as it is the truth under the oath he has taken.

And he is twenty-five years old more or less, and he did not know how to sign his name. The *corregidor* signed.

Francisco Roco de Villagutierre

Before me, Jorge López de Lira, notary.

9.4 Testimony of Martín de Texada

In the town of Santiago de Sandia, province of Carabaya, March 19, 1611, the *contador* Francisco Roco de Villagutierre, *corregidor* of this province, for the investigation, ordered to appear before him a *mestizo* boy who did not know his age but looked to be ten or twelve years old, more or less. He said he was named Martín de Texada and was born in this province, where his natural mother[37]—named María Ureña—is from, of the *ayllo*[38] Patanbuco of this town. At present he serves Diego Ortiz de Bolunbiscar. And from him the *corregidor* received the oath in conformity with the law, and having done it well and completely, he promised to tell the truth.

And being questioned in accordance with the intent of the judicial edict of these legal proceedings, and by them, he said that almost a year ago he left this town for his master's *estancia* in the Nequeneque valley, traveling with Damián de Morales and a *negro*, who was then owned by his master and is now with Juan Fernández Fraysancho. And they arrived in the *estancia*, and one day [his] master, Diego Ortiz de Bolunbiscar, went to another, neighboring *estancia*, leaving in his *estancia* Damián de Morales, this witness, and the *negro* named Antón. And after his master had left, Damián de Morales called [him] and ordered him to go and help an *yndio* of his called Pedro—this witness does not know where he was from, though Pedro said he was from the area around Cuzco and that he was an ordinary tailor—and that he help Pedro round up a mule of his that was loose in the pampa, and so [he] went to help. And when he returned Antón Negro told [him] that Damián de Morales had called him to the central hall and had given him a jug of wine that he had taken out of the pantry, and that the *negro* had not wanted to drink it and so had thrown it out because he thought that [Morales] had put some potion in it to get him drunk, and this witness knows nothing else. And on the other day a *mulato* named Francisco, who is in the *estancia* of his master, told this witness how the *negro* Antón had told him that Damián de Morales was a *puto* and that if the judicial officials learned of it they would have to arrest him and burn him, and he knows nothing else.

Asked if, when [he] and Antón Negro and Francisco Mulato were dining in the kitchen, the *yndio* of Damián de Morales had come and asked for the *negro* Antón, saying that his master was calling for him, this witness said that he did not eat in the kitchen with the others but in the central hall where he was alone with his master.

Asked if after a good length of time that or another night the *negro* Antón had come to where [he] and the *mulato* Francisco and Antonio de Andrada were, and had told them how Damián de Morales had wanted to fornicate with him and give him money, he said that he does not know anything about what the question refers to other than that the following day the *mulato* Francisco told him that the *negro* Antón had told [Francisco] that Damián de Morales had wanted to fornicate with him and give him money.[39]

Asked where this witness was sleeping and with whom, he said that every night of the two that they were in the *estancia* [he] slept in the central hall where his master was sleeping, and that Damián de Morales slept alone in an alcove in the same hall.[40]

Asked if [he] saw, understood, or heard that Damián de Morales may have slept with some man in the daytime or at night, or that they may have closed themselves in a suspicious location, speaking in secret, he said that he did not know nor see anything more than what he has said.

Asked how many days Damián de Morales traveled in the company of this witness, his master, and the *negro* Antón, and to where, he said that they were two days in the *estancia* of Nequeneque and that they then left for the *estancia* of Omabamba,[41] arriving in one day. And the following day Damián de Morales left for the mines of Aporoma with his boy, and [this witness] and his master and the *negro* Antón stayed in the *estancia* of Omabamba where they were for three days, and at the end of those days his master, [this witness], and the *negro* left for the mines of Aporoma. And then [he] changed his statement, to say that the *negro* had fled from his master in the *estancia* of Omabamba, heading towards the province of Sangabán, and that [he] and his master travelled alone to this town of Sandia from where his master sent the *mulato* Francisco and an *yndio* called Domingo to the province of Sangabán to go after the *negro*.

Asked that if some night or day [he] has seen or has heard that Damián de Morales or any other person may have offended God our Lord in the *pecado nefando*, he should say who he heard it from and who those persons are, he said that he knows nothing about what the question asks, nor has he seen any more than what he has stated.

Asked where the *yndio* Pedro, servant of Damián de Morales, is, and [where] Damián de Morales himself is, he said that he does not know where they are other than that he has heard that Damián de Morales has gone towards Cuzco,[42] and that a little over eight months ago, when this witness was with his master in Aporoma, Damián de Morales told his master that the boy Pedro had fled from the town of Para.[43] And he does not know anything else, nor where they are, and this is the truth under the oath he has taken.

And he did not know his age, but he looked to be about ten or twelve years old, and he said he knows how to sign,[44] and he signed with the *corregidor*.

> Francisco Roco de Villagutierre
> Martín de Texada
>
> Before me, Jorge López de Lira, notary.

9.5 Testimony of Juan de Nofuentes

In the town of Santiago de Sandia, province of Carabaya, March 30, 1611, Francisco Roco de Villagutierre, *corregidor* and *justicia mayor* of this province for the King our Lord, for the investigation of what is contained in the judicial edict governing these legal proceedings, ordered to appear before him Juan de Nofuentes, *vezino* of this province. And from him he received the oath by God our Lord and a sign of the cross that he made with the fingers of his right hand, and having done it well and completely, in conformity with the law, he promised to tell the truth.

And being questioned in accordance with the judicial edict, he said that about thirty days ago, more or less, when he was in Huancané in the Collao, a Juan Alvarez told [him] that Alonso Fernández de Córdoba had told [Alvarez] how he had gone into the mines of Aporoma to collect some gold that he was owed by Juan Bichaco. And in the mines a *negro* of Pedro Ximénez told Alonso Fernández de Córdoba that there were *putos* in this province and that Damián de Morales was one. And one night Damián de Morales, who was dressed in the clothing of an *yndia*, called the *negro* and told him to do his business.[45] And the *negro* said to him that he was scandalized, and then Damián de Morales had said to the *negro*, "Don't be afraid as your master, Diego Ortiz de Bolunbiscar, also knows how to do it."[46] And that is what Juan Alvarez told this witness, and nothing else, and that Alonso Fernández de Córdoba said that he had written all of this to the señor *presidente*.[47]

Asked if he knows, has seen, heard or understood that some person may have offended God our Lord in the *pecado nefando*, he should declare who these persons are, who has heard it said, seen, or understood it, he said that he has never seen, heard, or known of any person who may have offended God our Lord as the question asks, and he has lived and resided in this province for more than ten years and has not heard more than what Juan Alvarez told him. And [he] was scandalized to see such impressive evidence like what Juan Alvarez had told him, and that's how it was. And [Alvarez] said to him that Alonso Fernández de Córdoba had evidence and a great bias against the aforesaid individuals.[48]

And this that he has said is the truth, under the oath he has taken, and he knows nothing else. And he said that he is fifty-six years old, more or less, and that the general [questions] of the law do not apply to him.[49] And he signed his name with the *corregidor*.

Francisco Roco de Villagutierre
Juan de Nofuentes

Before me, Jorge López de Lira, notary.

9.6 Testimony of Antonio de la Rocha

In the mining settlement of Aporoma, province of Carabaya, April 28, 1611, the *contador* Francisco Roco de Villagutierre, *corregidor* and *justicia mayor* of this province for the King our Lord, for the present investigation, ordered to appear before him Antonio de la Rocha, *vezino* of this province, from whom he received the oath by God our Lord and by a sign of the cross that he made with the fingers of his right hand. And having carried it out well and completely, in conformity with the law, he promised to tell the truth.

And being questioned in accordance with the intent of these legal proceedings, he said that about six months ago, more or less, one day [he] was going to the kitchen in his father-in-law's house to ask for a little tobacco from Antón Moreno,[50] the slave at that time of Pedro Ximénez. And [he] said to the *negro*, "Morales, who was *protector* of this province, is under arrest for a fight he had with the *contador* Francisco Solórzano de Gobantes, which grieves me." And Antón Negro responded to [him], saying that Damián de Morales was not a Spaniard but a *puto*. And [he] asked [Antón Negro] why he said that, and he answered that when [he was] in the *estancia* of his old master, Diego Ortiz de Bolunbiscar, which is in the Nequeneque valley, one day, when Diego Ortiz de Bolunbiscar wasn't there, Damián de Morales called for the *negro* and gave him a little wine. And then Damián de Morales told the *negro* that he liked him very much, and he put his hand through the opening of the pocket in the breeches worn by the *negro*, and he patted him on the buttocks two or three times, saying that he liked him very much and that he would give him money. And the *negro* said to him that he wasn't a Spaniard but a demon, and he recommended him to Our Lady of Copacabana.[51] And a little later Damián de Morales put black on his hands and his face, and he put on the clothing of an *yndia*, an *azo* (skirt) and *lliquilla* (shawl),[52] and he got into his bed and called the *negro* Antón, telling him, "Come here, I like you very much Antón." The *negro* told this witness that he had replied to Damián de Morales that if he hadn't been a friend of his master, Diego Ortiz de Bolunbiscar, he would have killed him. And soon the *negro* left and never more did he want to see him, and Damián de Morales pursued him for three days. And all that he has said was told to this witness by Antón Negro in the kitchen, and it is the truth and what [he] knows under the oath he has taken.

Asked if [he] knows, has seen, or has heard of any person who may have committed the *pecado nefando* against God our Lord, and who the persons are, and from whom he heard it, he said that he doesn't know of anyone who has committed the *pecado nefando* nor has he heard it said.

And this is the truth and what he knows and nothing else, under the oath he has taken. And having been read word-for-word what his testimony contains, and having understood it, he said that it is correctly written and he affirmed it and ratified it, and if necessary he will say it again. And he said that none of the general questions of the law apply to him in what he was asked, and that he is about fifty years old, and he signed with the *corregidor*.

Francisco Roco de Villagutierre
Antonio de la Rocha

Before me, Pedro Díez Vellido, notary.[53]

9.7 Testimony of Juan Alvarez

In the mining settlement of Santiago de Buena Vista, province of Carabaya, May 12, 1611, the *contador* Francisco Roco de Villagutierre, *corregidor* and *justicia mayor* of this province for the King our Lord, for the investigation of this case ordered to appear before him Juan Alvarez, resident in this province, from whom he received the oath by God our Lord and by a sign of the cross that he made with the fingers of his right hand, and having done this well and completely, in conformity with the law, he promised to tell the truth.

And being questioned in accordance with the intent of the judicial edict, he said that a little more than four months ago, when [he] was in the mining settlement of Aporoma, Francisco Chamizo The Elder brought with him a refrain or couplet that had reached wherever people got together in small groups; it went like this: "Captive I am, I will not say of whom; Tell it to Morales that I am his."[54]

And [he] remembers that he heard this said when he was in the mining settlement in the company of Cristóbal Osorio de Quiñones, *teniente* of the settlement, and of other people whose names he cannot remember. And Francisco Chamizo said to Cristóbal Osorio de Quiñones: "Put a stop to this, Your Mercy señor *teniente*," and [Osorio de Quiñones] replied that he had to put a stop to it. And Francisco Chamizo told him what the *negro*, who is owned by Juan Fernández Fraysancho, had said, which is that Damián de Morales had wanted to fornicate with him, as one time he was in an *estancia* of Diego Ortiz de Bolunbiscar, whose slave he had been, in the Nequeneque valley. The *negro* said that he had arranged for an *yndia palla*[55] to come at an unearthly hour to a small unoccupied hut, all of which had been arranged by Damián de Morales. And at the agreed upon hour the *palla* came, and the *negro* went to advise Damián de Morales as he had been ordered to do; and going to the hut he saw that it was Damián de Morales who was dressed as a *palla*, and who spoke to him and began to lift up his clothes, putting his hand in his fly, telling him that he had a very nice body.[56] And the *negro* said to him, "Then you are not Morales;[57] I have to tell this to my master, Diego Ortiz de Bolunbiscar." And Damián de Morales had then replied, "Keep quiet Antón, your master also knows." And this witness heard this said by Francisco Chamizo in the mining settlement of Aporoma. And Cristóbal Osorio de Quiñones had replied [to Chamizo], "Damián de Morales isn't here now as he has already gone; soon the *corregidor*, who is now coming from Chuquisaca,[58] will be in the province and he will put a stop to this."

And likewise, this witness has heard this said by many others whose names he cannot remember, other than Alonso Fernández de Córdoba, who he heard talk about this in the town of Huancané. And [he] heard Fernández de Córdoba speak of how he had entered the settlement of Aporoma to collect some pesos that Juan Bichaco owed him, and Juan Bichaco hadn't paid him because Francisco de Aguirre had obstructed him so that he would not be paid. And for that reason [Fernández de Córdoba] had said to this witness that Francisco de Aguirre and the *corregidor* had to pay him. And he said that the *corregidor* must also be a *puto* as he had given to an *alguazil* (bailiff) he had, named Hernando, lace collars and shirts, ordering them to be made for him and then giving them to him later. And this is what he knows.

Asked if he knows, has seen, heard, or understood by some way or fashion that some person may have offended God our Lord in the *pecado nefando*, he said that he knows nothing more than what he has heard and has said. And what this witness heard from Alonso Fernández de Córdoba he heard for himself and without doubt from a biased man, and [Fernández de Córdoba] complained that as Juan Bichaco had not paid what he owed him he would raise a thousand false testimonies. And [he] knows no person who may have offended God our Lord in the *pecado nefando*, and this is what he knows and is the truth under the oath he has taken. And he said that Alonso Fernández de Córdoba has gone with the Conde de la Gomera to Guatemala, and this witness doesn't know where he, or Francisco Chamizo, is.

And having read this and understood it, he said that it was correctly written, and he affirmed it and ratified it.

And he said, likewise, that when Alonso Fernández de Córdoba told [him] what he has said, he also told him how he had denounced the *corregidor* for taking out of the province of Carabaya 26,000 pesos in gold dust before deducting the royal fifth, and he showed a letter to this witness that he had written about this to the *Contaduría mayor* of this kingdom.[59]

And this is what he heard said to him, under the obligations of the oath, and he said that the general questions of the law do not apply to him. And he is thirty years old more or less, and he signed with the *corregidor*.

> Francisco Roco de Villagutierre
> Juan Alvarez
>
> Before me, Pedro Díez Vellido, notary.

9.8 Corregidor *Francisco Roco de Villagutierre Orders That Damián de Morales be Brought to the Jail in Sandia and Punished*

In the mining settlement of Santiago de Buena Vista, province of Carabaya, May 12, 1611, the *contador* Francisco Roco de Villagutierre, *corregidor* and *justicia mayor* of this province, for the King our Lord, having seen these court records ordered that there be dispatched a court order, based on the contents of these proceedings, against Damián de Morales so that he may be brought to the jail in the town of Sandia and punished according to justice. And he signed.

Francisco Roco de Villagutierre

Before me, Pedro Díez Vellido, notary.

NOTES

ACKNOWLEDGMENTS   I would like to thank the directors and staff of the Archivo Nacional de Bolivia in Sucre, the Archivo de Relaciones Exteriores y Culto in La Paz, and the Archivo General de Indias in Seville. Research for this project was funded by the Social Sciences and Humanities Research Council of Canada and Simon Fraser University. My thanks as well to Joanna Spurling for making the first transcription of this document, Richard Boyer for comments on a near-final draft, and Pete Sigal for bibliographic suggestions and feedback following a conference paper I gave on the case several years ago.

1. All intimate acts between members of the same sex were sinful and often subsumed within the broad definitions of "sodomy" and "abominable (or unmentionable) sin" that were prevalent at the time, but the courts were particularly concerned with anal intercourse, and those convicted of the act typically received the harshest punishments.
2. There are still relatively few studies on the abominable sin in colonial Latin America. See Serge Gruzinski, "Las cenizas del deseo: Homosexuales novohispanos a mediados del siglo XVII," in *De la santidad a la perversión: O de porqué no se cumplía la ley de Dios en la sociedad novohispana*, Sergio Ortega, ed. (Mexico City: Editorial Grijalbo, S.A., 1986), 255–81; Lee Michael Penyak, "Criminal Sexuality in Central Mexico, 1750–1850" (University of Connecticut: Ph.D. dissertation, 1993), 245–309 (which includes a brief discussion of the sparsely documented topic of sexual relations between women; see pp. 288–92); Richard C. Trexler, *Sex and Conquest: Gendered Violence, Political Order, and the European Conquest of the Americas* (Ithaca: Cornell University Press, 1995); and Geoffrey Spurling, "Honor, Sexuality, and the Colonial Church: The Sins of Dr. González, Cathedral Canon," in *The Faces of Honor: Sex, Shame, and Violence in Colonial Latin America*, Lyman Johnson and Sonya Lipsett-Rivera, eds. (Albuquerque: University of New Mexico Press, 1998), 45–67. On the Council of Trent's reforms and sexuality, see Asunción Lavrin, "Sexuality in Colonial Mexico: A Church Dilemma," in *Sexuality and Marriage in Colonial Latin America*, Asunción Lavrin, ed. (Lincoln: University of Nebraska Press, 1989), 47–95. For a medieval European example of a *pecado nefando* accusation used to defame an adversary, see James A. Brundage, "The Politics of Sodomy: Rex V. Pons Hugh De Ampurias (1311)," in *Sex in the Middle Ages: A Book of Essays*, Joyce E. Salisbury, ed. (New York: Garland, 1991), 239–46. There is an extensive bibliography on sexuality (and the abominable sin) in medieval and early modern Europe; see, for example, Rafael Carrasco, *Inquisición y represión sexual en Valencia: Historia de los sodomitas (1565–1785)* (Barcelona: Laertes, 1985); Guido Ruggiero, *The Boundaries of Eros: Sex Crime and Sexuality in Renaissance Venice* (New York: Oxford University Press, 1985); Michael Rocke, *Forbidden Friendships: Homosexuality and Male Culture in Renaissance Florence* (New York: Oxford University Press, 1996); and Jacqueline Murray and Konrad Eisenbichler, eds., *Desire and Discipline: Sex and Sexuality in the Premodern West* (Toronto: University of Toronto Press, 1996).

3. The *protector* was supposed to serve as an advocate for indigenous people in his jurisdiction. When Damián de Morales received the post in 1607, he was formally instructed to help the "yndios" (Indians) in their work and their disputes, aiding them in any legal suits and making sure that they were treated well and paid for their labor (Archivo General de Indias [hereafter AGI] Charcas 55).

4. Slaves were often referred to only by a single Christian name sometimes followed by "Negro," though to differentiate them, their place of origin or ethnicity might be added, as in Antón's case ("from the land of Congo"). James Lockhart, *Spanish Peru, 1532–1560: A Colonial Society* (Madison: University of Wisconsin Press, 1968), 176.

5. Magistrates used hearsay as an important element in their investigations, relying on information networks to seek out key witnesses and possibly other guilty parties. But judges did not treat all evidence equally. While hearsay was admissible in abominable sin cases and could be used to build a behavioral profile thought to indicate guilt, a severe punishment required either confession or "credible" eyewitness testimony of the accused caught in the act (and witness credibility was often questioned, based in part on *calidad* or status).

6. See Penry's chapter in this volume for a discussion of *reducciones* in the Andes.

7. Archivo Nacional de Bolivia (hereafter ANB) Minas T. 123 No. 7 1614 ff. 28–39v.

8. On colonial Carabaya, see Jean Berthelot, "Une Région Minière des Andes Péruviennes: Carabaya Inca et Espagnole (1480–1630)" (Ecole des Hautes Etudes en Sciences Sociales, Université de Paris X - Nanterre: Thèse pour le doctorat de 3e cycle, 1977). Both Lockhart (*Spanish Peru*, 178, 181, 185, 191) and Bowser (*The African Slave in Colonial Peru, 1524–1650* [Stanford: Stanford University Press, 1974], 13, 17) discuss slave and free African labor in the Carabaya mines.

  There was a close connection between Carabaya and the neighboring Andean highlands. Some of the early mine-owning families also had *estancias* in the *altiplano*. Diego Ortiz de Bolunbiscar, who owned the ranches in the Nequeneque valley, held mines in Aporoma that had first been claimed by his maternal grandfather. Similarly, a man named Juan Bellido had mines that had been in his family for decades, while he also owned a highland *estancia*, with a sizeable herd of one thousand three hundred cows and two thousand sheep (ANB EC 1607 No. 5). On the early Spanish mine owners in Carabaya, see Berthelot, "Une Région Minière," 310–14.

9. The entire document is twenty-four folios in length (roughly forty-eight pages); the record of Roco de Villagutierre's inquiry occupies the first ten folios.

10. The witness Antonio de la Rocha (9.6) refers to this quarrel between Morales and Solórzano de Gobantes.

11. ANB EC 1612 No. 9 f. 24.

12. I first found this document as a handwritten copy made earlier this century for the Bolivian Ministry of Foreign Affairs (Archivo de Relaciones Exteriores y Culto, D1-1-108 No. 486) and then later consulted the original in Seville (AGI Charcas 55). While I have focused here on Damián de Morales's career after he left the mining region, he actually received his first Crown posting in 1601, and before becoming *protector* in 1607 he had been *teniente* in both Pacajes (just to the south of Lake Titicaca) and Carabaya. All of the official commissions in this 1631 manuscript refer to Morales by his full name—Damián de Morales Uçabal (the matronym "Uçabal" does not appear in the records of the *pecado nefando* investigaton).

13. Huancavelica was an important mercury mine (mercury was used to extract silver metal from ore). The province of Cotabambas y Omasuyos was located in the district of Cuzco.

14. Normally the incumbent carried out the *residencia*, but in this case the incoming *corregidor* was a direct relative of the outgoing official, so Morales was appointed.

15. For a study of English and Dutch incursions on the Peruvian coast, see Peter T. Bradley, *The Lure of Peru: Maritime Intrusion into the South Sea, 1598–1701* (Basingstoke and London: The MacMillan Press, 1989).

16. For a detailed study of such networks, see Richard Boyer, *Lives of the Bigamists: Marriage, Family, and Community in Colonial Mexico* (Albuquerque: University of New Mexico Press, 1995), 167–217.

17. As far as I know, the first publication on the subject for Spanish America did not appear until 1986 (Gruzinski, "Las cenizas del deseo"), though many researchers must have come across *pecado nefando* trials. In 1980 Gunnar Mendoza, for decades the director and cataloguer of the National Archive of Bolivia, pointed out that this was an area of research that had received little or no attention from historians (Gunnar Mendoza L., "Guía de Fuentes

Inéditas en el Archivo Nacional de Bolivia para el Estudio de la Administración Virreinal en el Distrito de la Audiencia de Charcas, Años 1537–1700," in *Guía de las Fuentes en Hispanoamérica Para El Estudio de la Administración Virreinal Española en México y en el Perú, 1535–1700*, Lewis Hanke, ed. (Washington, D.C.: Organización de los Estados Americanos, 1980), 75. Work on this case and others now forms part of a larger project I am carrying out on the abominable sin in the early colonial Andes.

18. In addition to following the conventions adopted in this volume (see introduction), I have modernized and regularized the spelling of personal names and places, though I have retained the original spelling for other Spanish or indigenous language words (e.g., *yndio, azo, vezino*, etc.). In order to increase the clarity of the text, I have added names or pronouns (always marked by the use of square brackets), frequently as substitutions for the highly repetitive references to "this witness"; I have also deleted the redundant phrase "and this [the witness] answers" ("y esto rresponde"), which appears frequently in the recorded testimony.

19. ANB EC 1612 No. 9, ff. 1–10v.

20. In its more general usage, the term "Collao" referred to the Titicaca Basin as a whole; in this case, though, the "province of the Collao" refers to the *corregimiento* (administrative district or province) of Collasuyo, located to the north of Lake Titicaca and just to the west of the district that held Huancané. Collasuyo was also known as Azángaro y Asillo, the names of its two principal settlements.

21. Located on the shores of Lake Arapa, the Villa de Betanzos was named after an early *encomendero* in the area, Juan de Betanzos, who wrote one of the first chronicles on the Andes (*Narrative of the Incas* [Austin: University of Texas Press, 1996]).

22. From *puta*, or female whore. In his 1611 dictionary, Sebastián de Covarrubias links *puto* with the *pecado nefando*, defining the term (in Latin) as "Notae significationis et nefandae" (*Tesoro de la lengua castellana o española* [Barcelona: S.A. Horta, 1943], 889).

23. This is a particularly tough passage to translate. The original is as follows: "que el dicho Damian de Morales daua ligeras donde estaua en esta prouincia y fuera della Diego Ortiz de Bolunbiscar y las mesmas ligeras daua el dicho Diego Ortiz de Bolunbiscar buscando al dicho Damian de Morales los quales ofendian a dios nuestro señor con el pecado nefando." The primary difficulty lies with the meaning of the enigmatic "daua [daba] ligeras;" I have read it here as moving quickly from place to place, but it could also mean flighty or frivolous behavior (though that does not really fit the grammatical context). The passage "en esta prouincia y fuera della Diego Ortiz de Bolunbiscar" also offers a challenge as it is not clear where the break should be—after "della" (assuming then that a conjunction is missing) or after "Bolunbiscar."

24. As Bibero has already said that everything he has reported up to this point came from his conversation with Hernando de Llamas, the sense here must be that he *also* heard all this from the carpenter Olivera.

25. Putina lies to the north of Huancané, about halfway between that town and the Nequeneque valley.

26. "y todas sus cossas" ("and all of his things"). From the context it would seem that "cossas" ("things" or "stuff") refers to expenses (and may even be a slip of the notary's pen, writing "cossas" for "costas" [expenses]).

27. "negro ladino en lengua española." *Ladino* was often used to refer to a non-European (indigenous or African) who was more broadly acculturated in Spanish ways (clothing, religion, language, etc.); in this context, though, it clearly refers specifically to the ability to speak Spanish.

28. In the 1570s the two districts of Carabaya and Sangabán were amalgamated into one *corregimiento* (or "province"). The original divisons, though, continued to be recognized locally as distinct entities. In this document, the witnesses' references to the "province of Sangabán" reflect the ambiguous meaning and usage of the term *province* in the colonial Andes.

29. *Pues* can be translated as "so," "well," or "then"; it is often used as a hesitation, marking a pause or shift in speech (it is very common in spoken Spanish today, especially in the Andean region). I have left it in Spanish to retain the conversational flavor that is so clear in the original document. However, where *pues* is used as a conjunction, meaning "since" or "for," I have translated it into English.

30. "que le queria mucho," which could also be translated as "he loved him very much" or even "he wanted him very much."

31. "anbi" in the document, probably from the Quechua or Aymara *hampi*, meaning medicine. Ludovico Bertonio, *Vocabvlario de la Lengva Aymara* (Cochabamba: Centro de Estudios de la

Realidad Económica y Social, [1612] 1984), 117; Diego Gonçález Holguín, *Vocabvlario de la Lengva General de Todo El Perv llamada Lengua Qquichua o del Inca* (Lima: Imprenta Santa María, [1608] 1952), 145. Thanks to Tom Abercrombie for suggesting this reading of "anbi."

32. "as bebido Anton"; according to Antón's recorded testimony, Morales always used the personal and familiar "tu" ("you") form in addressing him, whereas Antón always replied with the more formal and respectful "vos." The contrast in their speech reflected the nature of their hierarchical relationship.

33. It is not clear what Andean language Antón spoke, and he may have been familiar with more than one. In this region of the *altiplano* the majority of the indigenous population spoke Aymara and/or Pukina; most of the Andean words used in this document, though, are Quechua.

34. In this area today people still keep ferocious watchdogs, either in their dwellings or, more commonly, housed in a small structure built right next to the front door.

35. The notary here copies down a significant grammatical error that Antón makes, "Estoy honbre [hombre]" rather than "Soy hombre," confusing two separate Spanish verbs (both of which can be translated by the English "to be").

36. Located in the highlands in the northwestern corner of the province of Carabaya (in the district of Sangabán).

37. The use of the term "natural mother" ("madre natural" in the original) indicates that Martín de Texada was born out of wedlock. While the court records note his mother's name and *ayllu* affiliation, his Spanish father is never identified. In reading Martín's testimony, you might consider in what ways it does (or does not) reflect his age, examining both his reported statements and the specific questions that he is asked.

38. The "ayllo" (more commonly spelled *ayllu*) was an Andean social group whose members controlled specific lands and/or resources and who considered themselves descended from a common mythical ancestor and a particular origin place.

39. "y le daua plata" (literally, "and he was giving him money") in the original. Martín's choice of the imperfect ("he was giving") rather than the preterite ("he gave") indicates that the money was offered but not actually given, a sense reflected in this translation.

40. "aposento de la dicha sala" in the original.

41. The *estancia* must have been situated in the *puna* (high plain) of Omabamba, an extensive area of high altitude grasslands that lies between Nequeneque and the Sandia valley.

42. Morales would have left for the Cuzco area to take up his new post in the *corregimiento* of Cotabambas y Omasuyos.

43. Para was located on an eastern sloping valley, north and west of Sandia.

44. Martín de Texada signs his name in large, bold, carefully formed letters, in a style between printing and cursive that would seem to derive from his youth and incipient literacy.

45. "que hiziese su officio" in the original.

46. Here I have deleted a line in which Nofuentes merely repeated that, at the time, Antón de Tierra de Congo was owned by Ortiz de Bolunbiscar.

47. A reference to the president of the Audiencia of Charcas.

48. From the context, "aforesaid individuals" must refer to Damián de Morales and Diego Ortiz de Bolunbiscar.

49. The "general questions of the law" inquired into the relationship of the witness to the interested parties in any litigation; by stating that the general questions do not apply, Nofuentes declared that he was not directly related to Morales nor otherwise compromised by him.

50. Antonio de la Rocha here refers to Antón as Antón Moreno (*moreno*: dark skinned; dark brown hair), though later he uses the more common Antón Negro.

51. Located on the shores of Lake Titicaca, Copacabana was an important Inka and pre-Inka religious center, and, from the late sixteenth century on, a major Christian shrine and pilgrimage site dedicated to the worship of the Virgin of Copacabana. See Sabine MacCormack, "From the Sun of the Incas to the Virgin of Copacabana," *Representations* 8 (1984): 30–60.

52. *azo* [*acsu*]: woman's skirt (Quechua); *lliquilla* [lliclla]: woman's shawl (Quechua). Gonçález Holguín, *Vocabvlario de la Lengva General*, 17, 213.

53. Note that in Aporoma and Santiago de Buena Vista, the *corregidor* employed a different notary. Díez Vellido was no doubt a member of the Bellido family I mentioned in note 8 above

(the variant spelling of his surname reflects the common practice of using v, b, and u interchangeably).

54. "Cautibo soi no dire cuio digalo Morales que soi suio." There is a nice, subtle play on words here, with "captive" referring both to Antón's slave status (slaves were often called "captives") and to his being an emotional captive, an object of desire.

55. *Palla*: noblewoman, elegant woman (Quechua). Gonçález Holguín, *Vocabvlario de la Lengva General*, 273.

56. "muy buenas carnes," which literally means "very nice flesh." In its plural form, as used here, *carnes* can also mean "fat"; it may then refer to Antón's girth, which Damián de Morales clearly found attractive.

57. Could this be a pun on Morales's name (on "morales," or morals)? In reporting what he heard about this conversation, Alvarez has Tierra de Congo using the "tu" form when he addressed Morales.

58. Chuquisaca, more formally known as La Plata (or Ciudad de La Plata, City of Silver), was the capital of the Audiencia of Charcas. It is now Sucre, one of Bolivia's two official capitals. For a late sixteenth-century case that took place in La Plata, see Abercrombie's chapter in this volume.

59. Fernández de Córdoba's communication to the chief auditing and accountancy office (the *Contaduría mayor*) may have had an immediate impact. In a letter to the king written on April 4, 1612, the viceroy referred to fraud involving the royal fifth in Carabaya. The concern was that mine owners and others had conspired to take out gold without deducting the *quinto* (the fifth) owed to the Crown (Berthelot, "Une Région Minière," 284).

DOCUMENT THEMES

African/Afro-Latin American Peoples; Crime; Economy and Work; Ethnicity; European-Mestizo Peoples; Gender; Gossip and Communication; Honor; Insults; Popular Culture; Race; Religion; Rural Life; Sexuality; Slavery.

SUGGESTIONS FOR FURTHER READING

Bowser 1974.
Gruzinski 1986.
Johnson and Lipsett-Rivera 1998.
Lavrin 1989.
Murray and Eisenbichler 1996.
Rocke 1996.
Ruggiero 1985.
Spurling 1998.
Trexler 1995.

C H A P T E R
10

"Wife of My Soul and Heart, and All My Solace": Annulment Suit Between Diego Andrés de Arenas and Ysabel Allay Suyo

(Huánuco, Peru, 1618)

Nancy van Deusen

INTRODUCTION

Marriages in colonial Latin America were considered sacrosanct; under exceptional circumstances, however, the ecclesiastical court would grant an annulment to dissolve the marital union. Unhappy spouses could request annulments for reasons of impotence, legal impediment, illegal degree of consanguinity, or most commonly, a lack of consent or freedom in selecting a spouse.[1] Annulment litigation records abound with tales of family members resorting to beatings, forced enclosure, or the denial of food and contact with siblings to coerce or threaten a recalcitrant young man or woman to marry an undesired partner.

The case of Ysabel Allay Suyo and Diego Andrés de Arenas falls into the latter category, the most common found in annulment suits. In 1618, Ysabel notified the *visitador* (inspector),[2] Miguel Budi de Azorín,[3] that she had been forced to marry Diego by the Mercedarian friar, Alonso Sarmiento, for whom Diego worked as a *yanacona* (personal retainer). Ysabel testified that her family resided in the *corregimiento*[4] of Huánuco, in a hamlet named Guachagaro; according to witnesses in support of Ysabel, Diego Andrés was a *forastero* (an outsider)[5], originally from the Cuzco area. Both were native Andeans, though Diego claimed to be a *ladino* (a literate, hispanized Indian). With the *visitador's* support, on March 28, 1618, Ysabel formally filed for an annulment before *licenciado*[6] Joan de Vega, the priest and ecclesiastical judge in charge of native Andeans in Huánuco. In their subsequent legal dispute, both Ysabel and Diego Andrés had access to the services of special lawyers, called *procuradores de los naturales*, who were charged with representing the interests of native Andeans.[7] As required by ecclesiastical law, throughout the proceedings Ysabel was held in seclusion (*depósito*) in the home of a well-known and honorable Spanish female citizen of Huánuco.[8]

In answer to Ysabel's complaint, Diego claimed that he and Ysabel had married of their own volition, that her parents had consented to the match, and that both his and her best men,[9] including some *caciques* (Andean authorities) from the village of Nombre de Jesús,[10] had financed the wedding festivities. Ysabel presented a number of eyewitnesses who testified to her resistance on her wedding day, including her refusal to give her consent during the marriage ceremony. As a countermeasure, Diego then called upon Gerónimo Ortiz de Mena, the principal *procurador de los naturales* in Lima, to write to the *vicario general* (vicar general, the head ecclesiastical judge) in an attempt to discredit the witnesses' integrity and veracity, in part questioning their connections to the plaintiff.[11] The ecclesiastical court then called several of Ysabel's witnesses to testify again. Perhaps fearing he was about to lose the case, Diego appealed to Ysabel's sentiments by composing a love letter; it was to no avail, however, and the case pressed on until March 9, 1620, when the *vicario general* in Lima, Dr. Feliciano de Vega, pronounced the sentence annulling the marriage.

He said, she said

Included in this chapter are nine document entries, presented here in chronological order, taken from the court records of the annulment suit between Ysabel and Diego. In the first entry (10.1) we hear Ysabel's complaint before the ecclesiastical judge in Huánuco, stating her reasons for requesting the annulment; in the next three we see her complaint corroborated in the testimonies given by three of the four witnesses who appeared on Ysabel's behalf. In the fifth entry (10.5) we read the love letter Diego Andrés wrote to his estranged wife. The sixth excerpt is from the request Gerónimo Ortiz de Mena made to discredit Ysabel Allay Suyo's witnesses. Entry 10.7 presents a fragment of additional witness testimony, called after Ortiz's letter to the *vicario general*. The eighth includes a formal investigation of the parish register in the village of Nombre de Jesús to find Diego and Ysabel's marriage certificate. And finally, the last excerpt contains the sentence issued by Dr. Feliciano de Vega, the ecclesiastical judge and *vicario general* in Lima.

These document entries raise a number of important issues, including the often conflicting legal and social jurisdictions between the colonial state and the church, gender relations, notions of honor and status among Andeans, and literacy and Diego's familiarity with European literary genres. The love letter itself is a treasure for colonial historians as it attests to the positive sentiments and intimate circumstances of individual lives.

THE DOCUMENT[12]

10.1 Ysabel Allay Suyo Petitions the Vicario to Present Witnesses

In the city of León de Guánuco[13] on May 18, 1618, *licenciado* Joan de Vega, *vicario* and pastor of the natives of this city, by order of His Grace, the archbishop of the City of the Kings [Lima][14] of the council of the King, and judge in this case, presented this petition in the name of Ysabel Allay Suyo:

[I], Ysabel Allay Suyo, by means of my attorney, in the lawsuit against Diego Andrés de Arenas over the annulment of the marriage for not having consented[15] nor willingly having married Diego Andrés [state that]: he [Diego] alleges in his statement he presented on May 7th that I willingly married him, and my parents and sister supported the marriage. I deny this; I never willingly consented, but, as I have claimed in other written documents, Father Alonso Sarmiento forced me to marry Diego against my will in the settlement of Guachagaro, [which is] outside of his parish, because he is his [Diego's] master,[16] and Diego served him. Diego Andrés is a *forastero* Indian, having come recently, less than one year ago. He confesses it in his testimony, which works in my favor.[17] At the same time, he makes other absurd assertions[18] that are false, all with the intention of running roughshod over me;[19] he does not declare the truth and is side-stepping the evidence. I will prove the contrary to what he says and alleges.

I ask and implore[20] that you rule that proof is necessary[21] to enact his legal order.[22] I am ready to do what is necessary and will present witnesses for the examination, wherever they might be, and they will tell the truth, and I ask that justice be served.

> Cristóbal de Taracoma y Contreras
> [Ysabel's *procurador*]

10.2 Testimony of Domingo de Ariçola

In the city of Guánuco, May 26, 1618, for the judicial inquiry[23] in the name of the plaintiff, Cristóbal de Contreras presented the witness Domingo de Ariçola, an inhabitant of Guánuco who was sworn in over the sign of a cross.[24]

To the first question he responded that he has known Diego Andrés de Arenas for about one year and Ysabel Allay Suyo for more than ten years. He knows that Diego Andrés de Arenas is not from this province, but from that of Cuzco, because he told this witness and he has also heard it elsewhere.

To the second question he responded that Friar Alonso Sarmiento of the Mercedarian Order married Diego Andrés de Arenas and Ysabel Allay Suyo in the settlement of Guachagaro. They called this witness to the home of the parents of Ysabel Allay Suyo in order to have witnesses present; and so it was, arriving at the home that is in the settlement of Guachagaro, near the big irrigation canal that serves this city, we found Friar Alonso Sarmiento there. Later they called Ysabel Allay Suyo, who was in [another] room in the house and did not want to come out, and even though they called for her to come out various times, she did not want to, and her mother went in to get her and brought her out crying. In the main room the padre (priest) asked her two times if she would marry Diego Andrés, and both times she said "no." This witness stood by her side and reprimanded her by saying why didn't she want to marry to make her parents happy, and that it was better to be in the service of God, our Father. Then Friar Alonso Sarmiento asked her again if she wished to marry, and this witness never heard her say "yes," and then the padre took her hand and that of Diego Andrés and married them. Ysabel was crying throughout, and after the wedding she returned to the room where she had been. And this witness asked the padre why he hadn't asked [the couple] to embrace, and he said, "you are right, I didn't," and they called for Ysabel to come out again and told her she had to embrace her husband, Diego Andrés, which she refused to do. Diego Andrés then threw his arms

Figure 7 A priest forces a young Andean man and woman to marry against their will (Guaman Poma de Ayala [1615] 1980, f. 573).

around her. Diego Andrés served Friar Alonso Sarmiento. The marriage is not valid because this witness never heard Ysabel Allay Suyo say "yes." An old Indian named Rucana was inside the house, and several other Indians whom this witness does not know were near the door.

To the third question he replied that he knows that Ysabel Allay Suyo always seemed very discontented after the marriage [had taken place] and fled from

Diego Andrés, and as soon as the padre finished the ceremony, he mounted a mule and returned to his *doctrina* of Nombre de Jesús. And this witness did not see nor hear if the padre had taken care of the legal requirements necessary and [carried out] the marriage banns established by the Council of Trent.[25]

To the fourth question he responded that he heard the padre tell Diego Andrés and Ysabel Allay Suyo to follow him, and the next day they went [to Nombre de Jesús], and Ysabel Allay Suyo told this witness that Diego Andrés has treated her very badly.

To the fifth question he responded that Ysabel Allay Suyo is a good Christian and under no circumstance would she try to seek a legal separation if she had not been forced to marry against her will.

10.3 Excerpts from the Testimony of Julian Rurru

[Excerpts from the testimony of Julian Rurru,[26] recorded in the city of León de Guánuco on June 30, 1618.]

Cristóbal de Taracona y Contreras,[27] in defense of Ysabel Allay Suyo, wife of Diego Andrés, presents before the judge Joan de Vega, Julian Rurru, from the village of Ycos in the *encomienda*[28] of doña Ysabel de Toledo, resident of this city, approximately thirty-nine years old. The judge swore the witness in over the sign of a cross.

To the first question he responded by saying that he only met Diego Andrés the day of the wedding and that he had known Ysabel Allay Suyo approximately ten years . . .

To the fourth question he responded that Diego Andrés, Ysabel Allay Suyo and her parents went to the village of Nombre de Jesús of the Guamalies, where they say that they were formally married.

10.4 Excerpts from the Testimony of Diego Xicxi

[Excerpts from the testimony of Diego Xicxi, recorded in the city of León de Guánuco on June 30, 1618. Xicxi was identified as a criollo[29] *and muleteer from Guánuco.]*

To the first question he responded that he has known Diego Andrés for one and one-half years and Ysabel Allay Suyo for more than ten years.

To the second question he responded that he knew Diego Andrés was a *yanacona* of Friar Alonso Sarmiento, and that in the settlement of Guachagaro, one day around vespers, the padre married Diego Andrés and Ysabel Allay Suyo. And in order to marry them they brought her out of a room where she had been hiding in the home of her parents. The padre asked her if she wished to marry Diego Andrés, to which she replied two times, while crying, "no." And Domingo de Ariçola, who was there in the main room of the house, went up to Ysabel Allay Suyo and said that she should do what her parents wanted, and then Friar Alonso Sarmiento asked her again, to which she replied "no." Then Felipe Manco, her father, said that she had to do what he wished, and the padre went up to her again and took her hand and that of Diego Andrés, and said "now say that you want to," but this witness never heard her say "yes." And then the padre asked Diego Andrés if he wanted to marry Ysabel Allay Suyo, and he said "yes," to which the padre replied that they were married. This witness heard Ysabel Allay Suyo say that because she had been forced to marry she did not have to live with Diego Andrés. And the settlement of Guachagaro, where the marriage took place, is in the parish of this city and not of the Guamalíes, which is where the friar Alonso Sarmiento was from. This witness was in the main room with Francisco Rucana,[30] who later left, and he saw that Domingo de Ariçola and Julian Rurru were in the entrance. And he knew that they had not announced the marriage banns, and this witness went to the house when the pastor was about to marry them.

10.5 Love Letter from Diego Andrés de Arenas to Ysabel Allay Suyo[31]

Praise Be the Holy Sacrament

My infinitely desired and beloved, my without equal and singularly loved and longed for señora and wife of my soul and heart and all my solace and comfort,[32] for to be given that in perfect union of the Holy Mother Church—I give you my faith and word, my Ysabel, of my good judgment[33] and my innermost feelings,[34] that I do not know what is wrong and what is happening to me because I find myself without willpower and memory, for to have, between us, the potential, in you, my Ysabel, sculpted and impressed by the hands of the most perfect love that my heart and soul feel for you.

My angel, how much more you delay in concluding the battle with me from which you have to emerge victorious with the desecration of the annulment, or I would emerge triumphant with the desecration of the Holy Mother Church. This battle is now necessary, señora, to wage in the valley of Jehoshaphat before the court of truth. Señora, a great deal of courage and strength is required [for that]. Well, you rose up and lit the fire of the first declaration[35] and discord between us, without considering the disastrous result [of that action] and, as I say, the more the sentence is prolonged and postponed, that much more I live without peace nor pleasure, and the longer I don't see you and I desire to see you, how much more it eats away at me and damages the soul and heart to see you. How much I hope and confide in God that I can once again enjoy you, it pleases me so much, and finally, from the dead I can return to life; and how much I imagine and suspect that you have to resist and make war upon me, how much I become infuriated. I catch on fire and burn alive in the flames and fire of cruel reason and wrath, inhumanely and desperately. I combat a fortress, and your parents and sister Juana, they were the perpetrators of this war, not you my dear. Because believe me, my señora, how much Helen of Troy was esteemed and beloved, so much so that all of Troy embraced her and it was destroyed and cost infinite lives. And so, my only señora, how much I die for you my beautiful Helen, and how much I love, esteem, and want you, and how much I desire to die, to be beneath your feet; if you could live for one thousand years, how much more we would embrace each other and destroy each other in accordance with our ready munitions, bullets and artillery. And so, my angel of consolation, because my God of heaven and earth lives, I will live in you, or without you I will die; I say no more. This because you, my Ysabel, are my life, my angel, my good, my solace, my happiness, my rest, my repose, my peace of mind, my gift, my honor, my refuge, my heart, my soul, my only señora and wife.

And finally, you, with whom I have embarked on the royal ship of the Holy Mother Church to navigate and cross, the two of us, in the sea of the world, a sea so tempestuous and with so many storms and dangers, with so many squalls and whirlpools, where so many souls, because they lose the light of hope and their courage and strength from the tasks God sends for their merit,[36] do not reach the gate of the blessed, they drown, are lost, and sink to the infernal depths. For this I ask you, my Ysabel, don't leave me nor jump off this sacred ship of the Holy Mother Church in which we are making this journey with God's blessing to the Promised Land that is the glory of Paradise. I beg you, my Ysabel, don't leave this war vessel of Saint Peter until, victorious, we disembark in heaven, because if you leave this ship to the sea of the dangerous world you would perish and drown in the infernal abyss. Although you should have faith in the compassion of God, because our Lord and God is very compassionate, in no way is His compassion or His mercy a reason or cause to offend His Divine Majesty more. I don't know what truth to tell you Ysabel, except that now, coming to the great realization and true recognition of having caused you such unfair distress and having caused your tears to fall without reason, it burdens my soul and heart, and I repent and cry when I remember when I caused you to fall to the ground when you, Ysabel, were planting potatoes above in the area near the cliff. I break down weeping, my Ysabel, when I remember how I injured your mouth for so many days. Oh heavenly God and Father, how blind, how far from reason. Married, we lived together, my Ysabel, for one year and five months; how hard, how rough, how cruel was I to a dove and lamb of God, who had been given for me to serve her in great faith and love. Forgive me señora, forgive me señora, forgive me sister, forgive me wife, for the love of the death and the passion of Jesus Christ. And you see that God has such great mercy in this life, and in the next we will live in peace and joy. Can you imagine what it would be like [to live] in the grace of God? I am lit up like a beacon[37] and very well provided for by the strength of His mercy. I say no more, only that if all this is not enough to convince you, there is nothing but arms and force. God is great, as I wish. From Lima, July 6, 1618.

Your true husband until you annul the
marriage, Diego Andrés de Arenas

Recently, some Indians of Guánuco told me that you were walking around free and unconfined, and, evidently, it was understood that you were causing me to lose my honor and self-esteem. I don't believe this, my señora Ysabel; I am confident in your virtue and honesty and purity and the watchfulness of your parents, but I do not confide your honor in your sister Juana. And, as I say, they told

admits

me, igniting my passion and anger. I wrote I don't know how many letters, and I sent you our rosary. With all this I don't know anything until you annul the marriage.

10.6 Excerpts from Gerónimo Ortiz de Mena's Petition

[Lima, October 13, 1618, fragments of a petition from Gerónimo Ortiz de Mena, *procurador general de los naturales*, in the name of Diego Andrés de Arenas, Indian] in his case against Ysabel Allay Suyo in her request for an annulment petition to His Majesty [the *vicario general*, Feliciano de Vega in Lima] to consider the following:

In the first place, Francisco Rucana is a senile, old Indian, over eighty years old, who normally is drunk, and he is an intimate friend of the parents of Ysabel Allay Suyo.

The Spaniard Domingo de Ariçola has been living in concubinage with the sister of Ysabel Allay Suyo and testified passionately only to oblige her and the parents of Ysabel Allay Suyo.

Julian Rurru and Diego Xixci are just ordinary Indians who eat and get drunk with the parents of Ysabel Allay Suyo and only testified to oblige them, so you should not have faith nor give credit to any of these testimonies.

To Your Majesty I ask and beg that Ysabel Allay Suyo be made to return to the marriage to be with her husband Diego Andrés de Arenas.

Gerónimo Ortiz de Mena

10.7 Testimony of Andrés Chanta

[*Excerpts from the testimony of Andrés Chanta, Spanish speaking Indian* ladino, *around twenty-two years old, recorded in the city of León de Guánuco on October 19, 1619.*]

To the first question he responded that he has known Ysabel Allay Suyo since she first had use of reason, and Diego Andrés for about three or four months.

To the second question the witness responded that one day he went to pay a debt in Guachagaro, a parish of Guánuco, and in passing by the home of Felipe Manco, the father of Ysabel Allay Suyo, they called him to be a witness at the ceremony . . .

To the third question he responded that he knows that Ysabel Allay Suyo walked around complaining that she had been forced to marry [against her will], and that one day she came to his house and asked his wife to hide her because she could not bear to see Diego Andrés. She cried and said that she should not have to live with him.

To the fifth question he knows that Ysabel Allay Suyo is a good Christian; he has seen her doing good works, and she has lived honorably and virtuously. Her life is the envy of many of the natives here who know her, and if the marriage had been consensual she would not have initiated this lawsuit.

10.8 Search for the Marriage Certificate and Testimony of the Caciques *and* Alcalde *of Nombre de Jesús*

In the village of Nombre de Jesús, on November 8, 1619, the very reverend padre García de Agüero of the Mercedarian Order, pastor and *comendador*[38] of the *doctrina* of the Guamalíes, received a letter from the Illustrious Sir Joan de Vega, judge and *vicario* of the city of León de Guánuco, asking compliance with its contents.

The padre *comendador* ordered the book where marriages are recorded to be brought forth, and having proceeded through all of the marriage certificates, [it became clear that] the record of Diego Andrés de Arenas and Ysabel Allay had not been entered in the book. For further justification, he ordered the *caciques* don Carlos Carpa, don Juan Carpa and don Miguel Paucar Chagua, the *caciques* and governors and *alcalde*[39] [to appear]. From each of them he received a sworn statement over a cross that they promise to tell the truth, and the witnesses [the *caciques*] said that as the pastor of this *doctrina* of the village of Nombre de Jesús, padre Friar Diego Sarmiento married Diego Andrés de Arenas and Ysabel Allay in the village of Nombre de Jesús, and they did not see the marriage [take place], and at the same time they know that for approximately one year they had lived together as man and wife, and that is the truth.

10.9 Sentence of the Vicario General *in Lima*

[Sentence pronouncement, City of the Kings (Lima), March 9, 1620.]

In the case requested by Ysabel Allay Suyo, Indian and inhabitant of the *repartimiento*[40] of Guamalíes, against Diego Andrés, Indian, I declare the marriage carried out by Friar Alonso Sarmiento of the Mercedarian Order to be nullified, because it was done against her will and by force, and because Friar Alonso Sarmiento married them outside the district of his parish, and because he is not the pastor of Diego Andrés and the others. With regard to this case, the marriage took place against the will of Ysabel Allay Suyo; she has been able to prove her case, and it is in conformity with the requirements of the law to declare the marriage to be null. As I have said, the marriage took place without her agreement, and because of that, she may elect the [marital] status[41] she wishes, and by His Grace [the pronouncement] is definitive and purified.

Dr. Feliciano de Vega

NOTES

ACKNOWLEDGMENTS   The author wishes to thank Brent Carbajal, Alan Gallay, Laura Gutiérrez, Director of the Archivo Arzobispal of Lima, Margarita Suárez, and Corrine Winter for their assistance and editorial suggestions.

1. The Council of Trent (1545–63) formally established lack of consent as grounds for annulment; this decree was reaffirmed in the Second Council of Lima (1567).

2. *Visitadores* were secular or ecclesiastical authorities in charge of special investigations in a *corregimiento* or a village.
3. This particular *visitador* was dispatched by Archbishop Lobo Guerrero to inspect the *corregimientos* of Huánuco in 1617.
4. A judicial and administrative district.
5. A *forastero* was an Andean who had abandoned his/her community of origin.
6. A title of an individual holding an advanced degree from a university.
7. Ysabel Allay Suyo requested Cristóbal de Taracoma y Contreras to be her defense attorney, and Diego Andrés solicited the support of Juan Ramos de Salazar.
8. Ecclesiastical law required the female spouse to be placed in temporary custody in an institution called a *recogimiento*, a convent, hospital, or an honorable home, to protect her from violence or other forms of retribution. She was to remain enclosed until the judge reached a verdict, a process which could sometimes last over a year.
9. "padrinos" in the original.
10. The village of Nombre de Jesús was located in the *corregimiento* of Huamalies and in the *doctrina* (ecclesiastical district of the regular clergy) where Alonso Sarmiento served as a Mercedarian friar.
11. Diego may have appealed to the principal *procurador de los naturales* in Lima because he had no witnesses of his own and his best tactic was to try to have Ysabel's witnesses discredited on the basis of bias.
12. This chapter is based upon an analysis of the annulment suit, "Ysabel Allay Suyo vs. Diego Andrés" 28 March, 1618, Huánuco, Archbishopric Archive of Lima, Nulidades, Leg. 7, 73 folios.
13. In this translation I maintain the colonial spelling "Guánuco" (now Huánuco).
14. Throughout the colonial period, Lima was also called Ciudad de los Reyes (City of the Kings), or Los Reyes.
15. "prestado con sentimiento" in the original.
16. The term *amo* (master) was also applied to slave owners. It can mean master, owner, or proprietor. Personal retainers or servants were common among priests.
17. As a recently arrived *forastero*, Diego probably had no immediate family in the vicinity, did not know community members well, did not aid in tribute payments, and may have been considered less trustworthy by local inhabitants.
18. "alega otras impertinencias" in the original.
19. "todo a fin de querer atropellar" in the original.
20. The phrase used here, "pido y suplico," is standard legal format.
21. "sentencia de prueva" in the original.
22. Diego Andrés had requested that his wife be returned to "hacer vida maridable" (literally, to live a married life) with him because her case could not be justified. She petitioned the judge to order that Diego Andrés prove that the allegations against him were not true.
23. "información" in the original. This introduced the central section of annulment proceedings, where witnesses were called forth to testify.
24. In accompanying documents, Ysabel Allay Suyo says that Ariçola is a Spaniard and a good Christian.
25. Banns of marriage, required by the Council of Trent, served as a public announcement of the betrothal. Usually, the local priest proclaimed the engagement and the couples' names from the pulpit. At that juncture, parishioners could disclose information that might impede the marriage from taking place.
26. I decided to edit certain portions of his testimony and those that follow, because the information repeats much of what Domingo de Ariçola said.
27. The spelling of personal names varies in the original document.
28. A grant made to a Spaniard which gave him/her the right to the labor and tribute payments of a specific group of native Andeans.
29. Generally the term *criollo* applies to American-born Spaniards, but in this case it refers to a hispanized, native Andean living in a city.
30. Francisco Rucana, an eighty-year-old Indian potter, also testified; I have excluded his testimony because it repeats what the other witnesses said.
31. Whether Diego composed the love letter remains a matter of speculation. As a *ladino*, he may have been educated by the priest whom he served, which would explain his use of biblical and classical references in the text. Certainly literacy among some Andeans, particu-

larly native elites, was not uncommon. However, the notary public of Huánuco actually recorded the prose.

32. literally gift, but figuratively pleasure, luxury or comfort.
33. "ojos" in the original, which literally means eyes but can be translated figuratively as good judgment or perspicacity.
34. "entrañas" in the original, literally entrails or insides.
35. Diego Andrés refers here to the complaint Ysabel filed before the ecclesiastical judge, which initiated the annulment suit.
36. "y por perder el ánimo y esfuerso en los trabajos que dios embía para sus mas méritos" in the original.
37. "me hacho" in the original.
38. A friar in charge of particular responsibilities within a monastery.
39. The chief official in an Andean village.
40. A term used interchangeably with *encomienda* in the Andes.
41. In this instance, the word "estado" refers to her marital status. The judge is saying that she may remain single or choose to marry.

DOCUMENT THEMES

Cultural Contact/Ethnogenesis/Resistance; Ethnicity; European-Mestizo Peoples; Family; Gender; Honor; Indigenous Peoples; Marriage; Popular Culture; Religion; Violence; Women

SUGGESTIONS FOR FURTHER READING

Flores Galindo and Chocano Mena 1984.
Lavallé 1986.
Seed 1988.
Stavig 1995.
van Deusen 1997.

CHAPTER

11

Favored Women, Subjected Indians: The Settlement of Pero d'Araujo's Estate in São Paulo

(1637–40)

Muriel Nazzari

INTRODUCTION

The document partly translated here, the *auto de inventário* (settlement of estate) of Pero d'Araujo, is one of thousands of such documents that have survived in São Paulo since the late sixteenth century.[1] Most were processed and filed by the *juiz dos órfãos*, the judge of orphans, who dealt with minor heirs, called orphans by the Portuguese even if only one parent had died. *Autos de inventário* incorporated all the papers, including the inventory (*inventário*), that were produced by the probatelike process of settling an estate under Portuguese law, and they took place whenever a property owner died whether or not the deceased left a will. They have been the main documentary source for much of the social history written about colonial São Paulo.[2]

The captaincy of São Paulo developed very differently from northeastern Brazil. Throughout colonial times it received little attention from the Crown because it had no mineral or agricultural wealth. In fact, shipwrecked sailors who married the daughters of Indian rulers were the first Portuguese inhabitants, joined in 1554 by the Jesuits who founded the town of São Paulo. The Jesuits converted many of the Indians from the surrounding areas and settled them in villages close to town, allowing the Portuguese settlers to hire them for a wage. During the sixteenth century the original settlers were joined by a handful of Portuguese couples, but by the end of the century, when the economic importance of the Brazilian Northeast had become well known, the population coming to São Paulo was mostly male. These new colonists included a few royal officials, penniless men who had not found a niche in the Northeast, and convicts exiled to Brazil by the Portuguese Crown. As the number of Europeans grew, there were not sufficient Indians in the Jesuit villages, and settlers came to resent Jesuit control over labor.

Toward the end of the sixteenth century, Paulistas commenced quasi-military expeditions, called *bandeiras*, to the backlands (*sertão*), overtly to discover

• *141* •

gold but covertly to capture Indians, thus remedying the problem of a scarcity of labor in the region.[3] *Bandeiras* continued throughout the seventeenth century, bringing back thousands of Indians. The Crown did not allow Indian slavery after 1611, but the Paulistas convinced the Crown to accept a system of Indian personal service to private individuals euphemistically called "administração" (administration). By studying *autos de inventário*, historians have been able to reconstruct many of the *bandeiras* and also learn how the "administration" of Indians actually worked. Pero d'Araujo's *auto de inventário* shows, as do others, that, though they were called free, Indians were inherited, bequeathed, bartered, and given away as gifts or in dowries. The only difference with African slaves in *autos de inventário* (at least through the 1660s) is that Indians were given no monetary value. Neither were there explicit references to the sale of Indians (though there is some evidence that Indians were actually sold by Paulistas, especially to other regions of Brazil). Thus the main difference between an African slave and an Indian "administrado" was that the latter had not become a legal commodity.[4]

Social historians have also used *autos de inventário* to study what kinds of property people owned and what crops they planted. Though São Paulo has sometimes been described as having a subsistence economy, the inventories themselves show considerable commercial production, which was not only sold locally but also to other regions of Brazil, especially wheat, flour, pork, marmalade, and cotton cloth, including sail cloth. They also show that practically all estates cultivated subsistence crops, mostly manioc, corn, and beans, to feed everyone on the estate.

The *auto de inventário* of Pero d'Araujo, which includes two inventories and a will, tells us a good deal about all of these topics, as well as about how the inheritance and marriage systems functioned. D'Araujo was a young man of twenty-four when he died only a few months after he married Izabel Mendes, and, judging from the *inventário*, a few months after he returned from a trip on a *bandeira* to bring back Indians.[5] As he had lived in the town of São Paulo with his mother, Ana de Alvarenga, whereas his future wife and her family resided in the nearby town of Santana de Parnaíba, they owned property in both settlements after they married, thus making two *autos de inventário* necessary. Pero d'Araujo's inventory shows what kind of property was highly valued in São Paulo at the time, such as clothes, swords, and silver, and conversely what kind of property was considered, perhaps surprisingly, to have no monetary value at all, such as land or Indians. It reveals the ambiguous terms Paulistas used when talking about their Indian *administrados*. This *auto de inventário* also includes the dowry João Mendes Giraldo gave his daughter Izabel, permitting us to evaluate which one of the spouses contributed the most property to the marriage. In addition, Pero d'Araujo's will provides an example of the place of religion in people's lives, and of how daughters were favored over sons.

I have also translated parts of the litigation by which Ana de Alvarenga wrested the guardianship of the infant heir, her grandson Pero, from his grandfather João Mendes Giraldo. This fact goes against our idea of what patriarchy was like. Or does it? Ana de Alvarenga represented the boy's *father's* lineage (the patrilineal side), whereas João Mendes Giraldo represented the boy's *mother's* side (the matrilineal side). Was gender the issue here or was it lineage? And if it was lineage, was it because of patrilineality or because of the prestige of the family? Interestingly, years later, when the boy was a young man receiving his inheritance from his guardian, he signed himself Pero d'Araujo de Alvarenga.[6]

Though these documents provide the only information we have on Pero d'Araujo, they nevertheless reveal many illuminating details on his way of life and on how he and his family earned a living. Why, for instance, would he risk his life on a *bandeira* when his father had died on one? Was the incentive economic? What business decisions did Pero's widow take? What goods did they produce for subsistence and/or for sale?

I have translated only parts of the two *autos de inventário* of Pero d'Araujo, which were bound together with his mother's.[7] I did not translate other documents, such as transcriptions of powers of attorney, oaths taken by appraisers, requests that witnesses appear, the list of debts owed by the couple, the receipts signed by beneficiaries of the will or by priests paid for the performance of masses, the lists showing how the moveable property and livestock were divided between the widow and the orphan, or the duplication of Izabel Mendes's dowry, which appeared in both inventories. I have also placed the documents chronologically, for example placing the will at the beginning whereas in the manuscript it was presented in the second *auto de inventário*.

THE DOCUMENT[8]

Auto de Inventário and Last Will and Testament of Pero d'Araujo, 1638.

11.1 The Judge of Orphans Orders an Auto de Inventário *Following the Death of Pero d'Araujo*

Inventory that Domingos Fernandes, judge of orphans, made after the death of the deceased Pero d'Araujo.

Year of the birth of our Lord Jesus Christ 1638, at the *fazenda* of João Mendes Giraldo, within the boundaries of this town of Santana da Parnaíba, Captaincy of São Vicente, parts of Brazil. On the fourth day of April of this era, in the *fazenda* of João Mendes, the judge commanded that this *auto de inventário* be carried out to list the property that remained from the death and decease of Pero d'Araujo. For which [purpose] he had Izabel Mendes, widow of the deceased, declare under oath on the Holy Gospel the property that between the two of them she owned with the deceased,[9] to which she said that she would tell what she knew, but the rest her father would tell because she did not know what dowry her husband had been promised and so could not list it, but her father knew and could declare for [her]. So the judge had João Mendes Giraldo swear under oath on the Holy Gospel that he would declare what he knew, and he promised to do so. Thus I prepared this *auto*, which he signed, as did the judge and I, Asenso Luis Grou, notary of the Court of Orphans, [who] wrote it . . .[10]

And then the judge asked João Mendes Giraldo if the deceased, his son-in-law, and his widowed daughter had any children, and he stated to the judge that it was only a short time since they were married and so they had no children but that his daughter was pregnant by [her deceased] husband . . .

11.2 Inventory of Pero d'Araujo's Property in Santana da Parnaíba

List and appraisal made of the property that was found and declared for this inventory.

One sword and dagger, and their necessary accessories, including belts and scabbards, appraised at 5,000 *réis*	5$000[11]
One [man's] wool suit, including a tunic and cape[12]	5$000
One pair of black silk sleeves	1$000
One [man's] light wool vest	1$280
A pair of used black garters	$160
A pair of used blue taffeta garters	$320
A pair of white leather shoes	$160
One pleated skirt, trimmed	3$200
One used serge skirt	2$000
A used lady's taffeta blouse	1$000
One new cedar chest measuring 6 palms (*palmos*), with its lock	2$000
One used chest with its lock	1$000
One smaller used chest with its lock	$640
One new cedar buffet	$640
Two tablecloths	1$280
Two hand towels	$400
Fourteen napkins	$400
Twelve china plates, six washbowls	$600
One china salt cellar	$100
Four china bowls	$160
One used pewter platter	$240
Four head of swine	2$000
Six *arrobas* of cotton	___13
Twenty bolts of cloth . . . eight hoes, six scythes, and six axes, all together	5$000
A chestnut horse	4$000

Free[14] *peças de serviço* ("pieces," or persons, to perform services)[15]

Singles: Apolonia; Maria; Antonia; Anzella, with a baby at her breast; Brizida; Ilena, with a baby at her breast; Maria; Genoveva; Cordula; Juana; Juana; Ana; . . .[16] Domingas; Anastasia; a young girl called Francisca; another young girl [called] Nicolasa; another young girl called Lucrecia; a young boy called Pedro.

Couples: Alonso; a daughter of Alonso called Izabel, and another boy, João, and his [Alonso's] wife Ana, with a baby at her breast; Paulo, with his wife, Ursula, and a baby at her breast; Inasio and his wife, Maria; João and his wife, Maria; Graviel with his wife, Apolonia; Henrique with his wife, Luiza; Vicente with his wife, [Marina]; . . .[17] with his wife Inasia . . .

João Mendes Giraldo stated that the people he declared are the people he had promised in dowry, and that besides these *peças* his deceased son-in-law had others, . . . and he had them in his *fazenda* in São Paulo where another inventory was made of the property he had and possessed [there]. And they should be included in that inventory, and so he did not declare them in this one, except for four *peças* that were here in this *fazenda*. And if the others were not listed in the other inventory, he would list them in this one . . .

João Mendes Giraldo declared that in the dowry list that he promised his daughter was one farm, with a house of two *lanços*, with a tile roof and walls made of *taipa de mão*,[18] [and] with its strip of cotton field, [all of] which he had not yet given her. And he had also promised five hundred *braças* of land he owned, and some other things he had promised in the list and had not yet delivered he would give to her, and because he could not remember all he would bring the list. He also said that in the list he promised his daughter two chairs, and that to buy them and four more he had given the deceased, his son-in-law, twenty-one *patacas*,[19] and the deceased had given the money to Pero da Silva who had it and was responsible for it . . .

11.3 The Justice of the Peace Orders an Inventory of Pero d'Araujo's Property in São Paulo

Inventory that the Justice of the Peace Pero Leme do Prado made of the property that was left by the death of Pero d'Araujo.[20]

Year of our Lord Jesus Christ 1638, on the fourteenth day of May of this year in this town of São Paulo, Captaincy of São Vicente of which the Count of Monsanto is governor and captain-general for His Majesty, in this town in the home of Pero da Silva, to which the justice of the peace Pedro Leme Prado came . . . with me and the appraisers, Manoel da Cunha and Manoel Alveres de Sousa, to make an inventory of all the goods and property that remained after the death of Pero d'Araujo, to carry out [this inventory] in this town and in this same house. And since Izabel Mendes, the widow of the deceased, was not in the house because she had gone to Parnaíba to the house of her father, João Mendes Giraldo, the judge asked Pero da Silva to take an oath on the Holy Gospels before me, the notary, to truly declare all property that remained at the death of the deceased.[21]

[Short routine delcarations follow, including the process of handing in the will.]

11.4 Pero d'Araujo's Last Will and Testament

And then I [the notary] added the will of the deceased Pero d'Araujo:

In the name of God amen. May everyone who sees this will and testament know that in the year of the birth of our Lord Jesus Christ of 1638, on the twenty-fifth day of the month of March of this year, I, Pero d'Araujo, resident of this town of São Paulo, being ill by the hand of God, in my bed, but with all my wits about me, and because I do not know when God will see fit to call me to his side from this present life, I have ordered my testament so:

First, I offer my soul to the Holy Trinity, Father, Son and Holy Ghost, three persons and only one true God, and I plead to our Eternal Father by the death and passion of his only-begotten son that he receive my soul with the eyes of his divine mercy, and I ask our Lord Jesus Christ by his divine wounds, who has already in this life granted me his precious blood and the worth of his travail, may he also grant me mercy in the life I expect, the prize of which is glory, and I implore the always Virgin Mary, our Lady and Mother of God, and the holy apostles Saint Peter and Saint Paul, and my guardian angel and my namesake saint and all the saints in the celestial court, may they intercede for me, and I implore my Lord Jesus Christ as one of his sheep, may he save me with his precious blood on the true cross, for I believe and profess everything the Holy Roman Church teaches.

Should God take me to himself, may my body be buried in the main church of this village in the niche of my grandfather, may he rest in peace, accompanied by the Brotherhood of Holy Mercy, with its banner, giving them the usual alms. I also wish to be accompanied by the Reverend Fathers of Our Lady of Mount Carmel, giving them the customary alms. I also want my body to be accompanied by the cross of the fire of purgatory, receiving the customary alms.[22] I command that after one month a service of nine lessons be performed in my memory in the same main church. I also request that nine masses to Our Lady of Mount Carmel be performed for me by her friars, and that the same friars say three masses for me at the altar of Saint John . . .

I declare that I am married before the church to Izabel Mendes, with whom I still have no son or daughter to be my heir. Only if she is pregnant, and God will that she deliver a son or daughter, then that child is my universal heir. If the child is a girl, I also bequeath to her the remainder of the third of my estate, but if it is a boy, I bequeath the remainder of the third to my wife Izabel Mendes.[23]

I declare that if no son or daughter is born to us, I name my mother Ana de Alvarenga as my universal heir, who will receive my estate, except for the third I have willed to my wife.

I bequeath two servants that I possess to my niece, daughter of Domingos Masiel, may they serve her as they have served me, and I beseech her to treat them well for they are free[24]. . .

11.5 Appraisal of Pero d'Araujo's Property in São Paulo

Appraisal

These houses of Pero da Silva, where he lives, were appraised—a house of two *lanços*, with their gallery,[25] made of *taipa de pilão*, with a tile roof, and with an orchard that touches on the property of the Fathers of the Company [of Jesus], and lying between the houses of Francisco de Proensa and Domingos Masiel. And the houses were appraised at 28$000 *réis*. Half of the houses belonged to the deceased since the death of his father Pero d'Araujo, so they belong to his heirs, [appraised] at

14$000 réis for Pero da Silva	14$000
Six new chairs at one thousand *réis* each	6$000
Four hundred and fifty *mãos* of this year's corn	4$500
Twenty-eight *alqueires* of sorted beans	2$800
Plus sixteen *alqueires* of last year's beans	$800
Five *arrobas* of bleached cotton	2$000

Pero da Silva declared that some wheat of the deceased remained in Jaraguá,[26] and that after it was threshed he would come and declare it in this inventory . . .

He also declared that in the Jaraguá farm there was a field of manioc that was worth 5$000 *réis*, and he declared under oath that he had already received 2$000 *réis*.[27]

One mare with its colt, appraised at 2$000 *réis*.	2$000

11.6 The Dowry of Izabel Mendes, Widow of Pero d'Araujo

Pero da Silva declared also that he had the list of what João Mendes Giraldo had promised the deceased in marriage, which list the judge commanded be added to this inventory so that its contents be recorded, as follows:

Dowry of Izabel Mendes[28]

Thirty *peças* of the people of this land, including twenty to till the soil—ten male *negros* and ten female *negras* with their families, and each one of them with the requisite tool.[29]

One farm with a house of two *lanços*, with a tiled roof and its accompanying cotton field.

Five hundred *braças* of my land.

One bed and its bedding, a wool mattress, two sheets, one blanket, one long pillow, and two small pillows. One cot.

Two suits of clothing for my daughter, one made of silk and one for everyday use. To go to church in style, the silk taffeta suit will include a cape, a coat, a skirt, and a jacket. The everyday suit will include a wool coat, a serge skirt, and a jacket.

One table, two chairs, a chest, linens, two tablecloths, six napkins, four hand towels, and the requisite china.

A couple of swine to start raising swine.

A house in the town of Parnaíba, if they live in Parnaíba. If not, I am not obliged to give the house.[30]

And if he wants me to, I will provide the food to feed them and their people for two years.[31]

What I hereby have promised includes the inheritance of my daughter that she received from her mother, Maria Alveres Correa, and I make this declaration so that he [Pero d'Araujo] will never claim her inheritance, and if he accepts this list I promise to deliver what I have listed if he marries my daughter. I sign today, November 9, 1637.

João Mendes Giraldo.

[At the bottom of the list, in the handwriting of the deceased, is the following:]

The marriage is concluded, giving me half a dozen chairs and a silver tumbler and four silver spoons, and one hundred *alqueires* of flour placed in the port of Santos.[32] Pero d'Araujo . . .

And Pero da Silva declared that João Mendes Giraldo, seeing the statement of the deceased, said before several persons that he would give everything he owed to his son-in-law.

Furthermore, Pero da Silva declared that João Mendes Giraldo, after the deceased Pero de Araujo received Izabel Mendes as his wife, declared that he gave them a further seven or eight *peças de serviço* besides those declared in the dowry list, so that the total he gave was fifty souls, big and little, and João Mendes Giraldo also gave his daughter gold earrings and two more silver tumblers and two silver spoons, besides the four listed, and everything is in the possession of the widow Izabel Mendes.

Pero da Silva declared further that after the death of the deceased Pero d'Araujo, he killed six pigs, which provided nineteen *arrobas* of pork and twenty-six *varas* of sausage and two jars of lard, which he had sold in the town of Santos . . . for a total of 11$430 *réis*, from which he paid Francisco da Fonseca Falcão 8$000 *réis* that the deceased owed him for a sword and its scabbard and a dagger and powder and shot that he gave him when he left for the *sertão* (backlands) . . .[33]

11.7 Pero da Silva Continues the Inventory of Pero d'Araujo's Property in São Paulo

Pero da Silva declared that he had two *patacas* worth of the rest of the pork, sausage, and lard.

Pero da Silva also declared that the people that the deceased possessed, which he brought from the *sertão*,[34] besides those he received in dowry, were the following:

Joana with her son Paulo, single. Juliana, single, with her two small children, a girl, Pomona, and a boy, Lourenço. Paul and his wife, old people. Romão, youth. Vasquo, youth. Plus four young women who are in the possession of the widow Izabel Mendes, named Nataria, daughter of Joanna, and Cordula, Floriana, and Maria. Plus another young woman named Cecilia . . .

Then the appraisers added the following to the inventory:

One used blanket	1$600
One embroidered cotton hammock	1$600
Six used hoes	1$440
Twenty used scythes	$640

11.8 The Judge of Orphans Names João Mendes Giraldo Guardian of Pero d'Araujo's Son

On November 6, 1638, in this village of Santana de Parnaíba in the home of the justice of the peace and judge of orphans, Domingos Fernandes, before him came João Mendes Giraldo, a *morador*. And in my presence [he] said to the judge that his daughter, Izabel Mendes, widow who remained from the deceased Pero d'Araujo, had had a baby boy by her deceased husband, and the boy was the universal heir of the deceased his father, and he therefore requested of the judge . . . that since there was an heir in this inventory he should have the division of the estate made between the heir and the widow, and he also requested that the inventory made in the town of São Paulo after the death of the deceased be joined to the present one, and that with one and the other the division be made, and he presented the other inventory to the judge. And he also requested that since the will of the deceased did not name a guardian for the orphan, the judge determine who should be his guardian.

And then on the same day of the same year the judge determined that since João Mendes Giraldo was the boy's grandfather . . . [he] should be his guardian . . . [and] that he should oversee the raising of this orphan, his grandson, and see that his property grow. And this was decided by the judge because there is in this village [no] relative of the deceased and of his lineage who could be a guardian of the orphan and because João Mendes Giraldo lives in this town and is the orphan's grandfather and is well-to-do . . .

11.9 Further Statements on Pero d'Araujo's Property and Izabel Mendes's Dowry

On November 12, 1638, in this town in the home of the justice of the peace Domingos Fernandes, in my presence appeared Manoel da Costa do Pino, proxy and representative of the widow,[35] making a request to the judge, saying that he had examined the inventories and learned that all the corn and beans that would feed the *peças de serviço* of the widow and orphan had been sold, so he requested that since there was no other means of subsistence than a field of manioc appraised at 5$000 *réis*, which the widow and her people were already eating since there was nothing else, he requested that it be left out of the inventory to sustain the widow and the orphan and their people since it helped both sides. And the judge considered the request and found it just to keep the appraisal of the field out of the inventory to support the pagans, for without it they would perish . . .

And on the same day and year João Mendes Giraldo appeared before the judge and stated that he had some more property to declare which he had inadvertently left out:

Six silver spoons	2$800
Two silver jugs	3$200

Plus a young man named Tomas with his wife Tomazia, plus two young girls, Ana and Maria, plus a young boy ten years old more or less named Pascoal. He also declared that in the house of Pero da Silva there was a little *mulatto* girl named Grazia who belonged to the deceased but was not mentioned in the São Paulo inventory, nor was another *negra*, a young girl named Iria . . .[36]

João Mendes Giraldo added that his daughter had ordered that the eleven *arrobas* of cotton previously listed in the *inventário* be spun and woven to help in paying her husband's bequests, and that it all amounted to one hundred *varas* of cloth that was sold for one *tostão* the *vara*, adding up to 10$000 *réis*.[37]

And then on the same day and year the judge added up the property that is declared in this inventory and according to the sum the whole property adds up to 105$110 *réis*, from which quantity is subtracted 13$988 *réis* that are the debts owed by the deceased plus the judicial costs of this inventory both in São Paulo and here, leaving 91$622 *réis* to divide between the deceased and his widow. And the judge commanded that they be divided giving each side their part . . .

And then on the same day, month, and year João Mendes Giraldo said to the judge that, among other things in the dowry, he had promised to the deceased his son-in-law a farm that he was now constructing, so he requested His Honor that it not be mentioned for the time being in the division of property, and that when it was finished João Mendes Giraldo would advise the justices to see whether he had completed it, as he had promised it to his son-in-law, and it should then be appraised to give the correct value to each of the two parts. And the judge commanded that the farm not be mentioned until it was finished . . .

11.10 The Division of Pero d'Araujo's Property

Division of Property

On November 16, 1638, in this town at the home of the judge in the presence of the guardian of the orphan Pero, son of the deceased, and in the presence of the proxy of the widow, I handed the inventories to the dividers so they could peruse them and make the division of property. And then both of them with me, the notary, who declared to them the further additions that had come in, inspected this inventory and according to what they found they made the division, dividing 91$622 *réis* between the widow and the deceased her husband, and the part of the deceased amounted to 47$811 *réis* and the same amount the widow's share of the moveable goods. And then responding to the command of the judge they took the third from the share belonging to the deceased, and the third amounted to 15$270 *réis*, leaving for the orphan Pero 30$540 *réis*. And the judge commanded that the dividers divide the property according to the accounts of those shares and the third, and the dividers did so as follows.[38]

[The division of moveable possessions and livestock is omitted here.]

And then the dividers divided the free *peças de serviço* between the deceased and his wife, subtracting three *peças* who died after the deceased, finding there were fifty-four head, counting big and little ones, who were divided according to the custom of this land, giving an equal share to the deceased and his widow, and each one had twenty-seven head . . .

Land

The dividers also divided five hundred *braças* of land in Juquerí[39] and gave their share to each of the parties—250 *braças* [each]—and from the 250 that belong to the deceased they separated the third, eighty-three *braças* [to go to the widow as per his will], and there remain 167 *braças* for the share of the orphan. And with this the dividers declared they had finished the division, and the judge considered them complete, asking the orphan's guardian and the widow's proxy if they agreed, and they said yes, and signed this which I [the notary] have written . . .

11.11 Ana de Alvarenga, Pero d'Araujo's Mother, Petitions Successfully to be Guardian of her Grandson

Ana de Alvarenga, resident of this town of São Paulo, declares that four months after Pero d'Araujo, her son, married Izabel Mendes, daughter of João Mendes, residents of Parnaíba, he died, and his wife was pregnant and the orphan Pero was born, heir to his father. And despite most of the property being in this town, especially houses and fields, they named João Mendes, maternal grandfather, guardian of the orphan, whereas, according to the law and *Ordenações*, book 4, title 102, par. 3,[40] when the mother cannot be the guardian the paternal grandmother should be the guardian. Since her daughter-in-law is married to Felipe Fernandes, in whose power is her grandson Pero, with all the property he inherited from his father, and since he [Felipe] is a stepfather, he dissipates his [the orphan's] property and does not raise him properly as she would do, wishing to support him with her own resources in this town where he can learn to read and everything else necessary for his good education, and she wants to see his property grow without spending it for his support. She therefore asks Your Honor to command that the orphan Pero her grandson be given to her . . .

On November 2, 1640, in this town of São Paulo of the Captaincy of São Vicente in the home of Pero da Silva, where the judge of orphans, dom Francisco Rondon de Quebedo, and I, the notary, went. And in the presence of Ana de Alvarenga, wife of Pero da Silva, grandmother of the orphan Pero, son of the deceased Pero d'Araujo, the judge had her [Ana de Alvarenga] take an oath on the Holy Gospels that she would be the guardian of the orphan her grandson and that as such she would raise him and educate him and administer his property in such a way that the orphan would have no loss in his property due to her, under the penalty of paying for such a loss from her own property . . . I, Manoel Coelho, notary of orphans, wrote this, and since Ana de Alvarenga does not know how to write, she asked her husband Pero da Silva to sign for her together with the judge. I sign at the request of my wife, Ana de Alvarenga, Pero da Silva. [dom Francisco Rondon de] Quebedo.

NOTES

1. Pedro and Pero were used interchangeably at this time. The spelling of other names (as well as many words) was not always consistent; I have used only one spelling in this translation.
2. Authors who have used *inventários* to study the family, women, and social relations in colonial São Paulo (and who write in English) include Muriel Nazzari, "Parents and Daughters: Change in the Practice of Dowry in São Paulo, 1600–1770," *Hispanic American Historical Review* 70:4 (1990), pp. 639–65, and *Disappearance of the Dowry: Women, Families, and Social Change in São Paulo, Brazil (1600–1900)* (Stanford: Stanford University Press, 1991); and Alida Metcalf, "Fathers and Sons: The Politics of Inheritance in a Colonial Brazilian Township," in *Hispanic American Historical Review* 66:3 (1986) pp. 455–84, and *Family and Frontier in Colonial Brazil: Santana de Parnaíba, 1580–1822* (Berkeley: University of California Press, 1992).
3. To learn more about the *bandeiras* organized by the Paulistas, see John Hemming, *Red Gold: The Conquest of the Brazilian Indians* (Cambridge, Mass.: Harvard University Press, 1978), especially chapters 12 and 13, and his "Indians and the Frontier," in Leslie Bethell, ed., *Colonial Brazil* (New York: Cambridge, 1987). See also Richard Morse's classic, *The Bandeirantes: The Historical Role of the Brazilian Pathfinders* (New York: Knopf, 1965).
4. To study the situation of Indians in São Paulo, see John Monteiro, "From Indian to Slave: Forced Native Labour and Colonial Society in São Paulo during the Seventeenth Century," *Slavery and Abolition* 9:2 (1988): 105–27 (Monteiro's work is mostly based on *inventários*), and Muriel Nazzari, "Transition Toward Slavery: Changing Legal Practice Regarding Indians in Seventeenth-Century São Paulo," *The Americas* 49(2) (1992): 131–55.
5. I calculated Pero d'Araujo's age from the fact that he was three years old in 1617 when the *inventário* of his father, also named Pero d'Araujo, was made after he died in the backlands on a *bandeira*. See Vol. 5, p. 171 of *Inventários e Testamentos: Papéis que pertenceram ao 1 Cartorio de Orfãos da Capital*, 44 vols. (São Paulo: Arquivo do Estado de São Paulo, 1922–77), hereafter referred to as IT.
6. Portuguese surnames followed no fixed rules. Individuals had great freedom to choose those they wished, and there were many who did not even bear their father's name.
7. An ellipsis marks those places where sections of the document were omitted.
8. Most of the surviving *autos de inventário*, especially those for the eighteenth and nineteenth centuries, are still in manuscript form, but Pero d'Araujo's is included in a published collection, Vol. 29, pp. 215–74 in IT. A manuscript *auto de inventário* can be anything from five pages to several hundred pages long, written on both sides. By the beginning of the twentieth century they were being typewritten.
9. Married couples owned what was termed community property, that is, property owned in common by both spouses, though the husband was usually the administrator. This last phrase in the document shows that the judge and notary considered Pero'Araujo's wife a co-owner of their common property.
10. Luis Asenso Grou used two words that I have translated as "notary," *tabelião* and *escrivão*. "Tabelião" is in fact the one that is closest to the English word "notary," for it means one who recognizes signatures and who registers deeds and other public documents. "Escrivão" is similar to the Spanish term "escribano" and has a much wider meaning than the English "notary." An "escrivão" performs many of the activities of a lawyer, and in modern Brazil and Portugal an "escrivão" must have a specialized degree like a lawyer's.
11. During the sixteenth and seventeenth centuries, the basic Portuguese and Brazilian monetary unit was the *real*, plural *réis*. There was a slow process of change through which the monetary unit became the *mil-réis* (a thousand *réis*), probably at the end of the eighteenth

and beginning of the nineteenth century. Long before that, however, as we see in this inventory, the dollar sign was placed between the digits for a thousand and one hundred *réis*.

12. In the remainder of the list I have not included the written phrases that repeat each item's value (in this case "appraised at five thousand *réis*").

13. The value given the cotton was unreadable in the original manuscript.

14. Because the persons listed here were all indigenous, and the Crown forbade Indian slavery, Paulistas always listed them as free though they were clearly listing them as property.

15. The term *peça*, or piece, was used in colonial Brazil to count or list slaves. Paulistas referred to their Indian laborers and servants as *peças de serviço*, a usage that reflected the ambiguity of their status. Technically, they were not slaves as there was no appraised value and they were listed as being free.

16. An unreadable name.

17. Another unreadable name.

18. This house had two *lanços*, rows of rooms, made of *taipa de mão*, thick walls with parallel supports of posts or wicker filled with mud that was then allowed to dry in the sun. It was a larger house than the one Pero d'Araujo owned in São Paulo (he owned only one *lanço*), but the construction was cheaper since the latter had walls made of mud mixed with stones. The house referred to in the dowry was also on a farm, whereas Pero d'Araujo's house was in town.

19. A *tostão* was a coin worth 100 *réis*, while a *pataca* was worth 320 *réis*.

20. In the original manuscript copy and in the published version, this second *inventário*, made in São Paulo, comes at the end, for it was added to the one made in Parnaíba.

21. From information in another *inventário*, that of Ana de Alvarenga, Pero d'Araujo's mother, we learn that Pero da Silva was his stepfather. See IT, Vol. 29, pp. 175–215.

22. This was the cross of a lay brotherhood. There were several lay brotherhoods in colonial Brazilian churches to which members of a congregation could belong, the most famous of which was called the Holy House of Mercy (Santa Casa da Misericordia). It was also a very elite brotherhood. The Reverend Fathers of Our Lady of Mount Carmel were Carmelite friars.

23. This last sentence suggests that daughters were favored over sons in seventeenth-century São Paulo. See my "Parents and Daughters," p. 650. See also *Disappearance of the Dowry*, pp. 21–22. Under Portuguese law, persons who had children or living parents did not have full testamentary freedom; they were not allowed to leave their property to whomever they wished. Two thirds of the estate of the deceased (in the case of married persons, their estate was only half of what they owned with their spouse) had to go to his or her legally mandated heirs: the children, or if there were no children, the parents. Only one third could be willed freely, which is what Pero d'Araujo is doing here. He uses the phrase "remainder of my third" because he means what is left after his funeral, masses, and pious bequests are paid for.

24. These persons, called servants here, were Indian *peças*, "free" yet bequeathed.

25. Houses could have one, two, or three *lanços* (rows of rooms). This house had two *lanços* (which is why it is also referred to in the plural, as "houses") with a gallery or porch in front. The house was made of *taipa de pilão*, thick walls made of mud and stones. Pero d'Araujo had inherited one half of the house, one *lanço* with a half a porch in front, from his father when he died. The other half belonged to his mother (and stepfather, after they married). When Ana de Alvarenga died, the orphan Pero inherited his father's share of her estate.

26. Jaraguá was in the vicinity of São Paulo.

27. Fields of corn or wheat were appraised, but the value calculated referred to the grain, not the land. Often the land did not belong to the owner of the corn or wheat, who squatted.

28. Wives brought much more property to marriage than their husbands, which is very evident in this *inventário*. See "Parents and Daughters" pp. 653–54, and *Disappearance of the Dowry*, p. 38.

29. The people referred to here were Indians. The first word used by the Portuguese to describe Indians in the São Paulo region was *negro* (black), and they continued to use that word throughout the sixteenth and seventeenth centuries. Indians were differentiated from Africans (of which there were very few until the eighteenth century) by calling an Indian "negro of this land" and an African "tapanhum negro" ("Tapanhum" was an Indian word meaning foreigner). Pero d'Araujo had no African slaves.

30. This sentence bolsters an argument I've made that dowries helped pressure young couples to live near the wife's parents. See my "Parents and Daughters," p. 652, and *Disappearance of the Dowry*, pp. 29–30.
31. He is here promising to feed more than sixty persons for two years.
32. Santos was a nearby port on the Atlantic from which ships left for Rio de Janeiro, Bahia, or Europe.
33. This example indicates how productive Indian servants were. See "Transition Toward Slavery," p. 141.
34. A direct reference to Pero d'Araujo's participation in a *bandeira*.
35. The widow had given a power-of-attorney to Manuel da Costa do Pino, and he was therefore called her *procurador*, which I have translated as proxy or representative.
36. As noted above, "negro" here refers to an Indian.
37. Another example of the productivity of Indian servants. See "Transition Toward Slavery," p. 141.
38. Here we see the estate left after debts were paid first divided between the deceased and his widow. Then his half of the estate was divided into thirds, two thirds for his necessary heir, his newborn son, and one third that he could freely will. The most common marriage property regime used in colonial São Paulo was full community property, which meant that each spouse owned half of all the property they held in common. So when married persons died, their estate consisted of only half of what they owned with their spouse. The spouse did not *inherit* half, but rather, retained half.
39. Juquerí was a village about eighteen miles from the center of São Paulo, but still within the municipal boundaries of the town.
40. *Ordenações* refers to the *Codigo philippino ou ordenações do Reino de Portugal*, the legal code promulgated in 1603 by which Portugal and its empire were ruled.

DOCUMENT THEMES

Cultural Contact/Ethnogenesis/Resistance; Economy and Work; Ethnicity; European-Mestizo Peoples; Family; Gender; Indigenous Peoples; Inheritance; Land; Marriage; Religion; Rural Life; Town Life; Women.

SUGGESTIONS FOR FURTHER READING

Hemming 1978.
Hemming 1987.
Metcalf 1986.
Metcalf 1992.
Monteiro 1988.
Morse 1965.
Nazzari 1990.
Nazzari 1991.
Nazzari 1992.

C H A P T E R
12

Catarina María Complains That Juan Teioa Forcibly Deflowered Her
(Mexico, 1693)

Richard Boyer

INTRODUCTION

Local governors and their assistants adjudicated petty disputes involving plebeians and peasants throughout New Spain. The records that survive of these local courts of first instance provide students with invaluable glimpses of life in Mexico's towns and rural districts. For most of the colonial period an *alcalde mayor* (governor) or his *teniente* (lieutenant), heard complaints involving disputes over land, taxes, extortion, insults, and injuries.

In the case[1] before us Catarina complained to Captain don Luis de Alipi, who called himself *justicia mayor* (chief justice) of the jurisdiction of Malinalco, a town in the present state of Mexico some twenty miles or so from Cuernavaca. The title might imply that he was on special assignment at the pleasure of the viceroy, or it might be that as *alcalde mayor* he was permitted to use the title in his role as judge to differentiate himself from subordinate judges who most likely would have been his *tenientes*. As well as *justicia mayor*, don Luis also refers to himself throughout (with a single exception found in entry 12.10) as "acting *juez receptor*" in lieu of a properly qualified scribe. In other words don Luis acted both as scribe and judge and therefore had to have witnesses present to ensure that he did not tamper with the evidence. The makeshift arrangement, common enough in outlying jurisdictions, underscores a lack of formality, if not of method, in local courts. Complainants, defendants, and witnesses in such settings speaking to and before members of their own community must have expressed themselves with fewer inhibitions than they would have before a superior court with its full complement of doormen, notaries, lawyers, advisors, and high court judges.[2]

Catarina and Juan resided in, and were native to, the district of Malinalco. I have found no population estimates for Malinalco in the 1690s, but by 1791, one hundred years after Catarina's suit, around six thousand non-Indians, divided between people classified as Spaniard or *mestizo* and with a smattering of *mulatos* thrown in, lived in the district. In very rough terms, at the time of Catalina's suit the district may have had some one thousand seven hundred Indian tributaries, married heads of households, which would have meant a total Indian population of five thousand or so.[3] Catarina, Juan, and Magdalena all lived in San Nicolás, referred to as a *barrio* (entries 12.1, 3, 8, 10, 11) as well as a *pueblo* (entries 12.1, 4, 7, 8), which means it had a separate identity as an Indian town subject to Malinalco but was not contiguous with it.

This is a short document, and unlike most others in this collection I have been able to include nearly all of it. Readers can therefore follow a complete sequence of litigation that includes, in this case, the attempt by Catarina's brothers to have the complaint removed to the higher jurisdiction of the General Indian Court. My translation tends more to the literal than the interpretive—although all translations require that one interpret at every stage—so that readers may have a close facsimile of the text to debate its meanings for themselves. My translation also leaves visible or underscores with notes shifts in tense and person that occur from time to time in the original so readers might, as I did, wrestle with their significance. One must keep in mind, of course, that almost all the testimony has been filtered through a translator and survives as a "document" only as don Luis or the scribe of the General Indian court transcribed it. Readers might want to think about the degree to which Catarina's and Juan's own "voices" emerge from the transcript and the degree to which they seem to be submerged in legal phrases, formulaic statements, or summary paraphrases.

THE DOCUMENT

[Title page] On the charge of Catarina María, Indian of *barrio* San Nicolás in this *pueblo* [Malinalco], against Juan Teioa, Indian of this *pueblo*, for having deflowered[4] her and so on.

12.1 Catarina María Files a Suit

In the *pueblo* of Malinalco on August 20, 1696, before me, Captain don Luis de Alipi, *justicia mayor* of the *pueblo* and its district, acting *juez receptor* with attending witnesses for lack of a royal public scribe in this jurisdiction, there appeared an Indian who, speaking through the interpreter Juan de Medina, said her name is Catarina María from *barrio* San Nicolás of this *pueblo*, and that she was bringing a criminal action against Juan Teioa, an Indian of the same *pueblo*, to the effect that with little fear of God and scorning royal justice the said Juan Teioa "took hold of me yesterday next to the house of an Indian named Magdalena, into which he put me and forced me,[5] thus robbing me of my virginity."[6] And in order that he be punished according to law and, for this purpose, that Magdalena be questioned as a witness for lack of other witnesses, may it please Your Honor to have them locked up with those already confined in this *pueblo*'s jail, and have Juan "repay me for the loss of my virginity."

She pleads for justice and swore this statement before God and the cross according to law. She did not sign because she does not know how. The interpreter signed with me.

12.2 Arrest Warrant

And having reviewed this petition, I enter this suit as presented and accepted, and order that the Indian Juan Teioa be locked in the public jail of this *pueblo*, and the said Magdalena be questioned as a witness and [also] be put in *depósito* until this case is decided. And thus I decreed, ordered, and signed.

12.3 Juan Teioa Is Apprehended and Questioned

In the *pueblo* of Malinalco on August 21, 1696, I, Captain don Luis de Alipi, its *justicia mayor*, acting as *juez receptor* with attending witnesses for lack of a royal public scribe, having gone to the Indian Juan Teioa's house, had him taken into custody by Domingo García, the bailiff of this court, and placed in the Malinalco jail. On his arrival there I had him appear before me and received his oath, which he swore before God our Lord and the sign of the cross according to law.

He promised to tell the truth, and on being questioned said his name is Juan Teioa of *barrio* San Nicolás in this jurisdiction, and that the Indian Catarina María sent him many love messages by way of another Indian named Magdalena, but the deponent paid no attention. And having persisted, she sent another message by the said Indian Magdalena, telling him [that] he was not a man, nor did he know how to do anything because he was not coming when she called. And a little before noon on the day the lawsuit refers to, Catarina María, passing near Magdalena's house where the deponent was, began to provoke him [like] a seductress.[7] Having gone into the house, Catalina threw herself on the floor for the witness and he deflowered her (*la estrupó*), after which she said "look what you've done, don't treat me badly, I love you very much."[8] And having said this, Catarina María went home, and he did not see her again until I, the *justicia mayor*, apprehended him.

He states that this is the truth in accordance with his oath, upon which it was affirmed and ratified. He states that he is twenty years of age. I signed along with the interpreter who was present and the attending witnesses.

12.4 The Testimony of Juan Teioa's Sister, Magdalena María

Immediately afterward on the same day, month, and year, I, the said *justicia mayor*, accompanied by the said attending witnesses for lack of a royal public scribe in this jurisdiction, had an Indian appear before me, who, speaking through the said interpreter, said her name is Magdalena María, that she is married and a *vecina* of *pueblo* San Nicolás. Through the interpreter I received her oath in which, according to law, she swore before God and the cross to tell the truth.

Asked about the lawsuit, she said that five or six different times the Indian Catarina María gave her messages for Juan Teioa on the subject of love and she passed them on to him. Catarina used her [as a go-between] because she lives near Juan's house. And one day—she does not recall the date—Catarina gave her another message telling her to tell Juan that he shouldn't be such an ingrate (*ingrato*), that she loved him very much, and it seemed he was no man nor did he have the nerve (*valor*) to meet her. The witness gave the message to Juan and even as she was doing so, Catarina went up to Magdalena's house, and called to Juan, and they entered this witness's house. Meanwhile, this witness went off to do her errands, and when she returned she found them very happy together, and according to what they told Magdalena, Juan had deflowered Catarina.

The witness states that this is the truth according to her sworn oath. She did not know her age but appears to be about twenty-eight, and the rules governing the disqualification of witnesses (*las generales de la ley*) do not apply to her. She did not sign because she does not know how. The interpreter signed, along with myself and the attending witnesses.

12.5 Careamento: *Accuser and Accused Face One Another in Court*

In the *pueblo* of Malinalco on August 21, 1696, I, the *justicia mayor*, acting with attending witnesses for lack of a royal public scribe in this jurisdiction, having seen that this case packs conclusive evidence, caused Juan Teioa and Catarina María to appear before me. I received their oaths through the interpreter, which they swore before God and the cross according to law.

They promised to tell the truth. Catarina María, asked if Juan Teioa had brought her to ruin, in his presence answered yes. To which Juan said it was true that he had been with her, but that in his opinion she had not been a *doncella*. And having proceeded with this *careamento* they both kept to their [earlier] statements, with Catarina María only adding that Juan must repay her the loss of her virginity, but that she did not wish to marry him.

I then had Juan Teioa put back into the local jail, and I personally took Catarina María to the home of doña Bernabela Vargas, *vecina* of this *pueblo*, and placed Catarina María in her custody. I charged doña Bernabela to keep her under guard and not permit her to venture outside her house until such time as this case has been decided, and she agreed to comply fully with my instructions.

This is all that took place before me, to which I bear witness in my official capacity. I signed along with my attending witnesses and the interpreter.

[The next entry, dated September 1, 1696, is an auto de cargo. *It formally notifies the accused that, based on preliminary information collected by the court, he is charged with a crime. Admonished to tell the truth, he must therefore make a* confesión, *that is, a reply to the* cargo, *whether to deny his guilt or to admit it. To help Juan defend himself a kind of advisor-guardian called a* curador, *at times referred to in this document as* defensor *or defender, will be appointed by the court. Although not named here, Francisco de Herrera, a man who apparently had no formal training in the law and certainly held no university degree, would eventually act as Juan's defender.]*

12.6 Juan Teioa Petitions the Court

In the *pueblo* of Malinalco on September 4, 1696, before me, Captain don Luis de Alipi, its *justicia mayor*, the following petition was presented:

I, Juan Teioa, Indian, locked in this public jail, appear before Your Honor, using the best ways and means that are provided in law and are available to me. And I say that the complaint Catarina Hernández brought against me that I ruined her using force and deceit, to this I say that many times she sent messages by my sister Magdalena that I should go see her, that she had something to say to me, until the day that I saw her. It was her fault, because she went into my sister's house, and it's true that being a man I quickly followed. But to unburden my conscience, I did not ruin her there. And so I don't want to marry her but willingly will pay her whatever Your Honor would order me to give for all that.

To Your Honor I beg and plead that you have the kindness to help me in this my entreaty, and in doing so I will thus find favor and mercy. And I swear to God our Lord that this my petition is not made with malice, but to achieve justice, expenses, and whatever is necessary.

[signed] Juan Teioa[9]

[The case had now reached the point where don Luis needed expert legal advice on whether it should proceed to trial or be dismissed. He sent the file for assessment to Dr. don Joseph de Morales, a lawyer (abogado) licensed to practice before the audiencia in Mexico City. Morales directed that the case proceed to prueba. This meant that he found Catarina María's charges to be plausible, and should be evaluated further by taking the case to trial. Morales specified that testimony already given should be ratified and, if necessary, witnesses reexamined. Juan should be assigned a defender—he used the term defensor rather than curador—who could help him give his confesión. The directive, dated October 2, 1696, went into the record above the signatures of both don Luis and don Joseph together with attending witnesses.]

12.7 Catarina María's Brothers Petition the General Indian Court

I, Cristóbal del Castillo y Texeda, royal and public scribe of the General Indian Court (*juzgado general de los naturales*) in this kingdom, certify and bear witness that in the said court, before His Excellency the Illustrious don Juan de Ortega Monterrey, bishop of the Holy Church in the city of Valladolid, viceroy, governor, and captain general of this New Spain, the following petition was presented, which, with the decree attached to it and the opinion of don Jacinto de Vargas Campuzano, the longest-serving *oidor* of this *real audiencia* and *asesor*[10] of the General Indian Court, is here recorded to the letter:

Your Excellency, we, Pedro Pablo, Juan Baptista, and Joseph Nicolás, Indians native to the *pueblo* and jurisdiction of San Nicolás Malinalco, as the legitimate brothers of the *doncella* Catarina María, appear before Your Excellency and state that an Indian named Juan, native of the *pueblo*, two months ago at nightfall grabbed (*cojió*) our sister and brought her with false promises to a empty cottage, where, applying every force, he deflowered her, giving her a promise of marriage, as our sister has declared under oath. Because he left her, [abandoned] except for her brothers, she wanted more [of a settlement] from the *alcalde mayor*. Although the *alcalde mayor* has Juan in jail, he is obviously siding with him because he has money; he says he is about to set him free and without [paying court] costs, while our sister is left ruined. In order that the damage to her have its proper remedy and the aforementioned Juan be punished according to law or marry Catarina María by way of compensation, the *alcalde mayor* should forward court documents to this court. If necessary we shall appeal all of them and file a grievance asking that they be declared null, or seek another remedy in which, if brought, we would protest, dispute, and accuse him with all due formality, sending proof for this purpose.

For all of which, we ask Your Excellency and plead, having made this appeal, that it may please you to order the *alcalde mayor* of this district or his deputy to remit to this court the records concerned with our complaint in the manner we have originally expressed, without anything being omitted, and in the interim, while this case is being decided, keep the prisoner [Juan] under strict guard as we have requested and that penalties be imposed on him that he must fulfill. Let someone [of the *pueblo*] who knows how to read and write be notified of this, together with witnesses, costs and so on.

[*After hearing the petition of Catarina María's brothers, Viceroy Monterrey ordered on October 5 that don Luis de Alipi send the information gathered so far on the case to the General Indian Court for review. But the documents were in Mexico City with don Joseph de Morales who was assessing them for the Malinalco court. Don Luis complied with the viceroy's order, on October 11, by asking Morales to turn the file over to the General Indian Court. And so he did. The viceroy then reviewed it in consultation with the Lord Licentiate don Jacinto de Vargas Campuzano, the senior judge of the* audiencia *and assessor general of the court. Then, on October 22 the viceroy remanded the case to Malinalco with the directive that within eight days don Luis de Alipi complete the collection of evidence and, with the advice of the assessor Morales, appraise it and pronounce a verdict. Afterward he was to file a report on the case with the General Indian Court.*]

12.8 Juan Teioa Undergoes Interrogation

In the *pueblo* of Malinalco on October 26, 1696, I, Captain don Luis de Alipi, *justicia mayor* of the *pueblo* and its jurisdiction, acting as *juez receptor* with attending witnesses for lack of a royal public scribe in this jurisdiction, went to the Malinalco jail in order to receive the *confesión* of an Indian held in this case, and, in the presence of his attorney, Francisco de Herrera, and the interpreter Juan de Medina, received his oath, which he swore before God and the sign of the cross according to law. He promised to tell the truth, and the following questions were addressed to him:

Asked his name, marital status, occupation, *naturaleza*, and age, he said his name is Juan Teioa, he is unmarried, his occupation is that of *gañan*, and his *naturaleza* is Indian native to *barrio* San Nicolás. He did not know his age but appears to be about twenty. And thus he answers.

Asked whether he knows the reason for his imprisonment, he said "because of a woman." And thus he answers.

Asked how he can say he is imprisoned because of a woman, if it is for having violently deflowered an Indian named Catarina María. Speak and confess the truth. He said that he denies what the question says, because when he was with Catarina María, it seemed to him she was not a *doncella*. And thus he answers.

Asked why is he saying he has not ruined Catarina María, when in his earlier statement he says he had. Speak and confess the truth. He said that he begs and pleads that the earlier statement be read out. And this being done, he said he stands by that answer, which he affirms and ratifies. And as for the deflowering, he does not know whether she was a *doncella* or not, since it was the first time he had been with a woman and he had no experience in such matters. And it will be seen that it happened because of the messages [Catarina María] sent him via the Indian Magdalena María. And thus he answers.

Questioned why he says the aforementioned [Catarina] was not a *doncella*, he said that as he has already said, he had not been with another woman and cannot explain it but one day—he cannot recall the date—Mateo Clemente, an Indian of the said *pueblo* of San Nicolás, told him, "Watch what you're doing; don't touch Catarina María with a ten-foot pole.[11] Even if [she] wants to marry you, you don't want to, because I know she's not a *doncella*." And thus he answers.

He was asked and reasked other questions concerning the case and said that his testimony is the truth in accordance with his oath, upon which it was affirmed and ratified. He did not sign because he does not know how. His *curador*, the interpreter, and the attending witnesses signed.

[Immediately following the confesión, *don Luis declares this part of the case completed and through the interpreter notifies Juan, once again, of the charges* (cargo) *and evidence* (prueba) *against him. Don Luis recorded, formulaically, that "[Juan] said he heard it, and this is the reply he gave." The interpreter and Francisco de Herrera, identified here as Juan's* curador, *signed, along with don Luis and the court witnesses. The next stage in the trial will allow for the presentation of arguments and supporting testimony for the defense, and following that, for the complainant.]*

12.9 Juan Teioa's Defender Argues His Case

In the *pueblo* of Malinalco on October 27, 1696, before me, Captain don Luis de Alipi, *justicia mayor* of the *pueblo* and its jurisdiction in the name of His Magesty the following petition was read:

I, Francisco de Herrera, *vecino* of this *pueblo*, on behalf of the Indian Juan Teioa, who is confined in the Malinalco public jail on account of the suit filed by Catarina María, contending that he deflowered her and so forth. I say that Your Honor would be well served to order that my client, Juan Teioa, be released from his imprisonment for the following reasons. First, he is a boy (*muchacho*) incapable of reason and, being timid as he is, did not have the nerve to commit an offense such as this, especially because he remains under his father's authority (*patria potestad*), and his parents and my client fear God and their own consciences. Secondly, even if my client had deflowered Catarina María, he should not be imprisoned or punished since it was proven in the proceedings that Catarina María pursued him with amorous advances, as the Indian Magdalena María of the *pueblo* testified, the same person who bore the love messages of the aforesaid. And in that house where they were, it is certain that the latter incited my client and in effect did incite him by lying down on the floor for him. Hence, there was no abduction or violence, but, properly speaking, a simple fornication.

For all these reasons, and those my client presented, Your Honor would be well served to order that the witnesses he [Juan] mentioned in his confession be examined, that he be released from jail, and that Catarina María be severely punished. This submission should likewise be understood as evidence for my client, and in all of this I ask and plead that you decree and order according to justice.

[signed] Francisco de Herrera

12.10 Evidence in Support of Juan Teioa, Indian (1): The Testimony of Lucas de la Cruz

In the *pueblo* of Malinalco, October 21, 1696, before me, Captain don Luis de Alipo, *justicia mayor* of this jurisdiction, and Juan de Como, *juez receptor*, with witnesses present for lack of a royal public scribe in this jurisdiction, Francisco de Herrera presented in his client's defense an Indian witness who said to me, before the interpreter Juan de Medina he would receive the oath that he swore before God our Lord and the sign of the cross according to law promising to tell the truth.

On being questioned about the record [of the case], he said that his name is Lucas de la Cruz, his occupation is hat-maker, he is married to Micaela Gerónima, and he is native to *barrio* San Juan. He said that what he knows and can say is that he knows the Indian Juan Teioa, on whose behalf he has been asked to testify, since he was born. He also knows Catarina María. And what he knows and can say is that it is common knowledge in *barrio* San Nicolás that she is a public and worldly woman (*muger pública y mundana*) and therefore it is quite certain that Juan Teioa did not bring her to ruin. He [also] knows that on various occasions Catarina María sent love messages to Juan Teioa with Magdalena María, who has been heard to say this many times. This is what he knows to be the truth according to his sworn oath, upon which it was affirmed and ratified.

He did not know his age, but appears to be over forty. The rules governing the disqualification of witnesses do not apply to him. He did not sign because he does not know how. The interpreter signed, along with myself and my attending witnesses.

12.11 Evidence in Support of Juan Teioa, Indian (2): The Testimony of Baltasar de los Reyes

Immediately after, on the same day, month, and year, before me, the *justicia mayor* with attending witnesses for lack of a royal public scribe in this jurisdiction, Francisco de Herrera, acting on behalf of his client, presented as witness an Indian who, speaking through the interpreter Juan de Medina, said his name is Baltasar de los Reyes, his profession, painter, married to María Catalina, and native of *barrio* San Juan in this jurisdiction. Through the said interpreter I received his oath, which he swore before God and the cross according to law.

Upon being questioned according to the record [of the case], he said that he has known Juan Teioa, on whose behalf he has been asked to testify, in this district for ten years. And he also knows Catarina María. And what he knows and can say is that he knows she was not a *doncella*, since this was common knowledge in all of *barrio* San Nicolás. And he knows also that Catarina María sent messages by Magdalena María, which she gave him so that he should meet her, but he didn't want to go, being a mere boy (*muchacho*). And he knew that the aforementioned enticed Juan.

And this is the truth [he stated] according to his sworn oath, upon which it was affirmed and ratified. He declared he is thirty years old, and the rules governing the disqualification of witnesses do not apply to him. He did not sign because he does not know how. The interpreter and the attending witnesses signed.

12.12 The Court Asks Catarina to Present Witnesses

And immediately after, on the same day, month, and year, I the *justicia mayor*, with witnesses present for lack of a royal and public scribe and through the interpreter Juan de Medina, notified Catarina María that the presentation of evidence was closing and she should present any witnesses that she might have. She said she heard, and doesn't have witnesses to present. And this was her answer. The interpreter signed, along with myself and the attending witnesses.

12.13 The Case Is Sent to Dr. Morales for Assessment

In the *pueblo* of Malinalco, October 28, 1696, I, Captain don Luis de Alipi, *justicia mayor* of the *pueblo* and its district, acting as *juez receptor* with witnesses present for lack of a royal and public scribe, having seen this case and the depositions given on behalf of the defendant Juan Teioa, and to comply with the order of the Most Excellent Lord Bishop Viceroy and of the assessor general of the General Indian Court, ordered and order that this case be brought for assessment to Dr. don Joseph de Morales, lawyer of the royal *audiencia*, with payment of four pesos as his fee so that he decide the outcome and the sentence and I of course will conform to whatever he should decree and decide. And I signed, along with my attending witnesses.

12.14 Dr. Morales Decides the Case

I received these documents today, November 7, 1696, Mexico City.

[Signed]

In the criminal litigation against Juan Teioa, a native of the *pueblo* of Malinalco, that followed from the complaint of the Indian Catarina María, saying that he violently deflowered her, and in regard to what was alleged and proven by Juan Teioa's defender, saying that the aforementioned [Catarina] provoked him and was not a *doncella* when he knew her carnally (*la conosió*), and the other issues I see in the file:

Upon reviewing the writs and the merits of the case, and considering what has come to light therein, I find that I must sentence and do sentence Juan Teioa to pay the full legal expenses, amounting to twelve pesos. Let him be released from the prison in which he is confined, and let him be absolved and held blameless with regard to the deflowering and the demand for damages that came from it. And let Catarina María be warned not to solicit Juan, or anyone else, nor to tempt them with provocative behavior, under penalty of being placed in a *recogimiento* in Mexico City for a period of six years. And let her be warned to live decently or marry. And if any violation occurs, my sentence is to be enforced unconditionally. I thus pronounced and order as [court] assessor.

[signed] Dr. don Joseph de Morales

Notes

ACKNOWLEDGMENTS   Peter Rogers compared my transcription of this document with a photocopy of the original and then made a preliminary translation. Omar Farouk recopied several pages that were missing from my original photocopy. A research grant from the Social Sciences and Humanities Council of Canada supported the research program from which this case is taken.

1. This document comes from Mexico's Archivo General de la Nación, Criminal, vol. 139, exp. 24, pp. 363–76.
2. As well they surely abbreviated some contextual descriptions and explanations that would have been self-evident to all members of the community but not, unfortunately, to us.
3. The population figures come from Peter Gerhard, *A Guide to the Historical Geography of New Spain* (Cambridge: Cambridge University Press, 1972), p. 171.
4. Throughout I have used deflower to translate *estuprar* (spelled throughout this document as *estrupar*), which in other contexts can mean rape. In fact Catarina uses the word more in the sense of rape at times when she emphasizes that Juan took her by force.
5. The Spanish is "en donde me metió y forsó." I have translated this literally but a more interpretive translation, one that would not be inaccurate, might read "into which he dragged me and raped me."
6. Note that the notary puts part of the complaint into the first person.
7. The text reads "le empezó a provocar con amores."
8. "Mira lo que has hecho, y no me pagues mal que yo te quiero mucho."
9. Because Juan did not know how to write (see the concluding section of 12.8), his name was signed for him here in a practiced hand that included an added flourish that rustics and the barely literate would never have attempted. But by whom? We do not know because there is no attribution. Yet the flourish is nearly identical to one that the court translator, Juan de Medina, attached to his signature. And because Medina surely had a hand in putting Juan's statement into proper form, as well as proper Spanish, it is likely that he signed Juan's name.
10. Assessors were lawyers, judges often were not. In this case the viceroy, sitting as a judge, would have been required by Spanish law to receive expert legal advice on what decision should be made and then he would make it.

11. The Spanish is "no te metas en nada con Catarina María." The forcefulness implied by the adverbial phrase "en nada" justifies the strong rendering in English. Without it, the translation might read "don't get involved with Catarina María."

DOCUMENT THEMES

Crime; Gender; Gossip and Communication; Honor; Marriage; Popular Culture; Sexuality; Town Life; Women.

SUGGESTIONS FOR FURTHER READING

Borah 1983.
Boyer 1994.
Boyer 1995.
Boyer 1998.
Seed 1988.

CHAPTER 13

On Her Deathbed, María de la Candelaria Accuses Michaela de Molina of Casting Spells
(Guatemala, 1696)

Martha Few

INTRODUCTION

The Inquisition in Guatemala was officially established in 1572 with the appointment of its first commissioner, don Diego de Carbajal. Inquisition cases investigated and prosecuted by Guatemalan ecclesiastical authorities fell under the bureaucratic control of the Tribunal of the Holy Office of the Inquisition, located in Mexico City.[1] Commissioners of the Guatemalan Inquisition heard complaints of religious deviance, including witchcraft and sorcery, pacts with the devil, blasphemy, concubinage, solicitations in the confessional, and the possession of prohibited books. The Inquisition's mandate to enforce religious orthodoxy included all peoples in New Spain, with the important exception of the colony's majority—the indigenous population—who had been formally removed from its jurisdiction by order of King Phillip II in 1571.[2] But while the Holy Office could not prosecute Indians for religious crimes, it still regularly called them to appear in inquisitorial proceedings as witnesses.

The following document is an excerpt from an Inquisition case of sorcery prosecuted against Michaela de Molina, a *mulata* resident of Santiago de Guatemala, in 1696. Guatemalan commissioner Dr. don Joseph de Baños y Sotomayor had heard rumors that Michaela de Molina, a candy seller, had cast a spell on María de la Candelaria, an Indian servant, causing her to become extremely ill and expel and vomit numerous items from her body.[3] Baños y Sotomayor decided to investigate the case and interviewed María de la Candelaria on her deathbed because she was too ill to leave her home. He also questioned two other witnesses, María's mistress doña Juana González, and doña Juana's teenage niece, doña Rafaela González. All three described María's illness in detail, including her symptoms of nausea, fainting spells, and body swellings, and the expulsion of various items through her nose and mouth, such as blood, rocks, and pieces of charcoal. They attributed María's illness to a series of arguments she had with Michaela de Molina and Michaela's two Indian friends, Gerónima

García and Teresa.[4] After assessing the evidence, Inquisition authorities convicted Michaela de Molina of sorcery in July 1696, seizing her house and goods, and imprisoning her in the public jail until May of the following year.

The witnesses in this case resided in the city of Santiago de Guatemala, a major urban center and the political and religious capital of the Audiencia of Guatemala.[5] In the late seventeenth century, Santiago de Guatemala had a population of about forty thousand inhabitants. In this multiethnic city, roughly 15 percent of the inhabitants were identified as Spanish, 20 percent as tributary Indians, and the remaining 65 percent as *gente ordinaria*, which included Africans (both free and enslaved) and *castas* (mixed-race groups).[6]

Included in this excerpt from Michaela de Molina's case is the *auto* (judicial decree) from commissioner Baños y Sotomayor and the three testimonies of María, doña Juana, and doña Rafaela.[7] While the commissioner deemed María's supernatural illness as serious enough to investigate, none of the religious and political officials who reportedly witnessed María's strange expulsions, including three priests, an *alcalde ordinario* (town council member and judge), a royal notary, and a constable, came forward to denounce the incidents nor were they called to testify.[8]

In analyzing this document, readers may want to consider the following questions. Why was María's illness seen as so important for the Inquisition to investigate? Could the illness have been related to pregnancy or childbirth? How do you explain the sworn testimony about its supernatural causes and highly unusual effects? What was the significance of María's illness, and the items that she expelled, for people in late seventeenth-century Guatemala?

THE DOCUMENT[9]

13.1 Dr. Don Joseph de Baños y Sotomayor Orders an Investigation into Acts of Sorcery

Auto concerning going to the house of doña Juana González to take the declaration of an Indian woman sick from *maleficio* (sorcery).

In the city of [Santiago de] Guatemala, on July 2, 1696, señor Dr. don Joseph de Baños y Sotomayor, dean of the cathedral of this city, apostolic commissioner, subdelegate general of the Apostolic and Royal Tribunal of the Holy Crusade in this court and its provinces, priest of His Majesty, first rector and professor of sacred theology in the Royal University of Saint Charles, judge provisor and vicar general of this bishopric, and commissioner and *calificador*[10] of the Holy Office of the Inquisition, said that inasmuch as it is public knowledge that a *mulata vecina*[11] of this city named Michaela de Molina, who sells candies, has put a spell on a female Indian servant of doña Juana González, a *vecina* of this city, and as this Indian woman is in danger of dying from the spell and no one has appeared to denounce this event, it is necessary and proper to ascertain the truth and to take a statement from the sick Indian woman and from the rest of the people who know about this. Therefore, I resolved to personally go, with the assistance of the present notary of the Holy Office, to the house of doña Juana González to take the statement of the sick Indian woman and through her determine that which is most necessary. I resolve, order, and sign it [this decree].

> Dr. don Joseph de Baños y Sotomayor
> Don Miguel de Carranza y Córdova,
> notary of the Holy Office

13.2 Testimony of María de la Candelaria

In the city of [Santiago de] Guatemala, on July 1, 1696, in the afternoon, a woman named María de la Candelaria was called to appear before Dr. don Joseph de Baños y Sotomayor, dean of the Cathedral of this city, etc.[12] She swore to tell the truth. She is an unmarried Indian servant of doña Juana González, a *vecina*[13] of this city. She says she is eighteen years old and she is in bed.

[María de la Candelaria] was asked if she knows or presumes why the señor commissioner of the Inquisition came to see her, and why she is called by the Holy Office.

She said that she presumes it is to learn from her about the things she has expelled and vomited, which she presumes are the result of an *hechizo* (spell). This evil was done to her by a *mulata* named Michaela de Molina, who sells candies in the streets, after she had some encounters with her over the past two years. The first time caused her mistress, doña Juana González, to become annoyed, because [María] had gone to a holy day celebration in 1694 where she dragged the *mulata* Michaela de Molina by the hair.[14] A few days after the fight, María de la Candelaria began to suffer from fainting spells, and she expelled blood from her mouth and nose. And even though [María and Michaela] later became friends again, they fought a second time over some issues. While this witness walked by the *mulata* Michaela's door after midnight, [Michaela] provoked [María] so that . . . who had made a neighbor pregnant . . .[15] and the noise of their voices caused her mistress doña Juana González to leave her house to [confront] the *mulata*. This fight occurred at the end of last October 1695. A few days later [María de la Candelaria] gave birth and immediately began to suffer constrictions in her chest, which caused so much anguish that she appeared to be in the throws of death, and she was deprived of her senses, her belly and heart swollen. She suffered from this for three months, and neither doctors nor midwives understood the illness. Two Indian women, with whom [Michaela] has a very close friendship, helped the *mulata* Michaela do evil to [María]. One of the Indian women lives in Michaela de Molina's house, and the other visits almost every day; her name is Teresa, and she is from the nearby town of San Cristóbal el Bajo. Teresa is known to be a sorcerer,[16] and [María] has heard it said that the Indian Teresa killed a *mulata* woman with *hechizos* and was imprisoned in the public jail of this city. María de la Candelaria also presumes that the Indian woman, who lives in [Michaela's] house, is from the town of Amatitlán and is named Gerónima García, also helped Michaela. This witness said that she had a fight with [Gerónima]

because she "carried on"[17] with a married Indian man whose wife is also a servant, with [María], in the house of doña Juana González. The Indian Gerónima later fled after the *justicia* (judicial officials) arrested the *mulata* Michaela de Molina and the Indian Teresa on the suspicion that they had done evil to the witness.

[María de la Candelaria] was asked with what *maleficios* (spells) or effects [Michaela, Teresa, and Gerónima] had experimented. She said that fifteen days ago, her mistress had sent her on an errand. She began to feel faint, and then suddenly she expelled blood from her mouth and nostrils; she was brought back to her house discharging blood. First she expelled through her mouth a lump of rags tied with string. Then she expelled through her mouth two *jicaras* (cups) of coal in the presence of her mistress doña Juana González and Father Mathias Lobo de Utilla, a secular priest.[18] Later, in the presence of the priest of Nuestra Señora de los Remedios,[19] don Francisco de Pontaza, the secular priest don Juan de Moncada, and her mistress, she expelled from her mouth another large lump of blue rags, inside of which was a large lock of hair; and then immediately three times she vomited from her mouth a huge amount of *zacate* (hay) and a small ball of soap. And from the Sunday of the feast of Corpus Christi,[20] almost continuously until the following Thursday, she expelled blood and many locks of hair through her nostrils. And finally, at the same time that a stone hit the window of the house of this witness, she expelled from her mouth many pieces of stone, of the same type that had been thrown [at her window], some large and others small. And on that occasion the *alcalde ordinario* of this city, Captain don Diego de Quiroga, was in her room, as was a royal notary.

[María de la Candelaria] was asked if she had any more suspicions that the *mulata* Michaela had done evil to her.

[María de la Candelaria] said yes, because after she began to feel the effects of the *maleficio*, which she attributed to her enemy Michaela, [Michaela] went to the house of doña Nicolasa González, the sister of her mistress, to apologize. [Michaela] said that she hadn't done the *maleficio* but that the Indian woman Teresa from the town of San Cristóbal el Bajo had done it. Teresa was angry with [María] for having had an illicit relationship[21] with her son-in-law, Pablo Vallejo, *vecino* of the town of Santa Isabel, located close to the city. And this witness says that it is true that she had an illicit relationship with Pablo Vallejo, the son-in-law of the Indian Teresa, but it happened after the three months that she was in bed so ill after having given birth. [María] said that the *mulata* Michaela had also apologized to an Indian named Thomasa[22] and said that the Indian Gerónima García caused the Indian Thomasa to get divorced [and] she turned into a bird,[23] and that Juana de Monasterios (alias la Chunchu[24]) told her this. And [María] presumes that Michaela, together with the two Indian women, had done the evil to her that caused her to suffer. All three wished her evil, and she was not on good terms with them. And on one occasion, in the countryside, Michaela had wanted her to take off her clothes; [María] told a tall man about this, someone she didn't recognize as it was nearly nighttime.

And this is the truth by the oath made. And having it read, [María de la Candelaria] said that it is well written, and that she did not give [her testimony] out of hate but only to discharge her conscience. She promised to keep the [testimony] secret. And not knowing how to write, she did not sign [the document], and the commissioner signed it for her.

> Dr. don Joseph de Baños y Sotomayor
> Before me, don Miguel de Carranza y
> Córdova, notary of the Holy Office

13.3 Testimony of Doña Juana González

In the city of [Santiago de] Guatemala, on July 2, 1696, in the afternoon, before Dr. don Joseph de Baños y Sotomayor, dean of the cathedral of this city, etc., there appeared, having been called and sworn to tell the truth, a Spanish woman named doña Juana González, who is a member of the Third Order of Saint Francis, is a *vecina* of this city, and is more than fifty years old.

[Doña Juana González] was asked if she knows or presumes the reason that she has been called before this Holy Tribunal of the Inquisition.

She said she presumes it is to learn from her about her Indian servant named María de la Candelaria, who is in bed doing very poorly, expelling foul things through her mouth and nose, which she presumes is from the *hechizo* done by her *mulata* neighbor named Michaela de Molina, who sells candies. The reason that she presumes this is because her servant, María de la Candelaria, had some fights with [Michaela], and not with anyone else. The reason the two fought was because Michaela de Molina became entangled with her servant [María de la Candelaria] over an Indian man from the town of Santa Isabel named Pablo Vallejo. And when this witness heard this news, she punished her servant. She presumes that María de la Candelaria did not want to continue with the illicit relationship with Pablo Vallejo. [Michaela de Molina] did evil to [María] because one night, while her servant was going by [Michaela's] door, the *mulata* provoked her so much that [María] attacked her. At this [point] a neighbor left [her house], arguing with the *mulata*, and then told this witness [what was happening]. [Doña Juana] left [her house] with a stick in search of the *mulata*, who had fled. A few days later her servant gave birth, and became ill with shortness of breath, fright, and shock, and also her heart and belly swelled up from which she suffered for three months.

[Doña Juana] was asked if she knew if Michaela de Molina knew how to cast spells and what basis she had to presume that she, and not another, had done evil to her servant, other than what she has already declared.

[Doña Juana] said that even though she had never heard that the *mulata* had used spells, she based [her belief on the fact] that Michaela de Molina has very intimate friendships with two Indian women, one named Gerónima García from the town of Amatitlán, who lived most of the time with Michaela de Molina in her house, and who, immediately after the last time María de la Candelaria became ill, fled who knows where. And the other is called Teresa, from the town of San Cristóbal el Bajo; she is the mother-in-law of Pablo Vallejo, with whom [doña Juana's] servant had an illicit relationship. The Indian Teresa is publicly known to be a *bruja* (witch), and she was held in the public jail of this city for two years for having killed a woman with spells. After two years she pretended to be very sick, and because of this she left the jail and escaped. Similarly, a young woman named Lorenza la Ginesa[25] was living on the same street as this witness; [Lorenza] lived with Pablo Vallejo, son-in-law of Teresa, [and] she became ill from nausea and fatigue under the same circumstances as María de la Candelaria. This witness saw [Lorenza] arise from her bed like a crazy woman, ripping the bed's canopy into pieces . . . ,[26] expelling blood from her mouth and nostrils, and with the swelling of her chest she tore at it with her hands as if she wanted to pull something out of it. And it is public knowledge that the Indian Teresa cast a spell on her, and that she died from it. This is the same way that her servant suffers. With the close friendship that the Indian woman has with the *mulata* Michaela she does not leave [Michaela's] house. [Michaela] is the one that María de la Candelaria has fought with, so [doña Juana] presumes that Michaela de Molina got help from the Indian women to do evil to her servant. And likewise, [doña Juana] presumes that it was [Michaela] because after María de la Candelaria began to expel these foul things, the *mulata* went to the house of her sister, doña Nicolasa González to apologize, saying that it wasn't her who had done evil to María de la Candelaria, it was the Indian Teresa. As well, María de la Candelaria told this witness how on one occasion she had informed a man she didn't know how the *mulata* Michaela de Molina had wanted her to take off her clothes publicly after climbing to the top of the Alameda fountain; [María] said that [doña Juana] should watch out for [be careful of] [Michaela], and that because of the entreaties of the men who were there with the *mulata*, she hadn't taken off her clothes.[27]

And [doña Juana] was asked how long her servant suffered, and what things she expelled.

[Doña Juana] said that for two years María has suffered from fainting spells so bad that it seemed she would die, with blood in her mouth and nostrils. [María] began to suffer more after her fight with the *mulata* Michaela last October, when she became ill with nausea and fatigue after she gave birth, which she has already described. And recently, about fifteen days ago, [doña Juana] sent [María de la Candelaria] out to sell bread, and they brought her back to the house very ill, expelling much blood from her mouth and nostrils. [María] told this witness how she had lost her senses at a house during a fainting spell. [Doña Juana] called a doctor to cure her, but neither the doctor nor the midwives understood the attack. For some days she was sick to her stomach, and while doña Juana held [María] in her arms, her servant expelled a bundle made of rags tied with string. On another occasion, in her presence and that of the secular priest Father Mathias Lobo de Utilla, María de la Candelaria expelled two *jicaras* of charcoal from her mouth. And later, in the presence of the priest [Lobo de Utilla], the priest of Los Remedios, don Francisco de Pontaza, the secular priest don Juan de Moncada, and the witness, María de la Candelaria expelled from her mouth another bundle made of a blue rag with a lock of hair, and three times she expelled much *zacate* from her mouth and a small ball of soap. And while Captain don Diego de Quiroga, the *alcalde ordinario* of this city, and the royal notary, whose name [doña Juana] does not remember, were in [María's] bedroom, they heard the bang of a stone that had been thrown at the bedroom window facing the street. After the stone was picked up and examined by everyone in the house, María de la Candelaria began to expel many large and small pieces of the same rock from her mouth. And the royal notary told the *alcalde* to come look at what the sick woman expelled, but the *alcalde* said it wasn't necessary, but they showed it to him anyway. And this witness says that from the Sunday of the feast of Corpus Christi until Thursday, [María] expelled a large quantity of locks of hair from her left nostril.

And having read [the testimony], [doña Juana] said that it was well written and that she didn't give it out of hate but only to discharge her conscience. And she promised to keep [her testimony] secret. Because she didn't know how to sign her name, [the testimony] was signed for her by the commissioner.

> Dr. don Joseph de Baños y Sotomayor
> Before me, don Miguel de Carranza y
> Córdova, notary of the Holy Office

13.4 Testimony of Doña Rafaela González

In the city of [Santiago de] Guatemala, July 3, 1696, in the afternoon, before Dr. don Joseph de Baños y Sotomayor, dean of the cathedral of this city, etc., there appeared after being called, a Spanish woman named doña Rafaela Gonzalez, who swore to tell the truth. She is a *doncella* (maiden), the natural daughter of doña Josepha González, in whose domain she lives; she is a *vecina* of this city and more than eighteen years of age.

[Doña Rafaela] was asked if she knows or presumes why she has been called before the Holy Office of the Inquisition.

She said that she presumes it is to know what happened with a servant of her aunt, doña Juana González, and the things that [María de la Candelaria] had expelled from her mouth and nostrils, which she presumes to be from a spell that a *mulata* named Michaela de Molina, who sells candies, had cast on the servant María de la Candelaria because she had a fight with the *mulata*. And this witness knew about this because she was often present in the house of her aunt, doña Juana González. There she heard about how María de la Candelaria had fought over a long period of time with the *mulata* in the countryside, and that [she][28] beat her. And even though [doña Rafaela] saw afterwards that María de la Candelaria suffered from long fainting spells, and from blood in her mouth and nostrils, she didn't have . . .[29] from which she could start similar accidents.[30] Also, [doña Rafaela] knew that about seven months later María de la Candelaria had fought one night with the *mulata* Michaela de Molina, and that a neighbor named María Antonia found them. This happened right about the time that María de la Candelaria was to give birth. After [María de la Candelaria] gave birth, she became ill from fright and fatigues, and she suffered for three months. And again, about fifteen days ago, more or less, she knew that they brought María de la Candelaria to her aunt's house very ill, expelling blood from her mouth and nostrils. After, this witness saw that [María] begin to expel some things from her mouth, such as a blue bundle. [Doña Rafaela] went to the house of her aunt, doña Juana González, to help, and she saw for the first time that María de la Candelaria had much nausea; she then expelled from her mouth a bundle wrapped in a white rag and tied with string made from century plant fiber. Tied to the bundle was a small corn husk. Captain don Diego de Quiroga, the *alcalde ordinario* of this city, and don Diego de Arguello, a royal notary, went to her aunt's house and were shown the two bundles that the servant expelled. The notary untied both of them, and inside of the bundles this witness saw that he found a bit of *cebo* that was in a husk similar to that of the *chicozapote* seed, a tangle of hairs around a tobacco cigar, a small piece of rose-colored taffeta from Granada, a black ribbon, purple thread, a human tooth, half a clove of garlic, a piece of cacao tied with thread, and a small bit of charcoal. And on this occasion the witness and the others were in the drawing room, and they heard a rock that was thrown with great force at the window in the bedroom of the sick woman. This witness went to see what it was, and found a large stone that appeared to be a clod of burned earth, and she showed it to the *alcalde* and notary. Right after, María de la Candelaria began to

Figure 8   An indigenous woman, who works as a servant in a Spanish household, carries water from the community fountain. She is wearing a *huipil*. (Mexico, early nineteenth century) (Linati [1828] 1956, plate 26).

have great nausea and she expelled from her mouth an enormous quantity of rocks, large and small, of the same type that was thrown at her bedroom window. [Doña Rafaela] also showed them to the *alcalde* and notary, and she told the *alcalde*, don Diego de Quiroga, to come and watch the sick woman expel rocks, but he responded that it was not necessary. Later, on a different occasion, [doña Rafaela] saw [María de la Candelaria] three times expel charcoal in pieces, as if it had been ground up. Judging that [María] was dying and had lost her senses, they asked for the *santo oleo* (holy oil).[31] The priest, don Francisco de Pontaza, from the church of Los Remedios, came and he anointed and absolved her according to the [Papal] Bull. And because the priest saw the things she expelled, he did not dare give her the sacrament. And after, this witness saw [María] expel crushed *zacate* from her mouth two or three times, and a small ball of soap and a chile in a tangle of thread. One of the times that [María] expelled charcoal from her mouth was the Thursday of the feast of Corpus Christi, at about four in the afternoon, and when this witness was at the window in the bedroom of the sick woman looking out into the street. She didn't see anyone. This witness then felt a piece of charcoal hit her on the shoulders, and another fell to the floor. Also, during this time this witness saw María de la Candelaria expel many balls of paper and rags from her nostrils, and some pieces of *huipil*. The last two balls her aunt doña Juana sent to [Dr. don Joseph de Baños y Sotomayor]. During many of these incidents the priest don Francisco de Pontaza, Father Mathias Lobo de Utilla, and the priest don Juan de Moncada were present, as was Antonio García, constable, María Manuela, *mulata*, and so many others, but with the fright caused by the incidents, she can not remember who they were.

And [doña Rafaela] was asked if she knew if María de la Candelaria had enmity with another person, or if the *mulata* Michaela de Molina knew about *hechizos* and used them, or if she consulted others to use them.

[Doña Rafaela] said she did not know nor had she heard it said that María de la Candelaria was enemies with another person other than the *mulata* Michaela de Molina [nor] if she uses or knows how to use *hechizos*. She has only heard that she [Michaela] has a close friendship with an Indian woman from the town of San Cristóbal named Teresa, and she has also heard that [Teresa] is a witch. And she has [a close friendship] with another Indian woman from Amatitlán named Gerónima, who fled when María de la Candelaria began to expel things, as she has already declared. And also, immediately after [María began to expel things], the *mulata* Michaela de Molina went to the house of her aunt doña Nicolasa González to apologize, saying that it wasn't she who had done evil to María de la Candelaria, but the Indian Teresa.

And this is the truth by the oath given, and being read [the testimony] [doña Rafaela] said that it was well written, and that she didn't give it out of hate, but only to discharge her conscience. She promised to guard the secret [of her testimony]. Because she doesn't know how to sign her name the commissioner signed [the testimony] for her.

> Dr. don Joseph de Baños y Sotomayor
> Before me don Miguel de Carranza y
> Córdova, notary of the Holy Office

NOTES

ACKNOWLEDGMENTS   This chapter is based on archival research carried out with the aid of an Edward Turville Dissertation Research Fellowship from the Department of History at the University of Arizona. I would like to thank Kevin Gosner, Christopher Lutz, B. J. Barickman, and Geoffrey Spurling.

1. Ernesto Chinchilla Aguilar, *La Inquisición en Guatemala* (Guatemala, 1953), 25, 33.
2. Before this date Indians were tried by the Inquisition; after the king's decree, Spanish officials created the *proviserato*, which functioned as an alternative to the Inquisition, to administer Indian religious orthodoxy.
3. In this essay, I follow the colonial racial-ethnic designations used to describe those who appear in Inquisition cases, such as "Indian" (*yndio/a*); "Spaniard" (*español/a*); and "Black" (*negro/a*). "*Mestizo/a*" was used to refer to a person of mixed Spanish and Indian parentage. In Central America, "*Mulato/a*" referred to a person of mixed parentage, part African and part Spanish and/or Indian. For more on racial/ethnic designations used in colonial Guatemala, see W. George Lovell and Christopher H. Lutz, eds., *Demography and Empire: A Guide to the Population History of Spanish Central America, 1500–1821* (Boulder and San Francisco: Westview Press, 1995).
4. Teresa's surname is not given in the documents.
5. The Audiencia of Guatemala formed part of New Spain, and roughly comprised present-day Chiapas, Guatemala (except the Petén), El Salvador, Honduras, Nicaragua, and Costa Rica.
6. Christopher H. Lutz, *Santiago de Guatemala, 1541–1773: City, Caste, and the Colonial Experience* (Norman, Okla.: University of Oklahoma Press, 1994), 110. *Gente ordinaria* was a term meaning "common people," and was used in parish registries to classify everyone except Spaniards and tributary Indians.
7. I have not included translations of the formal ratifications of the women's testimonies nor the final letter convicting Michaela de Molina because of space constraints and because the sections do not contain much new information.
8. Some scholars who have studied the Inquistion in New Spain have argued that colonial authorities did not take the use of love magic and sorcery among Indians, Africans, Spaniards, and *castas* very seriously. For example, in her pioneering work on love magic and witchcraft in late colonial Mexico, Ruth Behar stresses the skepticism of Inquisition authorities with regards to claims of women's witchcraft, pointing to the leniency of punishments and the tendency of women to make self-denunciations ("Sexual Witchcraft, Colonialism, and Women's Powers: Views from the Mexican Inquisition," Asunción Lavrin, ed., *Sexuality and Marriage in Colonial Latin America* [Lincoln, Neb.: University of Nebraska Press, 1989], 178–206, and "Sex, Sin, Witchcraft, and the Devil in Late-Colonial Mexico," *American Ethnologist* 14 [1987], 35–55). This case, and other evidence from seventeenth- and eighteenth-century Guatemalan Inquisition records, however, suggest that official attitudes toward women's love magic and sorcery in New Spain varied temporally and regionally. See Martha Few, "*Mujeres de Mal Vivir*: Gender, Religion, and the Politics of Power in Colonial Guatemala, 1650–1750," Ph.D. dissertation, University of Arizona, 1997.
9. This document comes from the Archivo General de la Nación (Mexico), Inquisición, vol. 689, exp. 7, fs. 189–201v.
10. Ecclesiastical official named by the Inquisition tribunal to censure books.
11. Citizen, or in some cases just resident, of a particular municipality. In many colonial contexts *vecino(a)* was restricted only to those who could vote for and hold municipal office. Here, though, the term is used more loosely, applied to women as well as men, and to Indians and *castas* as well as Spaniards.
12. The court records repeat all of Baños y Sotomayor's official titles, hereafter substituted with "etc."
13. The attribution of *vecina* is ambiguous here, as it could refer to either María de la Candelaria or to doña Juana González.
14. "y el primero fue por (. . .) ocasionado disgusto con su ama doña Juana Gonsález por haverla (. . .) como la dha decl. avía hecha una entrada en una fiesta (. . .) de la Cruz el año pasado de 94." The translation is somewhat difficult here as a number of words are unreadable in

the text. The testimony appears to refer to a fight between the two women during the fiesta celebrating the *Día de Santa Cruz* (Day of the Holy Cross). Cutting and pulling hair were both insulting and degrading to women in colonial society; they signified attacks on one's personal honor. See Sonya Lipsett-Rivera, "*De Obra y Palabra*: Patterns of Insults in Mexico, 1750–1856," *The Americas* 54(4) (1998), 511–39.

15. "que se venían a los ma(. . .), lo qual embarazó una vecina." The meaning of this section is ambiguous; as part of one word is illegible, it is difficult to offer a more precise translation.

16. "hechicera" in the original.

17. The phrase used is "traía inquieto," which literally translates into "caused a disturbance or worry"; it suggests that the two were having an illicit relationship. Later references to their relationship confirm this interpretation.

18. The secular clergy mainly administered among Spanish colonists, while the regular clergy worked to convert and administer indigenous groups. The regular orders active in the conversion of indigenous groups in Guatemala were the Franciscans, Dominicans, and the Mercedarians.

19. Nuestra Señora de los Remedios, or Our Lady of Sorrows, was the parish church of Los Remedios in Santiago de Guatemala.

20. "infraoctova de Corpus" in the document. The feast of Corpus Christi celebrates the body and blood of Jesus Christ, highlighting the redemptive effects of the sacrament. Richard P. McBrien, ed., *The Harper Collins Encyclopedia of Catholicism* (New York: Harper Collins Publishers, 1995), 369.

21. "mal amistado" in the original.

22. Thomasa must be a neighbor or friend of María de la Candelaria.

23. "Y tambien dice se disculpa la dha mulata Michaela embiando a decir a casa desta decl a una yndia llamada Thomasa que la Yndia Gerónima García descasava a la dha Yndia Thomasa, se volbiá pájaro, y que se (. . .) dicho Juana de Monasterios (alias la Chunchu)." This is a convoluted section of the document that makes translation difficult. *Volver pájaro* could be a colloquial expression; however, I have chosen to translate "se volbiá pájaro" as "she turned into a bird." Guatemalan Inquisition and criminal records show that inhabitants of late seventeenth-century Guatemala believed that certain community members, especially Indians and women, had the power to transform their own bodies and the bodies of others into animals and birds through the practice of sorcery and witchcraft. See Martha Few, "Illness Accusations and the Cultural Politics of Power in Colonial Santiago de Guatemala, 1650–1720," Working Paper, International Seminar on the History of the Atlantic World, Harvard University, August 1998. Kay Warren has noted that in contemporary Kaqchikel Maya accounts, *rajav a'a*, or shape-shifters, frequently women, were a gendered metaphor for betrayal of the community during the political violence in Guatemala in the 1970s and 1980s. See her essay "Interpreting *La Violencia* in Guatemala: Shapes of Maya Silence and Resistance," in Kay B. Warren, ed., *The Violence Within: Cultural and Political Opposition in Divided Nations* (Boulder and San Francisco: Westview Press, 1993).

24. The meaning of her alias is unclear. In pre-Columbian and colonial Peru, *chunchu* was a pejorative term (essentially meaning savage) that the Inkas and other Andean agropastoralists used for the forest peoples of the Amazon. This usage may have spread to colonial Central America.

25. La Ginesa is her alias or nickname; its meaning is unclear.

26. This is unreadable in the document.

27. Unfortunately, there is no other contextual information in the document that might help in interpreting the references to Michaela de Molina wanting María de la Candelaria to take off her clothes.

28. It is unclear if María beat Michaela or vice versa.

29. This is unreadable in the document.

30. The meaning of this is unclear. The original reads "pero que no tubo (ma . . .) de que se podrian originar semejantes accidentes."

31. *Santo oleo* is holy oil used for anointing the sick and the dying; the priest had probably been called to administer the last rites. This oil was generally consecrated by a bishop on Holy Thursday, but could be blessed by a priest in an emergency. McBrien, *The Encyclopedia of Catholicism*, 931.

DOCUMENT THEMES

African/Afro-Latin American Peoples; Crime; Cultural Contact/Ethnogenesis/
Resistance; Ethnicity; European-Mestizo Peoples; Gender; Gossip and
Communication; Illness/Disease/Injury/Medicine; Indigenous Peoples;
Inquisition; Insults; Popular Culture; Race; Religion; Sexuality; Town Life;
Violence; Witchcraft; Women.

SUGGESTIONS FOR FURTHER READING

Behar 1991.
Cope 1994.
Farriss 1984.
Few 1995.
Gutiérrez 1991.
Lutz 1994.
Perry and Cruz 1991.
Silverblatt 1987.

CHAPTER
14

Dance of the People: The Chuchumbé
(Mexico, 1766)

Sergio Rivera Ayala

INTRODUCTION

The year 1766 was an important one in Mexico because it represented a turning point in New Spain's political and social life. In February of that year, Mexico City's *cabildo* complained to the Crown about the despotic and disrespectful measures that the new inspector general of the troops, Juan de Villalba, was using when he levied militia forces. According to the creole aldermen, Villalba had no consideration for the prerogatives of the elite in grouping them with commoners in militia units. Even worse, he made no attempt to appoint them to positions in the ranks of the officers in the new militia. The inspector general's attitude, which reflected the Spanish Crown's new policies in all their possessions, exacerbated the anger of New Spain's society particularly because it reminded them of their subordinate position in a time when creole national consciousness was building momentum.

A second event in 1766 can also be linked to the Spanish Crown's new policies. In August the Inquisition began to investigate a denunciation made by fray Nicolás de Montero of the Mercedarian Order. Fray Nicolás reported that in the streets of Veracruz "*mulatos* and people of mixed race . . . soldiers, sailors and other riffraff" practiced a dance called "el chuchumbé" in which the dancers (male and female) often touched each other in provocative ways, even "rubbing belly to belly." The chuchumbé, according to the denunciation, was characterized as "lewd and provocative of lasciviousness, causing grave ruin and scandal to the souls of Christendom and in prejudice to the conscience . . . and offense to edification and good customs." Because those who denounced these songs only reported the words, the music is lost to us. However, the descriptions of the dance together with the lyrics provide a good example of the richness of Mexico's popular culture of that period.

These two separate incidents—with no apparent connection—reflected the new policies implemented by Spain in its quest to establish tighter control of its colonies.[1] The new ideologues of colonial governance, men of the Enlightenment, believed that the state should play the leading role in constructing rational and productive societies. Disorderly cities, with the lower classes in control of the streets, were incompatible with that view.[2] For that reason, it was necessary to put an end to any kind of activity that was not considered proper to the new Enlightenment mentality. Thus, a dispute for the public space took place between the authorities and the people.

For the people of Veracruz, the inspector general of the troops, Juan de Villalba, appears precisely as the tool of disciplinary power. In some of the verses of the couplets of the chuchumbé, at least as perceived by the lower classes, Villalba embodied the policies of colonial government in Mexico.

The Holy Office of the Inquisition, since its establishment in 1571, had served as a coercive instrument of the Crown and the Church to preserve the unity of the Catholic faith against heresy. Thus, state and church were very much connected. And as part of these institutions, the Mexican Inquisition naturally tried to silence *anyone* who challenged the religious foundations of the Spanish monarchy during a period that marked the beginning of the end of colonial structures in Spanish America. In the second half of the eighteenth century, the Holy Office paid particular attention to numerous complaints from people who felt that colonial Mexicans were abandoning the precepts of the Catholic Church and moving more towards disorder and diversion.[3] Ironically, the same people who were shocked by popular diversions such as the chuchumbé ensured that a record of them survived in documents such as the one before us here.

The words of the chuchumbé show the worldview of the lower classes: a mixture of religiosity and earthly pleasure, a jubilation of life and death, a celebration of eroticism and violence, all surrounded by popular laughter. Readers will find, then, that the chuchumbé provides us with glimpses of lower class mentalities and preoccupations, as well as some sense of the richness of popular speech in which words have different meanings depending on the context. Let us examine the chuchumbé as it was preserved in the files of the Inquisition.

THE DOCUMENT

El Chuchumbé

A Mercedarian friar[4]
stands at the corner
lifting his robes
showing[5] the chuchumbé.[6]

Whether you are ready,
or not,
I have to blow on your chuchumbé.

That old devout woman
who comes and goes to San Francisco
takes the father, gives the father,[7]
and he is the father of her children.

From my chuchumbé,
of my *cundaval*,[8]
get ready,
I am going to provide for you.

The demoness of the *china*[9]
from the Merced neighborhood,
and how he moved
giving her the chuchumbé.

Whether you are ready,
or not,
I have to blow on your chuchumbé.

Figure 9   Men who made up part of the civil guard of Alvarado, a port located just south of Veracruz. It was in this region that the chuchumbé was particularly popular (Linati [1828] 1956, plate 33).

You are Marta the pious[10]
as for your charity,
no pilgrim leaves
unaided by you.

If Your Worship wishes,[11]
I would send you
the junk of *verinduaga*[12]

On the corner there are knifings
Dear God, what will become of me?
They kill each other
for what I have here.

If Your Worship does not wish
to come[13] with me,
señor Villalba[14] will punish you.

Furious animal a frog,
a light lizard,
and braver is the cunt
that blows on this dick.[15]

If Your Worship does not want
to come with me,
señor Villalba will punish you.

And if you do not come willingly,
señor Villalba will give you the prize.[16]

I married a soldier,
promoted to squadron corporal,
and every night His Worship
wants to mount the guard.[17]

Do you know Your Worship that,
Do you know Yo' Worship that,
You are, Your Worship, called
cantor of the mass.[18]

My husband went to the port
to mock[19] me;
he has no choice but to return
for what he left here.

Whether you are ready,
or not,
I will provide you with my
chuchumbé.

And if I do not provide,
I will provide you[20]
with what hangs from my
chuchumbé.

What can a friar give you
even with all his love?
A few shreds of tobacco
and a prayer when you die.

The chuchumbé of the *doncellas*,
they with me, and I with them.

The man standing on the corner
he who supports me,
he who pays my rent
and he who clothes me.

And for the relief of wives
to live nude and licentiously.

Death was without clothes
seated at a desk,
and his mother told him
aren't you cold, devil?

Come with me,
come with me,
I am a soldier of the yellows.[21]

Death passed by here,
with his needle and his apron,
asking at every house,
are there old clothes to mend?

Does Your Worship know that,
Does Your Worship know that
they have called Your Worship
a Lenten whore?

Death passed by here
giving me the evil eye,
and singing I said to her:
don't hurry, old bag!

If Your Worship wishes,
and will not get angry,
carry the cage that will be yours.

Death was without clothes
seated on a stool,
on one side he had *pulque*[22]
and on the other *aguardiente*.[23]

Does Your Worship know that,
Does Your Worship know that,
that I will enlist
and I will take Your Worship.

When my mother gave birth to me,
it was in a belltower,
when the midwife came
they found me ringing the bells.[24]

Ring and ring
they call Your Worship.
I will tell you if you don't get mad.
When my husband left me
there was nothing to eat,

and so rather I looked for it
dancing the chuchumbé.

Does Your Worship know that,
Does Your Worship know that,
they are calling Your Worship
ass wagger.[25]

My husband has died,
He is with God in His heaven
and I hope He holds him tightly
because I never want him to come back.

Chuchumbé of my *cundaval*,
get ready, so I will
provide you,
so if I don't provide, I will supply,
with what is hanging from my
chuchumbé.

The Jesuit's demon,
with such a big hat,
used a whip
as big as his father.

If Your Worship wants,
and will not get mad,
you will be called *fornicadorita*.[26]

NOTES

1. Also, one year later, in 1767, the Spanish Crown expelled the Jesuit Order from all their territories.
2. See Pedro Viqueira Albán, *¿Relajados o reprimidos? Diversiones públicas y vida social en la ciudad de México durante el Siglo de las Luces* (México: Fondo de Cultura Econoómica, 1987), p. 232 (forthcoming in an English translation *as The Decline of Propriety: Public Diversions in Eighteenth-Century Mexico City* (Wilmington: Scholarly Resources).
3. Viqueira makes this point throughout his book.
4. Note the Mercedarian friar who appears on a street corner in this first couplet anticipates a reference to the same neighborhood—"the Merced neighborhood"—below. It is of interest that a friar of the Mercederian order denounced the chuchumbé to the Holy Office.
5. The verb in Spanish is "enseñar," which means "to show" but also can be "to teach."
6. Throughout the text the word "chuchumbe" refers to the penis.
7. In this case, father means not only a priest but also a biological father.
8. The meaning of this word is unknown.
9. In this instance, *china* does not refer to nationality. It means "a girl of the people who used to live serving no one and with a kind of liberty at the expense of a husband or a lover or by her own industry. She was a *mestiza* and was also distinguished for her cleanliness and beauty." Francisco J. Santamaría, *Diccionario de mejicanismos* (Mexico City: Editorial Porrúa, 1959), p. 391.
10. Here, "Marta la piadosa" could be a reference to a comedy of the same name by the famous seventeenth-century Spanish playwright Tirso de Molina. In this play Tirso satirizes religious hypocrisy, also a theme of this particular couplet. More immediately, perhaps, it conjures up the person and character of Saint Martha, sister of Lazarus and Mary of Bethany. Martha provided Jesus with hospitality and has become the patron saint of hotelkeepers. In the chuchumbé, however, such hospitality is more related to sexual favors for special "pilgrims."

11. Here and elsewhere note that the gender of the speaker can change.
12. The reference here is to Captain Francisco Berinduaga, an officer who served under Juan de Villalba.
13. In Spanish the verb "to come" (*venir*) has the same sexual connotations as in English.
14. Señor Villalba, as we noted in the introduction, is none other than the new inspector general of the troops, Juan de Villalba.
15. The Spanish verb *soplar* (to blow) carries a sexual connotation similar to "blow" in English. In this context, however, the *papo* (cunt) gives the blow to the *pija* (dick), which means sexual intercourse rather than fellatio or a "blow job."
16. The comment is meant to mock Villalba's tactics.
17. The Spanish verb *montar* (to mount) can have the same sexual connotation as in English.
18. Editors' note: The cantor was a man appointed by, and thus a dependent of, the parish priest. He "assisted the priest in celebrating mass and led the choir in the sung masses" (William B. Taylor, *Magistrates of the Sacred: Priests and Parishioners in Eighteenth-Century Mexico* [Stanford: Stanford University Press, 1996], 333). The position of cantor brought both income and prestige.
19. The verb in Spanish is *burlar*, which means "to mock," but it can also mean "to be unfaithful to," "to seduce," or "to take the virginity of." The port refers to Veracruz.
20. Depending on the context "aviar," which I have translated as "provide," can also mean "prepare" or "supply."
21. I do not know what "soldier of the yellows" refers to. It may refer to a regimental insignia.
22. A traditional Mexican alcoholic drink that is made from the fermented sap of the maguey cactus.
23. Cane brandy.
24. "Ringing the bells," *repicando las campanas*, is a double entendre that can also refer to sexual intercourse.
25. The term "ass wagger" refers to the movement of the sexual act, as well to a woman who, as she walks, accentuates the movement of her hips.
26. Editors' note: The Spanish word "fornicador" means fornicator. The ending "ita" in Spanish often signifies "little" or a sense of endearment. The ending also implies a reference to a woman rather than a man. Readers might want to speculate, then, on how the term applies to the person referred to as Your Worship.

Document Themes

European-Mestizo Peoples; Gender; Governance, Colonial; Insults; Popular Culture; Sexuality; Town Life.

Suggestions for Further Reading

Brading 1991.
González Casanova 1986.
Pérez-Marchand 1945.
Perry and Cruz 1991.
Rivera Ayala 1994.
Saldivar 1980.
Viqueira Albán 1987.

C H A P T E R
15

Drinking, Gambling, and Death on a Colonial Hacienda
(Quito, 1768)

Ann Twinam

INTRODUCTION

In February 1769, fifty-six-year-old don Joseph de Grijalva y Recalde was convicted of murdering his third wife, thirty-two-year-old doña María Freyre. Her death occurred after a night of drinking and partying that took place on Sunday, November 13, 1768, on their hacienda San Joseph, located outside the town of Urcuqui, in the jurisdiction of Otavalo, north of Quito. Don Joseph's wealth and prominence made this the Ecuadorian "crime of the century," and it remains a fascinating case even today, given the ambiguity over whether he actually committed the crime.

At the time, ninety-three witnesses provided almost a thousand pages of testimony. They recounted incidents before the fateful party, detailed the twenty-four hours before and after doña María's demise, traced don Joseph's flight and capture six months later, and told of his imprisonment and trial in Quito. Don Joseph, his immediate family, friends, servants, and slaves provided depositions, as did hostile witnesses and officials who investigated the case.[1] Their testimonies underscore how murder can be a "time-freezer," for those involved in such a traumatic event vividly remembered details of daily life and daily interaction usually lost to historians, but that were then preserved in court records.[2]

Here we have space for only a selection of testimony from this large document that contains telling and sometimes surprising insights concerning gendered, hierarchical, and ethnic interactions on a late eighteenth-century Ecuadorian hacienda.[3] The devil here is definitely in the details as "microbursts" of testimony reveal relationships between husband and wife, father and son, and between members of this elite family and their mulatto and slave servants and Indian workers. Additionally, readers can find rare glimpses of popular pastimes including walking, card-playing, and drinking.

Not only does this document provide insights concerning life on a late eighteenth-century Ecuadorian hacienda; it also raises a question concerning a death: "Did don Joseph murder his wife?" Any judgment on this issue must assess the reliability of witness testimony. For example, should the depositions of don Joseph's relatives and dependants be discounted because they are slanted in his favor? How much evidence is circumstantial? How much is hearsay? Can an exact chronology of events be constructed? Did testimony change over time, and if so, why? Could witnesses who were so drunk plausibly remember what happened?

Much like the classic Japanese murder film *Rashomon*, important evidence in the case unfolds through the differences between witnesses' perceptions and subsequent testimony concerning the same events. Each observer has only part of the picture; sometimes witnesses reveal more than they may have realized. Only by tracing the movements of witnesses and putting their stories together does the broader outline of events begin to emerge. Since the usual procedure was for respondents to answer a list of questions prepared by the state or by the defense, they often parroted the content of the interrogatory in the affirmative. Sometimes, however, their own uncoached voices emerge; readers should watch for these moments. The first selections provide a narrative of the events on that fatal Sunday and Monday followed by a selection of testimony on key topics, final "confessions," the judgment, and a modern postscript from an expert witness.

The Cast of Characters

The Family

- **don Joseph de Grijalva y Recalde**: *hacendado*, husband of the deceased, his third wife doña María Freyre, accused of murdering her
- **doña María Freyre**: wife of don Joseph, known familiarly as Marica, mysteriously deceased
- **don Mariano Grijalva**: the second son of don Joseph
- **doña Manuela Lomas**: the wife of don Mariano, daughter-in-law of don Joseph
- **don Antonio de Grijalva**: the nine-year-old son of don Mariano and doña Manuela, grandson of don Joseph
- **doña María Laso**: an earlier deceased wife of don Joseph

Relatives

- **Dr. don Joseph Osejo**: a relative of don Joseph, priest, chaplain and administrator on the hacienda
- **don Francisco Osejo**: a cousin of don Joseph
- **don Jasinto Grijalva**: a *mayordomo* of the hacienda
- **don Joseph de Thorres**: a cousin of doña Mariá and an enemy of don Joseph

Servants and Slaves

- **Cathalina Sánches** (*la talona*): servant of Dr. don Joseph Osejo
- **Pascual Polo**: a black slave and harpist

- **Bernadina Mina**: a black slave and servant
- **Juan Benites** (Juanico): a mulatto slave
- **unamed** *negritas* who were servants or slaves

Others

- **Anna Rebelo**: a hacienda resident or neighbor
- **don Antonio Fernández**: a resident of the hacienda
- **Manuel Cárdenas**: a visitor to the hacienda on business
- **don Justo Fraga**: a family friend and business partner of don Joseph
- **Thomas Lomas**: a healer.
- **Rosa Almeyda**: a free *parda*
- **Mariano Unda**: a free *moreno*, helper to local officials
- **Julia Alvarrasín**: the woman who cleaned (scratched) doña María's neck

THE DOCUMENT

15.1 Excerpts from the Testimony of Cathalina Sánches, Alias La Talona (the Nimble)[4]

[Cathalina, about fifty years old, is the servant of priest doctor Joseph de Osejo, adminis-trator of hacienda San Joseph.[5] She gave her sworn statement at hacienda San Joseph, un-der guard, on December 2, 1768.]

She said . . . her occupation has been to knit stockings and caps with cotton thread . . . she has maintained herself in the service of the doctor for sixteen years, more or less, caring for [his] clothes and kitchen. And when the doctor began to administer this hacienda . . . about a year and a month ago, she had to accom-pany him. . . .[6]

Don Joseph arrived [around six A.M.] that Sunday after having spent four days at hacienda San Francisco in the company of don Francisco Osejo, don Justo Fraga, and don Mariano Grijalva. And don Joseph carried a guitar in his hands saying that he had taken it from an Indian to excuse his drunkenness. At which time doña María Freyre and doña Manuela Lomas left [the house], making them welcome and saying they had looked forward to their arrival so they could have the pleasure of listening to some good violin and flute music [and] they entered into the living room (*sala principal*). And then doña María went into her room and returned with some *aguardiente*, and gave it to the musicians. . . . And as don Mariano Grijalva with don Joseph and the others were in the study, they began to drink. . . . [But af-ter a time] . . . don Joseph [said] not to drink [anymore] because we have to hear mass, upon which they stopped and left for the oratory. And after hearing the mass, they had lunch, and after the meal, the men went to the card room to play.

At that time she [Cathalina] entered her room, lay down on the bed, and slept until [doña María and doña Manuela] entered her room. They woke her and invited her to go for a walk. And, although the witness had aching legs, to give pleasure to the señoras she determined to accompany them.[7] And they went to the house and garden of doña Anna Rebelo where they entered and picked some chilies that are called in the Inka language *guascaicho*,[8] and doña María asked to take some, using a piece of muslin that she had her *negrita* carry. And even though the witness told her not to take them because they could do [her] harm, doña María picked two peppers, and taking out the seeds she gave a small piece of the tip to the witness, and having tasted it she found it to be very hot, and therefore did not eat it. And later they went to the house of an Indian woman, and, entering the garden, this witness and the señoras picked some peppers called *chibatillos*. They took a few potatoes from the same garden and returned to this hacienda. And on the road they bought *chochos*, and arrived [at the hacienda] around five thirty in the afternoon. At which time don Joseph left the card room, and, approaching the señoras, said: "*Madamas*, you have walked a lot and diverted yourselves, what do you carry?" And they responded that they brought some peppers and, as he approached the witness, she said she also brought some *chochos*.

[As night arrived] don Joseph, don Mariano, don Antonio Fernández, Manuel Cárdenas, don Jasinto Grijalva, Dr. don Joseph Osejo, and the witness entered the study. And giving the witness the guitar that don Joseph had brought, don Mariano ordered her to play, and applauding the notes of the guitar he told her to sing some songs. So the witness sang [as the men] drank a *punche* they had prepared, and after a short time don Mariano said that the *madamas* should also come to enjoy themselves. . . . And when the señoras entered, the witness saw that they came with boiled eggs, and doña María gave her an egg and doña Manuela half of another, and they happily began (*empesaron con la alegría*) to help themselves to two rounds of the same *punche*. . . . But as [doña María] said that the drink would do her much harm, and that it would be better to drink wine, don Joseph said "No problem" (*en hora buena*) and, taking a flask of wine from the liquor case, he gave it to the señoras, to the witness, and to the rest of the servants.[9] And in the same way, he returned to repeat another time, and he put what remained in the flask on top of the table. . . . And don Jasinto Grijalva who was drunk (*caliente de la cabesa*) overturned the leftover wine into the punch bowl, and [don Joseph], taking the bowl, threw it on top of don Jasinto's head, who then left. . . . And as they were all happy and drunk [don Joseph] took out another flask of wine . . . and they continued drinking. And as the witness was very drunk with the mixture of the liquors, she tried to leave. . . . [but] don Joseph held her by the elbow, pulling her inside [the study]. She sat on the sofa, and as she saw that he was mad, she stayed. And in this way the party continued until doña María, as she was happy (*alegre*) began to sing and dance, and doña Manuela joined her as they continued to drink wine. . . .

At which time don Mariano arrived and said "enough of the harp" and the entertainment stopped. . . . Doña María said now that there is no music let us play the card game, *juego de burro*. To which don Joseph responded, "All right, but it has to be with the condition that the loser has to drink a glass of wine," and the bet was accepted. Doña María began to play, and don Joseph having lost the first hand . . . don Mariano took him and gave him a glass of wine. And the second game doña María lost, and when giving her the corresponding glass of wine she

Figure 10 Musicians and dancers celebrating in the late eighteenth-century Andes (Martínez Compañón [1790] 1936, plate 33).

said: "Son, not so much," and making a gesture with her hand, she toppled the glass, which fell on the ground and broke. And don Joseph became angry, declaring: "Heaven preserve me from women that are so silly, and friends of speaking with their hands." And doña María, to appease him, said, "*Taita*, don't be mad, if it is because of the glass, I have another that I will bring." To which don Joseph responded that it was not because of the glass, because he had plenty in the study. Then don Mariano called the witness to go and order dinner to be brought.

15.2 Excerpts from the Testimony of Don Mariano Grijalva

[Don Mariano, twenty-nine years old, is the son of don Joseph Grijalva. He gave his sworn statement at the Quito public jail to escribano Juan Mateos Lavarredez on July 6, 1769.]

That having stopped playing [cards], doña María wanted to go outside to relieve herself, and since this witness knew that she was very drunk, and because of the risk that she might fall onto the patio . . . he followed in a hurry and after him don Joseph Grijalva, his father. And observing that she had fallen on the ground, these took her in their arms and put her in the room that she had left, leaving her on the sofa covering her with a cape. And she remained sleeping or deprived of her senses, and they left her in the study. . . .

He said that with the excess of drink and the variety of liquors now mentioned they were so drunk out of their minds (*enajenados de sus sentidos*) that Cárdenas fell next to the harp and remained sleeping, and Jasinto Grijalva was so intoxicated that in place of the *aguardiente* that he had ready to make the *punche* he put wine in its place. Don Joseph Grijalva became angry because of this mistake and took the punchbowl and threw it at Jasinto and it broke, after that they stopped drinking *punche* and continued with the wine and straight *aguardiente*.

Dr. don Joseph Osejo was so drunk in the study that don Joseph called for a servant to carry him to his room. In company with Cárdenas, don Joseph and the witness left and put doctor Osejo in bed. They returned to the room where they had been [the study] and found only Cathalina Sánches and the harpist, and they left. And the witness with don Joseph locked the door of the study leaving inside the sleeping doña María in company of a son [Antonio] of the witness after which everyone went to bed.

15.3 The Testimony of Cathalina Sánches, Alias La Talona, Continues

[From Cathalina's statement, given at hacienda San Joseph, December 2, 1768.]

[After don Mariano ordered her to procure dinner.] And having left the study and entering the *sala principal*, she could not find the door to the kitchen; she [drunkenly] wandered trying to see if she could find it. Doña Manuela Lomas came and heard a noise, she asked who it was, calling the witness by her name. To which she responded, "Señora I can't find the door because my head is spinning." After which, taking her hand, [doña Manuela] took her to her apartment (*aposento*) and ordered dinner to be brought, and insisted that the witness eat, advising her that in taking something to eat it would take away her drunkenness. Shortly after that don Mariano entered swearing, "Cursed be my fortune" (*Mal haya mi fortuna*). And as doña Manuela saw that her husband was angry, she left the room during which time the witness assumed that don Joseph de Grijalva and doña María remained alone in the study. Don Mariano [then] left the apartment of the señora. Immediately doña Manuela reentered [her room and] on that occasion shared with the witness that she was upset with don Joseph. She had left to bring her son to [put him to bed and] don Joseph had spoken to her in an imperious voice, and demonstrating anger, he had told her "to go away and to leave it."[10] She replied that she came to fetch (*a llevar*) her son, he repeated "to leave it, that now there was no need," to which doña Manuela had replied, "Señor, as he is my son it worries me and I come to take him." But because [don Joseph] did not consent, she had returned [to her room]. [All of] which the señora expressed to this witness, in an emotional way. And [the witness] does not know when don Mariano left the room of doña Manuela if he returned to the study or not.

And eating with doña María [in her room] they heard the bustle of the servants and slaves who were coming and going [in the hall], that from what she remembered included the voices of the mulatto Juanico and the black Pasqual. And according to what she understood, they left mad, saying what was the use of the masters asking for food when they did not want to eat?

And since this witness was affected in the head, she asked doña Manuela if she would do her the favor of ordering her *negrita* to bring a light so she could go to the room of her master, Doctor Osejo. . . . She remained there and slept until the next day.

Around five-thirty in the morning don Joseph de Grijalva entered the room of the doctor, and approaching the witness asked her how long she was sleeping [because] she [had] to fix those curtains.[11] So the witness got up to begin that task. . . . And . . . don Joseph arrived and . . . the witness heard him tell Doctor Osejo . . . [about] a baptismal celebration . . . in the city of Quito . . . [when] doña Mariana Laso . . . had become so drunk that she slept a day and a night, and that after that she had come to hate . . . drink. Don Joseph said that [drinking] could do much harm, and . . . it seemed that the same had happened with Marica, for she had thrown up a fat and large worm and still hadn't awakened even though the day was advanced. . . .

By then, it was about six in the morning more or less. . . . Doña Manuela Lomas approached the witness and told her that she came to wake up doña María Freyre. For fear of her father-in-law, don Joseph, she had not been able to call in a loud voice, but instead right at the door she had called two times in a low voice saying, "Doña María, doña María." And since she feared that don Joseph would become angry with this because he shouted over just about anything, she had not dared to raise her voice because he might hear. Doña Manuela told this witness that [doña María] was sleeping a long time because it was late (ser mucho dormir, por ser muy de día). Then the black [slave] Bernarda arrived and told doña Manuela [it was time] to eat, and the latter responded how could she do this without doña María. [Bernarda] . . . said to eat, and when doña María awakened, she would give her something to eat.[12] And . . . around seven in the morning don Mariano Grijalva left his bedroom and, approaching his father, told him that he had been very drunk, but even so, he wanted a drink of wine because his body felt very weak. And although he had aguardiente, it was very bad and he could not take it, and so could he lend him the key to the study [where the liquor was stored]. And taking the key from his pocket, don Joseph gave it to his son who passed to the study.[13] And in a short while the son of don Mariano [Antonio] came and said, "Grandfather, Mama Marica is dead. . . ." And then don Mariano came out and said to don Joseph, "Sir, señora Marica is dead. . . ."

15.4 Testimony of Don Justo Fraga

[Don Justo, age thirty-four, is a friend and business partner of don Joseph Grijalva. He gave his sworn statement to escribano Juan Mateo Lavarredez on July 1, 1769.]

He said that Monday he returned to the hacienda San Joseph . . . entering [the house] around ten-thirty or eleven in the morning. He found a body in the drawing room, and asking a servant who had died, was told that it was the señora, wife of the master. And not wanting to believe it, the witness approached the body and uncovering the face, knew that it was María Freyre. He perceived that she had shed blood through the mouth and nose . . . and also . . . that beneath her ear she had a triangular-colored mark of [about] two fingers [width] and her nose was reddened with blood. The witness then passed to the room where don

Joseph de Grijalva was, to give him his condolences. Don Joseph said that the death of his wife had been from a great apoplexy resulting from the harmful things that she had eaten the previous day including peppers, [and] *rocote* with salt during the walk that she took, and that she drank *punche*, wine, and *aguardiente* and . . . on the patio threw up a worm, and they had put her to bed on the sofa. That night she had thrown up much blood that this witness saw on the sofa where they found her dead that Monday.

The witness said that he saw a woman—he doesn't know her first name but her last name is Alvarrasín and she is the wife of a silversmith—approach the body of the dead women with the intention of preparing it [for burial]. And she began to clean the throat with a cloth wet in water that ran down the neck, cleaning the blood, and, arriving at a discolored spot, she said, "A dead body doesn't feel," and she used the cloth with force. At which time they called the witness outside . . . leaving that woman in the expressed task.

He said that persons at the hacienda San Joseph told him that don Joseph Thorres had arrived hastily and with haughtiness (*acelerado y con orgullo*) saying that his cousin had died because don Joseph de Grijalva had strangled her. Moreover, [after] seeing the body, [don Joseph Thorres] went to the hacienda of El Ingenio to tell the same to the brothers of the deceased. They also went to see the dead woman. And on arriving at the hacienda, they pronounced similarly, that Grijalva had strangled and killed their sister, because the small [amount] of punch that she had drunk would not have been enough to kill her. The Freyres therefore called the governor and witnesses to scrutinize the body, which in effect is what happened.

15.5 Testimony of Mariano Unda

[Mariano, age twenty-five, is a free moreno. *His work is to assist local officials. He gave his sworn statement in Urcuqui to escribano Joaquin Guerrero on November 14, 1768.]*

This witness said he helped hold the light that the judge and the notary used to examine the cadaver of doña María. And the witness saw signs of fingers on both sides of the throat as if she had been choked with the hand. She also had blackish bruises on the neck on one side and on the other, in the middle she had scratches as if by fingernails. Her face was swollen, her mouth open, her lips darkish and also swollen. And she had blood from the mouth and nose on her face. . . .

15.6 Testimony of Thomas Lomas

[Thomas, age sixty-two, is a healer. He gave his sworn statement to escribano Juan Mateo Lavarredez at the Quito public jail on July 6, 1769.]

. . . Before [don Joseph and doña María] married, the parents of doña María called this witness to the hacienda of El Ingenio to apply some medicines. . . . Doña María had back pain and some marks on her face that he reduced with fresh drinks, and after her marriage he visited the hacienda . . . for the same back pain . . . continuing this medicine on various occasions. . . .

He went that Monday [to the hacienda San Joseph and] saw the body. And when the brothers of the dead woman uncovered her face, he saw that she had bled through the nose and mouth and that she had a colored mark beneath the ear and a bruise on the nose. Doña Manuela told the witness to wash the face with vinegar, which he did, observing with particular care that the whole face and the throat did not have more marks than stated.

15.7 Testimony of Don Justo Fraga Continues

[From don Justo's statement, given to escribano Juan Mateo Lavarredez, July 1, 1769.]

He said he has known don Joseph de Grijalva for many years and knows that he comes from good and honored ancestors, quiet, pacific, of known nobility. And as for the relationship that don Joseph had with his wife, doña María Freyre, he can only say one thing. Over a period of five months that this witness resided on the hacienda San Joseph . . . the witness never saw that there was discord between don Joseph and his wife. On the contrary he saw that he treated her with much love and affection sleeping together and living in the same dwelling. . . .[14]

He said . . . that doña María Freyre suffered from and complained of pain in the back and stomach, that she had a pale color and those persons close to her could perceive that her breath was foul. He also saw that sometimes the spit that she threw up contained blood and other matter. . . .

He said, that the days preceding the Sunday when doña María died she found herself . . . suffering more than at other times with chills and abnormalities. The witness knows this because doña María herself told him.

15.8 Testimony of Juan Benites

[Juan, age twenty-five, is the slave of don Joseph de Grijalva. He gave his sworn statement to the jues comisario Pedro Fernández in the pueblo of Urcuqui on June 10, 1769.]

He said, that on a certain occasion in which they were having a party (*en que se ofresio alegria*) in the study of don Joseph two months before . . . this event, doña María left the study and said: "Juanico, I can't make it to my rooms by myself." At this time the witness perceived that she breathed very smelly breath, and having put her in her bed, he left. And the next day the witness passed to see how she had awakened. And he told her "Come my mistress, take a drink (*un traguito*), and cure one problem with another," to which she responded, "No son, I have a stomachache, heat a little water, I want to throw up."

15.9 Testimony of Doña Manuela Lomas

[Doña Manuela, age twenty-five, is married to don Mariano and is thus don Joseph Grijalva's daughter-in-law. She gave her statement at hacienda San Joseph on December 5, 1768.]

[Sunday night immediately after the fiesta broke up] the witness was going to the *sala principal* passing the corridor that leads to the study, where in the door she encountered don Joseph de Grijalva and don Mariano her husband whom she asked,"Do you want to dine?" And as don Joseph said to let whoever wanted to eat to do so, she returned to her room and ate with Cathalina. And after a short while, don Mariano entered and became angry with her, for it was now his custom to become irritated even without reason.[15] And to avoid him, she left for the main room, and shortly afterward, she saw that don Mariano left [their room] and so she returned and shared her unhappiness with Cathalina. But then she remembered that her son had remained in the study, [and she was] full of concern although some time had passed, [and] she returned with her *negrita* to carry her son [to bed].[16] She then encountered don Joseph seated on the steps next to the door of the study. He asked the witness as he stood up, what he could do for her. She said she came to fetch her son. And approaching the witness [he said] in an angry voice to, "Leave it. At this hour you come with this?" To which the witness responded, "Señor, I have always cared for him as a mother." And as he said again to leave it, he gave her a push, and without pressing, seeing he was angry, she returned to her room leaving the boy in the study. . . .

Since her son had remained the night of the party in the study, the witness asked him the second day [after] the death and afterwards on other occasions she has questioned him with much care [to find out] if that night he heard any sound or some voices. To which he has responded that he heard no sound, only that having awakened late in the night he began to call doña María various times, and as she did not respond he approached and, groping [in the dark] he encountered the señora whom he touched. And he found that she was cold without any heat whatsoever, and even though this scared him, he made the comment that such cold could have been because she had been drinking. After which he had . . . slept until the morning when his grandfather entered with Manuel de Cárdenas and, taking a hat, reclosed the door of the study.

15.10 Testimony of Rosa Almeyda

[Rosa, age forty, is a free, unmarried parda. *She gave her sworn statement at the town of Tumbabiro to don Macheo Garcia de Benalcazar,* juez comisario *on November 16, 1768.]*

And in the darkness, the black people (*la gente negra*) were keeping wake over the body [when] don Joseph de Grijalva commanded once, and [then] another time that they should not make such sounds.[17] And then a black said secretly, "Well, because he strangled her, we should not even make noise."

15.11 Reexamination of Don Mariano Grijalva

[Given at the Royal Quito Jail to Dr. don Isidoro de Santiago Albear y Artundeaga, oidor, *on December 20, 1768 (more than five months after his first statement).]*

[Question:] You remained the last of all the invited guests in company of your father until he closed the door of the study . . . and it is not credible that after going outside and passing some time that for such a trifling reason you would make such an exclamation.[18] At that hour, one presumes it to have been a superior reason. . . . Tell what it was without keeping it secret and hiding it, because it is a fact on which this investigation principally rests.[19] And since it is proven, it will be necessary to use the means of torture so that you give the real and true motive.

He said that having remained alone with his father in the study after everyone had retired, [including] his wife doña Manuela Lomas, the witness left to look for dinner and to see his horse. He believes he spoke of this trip [to visit his horse] in his earlier deposition without saying why he went, or he doesn't remember what he said. And after that short visit he returned to the study where he had left his father alone. He found him outside in the corridor with the door shut and the key in his hand. [His father] gave it to him telling him to take it, and saying exactly the following words, "*Hombre*, it seems that Marica has died." And the witness responded, "Señor, don't say that, because if that has happened you will suffer, and we will all pay for what has occurred in this cursed party (*esta maldita función*)." After these words his father retired without saying a word. And the witness . . . entered his room overcome with pain and sentiment, tearing out his hair and cursing his fate and his fortune (*su suerte y su fortuna*), for he loved his stepmother, as is commonly known, and he loves his father. And that is what happened. And it could be seen that the witness was torn with sharp pain and feelings of his heart. . . .

15.12 Testimony of Don de Joseph de Grijalva

[Don Joseph, age fifty-six years, is married to the deceased and is the prime suspect in her death. He gave his sworn statement at the Royal Jail in Quito to Dr. don Isidoro de Santiago Alvear, oidor, on May 8, 1769.]

Because it was late and everyone was drunk (*estaban todos ebrios*) he called to [his son] don Mariano, and going with him to close the door of the study the witness found Cathalina on the lowest step [of the staircase] near the door outside the study. The witness entered followed by his son don Mariano and seeing that doña María was on the sofa, he approached to see her up close, and she seemed dead, saying to his son don Mariano [that] it seems that Marica is dead or drunkenness has made her appear so. It appeared to the witness that Cathalina had provoked a fit, for she was the only one who had remained in the study. . . .[20] He went with his son to close the door . . . he resolved to leave her as he was accustomed to do other times leaving his little grandson, the son of don Mariano, as company for her, and he closed the door. . . .

[And on Monday] don Joseph de Thorres entered [the witness's house] with a saber in his hand, saying with various arrogant and threatening words that his cousin had died of strangulation. And shortly before this the witness had heard . . . that a woman married to a silversmith of Urcuqui named Joachim had been present when the blood was cleaned from the dead woman. . . . And the woman had scratched the neck saying, "A dead body doesn't feel." From this the witness inferred . . . that she had been sent by Thorres, given the friendship she had with him, to make those marks that she had done, that this witness did not see, [to serve] as evidence that [doña María] had been strangled and to blame it on the witness.[21] For [Thorres] has always hated all his kin (*parentela*) this witness as well as his son don Mariano, with whom there has been several quarrels that led to blows, originating from the hatred that the brothers of the dead woman have for not having been given what they asked. . . .[22]

[Question:] The most principal point is this. You, having judged that doña María was dead after scrutinizing her in the study and suspecting that Cathalina had done her harm, did not begin the least investigation. Nor [did you] question her, considering her [to be] an enemy and perpetrator of a great cruelty against your own wife. Nor [did you] call the family so they might see if she were really dead, or [if she] might be helped medically, or [if she might be] absolved of her sins since there was a priest in the house to do it. And there is no doubt that the greatest and gravest consternation that can occur to a husband is seeing his wife [in such a state]. [Yet you] calmly retired, leaving her locked in, a thing that one would not do with a stranger, nor even with the most unhappy house slave.

He responded that he made no commotion . . . because the same had happened other times [with doña María] remaining in the same condition overwhelmed by *punche*. And he did not want to cause a clamor in the house without evidence until seeing in the morning what happened. And upon removing the body they told him that it was bleeding, so he made no stir with Cathalina attributing the death to a fit of illness. . . .

He says that he returns to swear beneath his word of honor and as a gentlemen that he did not put his hands on doña María nor was he the last alone with her in the study. And if his son don Mariano and if persons . . . affirm [differently] . . . they were mistaken or confused because of the *punche* and liquors that they had drunk. . . .

[Question:] What motive did you have to leave the conveniences of your house, to abandon your sons and to expose yourself to the dangers of health and life, by fleeing toward the deserted mountains on foot and through craggy roads crossing turbulent rivers? What man of [your] class would make such a journey unless his life was threatened when not even the delinquent blacks, *zambos* or Indians of this city [Quito] have been accustomed to flee their transgressions to that ruggedness? . . .

[He says that] knowing that the *corregidor* of the villa [Urcuqui], his capital enemy, looked for him . . . to catch him charging him as aggressor in the death of doña María, he determined to find his way into those mountains.

15.13 The First Judgment. Given by Dr. Galdeano. Quito, February 16, 1769

The *fiscal* says that Your Lordship ought to declare don Joseph de Grijalva the author and perpetrator of these disgraceful acts. . . . And in respect to the justifiable rigor of the civil laws . . . it would be useless for the *fiscal* to insist that don Joseph de Grijalva be whipped publicly before everyone and that he be put in a leather sack along with a dog, a rooster, a snake . . . and with the mouth of the sack sewn, to throw it in the sea or in the river closest to the place where he committed such great wrong. Not only has this been abolished in the Catholic Kingdoms of Spain, but also in farther kingdoms. . . . And so the *fiscal* must be content to ask for the ordinary pain of death by hanging or garrote.

15.14 The Second Judgment. Given by Dr. Galdeano, Quito, November 3, 1769[23]

No other could have committed such a scandalous attack but don Joseph Grijalva . . . who publicly manifested the tedium caused by [his wife's] company. . . . Don Joseph de Grijalva was the last who remained in the room with his wife, and he was the first to announce her death to his son. . . . It only remains to satisfy the public, revenging the death of an innocent woman whose blood is calling for corresponding satisfaction. . . . Even the most rustic suffers and understands the weakness and frailty of the feminine sex, and the confidence that women place in the company of their husbands, which reasons argue the absence of defense that don Joseph de Grijalva can raise in defense of his own life.

15.15 The Last Testament of Don Joseph de Grijalva. Quito, February 22, 1770

Don Joseph de Grijalva y Recalde . . . in this court jail for uxoricide (wife-murder) that was maliciously and rashly conspired by the relatives and brother of doña María Freyre, when her death occurred naturally because of the illnesses that she already suffered. . . . And this royal court sentenced me to exile in Valdivia.[24] Because of the contingency of an extended road and seas to cross, I make this my testament.[25]

15.16 Report on the Death of Don Joseph de Grijalva En Route to Exile in Valdivia

[Statement by priest Doctor Juan de Era, of San Juan de Vilba, March 24, 1770.]

The mule on which [don Joseph] was mounted swerved from the exact route of the pass [of the river] on that side and went over into a swirl of violent current (*chiflon de corriente violenta*). . . . With little fight the mule fell over, throwing don Joseph de Grijalva into the current. . . . [He] was carried [downstream] with great violence . . . and his front and head struck the river rocks. . . . In this church [of San Juan], the body of the deceased was buried.

15.17 Evaluation of the Health of Doña María Freyre

[Excerpt from a letter written by Dr. Malcolm Meyn Jr., M.D., to Professor Ann Twinam, October 18, 1995, Cincinnati, Ohio.]

There is no question that doña María Freyre had anemia secondary to chronic blood loss. The "pale color" of the skin is characteristic of the chronically ill with low hemoglobin. The blood loss was probably secondary to gastrointestinal hemorrhage, probably coming from the esophagus or stomach. The vomit described as blood . . . probably comes from the esophagus, posterior pharynx, or upper stomach. An entrapped or "sliding" "hiatal hernia" with ulcerations in the upper stomach or lower esophagus is also a likely bet. This could also explain why her problem was chronic.

From the description of the last night, it would appear doña María had a drinking problem . . . . Drinking encourages the formation of ulcers in the esophagus and stomach. If the drinking goes on for a prolonged time, the liver is permanently damaged and a condition known as "portal hypertension" develops, which in turn can lead to a sometimes fatal condition of "esophageal varices" or dilated veins in the lower esophagus . . . that are thin walled and rupture easily. . . . After a few minor bleeding episodes a major bleed occurs and the patient bleeds to death. The description of "fetid material" coming from her mouth and the description of "bad breath" are characteristic of any one who chronically vomits blood. . . .

To sum up, I believe that doña María had a chronic bleeding problem from the upper gastrointestinal tract that caused anemia. A likely possibility of the cause of bleeding was a hiatal hernia with ulceration of the lower esophagus or upper stomach aggravated by heavy drinking. This would not ordinarily cause sudden death unless there was massive hemorrhage at the end. If she were a chronic alcoholic with a swollen belly, then ruptured esophageal varices would have to be in the differential diagnosis. This could, in fact, cause death after a bout of heavy drinking.

NOTES

1. This case is located in the Archivo Nacional de Ecuador (Quito), Criminales, 15-11-1768, Cr. 57; 25-9-1769, Cr 58; 11-16-1770, Cr. 59. Don Joseph de Grijalva's last testament is in the Archivo Nacional de Ecuador, Archivo Notarial de Phelipe Santiago Navarrette, Años 1770–1771 (Feb. 22, 1770).
2. For a provocative methodological commentary and analysis of a murder case see Ranajit Guha, "Chandra's Death," in Ranajit Guha, ed., *Subaltern Studies V: Writings on South Asian History and Society* (New York: Oxford University Press, 1987): 135–65.
3. Since the documents concerning doña María's death number almost a thousand pages, the testimony presented here is necessarily only a small, albeit an important, part of a very complex case. I have used the standard elipsis (. . .) to show when material (from a few sentences, to paragraphs, to pages) has been edited from a witness's testimony. I have chosen transcripts that essentially tell the tale through the voices of Cathalina, doña Manuela, and don Mariano and that trace the events leading up to the death of doña María and the charges and eventual fate of don Joseph. All those who were present at these events testified; there are many other witnesses who are not included here. Lack of space has also made it impossible to present many other aspects of the case. Witnesses testified on both sides of the

following issues: that don Joseph had put opium in doña Maria's wine, that he had tried to cover up marks on doña Maria's face, that he despised his wife and had killed her in order to marry his sixteen-year-old niece, doña Josepha [Pepita] Osejo, and that Cathalina *la talona* was a go-between in that relationship. There are many other documents dealing with the search, eventual capture, and trial of don Joseph. Depositions were taken from principals several times over a period of years and there were some changes (see, for example, don Mariano's differing accounts) in testimony. Yet readers should know that none of the remaining documents contain definitive proof of don Joseph's guilt or innocence. The translated testimony of this selection provides the fundamental information necessary to consider whether or not a homicide had been committed.

4. Presumably a nickname derived from Cathalina's unusual dexterity with knitting needles.
5. It was not uncommon for priests to have additional occupations.
6. Cathalina's words were "huvo de acompañarlo," perhaps to emphasize her absence of alternatives, perhaps not surprising for a fifty-year-old woman without other means of support.
7. Perhaps Cathalina uses the word "determinó" to show she "determined" to go with them, to signal that as a servant, even a superior one, she really didn't have much choice.
8. Presumably Quechua. The testimony contains several places where both elite women and female servants use Quechua terms to refer to food.
9. This may have included the slave Pascual who was playing the harp. Testimony also makes clear that the study was usually kept locked because this was where both *aguardiente* and the much more expensive imported wine (the latter in a specially locked case) were stored. Elsewhere Cathalina notes that although servants might drink punch, it was unusual for them to be offered wine.
10. The nine-year-old had been locked in the study with the comatose doña María after the party.
11. In another part of her testimony Cathalina explains that the washing and drying of these linens was the major reason she stayed overnight at the hacienda, as she had actually wanted to go into town.
12. Although servants were at the beck and call of the family, they did seem to have some control over aspects of the domestic routine. There seems an expectation that the family would be present and would eat at those times when meals were served.
13. Testimony not presented here makes clear that don Joseph had the key when he locked the door of the study with doña María inside after the party. He gave don Mariano the key outside the study door. Very early in the morning Manuel Cárdenas had to leave and needed his hat from inside the study. Don Joseph woke up don Mariano, took the key, retrieved the hat, and relocked the study. He probably let his grandson out at that time.
14. It is worth noting that the couple had not gotten along immediately after their marriage, for don Joseph had tried to have the union annulled three days after the ceremony. Pressure by both the bishop of Quito and the president of the *audiencia* forced a reconciliation and the couple had been living together for five years before doña Maria's death. See Fernando Jurado Noboa, *Los Descendientes de Benalcazar en la formación social ecuatoriana, siglos XVI a XX* (Quito: Amigos de la Genealogía, 1984), pp. 162–68.
15. This is a critical part in her testimony, for she innocently assumes he is swearing because he is mad at her. Royal officials clearly think there is another interpretation given don Mariano's later testimony.
16. Presumably she was not too worried, given it was past midnight and she assumed her son was asleep. However, she wanted him to sleep in his own bed, rather than the sofa in the study.
17. Most likely they were wailing and grieving over the death of their mistress.
18. Don Mariano's problem is that he has to explain why he was cursing his fate in the bedroom in front of his wife after he had left his father. In an earlier testimony, he suggests he was upset about the incident where he handed the glass to doña María, it broke, and don Joseph became angry. The visit he refers to was a very brief one—he went outside and checked on his horse.
19. Royal officials ask the classic question, what did don Mariano know, and when did he know it?
20. The blame on Cathalina fit into other witness testimony that the women did not get along.
21. Some witnesses testified they were having a sexual affair.

22. Don Joseph uses a traditional Spanish defensive tactic here, to blame the charges against him on his enemies.
23. The sentence also included the confiscation of half of don Joseph's goods. Others who received sentences included don Mariano de Grijalva, don Thomás de Lomas, and Cathalina *la talona* on the presumption they withheld relevant testimony.
24. The death sentence was eventually commuted because the evidence was circumstantial, because of don Joseph's prominence, and his age. As his lawyer pointed out, sentence to ten years exile in Valdivia was effectively a death sentence.
25. Don Joseph was not totally truthful in this testament, for he lied about an illegitimate son he had fathered as a result of a broken promise of matrimony (*palabra de casamiento*) between wives two and three. His testament declared: "I do not have a natural son, that even though [they] are raising a boy named Ramón, he is not mine." Yet, don Joseph clouded the issue for he then left the boy 200 pesos, "because he raised him." Years later family members testified that don Joseph had left "a short note" to his eldest son to "look on don Joseph Ramón "as a brother" given that he was "born from his loins." Yet this prevarication does not mark don Joseph as an inveterate liar, for he was following traditional norms. It was understood that fathers of illegitimate sons might refuse officially to recognize them in last testaments; it was equally customary for them to make private arrangements for such offspring to receive maintenance and care. See Ann Twinam, *Public Lives, Private Secrets: Gender, Honor, Sexuality and Illegitimacy in Colonial Spanish America* (Stanford: Stanford University Press, 1999). Don Joseph's will is in Archivo Nacional de Ecuador, Archivo Notarial de Phelipe Santiago Navarrete, Años 1770–1771, Feb. 22, 1770; the comments on his recognition are in Archivo General de Indias-Seville, Quito 362, n. 35, 1797.

DOCUMENT THEMES

Crime; Ethnicity; European-Mestizo Peoples; Gender; Illness/Disease/Injury/
Medicine; Marriage; Popular Culture; Rural Life; Violence; Women.

SUGGESTIONS FOR FURTHER READING

Boyer 1989.
Jurado Noboa 1984.
Newson 1995.
Powers 1995.
Stern 1995.
Twinam 1999.

CHAPTER
16

Letters of Insurrection:
The Rebellion of the Communities
(Charcas, 1781)

S. Elizabeth Penry

INTRODUCTION

With the collapse of the colonial state and the establishment of republican regimes in the Andes in the early nineteenth century, new constitutions promulgated universal suffrage. Creoles, nevertheless, found ways to preserve their positions of privilege by denying rights of citizenship to those deemed ignorant, such as the laboring rural and urban peoples called "Indians." In particular, suffrage depended on ownership of private property and on literacy tests designed to deny the vote to unlettered native Andeans whose land rights were based on collective titles. The obverse of these tests meant that those who were literate and who held private land titles were no longer defined as "Indians."[1] This supposition of "Indian" ignorance and backwardness went hand-in-hand with the idea that "they" could not be good citizens or Christians. Late colonial documents are replete with calls for a new conquest, designed to bring civil society and religion to ignorant rural people. Yet, the archives of the late eighteenth-century Spanish colony also contain numerous examples of letters written by, and addressed to, Andeans. These letters clearly indicate literacy in Spanish as well as a fundamental grasp of the ideas of the rights of communities. Where did these ideas come from and how did they find their fruition in Andean society? A brief look at the organization of Andean society sets the stage for the documents in this chapter.

Before the Spanish Conquest, most Andeans lived in small hamlets widely dispersed across the countryside. These tiny villages were part of large-scale "kingdoms" of different ethnic and language groups that made up the Inka empire.[2] For Spaniards, however, civilized life was only possible in an urban setting. In early modern Spain, there was no unincorporated territory; that is, every bit of agricultural land across the countryside legally belonged to a town, and one held civil rights based on town citizenship.[3] This organization of space, and the assumption that urbanity bred civility, was transferred to the Americas and found its fullest expression during the administration of Viceroy Francisco de Toledo (1569–81).

Toledo's policies marked a watershed in Andean history with the imposition of a radically new form of social and economic life through the creation of *reducciones*, or resettlement towns. Numerous small hamlets scattered across the countryside were destroyed, and Andeans were forcibly resettled in large communities modeled on Spanish towns. These uniformly grid-patterned towns were designed to "civilize" the "Indians" and to distance them from native religion while facilitating their conversion to Christianity and the mobilization of their tribute and labor to colonial purposes. The *reducción* towns, with their central plaza and straight streets, would make the Andeans into "true men," implying, of course, that in the countryside they were brutes.[4] Although over the course of time, settlers in these new towns drifted back to some of the older hamlets, the *reducciones* remained important religious and administrative centers, containing both the church and the local government. The *reducción* became known literally as the "head town" (*cabecera*), while settlements in outlying areas were subject to it. Larger settlements became its annexes, while very small settlements of just a few families were mere hamlets.[5]

In Castile, citizenship in a municipality formed the basis for participation in town-based democratic self-rule. With the Castilian municipal government as the prototype for *reducciones*, Viceroy Toledo created Spanish-style town councils, or *cabildos*, partly to counterbalance the authority of the hereditary *cacique*,[6] the local native lord. Technically the *cacique* could not veto the *cabildo's* decisions. The *cabildo* officers, including the *alcalde*, were to be elected annually from the ranks of commoner Indians. *Alcalde* is often translated as mayor, but in effect the *alcalde* also acted as a municipal judge, hearing small claims cases. According to Toledo's decrees, the *cacique* could not be elected to the office of *alcalde*. Further, the *cacique* was ordered not to interfere in the annual elections of the council members.[7] Although the duties of *cabildo* members overlapped slightly with the *cacique*, in practice *caciques* continued to dominate local politics in the Andes. By the late eighteenth century, however, town councils had begun to play an active role in curtailing the power of the *cacique*.[8]

As the only Spaniards originally allowed to live within the *reducción*, priests could exert a tremendous influence over their parishioners. Drawings by the seventeenth-century Andean author Guaman Poma de Ayala illustrate rural priests alternately helping their parishioners by writing legal petitions, and then abusing them with beatings and excessive charges.[9] Viceroy Toledo had encouraged the close relations of priest and *cabildo* by requiring that *cabildo* officers assist the priest in catechism and conversion. Many times communities turned to their priest as a defense against the abuses of their *caciques*. Priests could show their displeasure and undercut a *cacique's* authority by refusing to bless him publicly, a ritual known as "dar la paz."[10] On the other hand, priests and *caciques* sometimes united in the economic abuse of the community. Conflicts between parishioners and priests increased during the last half of the eighteenth century as priests hesitated to implement the lower charges for priestly services introduced by the Spanish Crown. Despite these frictions, many priests were accused of being accomplices during the eighteenth-century rebellions.

Foundations for indigenous writing were also laid within the *reducciones*. Viceroy Toledo required each *cabildo* to have its own indigenous scribe and an archive to hold important papers. There is little early evidence for these scribes, but by the eighteenth century these plans had become a reality. While most Andeans remained illiterate, the letters in this chapter, addressed to and/or signed by *cabildos* or their members, point not only to a degree of literacy within rural towns, but also to the significance of literacy. The labored efforts to gain control over the conventions of written Spanish demonstrate that colonized Andeans understood the power of the written word. These documents are a bit unusual for the colonial Andes in that they are communications among indigenous people. No Spaniard was intended to read them. In many cases, historians are forced to tease the Andean voice from court cases, legal petitions and church or state inspection tours, all records produced for the Spanish colonial state.[11] If not for the general rebellion of the 1780s, these particular letters would not have been written or preserved.

What has been termed the "Age of Andean Insurrection" found its culmination in the early 1780s, as revolt extended from the region of present-day Colombia and Ecuador into what is now Argentina.[12] These uprisings in colonial Peru and Bolivia have been named for their most famous leaders. Tupac Amaru, a hereditary *cacique* who claimed descent from the Inka executed by Viceroy Toledo, sparked the revolt in the Cuzco region. Near present-day Potosí, Tomás Catari is credited with fomenting rebellion. Tupac Catari,[13] who took his adopted name from his two predecessors, twice laid siege to the city of La Paz. Unlike Tupac Amaru, neither Tomás Catari nor Tupac Catari were members of the hereditary nobility. Despite the prominence accorded these three individuals, most of the action during this time of rebellion (at least within the Audiencia of Charcas) took place under the leadership of people whose names are largely lost to history, people who were leaders within their own towns. This is because insurrection in Charcas began at the community level, generally in places where townspeople wanted to depose an unpopular *cacique*. Although not typically thought of as royal officials, *caciques* were salaried representatives of the colonial state; attacks on *caciques* were acts of treason which the Spanish could not ignore.

In this chapter, the focus is on those lesser known rebels. Included are letters written specifically to, by, and for indigenous peoples. They differ, then, from the correspondence or proclamations of the more famous indigenous leaders, which were generally written for Spanish consumption by official scribes and that provide "official" interpretations for the uprisings.[14] Also included are letters from the priests who discovered these missives and sent them on to the civil authorities. The rebel letters contained here—and their extensive circulation—suggest that there was likely a much higher rate of literacy during the colonial era than previously thought; they also indicate the importance of *reducción* towns and their annexes as loci of identification for indigenous people. No references are to be found here to prehispanic "ancient ethnic kingdoms" or messianic new Inkas who would restore such primeval polities; instead these calls go out to communities in the name of God and the Virgin Mary.[15]

The following letters were written between January and March 1781 within the Audiencia of Charcas, in an area that is now part of modern Bolivia.[16] The first letter (16.1), signed by "Nicolás Catari[17] and the Communities," calls on towns in the region to halt the movement of Spanish troops. Neither Nicolás nor the people whom he addressed were members of the hereditary indigenous elite; instead, this plea was sent to present and past town council members. The letter fell into the hands of the priest of Tinquipaya, after it was taken from Pedro Suyo, *alcalde* of Tinquipaya. In the second letter (16.2), the priest of Tinquipaya forwards Nicolás Catari's call to arms to Spanish officials in Potosí and describes how the *alcalde* became governor of the town. The *alcalde* replaced an unpopular *cacique* who was forced to flee for his life, in his words, "disguised as an Indian." Although an Indian himself, this *cacique* would not stoop to dress in a common poncho.

The third letter (16.3), written to the *cabildo* of Colpacaba and calling for assistance, was also captured by a local priest (16.4). Note that while the call to arms is made in the "name of Holiest Mary," the priest still insists that Andeans want to "live without GOD[18] or King." Here, the priest provides clues about rebel organization, reporting how and under what authority indigenous troops were dispatched.

The final document (16.5), a circular letter to rebel communities, traveled across two provinces and seven different communities before being captured near the town of Yura in March 1781.[19] In each indigenous settlement, the letter was signed by a local representative.

Taken together, these letters from rebels offer as clear a statement of meaning from the point of view of indigenous participants as a historian could hope to find. Unlike official statements of cause (prompted by Spanish interrogations), these tragic and simple communications between towns reveal the organization, language, and method of community-based rebellion. They also show the vital importance of literacy and of Andeans' comprehension of its importance. As people gathered for weddings or other festivals that brought communities together, these widely circulating letters were read out loud to recruit Andeans to the cause of community-based insurrection. The political philosophy implied in the language of these letters is neither wholly Spanish nor ancient Andean. Instead, Andeans had taken Spanish imposed town-based institutions and redefined them to create their own distinct identity as communities.[20]

THE DOCUMENTS[21]

16.1 Letter from Nicolás Catari and the Communities to the Past Principales of Yocalla and Tarapaya

To the señores, past *principales*,[22] of the communities of the parish of Yocalla and Tarapaya.

My very esteemed and dear ones. Immediately upon seeing this you must make every effort to communicate and notify everyone using every means possible. We are doing our part here. We have heard the news that the soldiers are heading out from all the large towns such as Chuquisaca,[23] Potosí,[24] and other places. For this reason I write to you, as we are the *indios originarios*[25] (natives) of all these *corregimientos* (royal districts), subject to the labors, first of God and of our Lord King and other governors. And considering this, you must do everything possible to prevent the soldiers from passing through,[26] since if they get past, they will finish us, and do whatever they want and whatever suits their will. And we, all of the provinces and communities of this side,[27] are working to prevent them from defeating us. I say to all of you that you should warn all the provinces and the communities of Indian people[28] so that they do their part, just as I advise. If you do not take care to defend yourselves you will see what hardships they will subject us to from then on. Thus, my brothers, I charge you not to ignore the soldiers who seek to leave Potosí.[29] I hope that you will also warn the people of Puna and Tomave, some of whom are tributaries.[30] Let God preserve you many years hence. From Macha town,[31] January 28, 1781. Your servants who wish to serve you.

> I Nicolás Catari and the *Comunidades*
> (Communities).

[The following appeared on the outside of the letter which was folded to form an envelope:]

To the señores, past *principales*, of the communities of the parish of Yocalla and Tarapaya.[32] May God protect you many years in
YOCALLA[33]
Let it pass hand-to-hand in power of the *alcaldes* of Tinquipaya without any delay because of its urgency.

Let all the people of the community of Tinquipaya come to this place, Cazcará.[34] Pedro Suyo [the *alcalde* of Tinquipaya] will take this immediately.

16.2 The Priest of Tinquipaya Forwards the Rebel Letter to Spanish Authorities in Potosí

Señor Governor Dr. don Jorge Escobedo y Alarcon
My Dear Sir, to whom I owe all respect:

The enclosed arrived in my hands at 4:00 this morning, and so without any loss of time, I send it to you for your information. This parish of mine finds itself without major upset with the exception of some (that they have told me are citizens of Macha), who took part in the tragedy of Aullagas.[35] The only other incident that I will tell Your Lordship about occurred on the day following the celebration of the Purification of our Lady, the third of February. Pedro Suyo (the same who was head of the past movements)[36] entered my room with a multitude of his followers and Indian allies, telling me that all his community wanted him for their governor, and thus would I give him the *bastón*.[37] I did it, but only after making him thoroughly aware that it would not be final until the royal *audiencia* was made aware of this because the naming [to office] would come from there. He responded to me that it was not important that they agree, that it was enough that I alone name him for governor.[38] I saw that because I had seen fit to do this, a change came over him and the others; they became serene. Since then there have been no problems here. Two [other] letters were found in his [Suyo's] possession with earlier dates. He showed them to me,[39] and the contents were essentially the same as this one. It was not possible to get them, though I tried, but he gave me his word that he would not get involved in anything else. That was the reason he was showing them to me. I will advise Your Lordship of what happens here. In the meantime, I pray to our Lord that he guard your life for many years. Tinquipaya, February 10, 1781. Joseph Varela y Bohorquez.

16.3 Letter Between Indigenous Cabildos in Paria Province[40]

To the *cabildo* of Colpacaba. To the señor *principal*.[41]

I have definite information on the news brought by the messenger. He says that more than twenty-five hundred soldiers have done great harm, and have humbled all of those of Peñas and Hurmires.[42] Just as many, they say, are coming by way of Chichas.[43] We will be surrounded this very night. Without a doubt they will arrive and wipe us out and none of us will be left in this province. Thus, for God's sake come as soon as you see this and take the news to everyone, as far as Culta, Cahuayo,[44] and Lagunillas, to all the hamlets.[45] Come in all fury with the greatest haste, in the manner of soldiers without an hour's delay. I beg you in the name of holiest Mary, to come, no matter what, all the *comunes*[46] as one. God our Lord will help us. Challapata. Changara.[47]

16.4 The Assistant Priest (Ayudante) of Culta Forwards the Rebel Letter to a Priest in Potosí

Señor Dr. don Mariano Ramon del Valle[48]
Culta, February 18, 1781
My dear friend and my Lord:

It is not possible to evaluate the frightening things that I live with in this parish. Every day we have more surprises with these Indians who want to live without either GOD or King, making themselves judges over their own legal cases[49] without any respect for GOD and his ministers. And it can all be attributed to the enormous rapacity with which, until the present, they have acted, taking lives and robbing from them when they can.[50]

I have certain news that the priest of Condo[51] is of a mind to flee to the Villa [of Potosí] to take refuge, because the Indians have been wanting to move against him and they have three reasons for this. First, he has hidden a *curaca*, whom they wanted to kill. The second is that they suspect that he wants to turn them over to the soldiers. And the third is that they are certain that the priest has money belonging to don Diego Cosido.[52] These are the reasons that they want to kill him, and they have said as much in this parish.

On the eleventh, there was a wedding and the following day a *cabo del año*[53] where many of our Indians, and also some from Macha and Tinquipaya,[54] met.

A short letter (which I have included with this) was read among them,[55] written by a *principal* from Challapata to this parish, as Your Mercy will see. And those from this parish, after having read it, met with those from Tinquipaya, begging them to go to Challapata, and that if they didn't, they would be lost. The next day, the *alcaldes* of our parish gathered together many Indians and dispatched each of them with two or three slings, bats, and other things for their defense.[56] On the same day, the 11th, the Indians were speaking in their gathering,[57] saying that the priest of Macha[58] had given them the keys of the church so that they could be on the lookout just in case the Spaniards or *cholos* or other people tried to enter there, so that by no means would they be able to take refuge in the Church.

"They[59] [the people of Macha] will do the same here, and in the manner that the priest of Macha has shown us, they will carry it out here.[60] They will go out to defend us. Also, the priest of Macha has shown us that it is equitable that weddings as well as all other things [the priest performs] will cost thirteen *reales*, according to the *cartas de favor* that our dead Catari brought to us.[61] This priest here has usurped them [the *cartas*] from us, and he has come out against us, trying to force us to pay the *tasa*.[62] He ought not to be doing that; rather he should defend us, but we will see about that."[63]

We have received news that the parish of Macha is without either priest, assistant, sacristan, or cantor because all of them are fugitives for what they have seen.[64] Also they have told us that they will not supply *mitanis* (laborers), *pongos* (house servants), nor any other things according to the *cartas de favor* written by Catari. In fact, I went to the annex of Cahuayo to oversee the election of the *alférez* and *mayordomo*,[65] and they would not supply a *pongo* or *mitani*, leaving me in the dark and dying of cold.

On the 15th, the *Jueves de Compadres*,[66] while I was going to marry some of my *filqueritos* (little parishioners), I met three Indians who were left over from those elected from our *alcaldes*.[67] One of them came up to me to ask what news I had of the soldiers. I, as if ignorant of everything, responded that I didn't know anything. But this wouldn't do; he thumped me on the side over my heart and told me that I had things hidden in my heart,[68] and that I didn't want to tell them anything. With this display, he took his leave, and they left very contentedly with their wives in the same manner as the preceding ones.[69]

I'm sending to Your Mercy thirty-three pesos that have been collected. We haven't had more receipts because those that have died, died suddenly and were poor.[70] Now we don't even have half a *real* for our expenses. I would very much appreciate it if you would do me the favor of taking care of the boy who carries this to Potosí,[71] until the Indians calm down or you come here yourself. At the same time, if there is something that you could offer me while here in my home, remember I have no other consolation here but you and your priests.[72] It hasn't been possible to get the burdock plants[73] because the Indians of Cahuayo aren't there now; they're in Challapata. I will appreciate it if you could get me some before you send the Indian back to me, and if you will advise me of your decision about what I have told you about all the frightening things that I live with in this parish. I want nothing more than to be in your company. And divine mercy permitting, things will become calm very soon so that we can live, serving our patron, our Lady of Mercy, whom I pray will prosper Your Mercy's importance for many years. That is my affectionate desire for you and your priests, to whom from my heart I commend myself.

Your faithful companion and trustworthy chaplain.

Joseph Balzeda.

16.5 A Circular Letter to the Communities

Señores *comunos* of all the province
My dear sirs,

I am informing you all that I have just arrived from the province of Cochabamba and the Cochabambinos and the *chapetones* (peninsular Spaniards) have united. They are coming, destroying towns; they have destroyed two towns, and thus Your Mercies, when you see this, prepare yourselves for our defense. Everyone should come immediately. Pass this letter to every town in this province of Paria. God protect us for many years. Poopo, March 7, 1781.

From Their Mercies, the *principales* of all the community of this town of Poopo, etc. For these reasons, whoever would resist this order, should suffer a vile death. As soon as you see this letter, hit the road, even if it's the middle of the night, for God's sake. In any case, the news that the priest of Poopo, don Manuel Aranibar, has given confirms that you should be well warned.[74] March 8, 1781.

[signed] *COMUNIDADES*[75]

Señores of the *comunidad* of Condo. When you see this, prepare immediately to leave for Poopo as the Cochabambinos and the *chapetones* have come together and they are destroying towns as they say in the letter. You all must warn Salinas[76] that we must join. Pass this letter.

Señores of the *comunidad* of Aullagas. When you see this, prepare yourselves as it says in the letter and come to Coroma. *Vale.*

Señores of the *comunidad* of Coroma. When you see this, prepare yourselves as it says in the letter. *Vale.*

Señores of the *comunidad* of Opoco. When you see this, prepare yourselves as it says in the letter and send it to Tomave immediately. *Vale.*

NOTES

ACKNOWLEDGMENTS   The research on which this is based was conducted in Spain, Bolivia, and Argentina during 1993–95 under the auspices of the Wenner-Gren Foundation for Anthropological Research, Fulbright/IIE, and the Graduate School at the University of Miami. The National Endowment for Humanities Dissertation Fellowship provided support for a year of analysis and writing (1995–96) from which this material is taken. I wish to thank Thomas Abercrombie and Geoffrey Spurling for their comments. Also, I wish to thank Tamar Herzog, who prodded me to take a closer look at "indigenous" literacy.

1. For in-depth studies of the Andean reaction to nineteenth-century liberalism, see Tristan Platt's "The Andean Experience of Bolivian Liberalism, 1825–1900: Roots of Rebellion in 19th-Century Chayanta (Potosí)" in *Resistance, Rebellion, and Consciousness in the Andean Peasant World: 18th to 20th Centuries*, Steve J. Stern, ed. (Madison: University of Wisconsin Press, 1987) and "Liberalism and Ethnocide in the southern Andes," *History Workshop Journal* 17 (1984).

2. On the pre-Columbian Andes, the classic work is by John Murra. See for example "An Aymara Kingdom in 1567," *Ethnohistory* 15(2) (1968):115–51 and "Andean Societies Before 1532," in *Cambridge History of Latin America*, vol. 1, Leslie Bethell, ed. (Cambridge: Cambridge University Press, 1984), 59–90. Karen Spalding's *Huarochirí, An Andean Society Under Inca and Spanish Rule* (Stanford: Stanford University Press, 1984) covers both pre- and postconquest society and also offers a culturally sensitive interpretation of the 1750 Lima and Huarochirí rebellion. Brooke Larson's *Cochabamba, 1550–1900: Colonialism and Agrarian Transformation in Bolivia* (Durham, N.C.: Duke University Press, 1998) offers a sweeping view of another region within the colonial Audiencia of Charcas.

3. Helen Nader, *Liberty in Absolutist Spain, the Habsburg Sale of Towns, 1516–1700* (Baltimore: Johns Hopkins University Press, 1990).

4. For more on *reducciones*, see Valerie Fraser, *The Architecture of Conquest: Building in the Viceroyalty of Peru, 1535–1625* (Cambridge: Cambridge University Press, 1990). The term "true men" comes from Juan de Matienzo's *Gobierno de Perú* (Paris: L'Institut français d'études andines, [1567] 1967), cited in Fraser, *The Architecture*.

5. The head town (*cabecera*) held a functioning town government, while annexes (*anejos*) generally had an incipient governing group. Smaller hamlets (*estancias*) were completely dependent on the nearby annex and head town.

6. *Cacique* was originally an Arawakian (Taino) term used for leaders in the Caribbean islands. The Spanish generalized this term to all indigenous hereditary lords, regardless of the language of the local people. In Quechua, the language of the Inka, hereditary native lords were known as *curacas*, sometimes spelled *kuraka*. Although the letters reproduced here likely were written by native speakers of Aymara, the term *curaca* is used in one of the letters. The Spanish continued the imperial Inka practice of privileging the Quechua language over other Andean languages such as Aymara and Pukina. On *caciques* and the delicate role they sometimes played as intermediaries, see Brooke Larson, "Caciques, Class Structure and the Colonial State in Bolivia," *Nova Americana* 2 (1979): 197–235, and Karen Spalding, "Social Climbers: Changing Patterns of Mobility Among the Indians of Colonial Peru," *Hispanic American Historical Review* 53 (1970): 645–64.

7. Toledo's mammoth plan remodeling Peru has been published as *Disposiciones gubernativas para el virreinato del Peru*, 2 vols. (Seville, 1986). Volume 2 contains detailed orders for the *cabildo* elections; see pp. 218–22.

8. It is difficult to track the evolution of local politics and the complex relations between *caciques* and *cabildos* because there are few surviving records of *cabildo* activities before the latter part of the eighteenth century.

9. See Guaman Poma de Ayala, *El Primer Nueva Corónica y Buen Gobierno*, ed. John V. Murra and Rolena Adorno (Mexico City: Siglo Veintiuno, [1615] 1980), 532–621.

10. The priest's blessing, literally "giving peace," involved passing the censer and the silver tray that held the Eucharist bread over the person to be blessed. This ritual was described in a synod held in Sucre in 1773, whose proceedings have been published under the archbishop's name, Pedro Miguel de Argondoña y Pasten, as *Constituciones Sinodales del Arzobispado de La Plata* (Cuernavaca, 1971). Failure to "dar la paz" was a source of conflict between priest and *cacique* in late colonial Charcas, leading several *caciques* to make formal complaints against their priests. Local priests clearly played an important role in legitimating authority. To compare this case to colonial Mexico, see William B. Taylor's superb study, *Magistrates of the Sacred: Priests and Parishioners in Eighteenth-Century Mexico* (Stanford: Stanford University Press, 1996).

11. Unlike colonial Mexico, there are few early *cabildo* proceedings or other records written in any native Andean language (for Mesoamerica, see James Lockhart, *The Nahuas After the Conquest: A Social and Cultural History of the Indians of Central Mexico, Sixteenth through Eighteenth Centuries* [Stanford: Stanford University Press, 1992], and Robert Haskett, *Indigenous Rulers: An Ethnohistory of Town Government in Colonial Cuernavaca* [Albuquerque: University of New Mexico Press, 1991]). The letters included in this chapter were written in Spanish,

but internal evidence within the letters indicates that they were written by people whose first language was not Spanish. For example, neither Quechua nor Aymara distinguish between Spanish "o" and "u" or Spanish "e" and "i"; documents written by native speakers of Quechua and Aymara usually contain these letters substituted for each other in ways that a native Spanish speaker would not mistake ("erse" for "irse," or "osurp" for "usurp" for example). Although quaint sounding phraseology carries over in documents Indians dictated to Spanish scribes, the distinctive spelling does not.

12. The term "Age of Andean Insurrection" is from Stern, ed., *Resistance, Rebellion*. The essays in that collected volume serve as a fine introduction to Andean rebellion.

13. The name Catari is spelled with a "C" in colonial documents, although in modern orthography a "K" is sometimes used. Political groups within modern Bolivia who take their names from these colonial heroes generally maintain the "C" spelling for Tomás Catari, and the "K" for Tupac Katari. The rebellion in the La Paz region is the subject of a recent doctoral dissertation by Sinclair Thomson, "Colonial Crisis, Community, and Andean Self-Rule: Aymara Politics in the Age of Insurgency (Eighteenth-Century La Paz)" (Madison, Wisc.: University of Wisconsin, 1996).

14. For Tupac Amaru's and Tomás Catari's letters and decrees, see Boleslao Lewin, *Tupac Amaru el Rebelde: Su época, sus Luchas y su Influencia en el Continente* (Buenos Aires, 1943). For a recent analysis of the illiterate Tomás Catari's official correspondence with Spanish officials, see Sergio Serulnikov, "Disputed Images of Colonialism: Spanish Rule and Indian Subversion in Northern Potosí, 1777–1780," *Hispanic American Historical Review* 76:2 (1996).

15. An older generation of scholarship frequently focused on Andean desire for a messianic new Inka. See the work by Lillian Estelle Fisher, *The Last Inca Revolt, 1780–1782* (Norman, Okla.: University of Oklahoma Press, 1966) and John Rowe, "El movimiento nacional inca" in *Tupac Amaru II–1780*, Alberto Flores Galindo, ed. (Lima, 1976). To put these arguments into perspective, see the article by Alberto Flores Galindo, "In Search of an Inca," in Stern, ed., *Resistance, Rebellion*.

16. This region had been part of the Viceroyalty of Peru until 1776 when the new Viceroyalty of Río de La Plata (Buenos Aires) was created. It is sometimes referred to as "Upper Peru."

17. Nicolás was a cousin of one of the better known rebels, Tomás Catari. Both were commoner Indians, not members of the hereditary nobility. Tomás, who had sought *audiencia* confirmation of *cacique* status, was already dead when this letter was written.

18. Capitalization follows original document.

19. For more on the rebellion in Yura, see Roger Rasnake, *Domination and Cultural Resistance: Authority and Power Among an Andean People* (Durham, N.C.: Duke University Press, 1988).

20. These issues are themes in my book manuscript, tentatively titled *The People Are King: Modernity and Popular Sovereignty in Colonial Indigenous Rebellion*.

21. Letters 16.1 and 16.2 are from the Archivo Nacional de Bolivia (ANB), SGI 1781#193 "Expediente que contiene la convocatoria por los Yndios alsados de Chayanta a los de otros Pueblos" fs. 1r-v & 3r-v. Letters 16.3 and 16.4 are from ANB SGI 1781 #42 "Expediente sobre los alborotos de los indios de Yocalla," fs. 1r-3r. Letter 5 is from ANB SGI 1781 #61 "Causa criminal contra Ramon Paca Bentura Pinto, Pedro Copacava, y demas reos prinsipales, comprehendidos en la sublevación Muertos, y Rovos perpretados en este Pueblo de Yura, y sus ynmediasiones etca. Jues El Señor Don Antolin de Chavarri, comandante de Milisias de la Provincia de Chichas, Año de 1781," f. 13. Copies of letters 16.1, 16.2, and 16.4 can also be found in Archivo General de Indias [Seville, Spain] Charcas 435, "Carta No. 7° / N 1 / Testimonio En que Constan las noticias de las Provincias Sublevadas y Providencias tomadas por el Señor Governador de Potosí Doctor Don Jorge de Escobedo / Año de 1781. / Pral."

22. As señor is frequently translated as "lord" in colonial documents, which implies nobility, and as the term *principal* is ambiguous, I have chosen not to translate either term. *Principales* could refer to commoners who had held office within the town government, but Spaniards sometimes used it generically to refer to all indigenous leaders, including *caciques*.

23. Chuquisaca, also known as La Plata in colonial documents, was the seat of the Audiencia of Charcas. Renamed Sucre in the nineteenth century, it now serves as one of Bolivia's two capitals.

24. The location of the famous silver mines in which indigenous people labored as *mita* (forced labor) workers.

25. *Indio originario* was a Spanish tribute category. In this context, Nicolás is referring to those who have a claim in local society, hence a brief definition would be "native."

26. Nicolás was writing this letter from the Chayanta province town of Macha. The two towns that the letter is addressed to, Yocalla and Tarapaya, lie between Macha and Potosí. He was urging the people of those towns to stop the troops before they could reach Macha.

27. "This side" ("este lado" in the original text) could refer to a geographic area, probably "this side of the mountains." Other possible interpretations could be that Nicolás was referring to a social division of some kind, or to those on the same side in rebellion.

28. The text reads "gente Yndianos" [sic], literally "Indian people." Grammatical and spelling idiosyncracies occur throughout the letter.

29. Nicolás knew that Spanish troops would be looking for him. This letter was written a few days after he had led a bloody assault on Aullagas, a Spanish mining center. That attack, which left more than thirty Spaniards dead, had been in retaliation for the death of his cousin, Tomás Catari. Tomás, who was accused of encouraging rebellion in the province of Chayanta, had been arrested in December 1780. On January 8, 1781, while being transferred to Chuquisaca (Sucre) for trial, the Spaniards escorting Tomás were attacked, probably in an attempt to free him. There is contradictory testimony as to what exactly took place next; some accounts claim that Tomás was summarily executed by firing squad in response to the attack, while others maintain that he died at the hands of his would-be rescuers. Whatever the case, following this Nicolás led troops that sacked and burned Aullagas, home to the militia officer who had ordered Tomás Catari's arrest. As many as four thousand Andeans attacked Aullagas with their slingshots armed with stones. Fighting in heavy fog and sometimes rain, the battle lasted for three days, while the Spaniards traded taunts with the Andeans and fought with guns, swords and attack dogs. ANB SGI 1781 # 53 "Expediente seguido con motivo de la sublevación de los indios de Aullagas, encabezada por Nicolás, hermano del caudillo Tomás Catari" contains reports from the battle front in Aullagas.

30. The text reads "gentes tributarios [sic]." The indigenous nobility (who generally served as *caciques*) were not subject to tribute, hence the term *gentes tributarios* [sic] refers to commoner Indians.

31. The text reads "de esta suya Macha," literally, "from this your Macha." This construction is not clear. The letter was not addressed to people from Macha; to translate this as "your Macha" makes very little sense. Macha was (and is) the name of a town. In preconquest times and during the early colonial period, Macha territory had been much larger. During the eighteenth century several towns were carved from former Macha territory. The people of these new towns acknowledged some links to Macha. Nicolás himself was from Chairapata, formerly Macha land, while his cousin Tomás was from Macha. In using this phrase, Nicolás seems to be specifying exactly where he is, in Macha itself, not just in land that pertained to, or once belonged to, Macha.

32. Yocalla and Tarapaya are both towns that lie on the road between Oruro and Potosí. Any troops moving from Potosí toward Macha would have to pass by them. Yocalla was a "vice parish" or annex of Tinquipaya. It also was the first major postal stop after leaving Potosí on the road to Oruro. Throughout the colonial period, even during the time of rebellion, and until the early twentieth century, Andeans were responsible for delivering the mail. Much to Spanish dismay, letters and official documents were sometimes opened and read before they reached their intended recipient. This helps to explain how Andeans managed to stay well informed of many controversies, such as the state's proposed changes for priestly charges. For a colorful description of the colonial postal service, see Concolorcorvo, *El Lazarillo, a Guide for Inexperienced Travelers between Buenos Aires and Lima* (Bloomington, Ind.: Indiana University Press, 1965). This translated reprint of a 1773 tongue-in-cheek report by a postal inspector offers anecdotes about the towns, the people, and their customs.

33. Yocalla was written in large capital letters in the center of the folded paper. In size it dwarfs the rest of the address.

34. I have been unable to locate Cazcará. It was not the name of any large town in the area. Possibly it referred to a fixed landmark (a hill, ravine, a large flat rock, etc), known as a *mojón*. A series of *mojones* were (and are) used to distinguish boundaries between territories of towns. Part of the annual duty of an *alcalde* was to officially trace the boundaries of his town by walking from *mojón* to *mojón*.

35. Here the priest refers to the attack on the Spanish mining town of Aullagas, described above. The Spanish were particularly frightened by the attack because the *coyarunas*, the urban indigenous miners, had joined forces with the "indios del campo," the Indians of the country-side. Normally these groups were considered enemies, and in the first day or two of the

attack on Aullagas, the *coyarunas* sided with the Spanish. Nevertheless, by the end of the battle, they were reported to have changed sides. This led the Spanish commander, Ignacio Flores, to warn that "one ought to never trust those who are not Spanish, because before the *coyarunas* regarded the provincial Indians as their capital enemies. In this case, there is nothing else to do but arm all the Spanish, and the semi-Spanish ("semi español," i.e., cultural *mestizos*), and all the Negroes or Mulattoes, with good arms." [Archivo General de Indies (Seville, Spain) Charcas 595 Flores to Vertiz, January 29, 1781].

36. During September 1780, there were various reports of rebellion in Tinquipaya. On September 17, an Andean from another province testified that Pedro Suyo had told him that the people of his town were rebelling against the *corregidor* because he was responsible for the death of an Indian. The man had been arrested because he was unable to pay for a mule that the *corregidor* had forced him to buy. Once in jail, he complained of severe stomach pain, but the *corregidor* had refused to release him. Forced purchase of goods, known as *repartimientos de mercancías*, or simply *repartos*, were a means by which royal officials augmented their salaries. The *corregidor* purchased a number of mules at a relatively low price and then forced Andeans to buy them at a higher price. When they refused or were unable to pay, they were simply thrown in jail. A second account of events in Tinquipaya came from the *cacique*, Juan Arque. In mid-September, Arque sent an urgent report claiming that Pedro Suyo was trying to depose him. Arque asked to be relieved of his duties, specifically in regard to tax collection, in favor of Suyo. He claimed that Suyo wanted to kill him and that he had only been able to escape Tinquipaya dressed as an "Indian," complete with poncho and the stocking-style cap with earflaps favored by Andeans (ANB EC #84 "Juan Evangelista Arque, indio principal y cacique de Porco, pide al protector general, amparo por el despojo de su cargo y por la tentativa de asesinato de que ha sido víctima").

37. The *bastón* (also known as a *vara*) looks like a small walking stick. It is sometimes quite ornate with silver head and tip and decorated with medallions or coins. It was (and is) a symbol of office. The parish priest sanctioned the office holder and carrier of the *bastón* by blessing him. This was an extremely important action that legitimated the authority of the office holder in the eyes of the community. When Pedro Suyo reportedly said that "it was enough" that the priest alone name him for office, he seems to reject the civil authority as represented by the *audiencia* in favor of the local religious authority.

38. The title "governor" referred to the *cacique*. During the rebellion, many communities deposed unpopular governors. A rapid change was taking place from hereditary *caciques* to ones elected by the community. Those elected were generally akin to Pedro Suyo; that is, those who had held prior offices within the community.

39. The fact that Suyo would show incriminating letters to the priest indicates the importance of the priest's role in the community. The priest then suggests that Suyo was seeking absolution for his actions.

40. Abercrombie makes use of the *cabildo* letter and cites other sixteenth to twentieth century indigenous writings from the same region in his *Pathways of Memory and Power: Ethnography and History Among an Andean People* (Madison, Wisc.: University of Wisconsin Press, 1998).

41. There is no date on this letter. It was probably written in the first week of February 1781. In the next letter, the assistant priest of Culta reports that it was read in Culta on February 11, 1781.

42. Towns located in the province of Paria, near Condocondo (also known simply as Condo), a *reducción* town mentioned in the following letter.

43. The colonial province of Chichas lay to the south, at the border of present day Argentina.

44. Culta and Cahuayo were annex towns under the jurisdiction of Condocondo.

45. "Estancias" in the original. Although it can be translated as farm or ranch, as used by Andeans hamlet would be the closest rendering in English. Rather than a single family operation, a small number of related families lived and worked in one small area. It was smaller that an annex, lacked any self-government, and was subject to the jurisdiction of a head town.

46. A reference to the *común*, or possibly to the *comuneros*. Another variation of this term, *comuno*, appears in the circular letter. *Común* can refer to commonly held land or to the common people. However, in these letters and in other testimony, the term (and its variants) also conveys a sense of community or assembly of the people; that is, the voice of popular sovereignty within Andean towns. The name *comunero* was given to community-based rebels

in sixteenth-century Castile. It was also the name of Paraguayan rebels of the 1730s. The following description of the political philosophy and the meaning of the *común* in colonial Paraguay could be applied to the Andean region: "Political authority . . . had been vested by God on the community or *común*. Therefore, the power of the *común* was above the power of the king. No law, no order, even if it came directly from the monarch, was valid until it had been approved by the *común* or its representatives. Similarly, no governor was legitimate who had not been accepted by the *común*. It was a complex political philosophy presented in simple words, and because the words were simple the philosophy caught hold in Paraguay, even among the illiterate of the countryside." From Adalberto López, *The Revolt of the Comuneros* (Cambridge: Cambridge University Press, 1976), 113.

47. Lagunillas and Challapata were also towns in Paria province, near Condocondo. Changara was an *ayllu* name from the town of Challapata. A pre-Columbian term with many meanings, at its most basic *ayllu* refers to a group of people who claim common ancestry and who collectively hold land. Changara could also be a slightly misspelled reference to a *principal* from Challapata, whose name was Chungara. In the following letter, the assistant priest refers to this letter as coming from a *principal* of Challapata.

48. Ramon del Valle was the parish priest for Culta to whom the *ayudante* reported and submitted fees collected for priestly duties. The *ayudante* was literate but not as well educated as a priest would likely have been. The letter reflects this.

49. The text reads, "haciendo Jueses de sus proprias causas," which implies that they had their own judicial/administrative system. According to Toledo's decrees, *alcaldes* were able to try small claims cases within the community. This could be a reference to that or to a more extensive and hybrid extralegal system.

50. From the context, this does not seem to be a reference to any specific robbery; rather, the *ayudante* seems to be indulging in hyperbole to impress his superior. In many ways this is a rather odd letter. Unlike the parish priest in Tinquipaya who wasted no time in forwarding the letter he discovered, the *ayudante* seems more concerned with his own personal status than with any impending attack on nearby towns. Not only does he take time to complain about his parishioners, at the end of the letter he pleads for a raise and to have the priest bring him some of his favorite medicinal herb!

51. Although under the civil jurisdiction of Condocondo, Culta had become a separate parish in 1779. The priest for Culta also served Cahuayo.

52. No explanation is given as to the identity of don Diego Cosido.

53. Literally, end of the year celebration. This refers to the commemoration of the first anniversary of a death.

54. Although it is not clear why the Macha or Tinquipaya people were in Culta for the festival, they were neighboring towns. A group of Culta people lived (and still live) within the jurisdiction formally claimed by Macha, and they celebrated festivals together. These multicommunity festivals suggest a means by which large numbers of people were mobilized in rebellion.

55. The text reads, "entre los quales se leyó una esquela," "a short note (announcement) was read among them." It is not clear whether the letter was passed around to be read individually, but it seems most likely that the literate among the group read the text out loud. This also points to the importance of the multicommunity festivals as a way of organizing action; people from Tinquipaya and Macha were in Culta when the letter was received. Note that these letters from Andeans were written in Spanish; there was no standard written Aymara orthography at the time. The sentence constructions are unusual and many times seem to be direct translations from Aymara.

56. Indigenous Andeans required special permission to carry swords or firearms. Their usual weapon was a rather large slingshot, which could accurately hurl a heavy rock with deadly force. In addition, whips and bats were used for close fighting. Women were known to put *wichuñas*, the weaving implement made from sharpened llama bone, to particularly telling use. Note here that the *ayudante* identifies the *alcaldes* as the ones who gathered people together and sent the armed troops out.

57. The priest used the word *bureos* to describe the meeting. In modern Spanish this translates as amusement, but an older usage would be tribunal or *junta*, or more generically, gathering.

58. The priest of Macha, don Gregorio José Merlos, was a close ally of Tomás Catari. Merlos later stood trial for his involvement in the rebellion. Priests were frequently accused of sid-

ing with the Andeans in this and other rebellions. See David Cahill, "Curas and Social Conflict," *Journal of Latin American Studies* 16 (1984):241–76.

59. Here the *ayudante* begins quoting the speech of the people from Culta.

60. Although it is not clear from the context what was meant by this, it likely refers to the priest Merlos's calls for abolition of the *repartos*, the forced sale of goods (see note 36). Another possibility is that this is a reference to reduced charges for duties performed by priests. Both of these financial burdens had been the subject of many complaints in the years leading to the rebellion.

61. Although he denied it, it was widely rumored that Tomás Catari had brought written notice of reductions in taxes, church duties, and forced labor from the viceroy. The *cartas de favor* appear to be a reference to these.

62. The *tasa* refers to tribute. In other words, the people of Culta believed that Tomás Catari had brought orders of tribute reduction that their priest and his assistant had hidden in order to force them to continue paying the higher rate. Accusations of this sort were quite common for the last half of the eighteenth century. In the 1750s, the Crown had ordered reductions for the fees paid to the priest for weddings, burials, etc. Many priests were accused by their parishioners of hiding the new list of charges while continuing to charge the higher duties.

63. The last line is literally "pero de todo lo verá," "but he will see it all." In this context the priest is reporting an implied threat which seems to merit a more forceful translation.

64. The priest Merlos had gone to Chuquisaca (Sucre) to plea for Tomás Catari. After Catari's death in January 1781, Merlos stayed on in the capital. Tomás's cousins, Nicolás and Damaso, believed that Merlos had been a negative influence on Tomás and they blamed Merlos for his death. Merlos was no longer welcome in Macha and could have been considered a "fugitive."

65. Both *alférez* and *mayordomo* refer to offices in Christian confraternities, organizations of parishioners which were responsible for celebrations of saints' days. These were annually rotating offices.

66. The Thursday before carnival that ushers in the Lenten season.

67. Again, the *ayudante* is a bit ambiguous. The original Spanish is "quienes havían sobrado de los electos de nuestros alcaldes." *Alcalde* was an annually rotating office, the highest elected civil post in a town. In order to qualify for the post, one had to have held lower civil and religious offices. What the phrase "left over" suggests is that there were a number of people within the town who had held sufficient posts to qualify as an *alcalde*. There were also *alcaldes* who served the church and priest. In these cases, it was not a civil office. A third possibility is that the *alcaldes* themselves had elected people. In this interpretation, it could be a reference to a *cabildo* meeting where officers of the community's confraternities were selected.

68. This phrase "things hidden in my heart" appears to be a direct translation of the Aymara construction meaning "to lie."

69. There is no specific indication as to whom the *ayudante* was referring other than the remainder of the *alcalde* candidates.

70. Again, this is a reference to the fees charged parishioners for priestly duties such as burials. If someone died suddenly and very poor, it would be extremely difficult for the priest or his assistant to collect their fees. The main sources of income for parish priests were the amount set aside from the *tasa* or tax collection and the charges for individual services such as burials, weddings, etc.

71. In other words, the *ayudante* sent the letter by a young boy but had not paid him for the delivery. He was asking the priest to cover the cost.

72. The *ayudante* seems to have been pleading for a raise from the parish priest. At the end of this line the *ayudante* refers to "sus padres"; while this could be a reference to his parents, it more likely refers to the other members of the Mercedarian order to which the priest and the *ayudante* belonged (as reflected in this translation: "your priests"). There was a Mercedarian monastery in Potosí.

73. The burdock plant (*lampazo*) is still believed to have curative powers. It is sometimes used as a diuretic, a purgative and according to a colonial era dictionary, a "stomach softener." Today the roots are sold in many health food markets to be cooked and eaten as a vegetable. The plant looks vaguely like a hollyhock.

74. There is no indication of what news the priest Aranibar might have other than to reinforce the warning of troop movements.

75. In the original, *COMUNIDADES* is in very large writing and is signed with a great flour-
    ish.
76. A town close to Condo.

Document Themes

Cultural Contact/Ethnogenesis/Resistance; Ethnicity; European-Mestizo Peoples;
Gossip and Communication; Governance, Indigenous; Indigenous Peoples;
Military/Rebellion; Popular Culture; Religion; Rural Life; Town Life; Violence.

Suggestions for Further Reading

Abercrombie 1998.
Gosner 1992.
O'Phelan-Godoy 1985.
Rappaport 1990.
Rasnake 1988.
Stavig 1988.
Stavig 1999.
Stern 1987.
Taylor 1979.

CHAPTER 17

Scandal at the Church: José de Alfaro Accuses Doña Theresa Bravo and Others of Insulting and Beating His *Castiza* Wife, Josefa Cadena

(Mexico, 1782)

Sonya Lipsett-Rivera

INTRODUCTION

Systems of honor in colonial Mexico meant that insults were more than just words. Utterances that defamed men and women of good reputation had to be answered or the slight to their personal status within the community would be permanent. Gossip underscored these taints, and although usually not as open, it could serve the same purpose as insults. Local elites believed that systems of honor applied only to them because only they could possess the high status that derived from their superior birth and lineage. From their vantage point at the apex of society, they looked down upon an undistinguished mass of commoners whose lack of virtue was patently clear and whose status could only be dishonorable.

Yet, from the other end of the social spectrum plebeians also conceived of themselves as possessors of honor. They might not compare themselves to a duke or a count, but within their local society they derived honor from proper conduct, legitimate birth, and sexual propriety. This honor was important in their everyday dealings, since they often needed credit and aid from neighbors and friends and thus depended upon relationships of trust. Moreover, plebeians distinguished between various hues of racial categories, which they associated with greater or lesser honor. While their perceptions varied from those of the dominant elite, plebeian self-identities were nevertheless important.

Although insults to an individual's honor had to be answered, reactions differed according to the circumstances. Could a social inferior attack and beat a social superior who had insulted him or her? Was a petition to the courts really a satisfactory rebuttal? In the document that follows, you will read how doña Theresa Bravo, an elite woman, reacted to inferences about her marital fidelity, and how José de Alfaro, a plebeian husband, responded when doña Theresa beat and insulted his wife. Their individual perceptions of the incident in question differed considerably, not only because they were opponents in a lawsuit, but also because of their distinct social standing. There is much left unsaid in this document. For example, José de Alfaro, the plaintiff, seems to believe that he can advance his cause by harnessing ill feeling toward don Diego Fernández, doña Theresa's husband and a colonial official. It is also clear that José de Alfaro holds don Diego Fernández directly responsible for the conduct of his wife, though doña Theresa's precipitous actions and don Diego's lackluster control over her brought dishonor onto his name. Yet, this was a plebeian perspective—part of the confusion of differing points-of-view found in this criminal complaint.

Documents such as this one are tantalizing because they allow us a glimpse of the tensions within a small town. But many criminal records are fragmentary and, just like this one, do not provide the whole file. In this document we see José de Alfaro and his witnesses argue his case, but we do not have the other side represented. We have to guess at how don Diego would defend himself and how this incident was resolved. No verdict is recorded, and so this case, like so many others, is instructive without providing a definitive resolution. It shows us the tensions in a small Mexican town and how women and men dealt with assaults against their name and body. It hints at larger issues, such as don Diego's status within the town, but these are left hanging.

The setting of the document, the town of San Juan Teotihuacán, in the valley of Mexico, also warrants some consideration. Although a major town of the region, and near the famous pyramids of the same name, the town, by the late eighteenth century, had become part of the intendancy of Mexico City. Thus, although a *cabecera*, it was within the orbit of the largest city of the colony. It was, however, not large. In 1791 a census recorded 895 people of Spanish descent, 388 *mestizos*, and 266 *mulatos*. Another count, done in 1804, noted 1,814 Indian tributaries.[1] Clearly San Juan Teotihuacán was large enough to have a varied, racially mixed population, but small enough that people knew each other and personal honor was vital to plebeians and elites equally.

THE DOCUMENT[2]

17.1 Alcalde Mayor *Don Thomas de Velasco Receives the Criminal Complaint*

Criminal proceedings as a result of the denunciation by José de Alfaro against doña Theresa Bravo, her daughter Theresa, and her sister Francisca, as well as a woman deposited[3] in their home, and don Diego Fernández, the husband of doña Theresa, for the mistreatment of his wife, Josefa Cadena. All are *vecinos* (residents) of this town. The presiding judge in this jursidiction is don Thomas de Velasco, *alcalde mayor* and commissioner.

To the *alcalde mayor* or his lieutenant (*lugar teniente*) in royal service in the town of San Juan Teotihuacán.

In the town and *cabecera* of San Juan Teotihuacán, on October 16, 1782, before me, Captain don Thomas de Velasco, *alcalde mayor* of this jurisdiction for His

Majesty, may God protect him, this petition and its contents are presented, in the presence of witnesses and in the absence of a notary.

17.2 The Petition and Criminal Complaint of José de Alfaro

I, José de Alfaro, resident of this town, by the proper channels of justice and without giving up the appropriate measure, say that on Sunday the thirteenth of this month, my wife, Josefa Cadena, was coming [out of church] after mass and passed close to doña Theresa Bravo, the wife of don Diego Fernández, *cobrador de las rentas de alcabalas y pulques* (official in charge of the collection of sales taxes and taxes on *pulque*).[4] Doña Theresa, using the pretext that my wife had brushed against her, which was not true, sprung forward, saying to her, "Oh, you black whore, you dare to brush against me." And throwing her to the ground, not only doña Theresa, but also her daughter, her sister, and the woman who was deposited with them and was in their company, hit her [Josefa] many times. Although don Diego was present, instead of trying to calm them, he said, "Give it to that black whore again." In this way, my wife came out of this attack with marks on her face and a big scratch. She has bruises all over her body because of the beating, and, since she is pregnant and now she is bleeding, we are worried about the unfortunate consequences of this encounter and that she might lose not only the baby's life but also her own.

In the above related events, doña Theresa and her husband, as well as the other accomplices, insulted my wife and me in a very grave manner and in all the ways imaginable. To a married woman, no insult is greater than to call her a black whore, since this offends her fidelity and her *calidad*.[5] Her honor is publicly known, and she is not a black but rather a *castiza*.[6] In regards to actions, none is worse than to have hit her all over her body and to have marked her face.[7] What makes all this much worse is that the insults occurred in public and in the presence of a numerous crowd who were leaving mass. Don Diego is a participant in this crime, not only because he did not prevent it as he should have and as would have been easy for him due to the power vested in him as a husband, but also because he encouraged his wife and the others who insulted my wife, to consummate the humiliation.

And since it is not just that this woman remains unpunished, and that my wife and I remain humiliated and insulted without proper redress, I file a civil and criminal complaint against doña Theresa, her husband, and the associated accomplices. I am justified in the admission of my complaint. It is proper that information be collected as a result of this petition, and this inquiry should also extend to the life and customs of don Diego. If it is true that he lives in disarray and scandal, he should be exiled from this town. The other cases pending against him in this jurisdiction should be gathered together with this one.[8] As a result of the criminal indictment, Your Excellency should arrest the guilty parties, and since don Diego is an employee of the *rentas*, his immediate supervisor, don José de Leon Peñaroja, should be informed so that this service will not be abandoned nor will it suffer.[9] Don Diego should be freed of the corresponding position and any secret tasks, so that Fernández can present himself at the prison. But, before all else, Your Excellency should send the two surgeons of this village to examine my wife and to declare their observations under oath. This will serve as the clearest proof of the crime about which the witnesses will testify. And having done all of this, you may deliver to me the judicial decrees to put my complaint in order. As such, and with all the appropriate protestations, I implore Your Excellency to provide justice. I swear and in lieu

[José de Alfaro] does not know how to sign.

[Signed by] Licentiate Manuel Cordero

17.3 The Alcalde Mayor *Issues Orders to Investigate the Complaint*

And seen and read by me, I received it as presented under the law, and in response to his petition, I must order and I so order, so that the basis of his complaint be shown, the information in the petition must be collected, extending to include the life and customs of don Diego and notification of the two surgical experts, don Felipe Antonio Herrera and don Bernabé de Castro, residents of this town, that they should examine Josefa Cadena, the legitimate wife of the complainant. They must swear and declare their findings according to the law and for the benefit of justice. By this decree, I so order and sign in the presence of witnesses. I certify.

Thomas de Velasco
José Segura and Juan Benavides,
witnesses

In the said day, month, and year, I, the undersigned *alcalde mayor*, acting in accordance with the above mentioned, ordered to appear in court don Felipe Antonio Herrera, master surgeon, with certification of the *protomedicato*.[10] In his presence, which I certify, I informed him of the parts of the order as they relate to him. He is to examine the person of Josefa Cadena and verify the blows that the petition alleges she received. He must declare the results of his examination in the appropriate form and in conformity with the law, according to his knowledge and experience. He stated that he had heard the order, that he understood it, and that he would follow these orders as soon as possible. He signed in the presence of the *alcalde mayor* and the witnesses who acted in the proper form. I certify.

Thomas de Velasco
Phelipe Antonio de Herrera
Juan de Benavides and José Segura,
witnesses

The same day, I, the *alcalde mayor*, made don Bernabé come to the court in his capacity as qualified surgeon, and in his presence, which I certify, I notified him of the sections of the previous order which correspond to him, that he must examine the body of Josefa Cadena. And he understood and said that he heard and will comply with the order. And he signed in my presence and that of my witnesses. I certify.

> Thomas de Velasco
> Bernabé Días Castro
> Juan Benavides, witness

17.4 Testimony of Don Bernabé Días de Castro, Qualified Surgeon

On the seventeenth day of the said month and year, before me, the undersigned *alcalde mayor*, and the witnesses, don Bernabé Días de Castro, qualified surgeon, appeared and said that, in compliance with the notification of the order, he went to the house where Josefa Cadena, legitimate wife of José de Alfaro, lives, and he found her there in bed and obviously ill. She was afflicted because she had been thrown to the ground while her hair was being pulled. And upon examination of her body, he found a scar from her right eyebrow to her hairline, a scratch apparently made by fingernails. She is a bit more than six months pregnant, and she has been hemorrhaging quite heavily through the natural passage— the mouth of the mother[11]—since last Sunday. He has not been able to contain the patient's loss of blood in such quantities despite the use of towels that his colleague surgeon, don Felipe Antonio Herrera, who has been attending her, ordered. And if the flow of blood cannot be contained with these remedies, he believes that she is at risk of a miscarriage. This is what he saw and observed in particular. And he can swear to it according to his loyal knowledge and understanding, and he swears by God our Lord and the sign of the holy cross according to the law that what he has testified is accurate and true. And he signed with me [the *alcalde mayor*] and the assisting witnesses. I certify.

> Thomas de Velasco
> Bernabé Días de Castro
> Juan de Benavides and José Segura,
> witnesses

17.5 Testimony of Don Felipe Antonio Herrera, Master Surgeon

On the same day, before me, the *alcalde mayor*, who has acted in the expressed form, don Felipe Antonio Herrera, Master Surgeon, appeared and said that in compliance with the notification of the order, he examined Josefa Cadena, whom he has been attending since the day of Sunday when her mother had called him to her side. The patient is six months pregnant, and as the result of a major disagreement that she had with other women, she was injured on her hips, thighs, and groin and showed all the symptoms of an impending miscarriage. He applied all the corresponding medicines and remedies to sustain her despite all the blood she lost, which happens in some pregnancies. And it is now the fifth day, and she has not had a miscarriage as a result of the medicines and remedies, which prevented a fever, and the fact that she did not suffer any brusque movements or blows to the hips. Otherwise, she only has a scratch to her forehead over the right eye. These are the details of his examination that he can declare, and he swears before God and the holy cross that what he has stated is accurate and true according to his knowledge and expertise. And he signed before me and my witnesses. I certify.

> Thomas de Velasco
> Felipe Antonio Herrera
> Juan de Benavides and José Segura,
> witnesses

17.6 The Alcalde Mayor Orders José de Alfaro to Present His Witnesses

On October 17, 1782, I, the undersigned *alcalde mayor*, who acts in the expressed form, made José Cadena, I mean Alfaro,[12] appear personally in this court to notify him that he must present his witnesses so that their information can be offered and understood. He [José de Alfaro] said that he heard and will comply with the order. And he did not sign because he did not know how, so I did in the presence of my witnesses. I certify.

> Thomas de Velasco
> José Segura, witness

17.7 Testimony of Don Manuel Delfin

On October, 18, 1782, to provide the information he has offered to give and that it is ordered received, José de Alfaro presented as witness a man from whom I took the oath that he made to God and the holy cross in accordance with the law. He said that his name is don Manuel Delfin, that he is married, of Spanish *calidad*, is forty years of age, and is a resident in this *cabecera*. He knows the person who presents him as a witness. And it is true that on Sunday, the thirteenth of the present month, he was leaving early mass in the company of don Diego Fernández, [the two of them] walking together to the place called Agua Fonda, [when] they heard shouts and turned around to see that Josefa Cadena was seated on the ground, in the company of her sister, and doña Theresa Bravo and her daughter Theresa and her aunt Francisca, as well as a woman deposited with them and many other women who he does not remember, were mistreating her with words.[13] Josefa Cadena got up and tried to hit them, and the young Theresa threw her onto the ground. He saw this because he went there to separate them, which he was able to do. But the others continued to mistreat her with very indecorous words and indecent expressions. And Chepa's [a nickname for Josefa] brother arrived and tried to defend her with indecorous words, and it was then that don Diego Fernández answered them with the same impurity and without stopping. And then, near the house of don Diego, the witness revealed that Josefa had said to doña Theresa that she was a whore and that no one had found a friend under her [Josefa's] bed. It was then that the fight began. All who participated were hit and scratched, but there was no use of arms. That is what he saw and knows of this case. As to the life and customs of don Diego, although he has heard various complaints since he is the administrator of the Royal Monopolies (*rentas reales*), he isn't sure about any of these things. It is true that he talks boldly and with insolence and other improper expressions. This is what he knows in particular and what he can declare in truth. Under oath he affirmed and ratified [his testimony], and he signed with me and my witnesses. I certify.

> Thomas de Velasco
> Manuel Delfin
> Juan de Benavides and José Segura,
> witnesses

17.8 Testimony of Manuel José de Ocampo

On October, 22, 1782, for the information that he is giving, José de Alfaro presented as witness a man who took the oath by God and the holy cross in accordance with the law, and under the oath he offered to tell the truth about what he might know and was asked. And he said that his name was Manuel José de Ocampo, married to doña María Josefa de Flores, Spaniard, twenty-eight years old and a resident of this town. On the thirteenth of the present month, in the house of don Juan Soto, having already left the early mass, he was in the door of Soto's house when he happened to turn his head and saw doña Theresa Fernández [Bravo] and Chepa the *chocolatera* (chocolate seller) fighting, but since he was far away he could not hear what they were saying nor did he see the beginning of the fight, nor did he know what they were fighting over. After, he went into the store, and he did not see or know what other persons were involved in the fight. As to the customs and life of don Diego Fernández, the husband of doña Theresa, he does not know if it is orderly or disorderly or anything else that is asked of him. He swears that he has told the truth according to the oath that he affirmed and ratified, and he signed it with me and my witnesses. I certify.

> Thomas de Velasco
> Manuel Joseph de Ocampo
> Juan de Benavides and José Segura,
> witnesses

NOTES

1. Peter Gerhard, *A Guide to the Historical Geography of New Spain* (Cambridge: Cambridge University Press, 1972), 274.
2. Archivo General de la Nación, (Mexico) Criminal, vol. 27, exp. 12, fol. 494–501, 1782.
3. Officials deposited a woman when she faced any kind of legal suit. For example, when a wife sued her husband for ecclesiastical divorce (that is, for separation in our terms) or accused a man of seduction or rape, the authorities had her placed in a house of good repute. The people who accepted such women into their houses, therefore, had to be well known

as honorable and of high moral standards. Don Diego's household—because the authorities had deposited a woman there—was clearly considered to be highly proper.

4. This position made her husband part of the local elite. He was in charge of collecting sales taxes as well as taxes on *pulque*, one of the most popular alcoholic drinks in Mexico.

5. The term *calidad* refers to the qualities that contribute to the person's overall reputation, one of which was race.

6. Colonial society created a vocabulary to designate racial mixtures. *Castizo* is often defined as the child of a Spaniard and a *mestizo* but more generally could be applied simply to someone of mixed ancestry.

7. The emphasis on the injury to Josefa's face is important. In New Spain facial injuries symbolized revenge. Men and women both tried to mark the faces of people who had offended them, very often for sexual reasons. Women marked another offending woman's face when the victim transgressed sexual boundaries by seducing a husband or lover.

8. Unfortunately there is no information provided about other complaints against don Diego.

9. As *cobrador*, don Diego was responsible for the collection of taxes.

10. The *protomedicato* was a medical regulatory board.

11. "por la via natural de abajo, boca de la madre" (i.e., the vagina).

12. The *alcalde mayor* here corrects his initial mistake, substituting Alfaro's name for Cadena.

13. "de rrasones."

DOCUMENT THEMES

African/Afro-Latin American Peoples; Crime; European-Mestizo Peoples; Family; Gender; Honor; Illness/Disease/Injury/Medicine; Insults; Marriage; Popular Culture; Race; Town Life; Violence; Women.

SUGGESTIONS FOR FURTHER READING

Cope 1994.
Gutiérrez 1991.
Lipsett-Rivera 1998a.
Lipsett-Rivera 1998b.
Martin 1990.
Pitt-Rivers 1966.

CHAPTER
18

Don Manuel Valdivieso y Carrión Protests the Marriage of His Daughter to Don Teodoro Jaramillo, a Person of Lower Social Standing

(Quito, 1784–85)

Christian Büschges

INTRODUCTION

Until the mid-eighteenth century, the church regulated the institution of marriage in Spanish America, emphasizing the freedom of individuals to marry according to their will and, if necessary, independently of their parents' consent. However, on March 23, 1776, the Spanish Crown introduced its own legislation, the Royal Pragmatic (*Real Pragmática*), to assert control over this important social institution. By 1778 the Crown had applied the Pragmatic to all of its colonies, and in subsequent years it issued a series of explanatory guidelines and supplementary decrees.[1] The Royal Pragmatic sought to protect families from socially "unequal" marriages and thus to preserve the traditional hierarchical social order. It required that children now obtain permission to marry from their father or, in his absence, from their mother, grandparents, or nearest adult relative or guardian. In cases where they married without parental authorization, the law allowed for their disinheritance.

The Royal Pragmatic resulted in a groundswell of lawsuits that contested its new regulations on legally acceptable marriages. The records of these lawsuits constitute a rich documentary source, one that offers important insights into contemporary views of inequality and the hierarchical ordering of regional social structures. Concepts of honor and nobility primarily determined the most important social distinctions, though they were in turn affected (and defined) by a number of other factors, including ethnicity and occupation.

The following document excerpts are part of a lawsuit tried before the Audiencia of Quito in 1784 and 1785, just six years after the Royal Pragmatic was promulgated in the Americas. The suit was initiated by Manuel Valdivieso y Carrión, a *vecino* (citizen) of Loja, a city located in the southern highlands of the *audiencia* district. In April 1784, Valdivieso wrote a letter to the *audiencia* president asking him to intervene in a dispute he had with Juan Teodoro Jaramillo; Valdivieso argued that Jaramillo, also a *vecino* of Loja, was of low social standing and had seduced his daughter Baltasara into marriage. For Valdivieso, such a marriage was clearly an offense under the Royal Pragmatic and would greatly dishonor his family; it had to be prevented at all costs.

As the *audiencia* superior court could only accept the case as an appeal from a lower provincial court, the president passed the suit down to the *corregidor* of Loja. At this point, Jaramillo formally challenged the legal basis of Valdivieso's case, arguing against the notion that he and his elected bride were socially unequal. He insisted that the marriage take place. After completing his investigation, but apparently without pronouncing a sentence, the *corregidor* sent the accumulated court records back to the *audiencia* in Quito.

The case ultimately generated extensive documentation; the court records fill 268 manuscript pages (134 folios). The case file includes copies or summaries of the documents presented to the court in Quito and the *corregidor* in Loja, the closing statements made by the lawyers representing the two parties in the suit, and finally the argument of the *fiscal* (crown attorney). While the litigation contains the arguments made in support of both Valdivieso and Jaramillo, the transcripts provide only slight evidence of Baltasara's point of view. Within the document summaries prepared by the Loja *corregidor*, there does appear Baltasara's statement that she had left her father's house after he had withdrawn his earlier consent to the marriage. While we lack the final decision of the *audiencia* and therefore do not know how the dispute turned out, we do know the *fiscal's* recommendations. In October 1785, drawing extensively on the points made by Jaramillo's attorney, the *fiscal* argued that the court should rule against Valdivieso's opposition to the marriage of his daughter with Jaramillo. He refuted the position that there was a considerable social distance between the two parties, and he stressed as well the consent Valdivieso had given to the marriage before his change of mind led to the dispute.

In the following excerpts the two parties present their opposing points of view. The first section contains a summary of previously recorded testimony prepared for the court on behalf of Valdivieso y Carrión. The summary condenses the depositions of ten witnesses who had responded to a lengthy set of questions designed to elicit testimony that would prove Jaramillo's social inferiority.[2] The court summary is followed by the detailed statements of the two opposing attorneys in the case, each laying out the legal basis of their client's claim.

The Cast of Characters

The following list of the main characters in the law suit and their kinship ties should help in negotiating the complex familial relationships referred to in the case:

- **Manuel Valdivieso y Carrión**: the plaintiff in the suit.
- **(Juan) Teodoro Jaramillo**: the defendant in the suit.
- **Baltasara Valdivieso**: Manuel's daughter and Teodoro's betrothed.

- **Juan Jaramillo and María Regalado y López**: Teodoro's parents.
- **Bartolo Gálvez**: María Regalado's second husband.
- **José and Francisca**: two of María's children who she had with other men (one of whom was named Tomás Aguirre).
- **Francisco Jaramillo**: Teodoro's paternal uncle.
- **Juan Jaramillo and Margarita González**: Teodoro's paternal grandparents.
- **Francisco Jaramillo**: Teodoro's paternal great-uncle.
- **Pedro Regalado y Ureña**: Teodoro's maternal grandfather.
- **Esteban (Regalado y?) Ureña**: Teodoro's maternal uncle.
- **Josefa Córdova**: Teodoro's former wife.
- **José de Herique**: Teodoro's close friend.

THE DOCUMENT[3]

18.1 Court Summary of a Questionnaire, with Recorded Testimonies, Presented by Don Manuel Valdivieso

[Asked] if they know or have heard publicly that it is well known and well recognized[4] that don Manuel Valdivieso and his ancestors have been of distinguished nobility and have obtained in Loja and other provinces the most honorable offices, they all confirm [that this is true].[5]

[Asked] if they know that doña María Aguilera, don Manuel Valdivieso's wife, and her ancestors have enjoyed an equivalent reputation, without any reduction of the noble privileges. All of them confirm.

[Asked] if they know publicly that don Juan Teodoro is of low birth, very inferior in origin and *calidad*[6] to don Manuel Valdivieso and his wife. Don José Vivanco says that he has not heard anything about it, either publicly or privately, that he is ignorant of the *calidad* of the parents of don Teodoro, that he has seen [Teodoro's] mother wearing lady's clothing, dressed as a *beata* (lay religious woman),[7] and that he has heard in public that Jaramillo was inferior in descent to don Manuel Valdivieso and his wife. Don Mariano Piedra [says] that he considered don Juan Teodoro a plebeian man and of low birth, but that he regarded him as neither mean nor ignoble,[8] and he knows Jaramillo's origin is very much inferior to that of don Manuel and his wife. Don Agustín Vásquez [says] that he has heard that he is not of noble birth, [but] that he also has heard that he is the grandchild of a distinguished gentleman.[9] Don Bernardo Aguirre [says] that he knows that the [honorific] 'don' was not given to Teodoro at first, but not because he was ignoble or mean; and he has considered him [Teodoro] a white man, and he has heard he descends from the Jaramillo family, which is reputed to be noble. No one can doubt that [the family] of Valdivieso and his wife is of the most illustrious kind. Don Mateo Vásquez [says] he has considered Jaramillo neither ignoble, mean, nor plebeian, [and] that he has known him as a Spanish man, but it is certain that he is not equal to don Manuel and his wife. Don Francisco Moreno [says] that he has not considered don Juan Teodoro a mean and ignoble man, and he does not know anything about his lineage; he has judged him to be a man not of the highest distinction but also not contemptible since he has seen him held in esteem and high regard. He also knows that he [Teodoro] is not an equal of don Manuel and his wife, and that during this lawsuit he has heard [things] in favor and in disfavor of the *calidad* of Jaramillo. Don José Murillo [says] that he has considered don Teodoro a white man and of inferior *calidad* to that of don Manuel. Doña Micaela Castillo [says] that she does not know if don Teodoro is a mean or ignoble man and that she has regarded him as a white and decent man.

[Asked] if they know that Jaramillo was a silversmith by profession, like his uncle Esteban Ureña. Don Mariano Piedra [says] that he has seen him in the silversmith's shop in the company of Esteban Ureña, but he is not sure if he was practicing this craft [though] he has heard this in public on the occasion of this lawsuit. Don Agustín Vásquez does not know if he was or was not [a silversmith]; he says that [Jaramillo] has led caravans of mules owned by Miguel Carrión, getting paid a salary for his work. Don Mateo Vásquez [says] that he saw [Jaramillo] as a child learning the silversmiths's trade in the company of his uncle Ureña, and after a short time he left it [the craft]; [don Mateo Vásquez says] that [Jaramillo] ran the *fábrica*[10] of the house of don Miguel Carrión at the rank of steward,[11] and he led the mules of don Miguel and his son, earning a salary. All the witnesses agree that Jaramillo served in the business and led Carrión's mule caravans . . .

[Asked] if they know or have heard etc.[12] Don Bernardo Valdivieso [says], concerning the paternal ancestors, he knows and has heard that the sons of don Juan Jaramillo and Margarita González[13] were regarded as plebeians, as were the maternal [ancestors] of Teodoro, and they did not hold any honourable offices. [Don Bernardo Valdivieso says] that Francisco Jaramillo is the great-uncle of don Juan Teodoro, and that the descendants of don Francisco have served, because of their family branch or line, in the top occupations. Piedra [says] that he does not know [if] the ancestors of Jaramillo had obtained honorable occupations or manual ones,[14] but that since his grandfather they have been reputed to be plebeians. Aguirre [says] that he does not know anything regarding [Jaramillo's] maternal [ancestors], but that the Jaramillos have served in honorable occupations. Don Mateo Vásquez [says] that he [has] heard that don Teodoro is related to and descends from Jaramillos, noble persons . . .

[Asked] if they have heard or known that don Juan Jaramillo etc. Don Francisco Riofrío [says] that on this same occasion[15] he has heard in various conversations that don Juan Jaramillo married Margarita González, reputed to be the daughter of an Indian woman from Saraguro.[16] Don Mateo Vásquez [says] that he has only heard that don Juan Jaramillo married badly and unequally for his noble station. The other [witnesses] do not know.

[Asked] if they know that Juan Jaramillo and González etc. Vivanco [says] that he only knows that the mother of Jaramillo had a son called José, and as a widow she married Bartolo Gálvez, a humble man who due to his poverty works as a *truquero*.[17] Don Mariano Piedra [says] that he did not know if María Regalado[18] was a plebeian, but that he has regarded her as such . . .

Don Mateo Vásquez adds that María Regalado was a white woman, and that he never saw her in the clothing of a plebeian. Moreno [says] that he did not regard María as plebeian. He knew that as a widow she had conceived José, the son of Tomás Aguirre, and Francisca, the daughter of another father, and that María married Bartolo Gálvez, and because he was a *truquero* [Moreno] considered him a man of low rank.

[Asked] if they know that María Regalado y López etc. Piedra [says] that he knew that she was the daughter of a Pedro Regalado Ureña, an ordinary man who neither deserved [the title of] don nor had obtained any office of honor. Doña Micaela Castillo [says] that she heard talk that Pedro was thought to belong to the second class and not be a distinguished gentleman . . .

[Asked] if they know that José Aguirre etc. Don Bernardo Valdivieso testifies that Francisca, sister of Teodoro, is the wife of Mariano Riofrío, bastard son[19] of an Indian woman. Piedra [says] that Riofrío is the son of an Indian woman. Don Agustín Vásquez [states] that it is said in public that Riofrío is the son of a gentle- man of distinguished nobility; although [Vásquez] has heard talk that [Riofrío] is a *mestizo*, he does not know anything about his mother. Aguirre [says] that he has heard it said that [Riofrío] is the son of an Indian woman and a gentleman . . .

[Asked that] they should declare if Francisco Jaramillo, brother etc. Don Bernardo Valdivieso [says] that on the occasion of the present case he heard don Bernardo Ríos say that don Francisco Jaramillo, Don Teodoro's uncle, had married Catalina Alvarez first, and then Victoria Tinoco, known to be a *mulata*. Don Agustín Vásquez affirms that Tinoco, wife of Francisco Jaramillo, was a free *mulata* in the ser- vice of doña Ana Valdivieso. Aguirre declares that this [was] publicly known . . .

[Asked] if they know that Josefa Córdova, Juan Teodoro Jaramillo's former wife etc. Vivanco [says] that he has regarded Josefa Córdova to be of second class origins. Don Mateo Vásquez [says] that Josefa [is] a white woman and that he has seen her wearing quite decent clothing. Moreno testifies that he regards Josefa not as a plebeian, although she is of humble birth, and that her father had mar- ried an Indian woman. One sister of Josefa had married Tomás Luna, a white man, but not of the plebeian kind, and the other [married] a *chapetón* . . .

[Asked] if José de Herique[20] is a child born out of wedlock[21] etc. Don Bernardo Valdivieso publicly clears him of the accusation[22] that he [José de Herique] was the son of an Indian woman. [Don Bernardo says] that at first Herique carried out the profession of a smith[23] and that he is an intimate friend of don Teodoro . . . Aguirre clears him according to what he has heard regard- ing the *calidad* of Herique, and adds that as an honorable man of good behavior and virtue he [Herique] has taken some measures to end the hostilities and dis- turbances occasioned by the proposed matrimony, and that, although many years ago he had worked as a smith, he now maintains himself as a trader (*mercader*), respected by everyone.

18.2 Petition Submitted to the Court by Ramón Jaramillo, Attorney for Don Manuel Valdivieso

I, Ramón Jaramillo,[24] attorney, in the name of don Manuel Valdivieso y Carrión, citizen of the city of Loja, in virtue of the power he has invested in me to act in the lawsuit against Juan Teodoro Jaramillo, concerning the marriage that he re- quests to doña Baltasara Valdivieso, daughter of my client, thinking himself no-

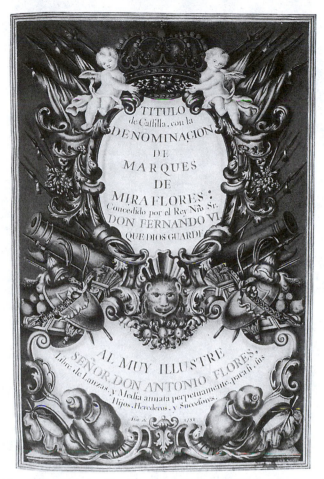

Figure 11 A title of Castile issued by King don Fernando VI to don Antonio Flores, making him a *marqués* (marquis) and giving to him and his heirs the rights of high nobility in perpetuity (1751) (Archivo Histórico del Banco Central, Quito. Fondo Jijón y Caamaño No. 599).

ble, and with the rest inferred, I say that in the name of justice [and] in order to serve the superior judgment of Your Highness, [you should] declare, with a just and clear judgment, that the named Jaramillo is plebeian and of humble birth and cannot and shall not enter into marriage with doña Baltasara. If she anticipates this decision with irregular and wrongful actions,[25] in contradiction to her known nobility and *hidalguía*, she should suffer precisely the penalties[26] prescribed in the latest publicly announced Royal Pragmatic (*Real Pragmática*), that all in these realms are ordered to follow, guard, fulfill and execute. The court should condescend to resolve and judge the case, both because the law is clearly on my client's side and because, despite the cunning lobbying[27] with which Teodoro has tried, with no other merit than his moneyed wealth, to aspire to a much higher station than that [appropriate to] his low birth, he does not cease to be the son of Juan Jaramillo, who was himself born of another don Juan Jaramillo and Margarita González, Val-

Figure 12 Like Figure 11, a grant of noble title which bestowed upon its wealthy recipient in the Andes the honors and privileges enjoyed by the highest levels of colonial society. In this case the king granted the title of *marqués* to don Antonio Sánchez de Orellana (1700) (Archivo Histórico del Banco Central, Quito. Fondo Jijón y Caamaño No. 578).

divieso, o Montesdoca, who, not knowing with certitude the identity of her father, must be classified as an Indian like her mother. Nor does Teodoro cease being the son of María de Ureña, known as the Maco Regala,[28] wife of the *truquero* Bartolomé Gálvez, both low people, who as such occupied the servile and mechanical stations appropriate to their birth. Because of his low birth, Jaramillo worked in the profession of silversmith under the shadow of his uncle Esteban Ureña, who instructed him publicly as an apprentice, until he went on to serve as steward in the house *fábrica* of don Miguel Carrión, and then as muleteer, or driver of his mules, a profession he carried out for many years in the company of don Pedro Javier Valdivieso, without neglecting all the activities with which he made his fortune.[29] He then bought the Catamayo hacienda, which has increased his means and made him conceited, so that, forgetting his humble beginnings, he claims not only to equal but even to exceed the distinguished *calidad* of my client. And his whole family, conspiring with their witnesses, who are of the same extraction as his, showing disrespect for the constant echo of the truth and the sacred religion of the oath, have insisted on ennobling their mean descent, not only through the [honorific] don, with which they prodigiously honor themselves, but also through nobility itself, which they ascribe to their ancestors, who, due to their contemptible *calidad*, never held any honorable position[30] of the kind held by subjects of distinction. And as [they have always carried out the] low, manual trades, they have not passed beyond being silversmiths and servants. Jaramillo himself, with all his fortune, hardly exudes the dignity of a steward of the city,[31] this being a position that the illustrious citizens of the most distinguished nobility have never obtained . . .[32]

That a corrupt or indulgent patron might give the title of don, which these days plebeian men often enjoy, does not mean that they therefore can constitute themselves as nobles without the requisites that laws and rights prescribe . . .

The unfortunate witnesses had wished to distinguish the family of the Ureñas, Regalados and López, who have earned nothing more than the honor of being either silversmiths or servants. Even if they might not have been of mixed origin, but had been Spaniards, they would not pass beyond the rank of *montañeses*,[33] who are commonly known as *mestizos* of a slightly better class than the children of an Indian woman and a Spaniard . . .

That is why the inequality which exists between Jaramillo and doña Baltasara is irrefutable, he descending from subjects of obscure birth and the lowest plebs, and she from the most distinguished, who, corresponding to their eminent nobility, have occupied the most honorable offices of the republic, as is consistent and publicly known.

18.3 Defense Submitted to the Court by Tomás García y Sierra, Attorney for Don Juan Teodoro Jaramillo

I, Tomás García y Sierra, in the name of don Juan Teodoro Jaramillo, citizen of the city of Loja, in virtue of the power he has invested in me to act in the lawsuit against don Manuel Valdivieso y Carrión . . . state that:

I will examine the foundations on which the complaint is based, and, as one cannot deny that don Manuel and his daughter doña Baltasara are accepted as noble and esteemed as such without dispute, it only remains to see if the lineage of my client has the claimed social distance to consider that matrimony is seriously offensive to the honor of the family of don Manuel, [considering] the [appropriate] degree [of relationship] laid out in the Royal Pragmatic of 1776. And in fact, the evidence given by both parties does not justify the [accusation of] low origin and extremely ignoble extraction which has been made against my client; on the contrary, the purity of his blood[34] and his *hidalguía* are demonstrated, all of which refutes the insults and invectives he has been exposed to . . . All his uncles and cousins, legitimate descendants of don Juan Jaramillo, have been regarded as persons of known nobility and distinguished *calidad*, for which reason they had obtained the best offices of that community (*república*)[35] and were married to women of the same class, as is entirely confirmed in detail by the certificate[36] presented by don Manuel Jaramillo, second cousin of my client and, at the moment, *alcalde ordinario*[37] of the city of Loja. This document should be kept in mind because it accurately enumerates the offices, honors, and marriages from the first don Juan Jaramillo, who was born in Alcalá de Henares . . .[38]

The copious number of witnesses that my client presented before the *corregidor*[39] confirmed unanimously that [Jaramillo's] ancestors, doña Margarita included, were not of the race of *negros*, Indians, and *mulatos* . . .

The nobility of his mother [is] impossible to deny, as it is confirmed by an extensive number of witnesses who affirm that they had known doña María, that she was the daughter of don Pedro Regalado de Ureña and doña Clara López de la Parilla, and that he [Pedro] was the son of the captain Antonio de Ureña and doña Isabel de Solórzano, and that doña Clara was the legitimate daughter of don Marcos López de la Parilla and doña Elena Román, all of them noble persons, free (*limpia*: literally, "clean") of people [descendants] from other castes . . .[40]

The Royal Pragmatic does not require a mathematical equality between prospective husbands and wives when it obliges the parents, relatives, or guardians to give their assent. And it only requires assent when matrimony does not seriously offend the honor of the family, declaring just cause for dissent in the case of a serious offense. And no one doubts that not every inequality is seriously offensive, since to be so it is necessary that the social difference be too striking and excessive . . .

All of this evidence [about the standing of Juan Teodoro] is enhanced by the extensive proof that my client has offered concerning his good habits and behavior. Although the opposing attorney characterizes this justification as useless and superfluous to this lawsuit, my client thought to present it as more relevant to the honor of his person, since he has well understood, by what the *arbitristas*[41] teach, that the political nobility that consists in good habits is better than the legal and civil one derived from blood, that moral virtue exceeds natural virtue, and that the nobility of heroic actions exceeds the nobility of blood. It is the same as when a philosopher, asked what nobility consists of, answers that in the case of the beasts it refers to the good constitution of the body, in the case of men to their good and laudable actions.[42] One may infer, then, that, far from being superfluous to the lawsuit, this evidence is most suitable to prove that my client has this double nobility that makes him worthy of the esteem that has been granted to his person in private and public acts in this neighborhood (*vecindario*). Also, it [has not] been proven otherwise that the office and profession [of steward of the city], to which he had been appointed in the year 1781, is appropriate only to plebeian men as, on the contrary, it has clearly been carried out by nobles . . .

When asked if the nobility loses its privileges through the practice of ignoble and mechanical professions, A.A. [the *arbitristas*] resolve that it is not denigrated if the nobility derives from blood and not from privilege, and that is the general opinion . . .

The earlier consent [of Manuel Valdivieso] was directed toward removing, through the remedy of matrimony, the public infamy that doña Baltasara must have suffered because of the illicit contact she had with my client for over two years,[43] without her parents having said a word in opposition in all this time . . .

It would not be reasonable to thwart this marriage of doña Baltasara, because, under these circumstances, no one would want her to be his wife, nor would it be possible for her to find another husband who, knowing about her former relationship (*amistad*), would extend to her the appropriate respect. It is also not tolerable that my client be scorned[44] when he aspires to grace through [the sacrament of] matrimony, having been valued during the illicit relationship, letting it be known through such irregular means that his notion of nobility prevails over [the obligations of] religion.[45] One should conclude from this argument, and from the sufficient proof I have presented to demonstrate the *hidalguía* of my client, that the petition of don Manuel Valdivieso should be declared unfounded and unjust . . .

NOTES

ACKNOWLEDGMENTS   I am very grateful to James Van Hook for revising my translation of the original text into English. I was able to consult the documents pertaining to this case while working in the National Archive of Ecuador in Quito during July and August 1995, thanks to a research grant provided by the Deutsche Forschungsgemeinschaft.

1. On the Royal Pragmatic, see Daisy Rípodaz Ardanaz, *El Matrimonio en Indias: Realidad social y regulación jurídica* (Buenos Aires: Fundación para la Educación, la Ciencia y la Cultura, 1977); Patricia Seed, *To Love, Honor, and Obey in Colonial Mexico: Conflicts over Marriage Choice, 1574–1821* (Stanford: Stanford University Press, 1988), 200–25; and Susan M. Socolow, "Acceptable Partners: Marriage Choice in Colonial Argentina, 1778–1810," in *Sexuality and Marriage in Colonial Latin America*, Asunción Lavrin, ed. (Lincoln, Neb.: University of Nebraska Press), 209–251.

2. I have included the responses to only some of the thirty-three questions asked of the witnesses. The surviving court documentation does not contain the original questionnaire.

3. Archivo Nacional del Ecuador/Quito, Sección General, Matrimoniales, caja 3, expediente 3-VI-1785: "[Au]tos de Don Manuel Valdivieso [y Carrión] con Don Teodoro Jara[mill]o sobre el matrimonio que pretende con Doña Baltasara Val[divies]o, seguidos en Loja ante el corregidor que los remitió al señor [Presi]dente, Regente, y su Señoría los pasó a este tribunal."

4. "pública y notoria" in the original. A critical defining characteristic of members of the *hidalguía*, or lower nobility, was that their status be "notoria," publicly known and recognized. An alternative term for *hidalguía notoria* was *hidalguía de solar conocido*, or nobility of known family line or lineage. Persons who received their noble status as a privilege granted by the Crown (*hidalguía de privilegio*) enjoyed a lesser degree of esteem, though in subsequent generations nobility by privilege (*hidalguía de privilegio*) could evolve into a publicly known and recognized nobility (*hidalguía notoria*).

5. "la absuelven todos" in the original.
6. The term *calidad* refers to a person's recognized social status and esteem.
7. A *beata* was a woman who led a religious life and wore a habit but who had not professed to be a nun and who continued to live in the community.
8. "Ruin ni vil."
9. "Caballero principal."
10. Here *fábrica* would seem to refer to the running of the family business in its entirety, including the operation of the mule train.
11. "Mayordomo."
12. Here the entire question is not included in the document; rather, the sentence fragment merely ends with "etc."
13. The paternal grandparents of Teodoro Jaramillo.
14. "mecánicos".
15. The occasion of the present lawsuit.
16. A village in the Loja region.
17. The term *truquero* probably refers here to the owner of a table on which a card game, called *truque*, was played (see María Moliner, *Diccionario de uso del español*, 2 vols. [Madrid: Editorial Gredos, 1984]). An alternate meaning might be the owner of an early form of the billiards table (see Real Academia Española, *Diccionario de Autoridades*, 3 vols. [Madrid: Editorial Gredos (1726–39) 1979]).
18. The mother of Teodoro Jaramillo.
19. "hijo adulterino" in the original.
20. José de Herique was a close friend of Teodoro's. As a person's reputation and rank was affected (and reflected) by the company they kept, Valdivieso tried to diminish Teodoro Jaramillo's social position by questioning the status of his friend José de Herique.
21. "hijo sacrilego."
22. The original here is "absuelve," but used in a different sense from that found at the beginning of this document excerpt (see note 5 above); here the term is used in its strict legal sense, meaning to acquit or clear.
23. "El oficio de herrería."
24. There is no indication in the document that Ramón Jaramillo was related to Teodoro.
25. That is, if Baltasara gets married before the final decision of the court.
26. The loss of all claims to inheritance.
27. "astucia y cabilasión."
28. There is no information in the document on the reason María de Ureña was given this nickname, or on its meaning.
29. Probably a reference to his occupations as a silversmith and steward.
30. "cargo."
31. "Mayordomo de la ciudad." At the beginning of 1781, Jaramillo was elected by the town council of Loja to the office of steward of the city and its hospital ("mayordomo de la ciudad y de su hospital").
32. Suggesting that the position was considered to be of too low esteem for people of high social status.
33. In the highlands of colonial Quito the term *montañeses* referred to *mestizos* who were held in higher social esteem than "ordinary" *mestizos* due to their lifestyle, higher status occupations, and claims to a higher purity of blood.
34. "Limpieza de sangre."
35. "República," in its early modern sense, derived from the Latin term "res publica"; in the early modern period *república* did not refer to a specific form of government or a nation-state but rather to a social and political community, an urban society organized politically (here the specific reference is to the city of Loja).
36. Unfortunately, the certificate was not included in the court records.
37. A member of the city council who served as a magistrate.
38. Spanish city near to Madrid.
39. A reference to the *corregidor* of Loja who initially tried the case.
40. "Castas."
41. "A.A." in the original. The economic and political decline of the Spanish monarchy, beginning in the latter part of the sixteenth century and continuing into the seventeenth, led to the publication of a number of pamphlets with prosposed remedies, or *arbitrios*; their au-

thors, who were people of different social origin, were referred to as *arbitristas*. In the eighteenth century the term was used less frequently, though the political, social, and economic changes brought about by the Bourbon reforms led to a renewed interest in publishing pamphlets commenting on the monarchy and its reforms. An alternative reading of the abbreviation "A.A." could be *abogados* (lawyers or attorneys). This interpretation seems unlikely, though, as Tomás García serves as the *abogado* for his client and *abogados* were hardly decisive authorities in the special subject of determining the true origin and essence of nobility.

42. "operaciones" in the original.
43. "Illicit contact" refers to sexual relations; it was not uncommon for couples to have sex once they were betrothed. However, it was critical that the marriage then be completed, otherwise the woman (in this case Baltasara) would lose her reputation. For a detailed discussion, see Ann Twinam, "Honor, Sexuality, and Illegitimacy in Colonial Spanish America," in *Sexuality and Marriage in Colonial Latin America*, Asunción Lavrin, ed. (Lincoln, Neb.: University of Nebraska Press, 1989), 118–55.
44. "se le desestime."
45. An enigmatic passage; the original is: "quando aspira a la gracia por medio del matrimonio, aviéndosele apreciado, quando constava la ilícita amistad, dando a conoser con tan irregular procedimiento, que prevalece en su concepto la nobleza a la religión." This would seem to stress Teodoro's unbroken will to marry Baltasara and his contention that while it might have been a sin to engage in premarital sexual relations, it was more important to act with nobility and ensure her reputation through completing the marriage.

DOCUMENT THEMES

Economy and Work; Ethnicity; European-Mestizo Peoples; Family; Gender; Honor; Inheritance; Marriage; Nobility; Town Life; Women.

SUGGESTIONS FOR FURTHER READING

Büschges 1996.
Büschges 1997.
Caro Baroja 1966.
Jaramillo Uribe 1965.
Konetzke 1951.
Ladd 1976.
Lohmann Villena 1947.
Maravall 1989.
Peristiany and Pitt-Rivers 1992.
Pitt-Rivers 1966.
Rípodaz 1977.
Seed 1988.
Stewart 1994.
Twinam 1989
Villamarín and Villamarín 1982.
Windler 1997.

CHAPTER
19

Permission to Marry: Eighteenth-Century Matrimonial Files
(Montevideo, 1786)

Susan Migden Socolow

INTRODUCTION

Matrimonial files (*expedientes matrimoniales*), a type of document found in the ecclesiastical archives of all churches throughout Latin America, contain the supporting evidence that was required before a priest could perform a marriage. Beginning in the mid-sixteenth century with the new laws formulated at the Council of Trent (1545–63), the Catholic Church worked to normalize the rules of marriage. Before Trent couples could marry without a clergyman being present; after Trent marriage came increasingly under the Church's control. In addition to making the services of a priest a fundamental part of a valid marriage ceremony, the council drew up a complex list of who could marry, and who could not.

The Church's more stringent rules of betrothal and marriage required prospective newlyweds to prove that they were not already married, that they were not too closely related to each other, and that they had not taken a religious vow of chastity or joined a religious order. Kinship relationships that would prevent marriage included not only blood ties, but also so-called spiritual ties or *parentezco espiritual*, which in these documents means being related as godparents to one's prospective spouse. In this selection we have six separate *expedientes matrimoniales* dated from 1786, which show how the rules on marriage drawn up by the Council of Trent affected the process of Catholic marriage in the Spanish American colonies.

While in theory all couples wishing to marry were to go through the same process, in the city of Montevideo, church authorities gathered the necessary information only if the groom-to-be was not locally born. San Felipe of Montevideo was the last sizable city created by the Spanish government in America. Founded in 1726, it was envisaged primarily as a military bastion to hold back Portuguese expansion in the region. But the city also commanded an excellent natural harbor, making it an attractive port for both legal and illegal trade. Initially commerce (or smuggling) was primarily with the Portuguese whose port city of Colônia da Sacramento (or simply Colônia) lay to the south, but who were also found throughout the area to the north. After Spain's commercial reforms of 1778, Montevideo was allowed to trade directly with Spain. And with a far better port than Buenos Aires, ocean-going ships preferred to anchor there and transfer goods by lighter across the river.

For at least the first twenty years of the city's existence, all men planning to marry would have been born elsewhere and thus been required to present the type of information contained below. As the years passed, although the number of people born in the city increased, the city and its growing economy served as a magnet for immigrants. The number of men marrying who were required to file an *expediente matrimonial* grew over time. The matrimonial files give us, therefore, evidence about the continual immigration of Europeans, as well as Americans from nearby regions (including Buenos Aires and the Mission district)[1] and African slaves. In spite of prohibitions against Portuguese and Brazilians migrating to the city, these documents make it clear that official policy did little to stop the movement of people across would-be frontiers. Readers will see evidence for the fluidity of territorial boundaries in eighteenth-century America and the relative powerlessness of states to control the movement of peoples across them.

The following documents may cause readers to wonder why ecclesiastical authorities drew little distinction between free and slave immigrants to the region in conducting marriage procedures. True, a free man initiated a matrimonial file by expressing his wish to marry whereas a slave's master or mistress had to initiate the proceeding. But once procedures began, both slave and free were required to present the same information.

What does an *expediente matrimonial* look like? Well, the first item in these files was a formal request filed by the groom-to-be requesting that Church authorities gather the required information. Once this petition was approved, the ecclesiastical notary questioned the groom-to-be under oath as to his marital status. The notary then immediately called at least two witnesses, always men, to attest to the information provided. To carry any weight in these proceedings witnesses had to be people who had known the prospective groom for some length of time and could swear to his bachelor status. The file was then passed on to the *vicario* who, finding everything in order, proceeded to call for a reading of the banns. These banns, a public announcement of the upcoming wedding, would be repeated in church for three successive Sundays. The publicity was an invitation for any member of the community to come forth with additional information that might prevent the wedding. If no one did so, the actual ceremony could take place.

In spite of the use of a boilerplate in drawing up these documents and the resultant repetition, they contain unique information—for example, the age and place of birth of both the groom-to-be and his witnesses—about individuals in the colony. In addition to providing data on marriage, they also give us a partial view of slave marriage. We do not have similar information about Montevideo-born slaves, but the *expedientes* do provide some rough measures of slave marriage as well as information about the age of the groom at the time of marriage. These documents can also be useful in studying literacy (or, better said, illiteracy) in a colonial society. Because only men were required to attest to their bachelorhood, we lack comparable information on the marriage age and literacy of the women who were marrying them.

In addition to allowing us to get an idea of the marriage rates and ages, the *expedientes* provide us with a picture of the geographical origin of Montevideo's population, both slave and free, as well as suggestions about the length of time they had been in the city. As to origin, readers may be surprised to see the apparent frequency of a pattern of bringing male slaves to Montevideo from Brazil rather than from Africa. The cases involving slaves demonstrate that one of the major slave trading routes for Montevideo was via Brazil. A careful reading of these documents, then, allows us to infer in rough terms some patterns of geographical mobility, socialization, friendship, and of networks of people joined together by common experiences.

The six cases that follow were all chosen from the *expedientes matrimoniales* files owned by the Archive of the Curia of Montevideo. In four of these *expedientes*, the couple wishing to marry are both slaves. In one case, a man born in Brazil is planning to marry a free black widow, and in another an Indian widower from the Missions district wishes to marry a *mestiza*. Readers will want to note both the formulaic nature of these files as well as their variation (both in the order in which information was solicited and the detail requested or provided) in mining them for glimpses of the lives for which they are the only remaining traces.

THE DOCUMENTS[2]

19.1 Nicolás de Zamora Seeks Permission for Two of His Slaves to Marry

Excellent *Vicario* and Ecclesiastical Judge:

I, don Nicolás de Zamora, *vecino* of this city, appear before you and state that I have two slaves named Juan and María Teresa, natives of [born in] Benguela,[3] and because they have asked me for permission to marry as our Holy Mother, the Church so orders, and they must therefore be sent for so that they can state that they are single and answer all questions related to holy wedlock, and therefore:

I request that you order that the above process take place.

As stated, in as much as what is requested in this petition is ordered by law, I name the present notary to take the necessary information.

[signed] Josef Eusebio González,
ecclesiastical notary[4]

In this city of San Felipe of Montevideo on September 3, 1786, as the *vicario* and ecclesiastical judge has ordered according to the law of marriage, I, the notary present, questioned the prospective groom under an oath made in the name of God, our Lord, and the sign of the cross, as required by law. He stated that his name is Juan Negro,[5] born in Benguela, and a slave of don Nicolás de Zamora, and has resided in this city for six years. He promised to state the truth as he knows it to all the questions that he is asked relating to his bachelorhood.[6] He further stated that he is single, neither engaged to marry nor under any promise of chastity nor a member of any religious order; neither is he related by blood nor marriage nor *parentezco espiritual* (hereafter godparenthood)[7] with the woman he wants to wed, María Teresa, black slave of the same master. This is the truth, given under the oath that he has made; he is twenty-eight years old and he does not sign this document because he does not know how to write. All of the above is witnessed by me.

[signed] José Eusebio González,
ecclesiastical notary

On the same day, month and year, as part of the same information contained in the request, I, the notary present by order of Your Grace, questioned a man under an oath made in the name of God, our Lord, and the sign of the cross, as required by law. He stated that his name was Juan Cardoso, black slave of don Simon Jauregui, born in the Congo and residing in this city. He promised to state the truth as he knows it to all the questions that he is asked. Concerning the bachelorhood of the prospective groom, Juan Negro, he stated that he has known him since he arrived in this land, and that he has always been a slave of don Nicolás de Zamora. He has always believed him to be a bachelor neither married nor engaged to marry nor related by blood nor marriage nor godparenthood with the woman he wants to wed nor has he given his word to wed any other woman. This is the truth given under oath, and he affirms and ratifies his statement. He is forty-eight years old and he does not sign this document because he does not know how to write. All of the above is witnessed by me.

[signed] Josef Eusebio González,
ecclesiastical notary

On the same day, month and year, I, the notary present by order of Your Grace, questioned a man under an oath made in the name of God, our Lord, and the sign of the cross, as required by law. He stated that his name was Juan Agustín, black slave of the señora Mariscala, and residing in this city. He promised to state the truth as he knows it to all the questions that he is asked. Concerning the bachelorhood of the prospective groom, he knows him as a bachelor who is neither married nor engaged to marry nor related by blood nor marriage nor godparenthood with the woman he wants to wed nor has he given his word to wed any other woman. This is the truth given under oath, and he affirms and ratifies his statement. He is twenty-nine years old and he does not sign this document because he does not know how to write. All of the above is witnessed by me.

[signed] José Eusebio González,
ecclesiastical notary

The above information having been seen by the *vicario*, he orders that the couple proceed to publish the banns in the matrix church[8] as the Holy Roman Catholic Church and the sacred Council of Trent have decreed. Thus it is ordered.

[signed] E. Juan Josef Ortiz

19.2 Bernardino Moreira de Silba Seeks Permission to Marry Leonor Pérez de Meneses

Excellent *Vicario* and Ecclesiastical Judge:

I, Bernardino Moreira de Silba, legitimate son of Manuel de Silba and Dominga Blanca de Olibera, born in the Capilla of los Remedios in the jurisdiction of Rio de Janeiro, and resident in this city for the last ten years, appear before you and state that to better serve our Lord, I intend to marry Leonor Pérez de Meneses, free black, widow of Gonzalo de Sosa, born in Rio de Janeiro and because I must give proof that I am free to marry, I present people who have known me and know me. Therefore:

I request that you order that the above process take place.

As stated, in as much as what is requested in this petition is ordered by law, I name the present notary to take the necessary information.

[signed] don Juan Josef Ortiz

In the city of San Felipe and Santiago of Montevideo, on January 10, 1786, as the *vicario* and ecclesiastical judge has ordered according to the law of marriage, I, the notary present, questioned the prospective groom under an oath made in the name of God, our Lord, and the sign of the cross, as required by law. He stated that his name is Bernardino Moreyra de Silba, born in the Capilla de los Remedios, in Janeiro,[9] and residing in this city for the last nine years. He promised to state the truth as he knows it to all the questions that he is asked relating to his bachelorhood. He further stated that he is single, neither engaged to marry, nor under any promise of chastity, nor a member of any religious order; neither is he related by blood nor marriage nor godparenthood with the woman he wants to wed, Lionora Peres de Meneses, the free black widow of Gonzalo de Sosa Nieba who died a year ago. This is all he has to say under oath, and he affirms and ratifies his statement; he is twenty-seven years old and he does not sign this document because he does not know how to write. All of the above is witnessed by me.

[signed] José Eusebio González,
ecclesiastical notary

On the same day, month, and year, I, the notary present by order of Your Grace, questioned a man under an oath made in the name of God, our Lord, and the sign of the cross, as required by law. He stated that his name was Juan de Matos, born in Janeiro and residing in this city more or less seven years. He promised to state the truth as he knows it to all the questions that he is asked. Concerning the bachelorhood of the prospective groom, Bernardino Moreyra de Silba, he stated that he knows him. He met him about twenty years ago in Janeiro and has also known him here because they have been soldiers together in the same company. He has always believed him to be a bachelor neither married nor engaged to marry nor related by blood nor marriage nor godparenthood with the woman he wants to wed. Nor has he given his word to wed any other woman. This is the truth given under oath, and he affirms and ratifies his statement. He is fifty years old and he does not sign this document because he does not know how to write. All of the above is witnessed by me.

[signed] José Eusebio González,
ecclesiastical notary

On the same day, month, and year, I, the notary present by order of your grace, questioned a man under an oath made in the name of God, our Lord, and the sign of the cross, as required by law. He stated that his name was Luis de los Santos, born in Paraguay and residing in this city nine years. He promised to state the truth as he knows it to all the questions that he is asked. In the matter of bachelorhood, he stated that he knows the prospective groom, Bernardino Moreyra de Silba. He met him in Colônia as a soldier and has also known him here all the time that he has been in Montevideo. He has always believed him to be a bachelor neither married nor engaged to marry, nor related by blood, marriage or godparenthood with the woman he wants to wed. Nor has he given his word to wed any other woman. This is the truth given under oath, and he affirms and ratifies his statement. He is twenty-two years old and he does not sign this document because he does not know how to write. All of the above is witnessed by me.

[signed] José Eusebio González,
ecclesiastical notary

The above information having been seen by the *vicario*, he orders that the couple proceed to publish the banns in the matrix church as the Holy Roman Catholic Church and the sacred Council of Trent have decreed. Thus it is ordered.

[signed] E. Juan Josef Ortiz

19.3 Don Josef Ortega Seeks Permission for Two of His Slaves to Marry

Excellent *Vicario* and Ecclesiastical Judge:

I, don Josef Ortega, *vecino* of this city, appear before you and state that I have two slaves named Pedro and Micaela, she born in Angola, and he in the Congo. They asked me for permission to marry as our Holy Mother, the Church so orders, and I said yes. I now requested that they be made to state that they are single and to answer all questions related to holy wedlock, and therefore:

I request that you order that the above process take place.

As stated, in as much as what is requested in this petition is ordered by law, I name the present notary to take the necessary information.

[signed] E. don Juan Josef Ortiz

In the city of San Felipe and Santiago of Montevideo, on February 9, 1786, as the *vicario* and ecclesiastical judge has ordered according to the law of marriage, I, the present notary, took an oath made in the name of God, our Lord, and the sign of the cross, as required by law from a man who stated that his name is Pedro Ortega,[10] born in the Congo and residing in this city for the last six years. He promised to state the truth as he knows it to all the questions that he is asked. And relating to the proof of bachelorhood he stated that he is single, neither engaged to marry nor under any promise of chastity nor a member of any religious order; neither is he related by blood nor marriage nor godparenthood with the woman he wants to wed, Micaela Ortega, born in Angola, a black slave of don José Ortega. This is all he has to say under oath, and he affirms and ratifies his statement; he is more or less twenty-eight years old and he does not sign [this document] because he does not know how to write. All of the above is witnessed by me.

[signed] José Eusebio González,
ecclesiastical notary

On the same day, month, and year, I, the notary present by order of Your Grace, questioned a man under an oath made in the name of God, our Lord, and the sign of the cross, as required by law. He stated that his name was Domingo, a black born in Angola and residing in this city for ten years. He promised to state the truth as he knows it to all the questions that he is asked. And relative to the bachelorhood of the person of Pedro Ortega, black slave, he stated that he knows him. He met him in Janeiro and has also known him here, seeing him frequently. He has always believed him to be a bachelor neither married nor engaged to marry, nor related by blood, marriage, or godparenthood with the woman he wants to wed nor has he given his word to wed any other woman. This is the truth given under oath, and he affirms and ratifies his statement. He is thirty years old and he does not sign this document because he does not know how to write. All of the above is witnessed by me.

[signed] José Eusebio González,
ecclesiastical notary

Next in reference to the information contained in the above request, I, the notary present took the oath made in the name of God, our Lord, and the sign of the cross as required by law, of a man who stated that his name was Manuel García Martín, black slave of Paula Martínez, residing in this city twenty years. He promised to state the truth as he knows it to all the questions that he is asked. And relating to the proof of bachelorhood of Pedro Ortega, resident, he stated that he met him twelve years ago in this city, that he has seen him frequently, that he has always believed him to be a bachelor neither married nor engaged to marry nor related by blood nor marriage nor godparenthood with the woman he wants to wed nor has he given his word to wed any other woman. He is forty-six years old and he does not sign this document because he does not know how to write. All of the above is witnessed by me.

[signed] José Eusebio González,
ecclesiastical notary

The above information having been seen by the *vicario*, he orders that the couple proceed to publish the banns in the matrix church as the Holy Roman Catholic Church and the sacred Council of Trent have decreed. Thus it is ordered.

[signed] E. Juan Josef Ortiz

19.4 Cayetano Manuel Seeks Permission to Marry Isidora Romero

I, Cayetano Manuel, Indian and widower of Rosa de Sayro, legitimate son of Toribio Manuel and Catalina Abuleyro, born in the *pueblo* of San Juan in the Missions district and residing in this city for the last five years, appear before you and state that I want to marry Isidora Romero, a *china*, legitimate daughter of Tomás Romero and Lorenza Ponzel, born in Buenos Aires and residing in this city for the past seven years. Because it is necessary that I prove my widowhood, and not having any documents, I wish to present witnesses from my town who will give testimony under religious oath. Therefore:
I request that you order that the above request be granted for it is justice.
As stated, in as much as what is asked for in this petition is ordered by law, take the information of widowhood which is requested. Thus ordered and signed.

[No signature]

In the city of San Felipe and Santiago of Montevideo, on May 4, 1786, as the *vicario* and ecclesiastical judge has ordered, I, the notary present, took an oath made in the name of God, our Lord, and the sign of the cross, as required by law from Cayetano Manuel. He promised to state the truth as he knows it to all the questions that he is asked about if he is the widower of Rosa de Sayro, Indian, who died years ago. He stated that it is true that he is the widower of the deceased Sayro, who died of smallpox more or less five years ago. Asked in which parish she was buried, he answered that in the cemetery of the very same church of San Juan. Asked if he had any impediment that prevented him from contracting marriage with Isidora Romero as he wishes, he stated that he had none, that he was a widower free to marry. This is the truth given under oath, and he affirms and ratifies his statement; he is twenty-eight years old and he does not sign [this document] because he does not know how to write. All of the above is witnessed by me.

[signed] José Eusebio González,
ecclesiastical notary

On the same day, month, and year, Bentura del Cobia, Indian, who works in the royal ovens (*hornos*), legitimate son,[11] from the *pueblo* of San Juan in Missions province and residing in this city for five years appeared before me. By order of Your Grace, I the undersigned notary received his oath made in the name of God, our Lord, and the sign of the cross, as required by law, in which he promised to state the truth as he knows it to all the questions that he is asked. Asked if he knows that prospective groom Cayetano Manuel is the widower of Rosa Sayro, he said that this is true, that Cayetano is indeed the widower of the late Rosa Sayro. Asked if he knows that Rosa died in the *pueblo* of San Juan, and if he was present in that *pueblo* when she died, he responded that he knows for certain that Rosa died in the above-mentioned *pueblo*. Asked how long ago Rosa died and where she was buried, he stated that she died three to five years ago. Asked if he saw her die or being buried, he responded that he was there when she died in the above mentioned *pueblo*, and that it is true that she was buried in the cemetery of San Juan because Rosa died of smallpox. This is the truth given under oath, and he affirms and ratifies his statement. He is thirty-eight years old and he does not sign this document because he does not know how to write. All of the above is witnessed by me.

[signed] José Eusebio González,
ecclesiastical notary

On the same day, month, and year, Diego de Cunigua, Indian, from the *pueblo* of San Juan in Missions province and residing in this city for five years, appeared before me. By order of Your Grace, I the undersigned notary received his oath made in the name of God, our Lord, and the sign of the cross, as required by law, in which he promised to state the truth as he knows it to all the questions that he is asked. Asked if he knows that Cayetano Manuel is the widower of Rosa Sayro, he said that he knows that, that he knew him while he was married to the late Rosa, and that lately he knows that he is the widower of the late Rosa. Asked where and how long ago she died, he answered that he knows that she died in the *pueblo* of San Juan in Misiones because he was there, and this was about five years ago, and she was buried in the church of the *pueblo* and that the priest was named fray Pedro Ernandes, and that he came to this city together with the prospective groom. This is the truth given under oath, and he affirms and ratifies his statement. He is twenty-nine years old and he does not sign this document because he does not know how to write. All of the above is witnessed by me.

[signed] José Eusebio González,
ecclesiastical notary

The above information having been seen by the *vicario*, he orders that the couple proceed to publish the banns in the matrix church as the Holy Roman Catholic Church and the sacred Council of Trent have decreed. Thus it is ordered.

[Not signed]

19.5 Don Josef Durán Seeks Permission for Two of His Slaves to Marry

Don Josef Durán, *vecino* of this city, appears before you and states that I have two slaves named Domingo and María, both of them Benguelan blacks. They asked my permission to marry as our Holy Mother, the Church, so orders, and they must therefore be sent for so that they can state that they are single and answer all questions related to holy wedlock, and therefore:

I request that you order that the above process take place.

As stated, in as much as what is requested in this petition is ordered by law, I name the present notary to take the necessary information.

[signed] E. Juan Josef Ortiz

In this city of San Felipe of Montevideo on June 15, 1786, as the *vicario* and ecclesiastical judge has ordered according to the law of marriage, I, the notary present, questioned him under an oath made in the name of God, our Lord, and the sign of the cross, as required by law. The prospective groom promised to state the truth as he knows it to all the questions that he is asked relating to his bachelorhood. He further stated that he is single, neither engaged to marry nor under any promise of chastity nor a member of any religious order; neither is he related by blood nor marriage nor godparenthood with the woman he wants to wed, María Durán, black slave of don Josef Durán. This is the truth, given under the oath that he has made; he is thirty years old and he does not sign this document because he does not know how to write. All of the above is witnessed by me.

[signed] José Eusebio González,
ecclesiastical notary

On the same day, month, and year, as part of the same information contained in the request, I, the notary present by order of Your Grace, questioned a man under an oath made in the name of God, our Lord, and the sign of the cross, as required by law. He stated that his name was Juan Negro, black slave of don Juan Ramos, a native of Benguela, residing in this city for twenty years. He promised to state the truth as he knows it to all the questions that he is asked. Concerning the bachelorhood of the prospective groom, Domingo, he stated that he met Domingo in Rio de Janeiro and has known him there and here, for they came together in the slave trade. He has always believed him to be a bachelor neither married nor engaged to marry nor related by blood nor marriage nor godparenthood with the woman he wants to wed nor has he given his word to wed any other woman. This is the truth given under oath, and he affirms and ratifies his statement. He is twenty-eight years old and he does not sign this document because he does not know how to write. All of the above is witnessed by me.

[signed] Josef Eusebio González,
ecclesiastical notary

On the same day, month, and year, I, the notary present by order of Your Grace, questioned a man under an oath made in the name of God, our Lord, and the sign of the cross, as required by law. He stated that his name was Josef de Texada, black slave of the colonel of the Fixed Regiment,[12] and residing in this city for the last six years. He promised to state the truth as he knows it to all the questions that he is asked. Concerning the bachelorhood of black Domingo, he has known him for the last six years in this city and has had a close relationship with him. Domingo has not given his word to wed any other woman, nor has he taken any vow of chastity, nor is he related by blood nor marriage nor godparenthood with the woman he wants to wed. This is the truth given under oath, and he affirms and ratifies his statement. He is twenty-six years old and he does not sign this document because he does not know how to write. All of the above is witnessed by me.

[signed] José Eusebio González,
ecclesiastical notary

The above information having been seen by the *vicario*, he orders that the couple proceed to publish the banns in the matrix church as the Holy Roman Catholic Church and the sacred Council of Trent have decreed. Thus it is ordered.

[signed] E. Juan Josef Ortíz

19.6 Don Eusebio José Vidal Seeks Permission for Two of His Slaves to Marry

Señor Priest and *Vicario*:

Don Eusebio José Vidal, lieutenant in the Dragoon Regiment and *vecino* of this city, appear before you and state that I have two black slaves named José Negro and Ana de la Concepción Negra, from Minas, and having asked me for permission to marry as our Holy Mother, the Church, so orders, and they must therefore be sent for so that they can state that they are single and answer all questions related to holy wedlock, and therefore:

I request that you order that the above process take place.

As stated, in as much as what is requested in this petition is ordered by law, I name the present notary to take the necessary information.

[signed] E. Juan Josef Ortíz

In this city of San Felipe of Montevideo on May 2, 1786, as the *vicario* and ecclesiastical judge has ordered according to the law of marriage, I, the notary present, questioned him under an oath made in the name of God, our Lord, and the sign of the cross, as required by law. The prospective groom promised to state the truth as he knows it to all the questions that he is asked relating to his bachelorhood. He further stated that he is single, neither engaged to marry nor under any promise of chastity nor a member of any religious order; neither is he related by blood nor marriage nor godparenthood with the woman he wants to wed, Ana de la Concepción, black slave of the lieutenant of the Dragoon Regiment don Eusebio José Vidal. This is the truth, given under the oath that he has made; he is twenty-eight years old and he does not sign this document because he does not know how to write. All of the above is witnessed by me.

[signed] José Eusebio González,
ecclesiastical notary

On the same day, month, and year, as part of the same information contained in the request, I, the notary present by order of Your Grace, questioned a man under an oath made in the name of God, our Lord, and the sign of the cross, as required by law. He stated that his name was Joaquín, black slave of don Manuel Soriano, a native of Bahia de Todos os Santos [Brazil], residing in this city for twenty years. He promised to state the truth as he knows it to all the questions that he is asked concerning the bachelorhood of José Vidal, black slave of don Eusebio José Vidal. He stated that they met in Bahia, and they arrived here in the same month. He has always believed him to be a bachelor neither married nor engaged to marry nor related by blood nor marriage nor godparenthood with the woman he wants to wed nor has he given his word to wed any other woman. This is the truth given under oath, and he affirms and ratifies his statement. He is twenty-nine years old and he does not sign this document because he does not know how to write. All of the above is witnessed by me.

[signed] Josef Eusebio González,
ecclesiastical notary

On the same day, month, and year, I, the notary present by order of Your Grace, questioned a man under an oath made in the name of God, our Lord, and the sign of the cross, as required by law. He stated that his name was Soterio, black slave of the commander of the Coast Guard (*resguardo*), a native of Bahia de Todos os Santos, and residing in this city for the last three years. He promised to state the truth as he knows it to all the questions that he is asked. Concerning the bachelorhood of José Vidal, he met José in Bahia and they were shipped together to this city to be sold. He has always known him to be a bachelor, who is neither married nor engaged to marry and has no impediment to undertake marriage with Ana de la Concepción Vidal, a native of Angola. This is the truth given under oath. He is twenty-eight years old and he does not sign this document because he does not know how to write. All of the above is witnessed by me.

[signed] José Eusebio González,
ecclesiastical notary

The above information having been seen by the *vicario*, he orders that the couple proceed to publish the banns in the matrix church as the Holy Roman Catholic Church and the sacred Council of Trent have decreed. Thus it is ordered.

[signed] E. Juan Josef Ortíz

Notes

Acknowledgments The author acknowledges with thanks the courtesies extended by Dante Turcatti, director of the Archivo de la Curia of Montevideo, where the documents of this chapter are housed.

1. The Missions district, or Misiones, lay to the northwest in the region of present-day southern Paraguay and northeastern Argentina. Its name came from the fact that it was the region where in the seventeenth and eighteenth centuries, the Jesuits had founded and effectively governed a series of mission towns to Christianize, educate, and protect local (chiefly Guaraní) indigenous peoples.
2. The documents translated, all dated 1786, come from the *Expedientes matrimoniales* section of the Archivo de la Curia of Montevideo. Their archival file or legajo numbers, corresponding to the order presented below, are 1, 4, 16, 13, 43, and 46.
3. A region of present-day Angola along the Atlantic coast.
4. Editors' note: The author has retained the variant spelling of personal names found in the marriage petitions. For example, González, the ecclesiastical notary, usually signed his given name as José, but four times in this document he uses the variant Josef.
5. Here Juan uses his race, "negro" or black, as his surname. His name could also be translated "black Juan."
6. In the Spanish text bachelorhood is referred to as "libertad" or "freedom." In essence being a bachelor meant that one had the freedom to marry.
7. Beginning the statement that "he is single," each groom-to-be swore that he had none of the attributes that would disqualify him to marry. Disqualifiers fell into two categories: personal attributes (for example, being already engaged to wed another person) and relationship attributes (for example, being too closely related to the bride-to-be).
8. The matrix church or "matriz" was the principal church of the city.
9. A frequently used abbreviation for "Rio de Janeiro."
10. Note that both Pedro and Micaela, his bride-to-be, have taken the same last name as their master. This occurred frequently in colonial Spanish America.
11. Although Bentura includes information on his legitimacy, he fails to include his parents' names.
12. An army regiment permanently stationed in Montevideo. Members of this regiment were professional soldiers as compared to the part-time members of the local militia.

Document Themes

African/Afro-Latin American Peoples; Gossip and Communication; Marriage; Migration; Religion; Slavery.

Suggestions for Further Reading

Boyer 1995.
Chandler 1986.
Lavrin 1989.
Martínez-Alier 1972.
McCaa 1990.
Miller 1990
Ramos 1975.
Seed 1988.
Socolow 1989.

CHAPTER
20

Felipe Edimboro Sues for Manumission, Don Francisco Xavier Sánchez Contests
(Florida, 1794)

Jane Landers

INTRODUCTION

Enslaved persons had legal rights in Spanish law that included the right to own and dispose of property and to buy their freedom and that of their family members. While many owners agreed to sell slaves their freedom without the intercession of the court, should the owner not be willing, a slave had the right to initiate a legal action called *coartación*. This required the court to determine the slave's "just price" as evaluated by two assessors, one selected by the slave and the second by the owner. An owner might challenge the evaluation and also might try to convince the court that the slave was undeserving, but even influential slaveowners had difficulty impeding solicitations for liberty when the law presumed it was the "natural" state of man.

Once the court set a "just" price for a slave, he made a down payment, became a *coartado*, and moved inexorably toward freedom. As soon as the slave had paid his owner the mandated sum, he received notarized manumission documents that detailed his full rights as a citizen in the community.

Coartación suits provide evidence about slave families, their occupations, and their economy. These records also demonstrate how owners and slaves negotiated their own relationship and how both employed reputation and community connections to try to achieve desired legal ends. As well, such suits illustrate the conciliatory nature of Spanish law, and how government officials, and even the contending parties, worked to achieve compromise.

In Spanish Florida the governor, Juan Nepomuceno de Quesada, his legal counsel, Josef de Ortega, and the government notary, José de Zubizarreta, formed the tribunal that adjudicated Felipe Edimboro's *coartación* petition and the challenge to it mounted by his owner, don Francisco Xavier Sánchez. Sánchez was perhaps the largest landholder in Florida and held important government beef and firewood contracts. His cattle empire comprised several thousand acres and stretched along the Diego Plains, north of St. Augustine almost to the Georgia border and west to the St. John's River.[1] Like most great Spanish landholders, Sánchez also owned urban properties, including a house on Marina Street and another two-story stone house on St. Charles Street in which he operated a retail store. Sánchez conducted business (including, his enemies alleged, an illicit slave trade) with companies stretching in a broad triangle from Baltimore down the Atlantic coast, to Havana, and east to Providence in the Bahamas.[2]

When Sánchez was away on business, his trusted Guinea-born slave and the skilled butcher of his cattle, Felipe Edimborough (aka Edimboro), acted as overseer of the one-thousand-acre San Diego plantation on which Sánchez kept a herd of eight hundred to nine hundred cattle, thirty to forty horses, and thirty-four slaves, including Edimboro's Guinea-born wife, Filis.[3]

The San Diego plantation was also home for Sánchez and his common-law wife, María Beatriz Stone (aka Piedra), a free mulatta born in Charleston. The couple lived together for almost twenty years and raised three sons and five daughters, all of whom Sánchez recognized at their baptisms. When the children grew older, Sánchez moved them into St. Augustine where they were attended by slaves of their own, including Filis. With their father's blessings and official dispensation from the bishop, three of Sánchez's quadroon daughters married white peninsular Spaniards and began their own households, while his twin daughters remained unmarried and lived together in the townhouse their father provided.[4]

In 1787 the fifty-one-year-old Sánchez married María del Carmen Hill, the seventeen-year-old daughter of a wealthy South Carolina family. María Beatriz Stone died three years later and left no property "due to her poverty." This formulaic phrase in her testament denoted her legal rather than actual condition, for as his treatment of his illegitimate children substantiates, Sánchez would have been shamed by such a failure of community-sanctioned responsibility. Sánchez's marriage to María del Carmen produced four legitimate sons and six daughters, and María del Carmen and her children apparently enjoyed an amiable relationship with the children of Sánchez's first union and served as godparents many times over for their children.[5]

Francisco Xavier Sánchez died on October 3, 1807, and with María Carmen's approval Sánchez's illegitimate children inherited houses, lands, and slaves valued at over 6,000 pesos. María and her eight young children could afford to be generous. When Sánchez's estate was probated it comprised nine plantations, grazing lands, slaves, cattle, nine townhouses and lots, and commercial interests valued at over $30,000.[6]

Of Edimboro we know that he was born in West Africa but became the slave of a British Floridian sometime in the 1770s. When that owner died, Sánchez acquired Edimboro at auction. Edimboro worked for Sánchez for the next twenty-two years during which time he and Filis began their extensive family.

Edimboro and Filis spoke English and considered themselves Protestants, but as this suit shows, they learned how to manipulate Spanish law and social conventions to advantage. In order to enhance their standing in the community and the success of their suit, Edimboro and Filis were baptized as Catholics on

July 15, 1794, and were formally married in St. Augustine's church on the 29th. Once free, the industrious couple made every effort to advance. They baptized all twelve of their children as Catholics, and their son Mariano attended the government school in St. Augustine.[7] Edimboro joined the free black militia and rose to the rank of sergeant, and his sons later joined him. They helped defend Spanish Florida against Anglo, Indian, and pirate enemies, for which military services Edimboro received a land grant from the Spanish government. Edimboro and Filis owned at least one slave who helped them work the land, and when Spain ceded Florida to the United States in 1821 Edimboro still held his homestead.[8]

Because he was illiterate and not a native speaker of Spanish, the court assisted Edimboro in several important ways to pursue his legal rights. A public attorney represented Edimboro, and he was allowed to choose his own interpreter. The governor's counsel also informed Edimboro of his right to have an assessment, and he named his own assessor.

The proceedings took place in the governor's house, which also served as the government headquarters for the province's main city and capital, St. Augustine. This Atlantic port city held about three thousand people in the 1790s, including Spanish officials and their dependents, a military garrison of about three hundred men, and a polyglot citizenry of Spanish, English, African, and Menorcan descent.[9] About one-fifth of the city's black population was free, and the notarial records for Spanish Florida show a regular pattern of self-purchase, as well as a lesser number of *gratis* manumissions.

Self-purchase was usually a slow and arduous process, as this case illustrates. It took Edimboro and his wife, Filis, twenty-two years to save enough money to buy freedom for themselves and their numerous children. Together they manipulated the *jornal*, the self-hire system widely practiced throughout Spanish America that allowed slaves to hire out their own time or practice their own occupations and crafts while retaining their earnings. In return the slave delivered an agreed-upon daily or monthly sum to his or her owner, but kept any surplus. Edimboro and Filis were supposed to give their *jornales* to their owner's mulatto children, whom he assigned them to serve, and whom, Edimboro charged, their father had failed to educate in Christian precepts. Instead the enslaved couple saved their hard-earned wages and purchased their freedom. The relative autonomy Edimboro and other slaves enjoyed in this community may be surprising to readers more familiar with the Anglo-Saxon system of chattel slavery. As you will note in his language and in the arguments he makes, Edimboro creatively tested the emancipatory potential of Spanish slave law and made it live up to its promise.

THE DOCUMENT[10]

Felipe Edimboro, black slave of don Francisco Xavier Sánchez, requests he be given his liberty as well as that of his wife and one child, also slaves of the same owner, based upon the assessments of experts.

20.1 Felipe Edimboro Requests Manumission for Himself, His Wife, Filis, and Their Five-Month-Old Daughter

Felipe Edimboro, black slave of don Francisco Xavier Sánchez, humbly declares that he has served his master for twenty-two years, and in that time his master has never had the least complaint as to his affection or service. The same is true of the declarant's wife, who has served their owner only slightly less time. This good service is worth more than the price for which he has requested liberty for the two, paying what is fair, or 250 pesos, for himself and the same for his wife, named Filis, and it is impossible to pay what is asked [by his owner] for each one, which is 500 pesos [apiece], a sum that is obviously unjust.[11] To earn that much is impossible, even if I worked excessively to collect it. Fair terms are the 500 pesos [total] that I could give. Further, don Francisco twice promised your exponent's liberty at no charge for having delivered his life and his hacienda from various persons who wanted to take all he had in his home.[12] In addition, I guarded his house with the expected exactitude while he made a trip to Havana to do important business, as the owner can testify, as could others. These facts make our request that you give us our liberty even more worthy of your consideration.

Moreover, he [Edimboro] has a five-month-old daughter for whose liberty he will give forty pesos, and with all this he will have accomplished the liberty of all of his family as well as his own.

Remaining at Your Honor's goodness and mercy, add [this statement] to the previous statement[13] to be given to don Francisco Sánchez, which appears to be correct, that the price should be 540 pesos. Awaiting the exact and great justice you administer. Florida, March 3, 1794. Because he does not know how to write he made an X.

[Signed] Felipe Arnaiz de Espinosa.

[Governor Juan Nepomuceno de Quesada ordered the petition reviewed by his legal counsel, don Josef de Ortega, and also ordered that Edimboro be advised of this action.]

20.2 The Government's Legal Counsel Requires Edimboro's Assessment and Proof of Marriage

I have reviewed this matter and find that the solicitation of liberty was contracted by judicial appraisal.[14] The exponent should be informed that that is his right and that a slave is so empowered [by the law]. And if he has not previously proven the legitimacy of his marriage with the black woman Filis, for whom he has also presented a petition for liberty, she should not be legally included in this petition. In such case, her petition should be forwarded separately.

[Signed] *Licenciado* [Josef de] Ortega,
[Governor] Quesada,
and José de Zubizarreta, public notary.

[The governor so ordered on March 11, 1794. The same day the notary notified Edimboro of the counsel's findings.]

20.3 Felipe Edimboro Responds and Selects an Assessor

Felipe Edimboro, black slave of don Francisco Sánchez, appears before you by means of an attorney to better observe the law, and states:

That I have been informed of your decree responding to my petition of the third of the current month, in which I asked that you concede my liberty, together with that of my wife and one child; in [your decree] doubts were expressed as to the legitimacy of my marriage, as well as the fact that I had not been evaluated as to the sum that should be charged for my ransom. With the greatest submission I will state all that occurs to me regarding the ruling.

As to the statement that I should be evaluated to obtain my liberty, I now understand that it should be thus, but I have the difficulty that should this happen, I will delay or never obtain that which I will nullify [my liberty]. For having given my owner the faithful service I rendered him, and for all the other circumstances that make me so valued, as most of the citizens of this province can testify as to my good habits and the rest that does me credit, it is clear that my master, as well as the persons to whom the task of the assessment is assigned, would all value me at such a high price that, no matter my desire to pay it, it would be impossible. For which reason I suggest that [because of] the personal services I have rendered him, such as saving his life on various occasions while accompanying him when he has needed my help, as my owner himself and others who serve him can tell you, he offered me my liberty as soon as the business in which he was involved was concluded. But since none of this was legally arranged, I have no other recourse but to ask for your intercession and that you authorize that I be allowed to pay the price at which I was purchased. For I believe that my master will be compensated for the additional value that I have acquired since the time of my purchase by the services just expounded.

As to the matter of the marriage, which in my petition I state to have contracted with Filis, also the black slave of don Francisco Sánchez, and by which we have a child, I can not call it legitimate, because it lacked the ceremonies required by the Catholic faith and it was only celebrated between ourselves, as is the custom among the rest of our kind of the British nation.[15] For which reason Your Majesty, with your well-known wisdom, will handle this according to your most prudent judgement. I hope that your kindness will incline you toward the most unworthy of those who implore your justice. Therefore, I beg Your Majesty to consent to what I have asked for with justice. I swear I have not proceeded out of malice and all the rest that is required.[16] Moreover, despite the above, and in case an evaluation is required, please accept don Miguel Ysnardy as my choice to appraise me according to his skill and fairness.

[Signed] Bartolomé de Castro y Ferrer
[Edimboro's counsel].

[On March 25, 1794, Governor Quesada ordered the notary to make a copy of Ed-imboro's petition and deliver it to don Francisco Xavier Sánchez. The governor also ordered the notary to advise Edimboro of this action.]

20.4 Don Francisco Xavier Sánchez Responds

Don Francisco Xavier Sánchez, a citizen of this city, appears before Your Majesty as required by law and by the proceedings initiated by my slave Felipe Edim-boro, soliciting his liberty, that of a black woman he calls his wife, and a daughter, all also my property, and I state:

That a copy of the petition has been delivered to me, and in order to reply in the proper manner, as I should, I ask that Your Majesty order my slave to appear before you, be sworn in, and declare clearly and openly, as required by law and under penalty of the law: firstly, how much money he has; how much of that is in jewelry and where and in what manner he acquired the sum; what daily or monthly *jornal* he ever gave me in all the time which he has been in my power; and lastly, by which extraordinary means unknown to me he acquired the sum that he presents in his first petition. And once his declaration is done, I ask Your Majesty to order that it be provided to me, so that with its contents I can reply in the appropriate form and with full understanding. Thus I swear I will proceed out of justice.

[Sánchez accepted don Miguel Ysnardy as Edimboro's assessor but asked the governor to replace Ysnardy as public interpreter for the rest of the proceedings. The governor named don Manuel Rengil, who accepted the commission of interpreter and swore to well and loyally carry out the functions of his office as he best understood them.]

20.5 Felipe Edimboro Testifies Before the Notary

In the city of Saint Augustine, Florida, on the said day, month, and year, there appeared before me to testify Felipe Edimboro, black slave of don Francisco Xavier Sánchez, whose oath I received by virtue of my commission and through the offices of don Manuel de Rengil, who swore him by God Almighty and the Gospel, according to the Protestant faith he professes, by which he promised to tell the truth as to all he knew and all he was asked about these proceedings, and he stated:

That he has 312 pesos in cash money that belong to him and of which he can voluntarily dispose, that he has no jewelry of any value that he could convert into cash and increase that sum that he has declared, and that this sum he acquired and saved, not only by his own great economy from a tender age, avoiding all superfluous expenditures that could waste whatever money he was given even since he was a child, but also because once he managed to save fifty pesos, his desire to conserve and increase his savings grew even stronger, and he managed to earn more, which in no way did the declarant squander, by hunting, fishing, killing some piglets for neighbors who hired him to do so, and through other licit means. His wife's continuous work washing clothes and making cakes contributed in no small way to arriving at the indicated sum, and all of this was done with the knowledge of his owner. He never gave his owner any *jornal*, for his obligation was to be a butcher and the owner received the agreed-upon compensation from the owner of the animals or the contractors with whom he dealt, although the declarant does not know how much his owner received or in what form. And the time the declarant worked for his own benefit was never at the expense of the duty to which his owner assigned him, and since his owner collected all the payments that were given for these services, the declarant has nothing with which to pay a *jornal* from his own means. The declarant notes that any time in which he was not working as a butcher, he remained in the house of his owner working at whatever he was told. He states that all he has said is the truth as demanded by his oath, that he is about forty years old according to his calculations, and he did not sign because he does not know how, and the secretary signed for him.

> [Signed] Manuel Rengil [Edimboro's interpreter] and José de Zubizarreta [public notary].

20.6 Don Francisco Xavier Sánchez Responds

Don Francisco Xavier Sánchez, citizen of this city, in the proceedings initiated by my slave Felipe Edimboro soliciting his liberty, that of the black woman he calls his wife, and of her child, all of them my property, and in response to the declaration that at my request my slave made by means of a public attorney as required by law, states:

That having read the declaration made by my slave, I find my slave's sworn statement false and without any merit because he swore by God Almighty and the Four Gospels, and it is well-known he professes no religion whatsoever, although he would like to make us believe with this oath that he is Protestant, but his sole and only religion is a lack of conscience. And in this he will always persist, if some divine omnipotence does not take pity on him, because his hardened heart is so controlled by lasciviousness that on the various occasions when I have encouraged him to study what is necessary to receive the holy sacrament of baptism and to follow and observe the teachings of God and his church, he has answered me with such libertinism and frivolous arguments that in truth, if humanity had not reigned in my Christian heart, I would have committed murder. And as it is known that the baptism of catechumens [persons undergoing instruction in the rudiments of Christianity] must only be administered to those showing full understanding of its complexity, never have I wanted, for the above-stated reasons, to force him to receive [baptism]. For such fundamental reasons I will in no way accept his sworn statement, and I annul it, admitting only that which to me is favorable.

And understanding as well as is possible the unfounded points in his false and ill-advised declaration, I will briefly give a concise narrative of the bad customs that I have observed in this ungrateful *negro*, omitting others, all of which I make available so that the righteous tribunal can proceed with the justice that it issues every day in its rulings. Even when my slave was the property of an earlier owner he was under my control and at my orders, and his duties were so light that they consisted of helping others of his class in field work. He had difficulty learning that occupation, as much for his little ability as for his lack of the necessary size, so after his owner died, he and other slaves belonging to the deceased were placed at public auction; and at that auction I purchased several slaves, among them Edimboro, paying a total sum for them all. And I applied him, as did his former owner, in whatever I needed done around the house or outside. He was not out of my sight a single day in all that time so it is not possible that he could have acquired the fifty pesos he states, nor even that he could have acquired the most minimal sum, because indisputably his fellow slaves would have notified me, and so that proposition is false. Once the cession of this plaza to Your Catholic King and señor,[17] may God guard him, was accomplished, and the governor señor don Manuel Vicente de Zéspedes was confirmed, I contracted with him to supply his troops and the citizenry with fresh meat for the period of eighteen months. And knowing the agility and inclination that my *negro* had earlier manifested for the occupation of butcher, helping others of this class, I resolved to give him that commission, although with some repugnance because I had noticed that he inclined toward thievery. And he did conduct himself that way in that task. With known and vile means was he able to acquire a growing sum, robbing me daily and with dissembling style, selling the innards, heads, tripe, and tallow of my animals to the citizenry, and particularly to all the Mahonese families, and although I repeatedly asked him to inform me what [those sales] were producing, I was never able to determine it as he told me all was lost and none of it could be used. All of which I had to suffer having never been able to find a way to control this [Edimboro's thieving] or discharge this task. But wishing in some way to correct this daily and exorbitant theft, I found another no less significant, for one day I decided to test it and found the same articles that my slave called wastes sold for at least six *reales* daily [eight *reales* equalled a *peso*]. And motivated more by curiosity than by the latter to visit the slaughterhouse where I had purchased him a house made of palm in which to live, which I was never able to get him to do, with some difficulty I forced open the door and was able to enter. Inspecting the few pieces of furniture in it I arrived at last at his bed, and in it I discovered a slab of meat that weighed three or four pounds. Holding him solely responsible for this unexpected find, he was proven a liar, and finally he asked my pardon and offered me compensation. As for that which I described earlier as wastes, not only did I determine on that occasion, but also on the occasion of finding the meat, that although he thought little of that of which he daily robbed me, not being bothered by the customary sales, [these acts] prove the false and improper means by which this *negro* has tried to embezzle, as well as the many inconveniences that the butcher also caused me by raising a certain number of pigs at my expense at the slaughterhouse, maintaining them on saleable products, of which, like the rest, he should have given me the profits. And when he felt the time was right he killed them, and wherever he found it most convenient sold them, adding the profits to everything else which he had robbed from me. But I do not want to hide from the just tribunal the deadly end of all this avid

accuses of theft, stealing

self-interest. Being, as I have earlier said, so inclined to cursed and lascivious liberties, as well as polluted by all manner of disreputable diversions, he contracted to rent the top floor of don Juan Villalonga's house, and most nights had rowdy dances there with suitable refreshments, and everyone well supplied repeatedly toasted the hospitality of don Francisco Sánchez's *negro*, Felipe Edimboro. Finally my [government meat] contract ended and with it the dances and the refreshments of my *negro*. His sudden departure[18] left two concubines abandoned, who better to satisfy his depraved vices he had kept with all they require. This is the end result of one with his many defects. He carried to my country home only a few items of clothing, and great offense to God Almighty to whom he swears and whom he does not know. I have observed the many and repeated insults because of which the one whom at that time he called his wife wanted to separate from him and their illegitimate marriage by any means, all of which proves he never had anything.

He also says in his declaration that she whom he calls his wife has collaborated to acquire the sum he presents, making cakes and selling them. That statement is false because as far as I know all she makes are some tortes of flour and honey that they call *queque* (cake),[19] which only blacks and poor boys eat. He also says that by washing clothes she acquired a certain number of *reales*, which, added to the rest stolen [from me], came to the total he presents in his last statement. In reality it is only on this occasion that I am made aware of this false information because I never gave my permission for this. She was assigned to care for my innocent family in town. And it does not seem right that during my frequent business trips to town, which was so distant from my home, I should have to waste time and patience to inspect what my black woman was laundering or to whom it belonged, always believing when I found her in the exercise of that task that she was simply fulfilling her obligation to comply with my orders. For this reason, not only should she inform me of everything that she has earned by this false and malicious means, but also a severe punishment should be imposed so that she will mend her ways in the future. Everyone knows, Sir, that everything my *negro* [Edimboro] has said is informed by an ignorant advisor[20] who wants to proceed without any erudition, much less experience or Christianity, but not only does he aspire to obtain by such unfounded and bad advice the means of my ruin, but also the ruin of my *negros*.

It is impossible for me not to inform the tribunal that the despicable proposition of my slave, citing and declaring that he has managed to accumulate the money he says he has with his fishing, hunting, and butchering of pigs, is so false that as a result of it he deserves a severe punishment, for it is well known that I have never granted my *negros* permission to spend workdays on such diversions, and having done so, it proves, as do the rest of their actions, that my interests have suffered, for they had the obligation to attend to their specific duties, and instead apportioned the time to their own malicious ideas. Feast days are the only time permitted for such [activities], and those they always spent sleeping, and when there was occasion, singing, playing musical instruments, and dancing, and also giving rein to their despicable vices. He also says that by butchering pigs he has been able to acquire a few *reales*, but this is a very limited possibility because [this is only done] at Christmas time, and then those who can, far from occupy-

not given permission to work outside duties

ing themselves in butchering, take advantage of the festivities, all of which is easy to verify. And as for the other kinds of animals, it would be even less likely, because everyone goes to the only slaughterhouse, where only beef is sold daily.

Sir, because some of my family lacked Christian instruction and sacraments, I decided to establish them in the city, assigning them one of the houses I own there, and at the same time [I gave them] two black women to live with them and contribute to their maintenance and decency. And I ordered them [the two black women] to give [my children] a daily *jornal*, and when work was not to be found, they were to present themselves for service in the house. And from these proceedings I find that only one of them complied with her obligations, and the other one, who is the one my *negro* calls his wife, forgot her obligations, and only spent her days doing laundry and making *queques*. At the same time I also ordered that my *negro* [Edimboro] provide a *jornal* daily for the support and aid of my family, believing, although not totally, that he would forget his lasciviousness, if not his deceitful way of robbing me, but once again I suffered the same misfortune for he persisted in his inveterate customs; for over the long period of seven years it was impossible, no matter how many attempts I made, to collect even a single *jornal*. My innocent family and I ignored this disobedience so as not to experience his veiled threats of flight. In the long run, I used him nine months, on two distinct occasions in those years, when I assigned him to be a butcher; three months [he worked] for don Guillermo Fleming, two for don Juan Leslie.[21] I also assigned him for two months to cut firewood, and one month to saw wood. And so it be known that I do not want to accuse him of all he deserves, I forgive him up to two years [of *jornales*] of the seven years he has robbed me, but he owes me five years of his *jornales*, it being well known and verifiable that not a day passed in which he did not earn at least four *reales* daily, taking care that his jobs were not made public, so that at no time could this or that individual testify [to his earnings], my irrational *negro* not understanding that in small populations such as this one everyone knows everything. He stubbornly took all these profits with obvious prejudice to my interests, and despite the many requests I daily made, it was impossible, no matter how many efforts I made, to collect a single *jornal* or collect any compensation That is certain, Sir.

I have stated that, as much as possible, I would attempt to contradict and make evident the unfounded points of his untrue declaration, but I must conclude that the many allegations that this false and treacherous *negro* makes so confuse, Sir, my limited genius, I must omit most of them, but not the following: that he continues to be charged that on two different occasions when he was butchering, don Joseph Sánchez[22] observed that my *negro* used the time so industriously and with such sagacity, that when Sánchez arrived to do his business, he found all the meat divided in small pieces, giving proof to embezzlement, for on other occasions he reprimanded him [Edimboro] not to do so, because of his suspicions, which were verified, and he corrected him quickly but too late. Lastly, Sir, to further incriminate the malicious craftiness with which the *negro* has proceeded, [I state that] on various occasions he has tried to get me to buy him shoes, and being aware of the malicious intentions, I replied that with all that he had embezzled from me he could buy them himself. And with great submission and hurt humility he answered and swore to me that I was not the owner of an embezzler, and he even demanded from me the shoes or their equivalent value. And [then] all of a sudden he presents and claims to own 312 pesos, without mentioning the many clothes it is evident he owns. Without doubt, Sir, I must infer one of the following propositions: that either he has used the false means that I have mentioned or, that taking advantage of my carelessness, he has robbed me in all the ways I have stated.

I ask and supplicate that you order him, without allowing him to make any new statements, to fully satisfy me for the presented sum, as the legitimate owner, and also that in the future my *negro* seek legally that which is required to achieve his freedom, without failing to show me what he is acquiring on his own time, and by what means, so that I will not consider myself deserving of them [Edimboro's earnings], as I now do. I ask justice and [protest] costs.

> [Signed] Don Francisco Xavier Sánchez
> and Rafael Saavedra de Espinosa
> [Sánchez's attorney].

[On July 1, 1794, the governor ordered that Edimboro be given a copy of Sánchez's statement, and he informed him that without prejudice to his solicitation for liberty, his case would be suspended until he answered his owner's allegations. He also ordered Edimboro to deposit the 312 pesos with the public notary, pending the tribunal's decision. On July 4, 1794, Edimboro deposited the 312 pesos as required.]

20.7 Through His Attorney, Edimboro Responds

Don Bartolomé de Castro Ferrer, public attorney, in the name of, and empowered by, Felipe Edimboro, black slave of don Francisco Xavier Sánchez, in his solicitation of liberty for himself, his wife, and his child, also slaves of the same, in the most proper legal form, appears and states:

That it would be a form of tyranny and a lack of subordination in my client to even deny the great calumnies and horrible sins that his owner imputes falsely to him in his last written declaration. But although his sad and unfortunate luck has placed him in the abject state of slavery in which he lives subjected, and in which he has always treated the señor with the most profound humility and punctual and exact service, nevertheless the sainted and pious laws entitle him to the full range of their benign protection, allowing him to claim in the present occasion the right to be represented and to reserve all the most favorable and pertinent elements of the law, and at the opportune moment to produce them in his defense.

It being well assured that the primary object of all tribunals is to investigate the truth, absolve the innocent, and condemn the guilty, allotting to each his due, I do not attempt to exaggerate by adding to the written record false narratives composed of sophisticated propositions and untrue consequences, such as those presented by his owner. On the contrary, I will condense as much as possible.

From the very beginning of his extended statement Sánchez launches against my client a thousand enchanted arrows whose venomous points will return to wound him. His object is none other than to keep my client and his family enslaved. He says that he rejects the sworn statement of his slave, Felipe, because he professes no religion whatsoever, and that he has tried to instruct him in the principles and precepts of Christianity but that [Felipe] never listened to his religious advice. But my client responds that he practices the Protestant faith as did his previous owner, who instructed him in it when he was still a young boy. My client is persuaded that if his owner, who is most active in his own interests, had zealously attempted the education of his slaves he would have quickly achieved it. He further states that he can hardly believe that his owner would spend the time indoctrinating those who are his slaves when he does not even do so for those who are his children. According to what he [Sánchez] himself confirms in his written statement, part of his family lacked Christian instruction, and he found it necessary to send them to the city to acquire it from some other person. If only by God it were true that Sánchez, full of pious zeal, had urged and encouraged my client to receive holy baptism and observe Christian precepts, teaching him the doctrine, to love God, and so know him better with the eyes of the soul. Well, then, if our Catholic monarch, may God protect him, only allowed there to be slaves in his dominions solely for the pious end that owners would instruct them in the faith, then they could make use of them for the space of ten years in recompense of this good deed, at the completion of which they should be given their freedom, it appearing to the Royal Majesty that in that time period they could have paid the cost of their purchase. But Sánchez, far from having done that to obey God, or the king, still opposes that which His Majesty provides in one of his royal decrees[23] (*reales cédulas*), and refuses to give liberty to my client, whether because of ambition or caprice.

Sánchez paints my client as an evil monster, mired in abominable and incorrigible vices, despite which, nevertheless, he desires to have in his home an irreligious *negro*, a disobedient and lascivious thief. Up to this point he has lived very satisfied with his habits and services, without complaining about them. Had Felipe committed such infamies and Sánchez not severely punished and corrected him, he [Sánchez] would have been an accomplice as a witness for those worldly crimes and responsible for those against God. And he reserved his vituperative charges for when my humble and dominated client came to ask his owner for his liberty. If, when he made him a butcher more than ten years ago, he already had suspicions of his disloyalty, why did he not assign him to field labor and choose another of his slaves in whom he had more confidence? Why, when he investigated and knew, as he maliciously states, that he sold the heads, innards, tallow, and intestines to the citizenry, especially to the Mahonese families, and that by this he defrauded totally his interests, did he not make an example of him by punishing him? Because, in truth, his conduct has never merited repression or punishment [but] rather praise and reward. From all these things, you may infer that my client committed none of these alleged crimes. And if he had, the noted malice of his owner, whose ambition wishes not only to enslave him, but also to extinguish his burning thirst to have the 312 pesos that, without failing in the least the obligations of the institution [of slavery], my client and his wife acquired with such fatigue and affliction, to shake off the heavy yoke of slavery, abominable to every rational creature.

Neither can I fail to put before you the implication, which in the last written statement Sánchez made, [and] which he later confessed openly and without a trace of truth, that my client had stolen everything as he supposes. He states, "But I do not want to hide from the righteous tribunal the regrettable results of all those badly served interests." And he immediately declares that they all embezzled at catered dances, and that once the [meat] contract was fulfilled, he [Felipe] did not take a single item to his house in the country except for a small quantity of clothing. Then he should not now argue that my client's actual 312 pesos are the result of all the thefts he attributes to him over a very long time period resulting from wastrel behavior in illicit diversions. With this he proves, although circuitously, that he earned the memorable sum with the sweat of his brow, and without defrauding in the least the interests of his owner.

Sánchez believes he injures his slave Felipe by calling illegitimate the marriage that he contracted with his consort according to the Protestant rites. On the contrary, a statement known to be the result of the shrill discourse of his owner will not injure in the least or have any force whatever against my client, once it is examined by the great wisdom of Your Majesty. Rather, it [Sánchez's shrill discourse] will absolve him [Edimboro] of all charges, insults, allegations of waste, and outrages, without any reflection on his honor and reputation while at the same time bringing dishonor to the very threshold of [Sánchez's] house. This is an inexplicable foolishness. For if my client is illegitimately married, he [Sánchez] consented to it and allowed that he live in cohabitation illicitly in his house. He knows full well that such illegal toleration is prohibited, as much by divine as by human law, and by doing so he would acquire the horrible renown of being a tolerator and fomenter of the vices of his slave. For which reason I hardly need to formulate any arguments in defense of my client, because with the very accusation he makes against my client, he also defends him, killing himself with his own weapons.

There is no truth to the charge that Sánchez touches upon as to the five years of *jornales* he says my client owes him, because in all the time my client was working for a salary for some citizen as a butcher or in other employments, the very same Sánchez received the *jornales* that [Felipe] earned. And otherwise he had Felipe occupied in serving him, the obligation of which he [Felipe] always punctually and faithfully fulfilled. And so [Felipe] is not obligated to give him a *maravedí*. And besides, no owner, much less that of my client, is so remiss that, seeing that his slaves fail to give him the stipulated salary daily, weekly, or monthly, he would not make them do so by reprimanding them, threatening them, and even punishing them, if they delay. Only my client's owner [is so remiss]; [he] must appear to the tribunal to have the patience of Job and a martyr's suffering in not having made in the course of five years any effort to be paid such a large sum, which would be almost impossible for my client to satisfy in his lifetime. One would have to admire Sánchez for having treated a well-behaved slave with such apparent kindness. But it is incredible that he would have done so with my client, who is in his current opinion the most depraved in the city.

Having thus answered the main points of Sánchez's statement, I will, for reasons of good will, leave all the rest unanswered, so as not to bother too much the patience of the tribunal by responding to allegations without any merit or importance. But fearing that such an omission might redound to the prejudice of, rather than in the favor of, he whom I defend, I will touch on the following.

Figure 13 The Villalonga house on St. George Street, St. Augustine, where Filis and Felipe Edimboro hosted dances (photograph courtesy of Ken Barrett, Jr.).

Without a doubt my client could have not only the 312 pesos he deposited according to your decree, but much more, which he has legally earned without failing in the obligations of a good slave. For the last ten years he has butchered the pigs of the townspeople in the winter, and they have always given him a peso apiece [per pig slaughtered]. During the rest of the year, when any resident wanted a cow butchered, after paying for his labor they always tipped him with the leftovers, which my party considers are those which Sánchez says he sold and got good money for. He was called to almost all the city dances, and was usually paid twelve *reales*, and sometimes he was paid two pesos a night. The wife of my client has also added to their savings making *queques* and doing laundry for people, with the knowledge of her owner, which now he denies. Once you have considered all the licit means which he has taken, without failing in any way to do what his owner ordered, you will not wonder how he was able to buy clothes and acquire the deposited sum, and this despite having spent something on the rent of the Villalonga house in which he put on honest [respectable] dances, with moderate refreshments for diversions and fiestas, which the blacks attended and for which they paid. Sánchez so embitters this matter that he gives the tribunal to understand that his slave Felipe expended considerable sums on banquets and in the maintenance of two concubines, a proposition which, for being so totally false, is worthy of the greatest disdain. The same is true regarding the pigs, which he [Sánchez] says my client raised at his expense and sold, appropriating his profit without any notification. My client has raised none at the expense of his owner, but did raise two or three at his own expense, and they were not raised at his owner's house. In this case Sánchez mentions frivolous things, lacking all convincing proofs.

Sánchez makes obvious to the tribunal the impious impulses of his diamond-hard heart by showing himself to be such an irrational adversary of his slave Felipe, who has so loyally served him, who has earned him so much, and finally, who two or three times saved him from the disastrous death that threatened him, showing himself eager to receive it [death] in his defense. In remuneration of all this, the great generosity of his owner has been to require him to pay a daily *jornal* of one peso, which should have been much less, because he did not cost 800 pesos.[24] Therefore, we ask that Your Honor accede to the liberty of my client on the same terms as he solicits in his first petition. It is justice I ask. I protest the costs caused by this hearing and which may incur in this controversy, and I swear that I do not proceed out of malice in what I have expounded; my only interest in this is the desire to defend the innocence of my client.

[Signed] Bartolomé Castro y Ferrer.

[On July 11, 1794, Governor Quesada ordered the preceding statement entered into the record and ordered a formal confirmation of Castro y Ferrer's power of attorney. The same day the royal notary notified both Edimboro and Sánchez, and Edimboro appeared before the notary and witnesses to reappoint Castro y Ferrer as his attorney. On July 16, 1794, the governor gave each party nine days to collect sworn testimony from witnesses,

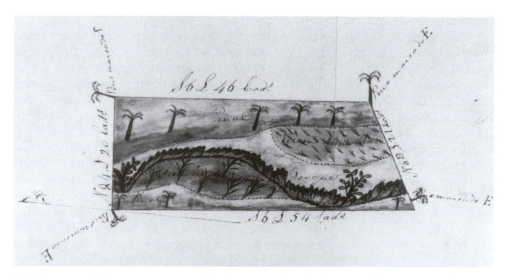

Figure 14 Watercolor survey of Felipe Edimboro's land grant (Spanish Florida Land Records, record group 599, series 990, Confirmed Spanish Land Claims, box 11, folder E-4. Courtesy of the Florida State Archives).

but Edimboro's counsel asked for an extension of another nine days because many of his witnesses lived outside the city. Castro y Ferrer also notified the governor that his client and Sánchez had agreed to discuss their dispute (controvers) *and that, as a result, they might obviate the rising expenses of the suit. The governor approved the requested extension on July 23, 1794, and the notary notified both parties.]*

20.8 Francisco Xavier Sánchez Responds

I, don Francisco Xavier Sánchez, resident of this city, in the proceedings which my slave Felipe Edimboro has initiated soliciting his liberty, come before you by means of the public attorney, as is my right in law, and state:

That having understood the grave prejudice that results from this litigation, my slave has seen fit to humbly supplicate me to grant his liberty at the assessed price, for which reason I renounce the statement I made so that this will take effect. I ask that you order the delivery of the money he has deposited, and likewise that you name an assessor to evaluate him. For my part I name don Juan Rodríguez of this city. And if the named [assessors] fail to arrive at an agreement, the tribunal may, according to the law, assign a third assessor. I ask justice, protest the costs, and swear.

> [Signed] Francisco Xavier Sánchez,
> Rafael Saavedra de Espinosa
> [public attorney].

[Governor Quesada so ordered on July 30, 1794, and the parties were notified. On August 5, 1794, the court suspended the investigation into Edimboro's earnings, allowing the slave's solicitation of liberty to proceed. It also ordered the assessors to declare Edimboro's good and bad properties, which made him more or less valuable, and to declare his value before the notary.

On August 12, 1794, don Juan Rodríguez, the assessor chosen by Sánchez, evaluated Edimboro at 525 pesos, basing that value on his "presence, as well as for his abilities and hard work, primarily in the job of butcher." Because don Miguel Ysnardy claimed reasons he could not serve as Edimboro's assessor, Edimboro's attorney asked to substitute don Pedro Peso de Burgos for the task. The court agreed, as did Peso de Burgos, and on August 14, 1794, the slave's assessor stated that he knew Edimboro very well and that his "conduct, abilities, love of work, and his presence" all made him commendable and worth a high price; however, considering that Edimboro was seeking his liberty, but also that his owner should not suffer prejudice and thus make it impossible for the slave to gain his freedom, he assessed Edimboro's value at 500 pesos. The court noted that the twenty-five peso difference between the assessments was not worth naming a third assessor, and on May 26, 1794, so notified don Francisco Xávier Sánchez. Sánchez responded that his slave was worth far more than the appraised price, and that in an ordinary sale he would not accept 800 pesos for him, as he had been offered on several occasions, both because he would lose Edimboro's services and because he was a skilled worker. But because Edimboro was seeking liberty and because he [Sánchez] had offered it to him earlier at 500 pesos, he would agree to that assessment and forego the twenty-five peso difference. The same day the notary notified Edimboro of Sánchez's agreement.

On August 29, 1794, Governor Quesada reviewed the case and ordered that Edimboro's 312 pesos be deposited with the public notary until such time as the slave completed payment of the 500 pesos at which he had been assessed. At such time, he ordered the notary to deliver the whole sum to Sánchez and issue Edimboro the certificate of liberty he solicited and to which he was entitled by the law and "by virtue of which he would be free and reputed as free, and could treat, and contract, testify in suits, and do all the things the laws authorize free persons to do." The governor ordered Edimboro to pay court costs of twenty-four reales and ordered the notary to notify all the parties. On September 1, 1794, Felipe Edimboro delivered the full 500 pesos to the royal notary, and was issued his certificate of liberty.]

20.9 Edimboro Petitions the Court

Felipe Edimboro, black slave of don Francisco Sánchez, by means of the public attorney, as a result of the proceedings that I pursued against my owner, that he concede me my liberty, to better proceed under the law, appear before you and state:

That as a result of all the deliberations, I was ordered to give 500 pesos for my liberty. Yesterday, without any reason whatsoever, my owner began to reprimand me severely, demanding that I give him the sum immediately, and if not, I would be sent to the countryside to labor for him. He added that he pursued his suit against me just because of my desire for freedom, and that, although he knew I was not really worth 500 pesos, because I dared to make a declaration to the authorities to obtain my liberty, he wanted to demand of me that exorbitant price. Nevertheless, Sir, I find myself ready to expose him in the act [of harassment], and I hope that the most just tribunal will pay attention to the repeated outcries I made to my owner about the amounts he proposes and will order what is most appropriate according to the law.

From the time this litigation began, don Francisco Sánchez required me to pay him five *reales* daily, basing it on one *real* per hundred pesos [of Edimboro's assessed price of 500 pesos]. He only released me from this demand on Sundays, but I asked him also to release me on all the rest of the feast days, as required by Church precepts, but he responded that he only relieved his *negros* of the *jornal* on Sundays and not the other solemn days of the year. He has not demanded this of the other slaves, and only charges me the *jornal* [on feast days] just as on the other workdays. I feel that this arises out of the struggle that he entered into against me, and I believe that the Catholic faith does not permit it, for it orders that believers should only spend feast days in the proper observances, and although I should say that I spent them as I did the other days, working, I did so for two reasons. The first was that my job required it so that the public would not lack the daily provision of meat that was sold [at the slaughterhouse]. The other was that, as a miserable captive, I desired, with this exemption on those days, to sustain my wife and children. But don Francisco Sánchez doesn't allow me any of this; rather, since the day I made my first representation in this litigation he has collected a peso daily, or the entire *jornal* I earn as a butcher. Furthermore, he also extracted a watch belonging to me, which was worth more than nineteen pesos and four *reales*. In virtue of all this, and because I am also ready to present the 500 pesos that he asks of me for my liberty, I ask that you order my owner to discount from that sum the five to eight *reales* he has received from my daily *jornales* in the time I have stated I worked on the feast days, and also that he return my watch, or its value, and that with this reduction, and with his receipt of the rest of the sum up to 500 pesos, I be granted my corresponding letter of manumission. For that reason, I ask it please Your Majesty to order done what I have asked. With justice [and] costs, I swear as required.

[Signed] Bartolomé de Castro y Ferrer.

[On September 1, 1794, Governor Quesada ordered this petition entered into the record and ordered the notary to deliver 500 pesos to don Francisco Sánchez. He added that if Edimboro wanted to begin a separate suit related to the new issues he could[25] and the tribunal would hear it and administer justice. Signed by Quesada, Ortega and Zubizarreta. The same day the notary notified both Edimboro and Sánchez and the matter was concluded.]

NOTES

ACKNOWLEDGMENTS   I would like to gratefully acknowledge the research support of the National Endowment for the Humanities, the Program for Cultural Cooperation Between Spain's Ministry of Culture and United States' Universities, and Vanderbilt University.

1. His main plantation, the San José, comprised more than eleven hundred acres, the Ashley, almost six hundred, and his original homestead, the San Diego, another ten hundred acres. Not only was Sánchez a government contractor, he was often the government's creditor. Accounts of the Royal Hacienda, Santo Domingo 2635 (1784–1795) and 2636 (1796–1819), Archivo General de Indias (hereafter AGI). For more on Sánchez, see Jane G. Landers, "Francisco Xavier Sánchez, *Floridano* Planter," in *Spanish Pathways in Florida*, Ann L. Henderson and Gary R. Mormino, eds. (Sarasota, Fla.: Pineapple Press, 1991), 168–87.
2. Inventory and appraisal of the estate of Francisco Xavier Sánchez, October 1808, Testamentary Proceedings, East Florida Papers (hereafter EFP), Bundle 309, folios 301–18, on microfilm reel 138, P. K. Yonge Library of Florida History, University of Florida, Gainesville (hereafter PKY).
3. Spelling, particularly of English names, varies widely throughout the Spanish Florida documents. I have chosen to use the most common spelling for this individual: Edimboro. For more on Edimboro's life, see Jane G. Landers, *Black Society in Spanish Florida* (Urbana and Chicago: University of Illinois Press, 1999).
4. The baptisms of Sánchez's illegitimate children are recorded in the Cathedral Records, Saint Augustine Parish (hereafter SAPR), Black Baptisms, vols. 1-3, on microfilm reel 284J, PKY. The baptisms of his legitimate children are recorded in vols. 1-4, on microfilm reel 284I, PKY. For marriages, see Black Marriages, SAPR, vol. 1, on microfilm reel 284L, ibid. For more on both these families see Landers, *Black Society*, op.cit.
5. Black Baptisms, SAPR, on microfilm reel 284 J and Black Burials, SAPR, on microfilm reel 284 D, PKY. Inventory and appraisal of the estate of Francisco Xavier Sánchez, October 1808, Testamentary Proceedings, EFP, Bundle 309, folios 301–18, on microfilm reel 138, PKY.
6. Ibid.
7. Black Baptisms, SAPR, on microfilm reel 284 J, and Black Marriages, SAPR, on microfilm reel 284 C, PKY. Roster of School Boys, March 26, 1796, SD 2531, AGI.
8. Review lists for the Free Black Militia of St. Augustine, 1802 and 1812, and Relation of the

Florida Exiles, August 22, 1821, Cuba 357, AGI. *Spanish Land Grants in Florida*, vol. 3 (Tallahassee: Works Project Administration), 43.

9. Census of 1784, EFP, microfilm reel 148. Mahon was the capital of Menorca, the smaller of the two Balearic Islands, located in the western Mediterranean and controlled by Spain. Spaniards called the residents of Mahon, Mahoneses, and residents of the island, Menorquines. This group came to Florida to work as indentured servants on the indigo plantations of Dr. Andrew Turnbull, and when Spain resumed control of the colony in 1784 they stayed. See Patricia C. Griffin, *Mullet on the Beach: The Minorcans of Florida, 1768–1788* (Jacksonville, Fla.: University of North Florida Press, 1991).

10. This document comes from Spain's provincial archives for Florida (1784-1821). This collection, known as the East Florida Papers (EFP), is found in the Library of Congress and is also available on microfilm. Felipe Edimboro's suit is found in Civil Proceedings, no. 25, July 6, 1794, EFP, microfilm reel 152. I appreciate the assistance of Eugene Lyon and David García, who helped me decipher several difficult sections in the manuscript.

11. At this time the Spanish peso was approximately equivalent to the U.S. dollar.

12. It appears that Edimboro dictated his first petition, which would account for the shifts between third and first person within this document. Edimboro's court-appointed attorney was responsible for the subsequent petitions, although the basic argument is still Edimboro's.

13. This portion of Edimboro's petition was an afterthought or postscript, and the previous statement he refers to is the one he had just submitted.

14. Owner and slave might simply come to an agreed price for the slave's self-purchase and avoid court intervention, but in contested *coartación* cases Spanish law required a judicial appraisal, meaning that owner and slave would each select someone to appraise the slave and help the court determine a "just price" for his/her liberty.

15. The Catholic church encouraged owners to allow slaves to be baptized and to marry, and respectable owners usually complied.

16. Spanish litigation records were very formulaic, and individuals sometimes abbreviated well-known phrases. In this case, because Edimboro's attorney has already included "I swear I have not proceeded out ot malice," "the rest which is required" might refer to the required oath on a cross or the statement protesting court costs.

17. Spain claimed Florida from 1565 to 1763, at which time it was forced by treaty to cede the colony to Britain. The Treaty of Paris returned Florida to Spain in 1784, and by the terms of the Adams-Onís Treaty Florida became a territory of the United States in 1821.

18. When his government meat contract ended, Sánchez required Edimboro to leave the city and return to work on the San Diego plantation.

19. Sánchez used the Spanish word "tortas" and the Anglicized "queque" to describe the flour and honey cakes Filis baked and sold. *Queque* is a term still used in many parts of Latin America.

20. Sánchez is referring here to Edimboro's court-appointed counsel, don Bartolomé de Castro y Ferrer.

21. Many persons of English descent became prosperous and influential in Spanish Florida. Some had remained in Florida after Britain retroceded the colony to Spain in 1763, and others had been attracted by Spain's liberal homesteading policy. Don Juan Leslie was an associate of the British merchant house, Panton & Leslie, which had a monopoly on Florida's Indian trade, and don Guillermo Fleming was the son-in-law of the wealthy Swiss planter Francisco Phelipe Fatio, and was himself a planter.

22. It is doubtful Sánchez refers here to his uncle Joseph, who would have been seventy years old in 1794, and his son by María Carmen Hill, Joseph Simeon, was not even born until 1797. This don Joseph Sánchez, then, might be his son Joseph who was born in 1771 and whose mother was the *mulata*, María Beatriz Stone.

23. Spanish slave law derives from Roman law and was codified in the thirteenth century in the *Siete Partidas*. This document, and the subsequent royal decrees on slavery, held that God made all men free and that slavery was *contra natura* (against nature) and so encouraged manumission suits such as Edimboro's.

24. In his statements to the court, Sánchez claimed to have been offered 800 pesos for Edimboro, not an unrealistic price for a skilled slave at the time.

25. I have found no evidence that Edimboro initiated another suit; it is possible that he and Sánchez came to some agreement in order to avoid further litigation and court costs.

DOCUMENT THEMES

African/Afro-Latin American Peoples; Cultural Contact/Ethnogenesis/Resistance; Economy and Work; European-Mestizo Peoples; Family; Manumission; Marriage; Popular Culture; Race; Rural Life; Slavery; Town Life.

SUGGESTIONS FOR FURTHER READING

Cutter 1995.
Hall 1992.
Hanger 1997.
Landers 1996.
Landers 1999.

C H A P T E R
21

"The Most Vile Atrocities": Accusations of Slander Against María Cofignie, *Parda Libre*
(Louisiana, 1795)

Kimberly S. Hanger

INTRODUCTION

Spain obtained the province of Louisiana from France according to provisions of the Treaty of Paris, signed in 1763, and effectively ruled it from 1769 until 1803. Louisiana had been part of the French colonial system since 1699, and thus with its acquisition the Spanish Crown found itself in a situation to which it was not accustomed: taking over, rather than giving up, American territory from another European power. For both the French and Spanish, Louisiana's value was mainly strategic. The Bourbon monarchs viewed the colony as useful primarily within the context of larger geopolitical considerations: neither wanted Britain to seize it. Although Spain, like France, considered Louisiana an economic burden, the Spanish Crown hoped to use it as a protective barrier between mineral-rich New Spain and England's increasingly aggressive North American colonies.

Founded in 1718 on the site of a long-established Native American portage point where the Mississippi River comes closest to the shores of Lake Pontchartrain, New Orleans was colonial Louisiana's principal urban center and port. The furs, hides, timber, and agricultural products of the Mississippi Valley region flowed through the city en route to the West Indies, the North American colonies, New Spain, and occasionally Europe. New Orleans also served as the entrepôt for slaves and various goods such as flour and cloth that colonials could not supply or manufacture themselves. By the late eighteenth century "the city that care forgot"[1] was a vibrant port, with people moving in and out, establishing relationships across racial and class boundaries, and generally challenging any kind of stable social order. The only nucleus to boast the title of *ciudad* (city) in all of northern New Spain, New Orleans had a resident population that grew from about three thousand to more than eight thousand during the era of Spanish rule, with a large transient population adding to this number. The percentage of *libres* (free blacks)[2] rose from 10 to 20 percent of New Orleanians over the same period; the rest of the population was about evenly divided between whites and slaves, with varying numbers of *indios* (Indians) and *mestizos* (persons of mixed Indian and white ancestry) residing in and around the city.[3]

When Spain assumed control of Louisiana, it installed its own officials, legal codes, and governing system.[4] The top administrator in the province was the governor general, and he, along with two *alcaldes* (judges) from the *cabildo* (city council), headed tribunals that heard civil and criminal cases originating in New Orleans or appealed from outlying posts. Decisions in these cases could in turn be appealed to the *cabildo* as a whole, and then on to the Audiencia of Santo Domingo, for litigants who were ordinary citizens, or to the governor of Cuba for those who held special privileges (*fueros*), such as members of the military or clergy.[5] An *escribano* (clerk or scribe) recorded all court proceedings. Most of the cases the governor and *alcaldes* heard make up a collection known as the "Spanish Judicial Records," which along with the "French Judicial Records" (those of the French Superior Council), are housed at the Louisiana State Museum Historical Center in New Orleans.[6]

The case of "Criminal Proceedings Pursued by don Pedro Favrot against María Cofignie, Free *Parda*, Concerning Slander," [7] most of which is translated in the following pages,[8] came before the governor general, Francisco Luis Héctor, el Barón de Carondelet, in June 1795. The governor usually adjudicated criminal cases, especially those in which one of the parties was favored with the *fuero militar* (judicial privileges granted to military personnel); the plaintiff Favrot was a captain in the fixed or permanent infantry regiment of Louisiana. When Cofignie allegedly insulted and harangued his daughter and indirectly his wife, Favrot petitioned the governor's court for redress. His original petition was written in French, the language of most New Orleanians, and translated into Spanish by Public Interpreter don Juan Josef Duforest. Favrot presented the testimony of two witnesses, and based on this evidence Carondelet placed Cofignie under house arrest because there was no women's prison at the time. Cofignie in turn provided her version of the events and played on the sympathies of the court as a poor single working mother with several children to support. Eventually Favrot settled for an apology to his wife and daughter, which Cofignie reluctantly made. The Spanish judicial system thus successfully mediated between competing interests to reach an acceptable compromise, while taking into account the race, status, and gender of each party. As in the Favrot-Cofignie case, the courts typically encouraged plaintiffs and defendants to reconcile their differences and admonished them to act according to acceptable rules of conduct.

Cofignie, however, did not give up fighting for what she believed to be just causes. The same month that Favrot brought charges against her, she petitioned a tribunal for the freedom of her brother, Antonio Cofignie. Antonio was a slave of María's former mistress, the widow of María and Antonio's white father, don Claudio Cofignie. It appears that don Claudio had verbally promised to give each of his three illegitimate children (María, Feliciana, and Antonio), born to his *grifa* slave Luison, 400 pesos to purchase their freedom. The girls had done so before don Claudio Cofignie's death in 1786, but Antonio had not, and now the widow refused to free him for that amount, demanding instead what María claimed to be an exorbitant sum. While María was in the process of seeking retribution, Antonio took matters into his own hands and ran away. His mistress then accused María of assisting Antonio and hiding him; ironically, María, who obviously placed much faith in the legal system, was thrown in jail once more, where she again called on the mercy of the court as a *pobre mujer* to release her so that she could support her family. Finally, a white planter in Opelousas, Louisiana, whose ties to the Cofignies are not clear, paid 1,100 pesos for the fugitive, with the promise that María would reimburse him that sum if her brother ever reappeared.[9]

As a single mother, María also struggled to care for her children. During the era of Spanish rule in New Orleans, Cofignie bore eight babies, the first in 1785 and the last in 1801; of these, three died in their youth. She had another daughter in 1806. The father of only one of Cofignie's children was identified in existing documents. Her son Josef Urra, a *cuarterón libre* born November 1797, was described in his baptismal record as the illegitimate son of Manuel Urra and the *parda libre* María Cofignie.[10]

Although Cofignie repeatedly appealed for mercy based on the fact that she had to work to support these numerous children, court records and censuses do not indicate her occupation. The most common jobs for free black women in New Orleans in the 1790s were laundress, seamstress, and seller; Cofignie most likely earned her living in one of these ways.

Many of those individuals who tested the boundaries of elite-defined acceptable behavior were free blacks like María Cofignie. Their position within New Orleans's hierarchy was not well defined, and, in fact, most *libres* did not choose to be demarcated as a separate group, preferring instead to be admitted to, and accepted by, white society. Although radicalized by the possibilities for equality with whites seemingly offered in the philosophies of the French and Haitian Revolutions, free blacks in New Orleans generally wanted to reform, not overthrow, the hierarchical Spanish social system that condemned them outright for being nonwhites and that failed to recognize their worth except as measured by skin color. Their challenges escalated in the revolutionary decades of the late eighteenth and early nineteenth centuries.[11]

The case that follows reveals many of these tensions. In their recorded statements, the litigants raise the issue of racial discrimination and comment, often implicitly, on distinct notions of personal honor, patriarchy, family, gender roles, and the meaning of freedom. Like all *libres* living in slave societies, New Orleans free women of color operated from an undefined, anomalous position, the middle section of a three-tiered hierarchy in which they were not truly free or slave, often not pure black or white. *Libre* women were also trapped in a patriarchal society that valued males more than females but that did not afford them the paternal protection due the weaker sex because ostensibly they did not possess honor and virtue, attributes only accorded whites. But as we will see in the following testimony, María Cofignie and other *libre* women did not suffer in silence.

THE DOCUMENT

21.1 Petition Presented by Captain Don Pedro Favrot

Don Pedro Favrot, captain of the fixed regiment of Louisiana, with the respect due Your Honor [Governor Carondelet], states that on the twelfth day of the current [month and year, May 1795] he had the honor of being presented to the tribunal of Your Honor requesting justice for the excesses María Cofignie, *mulata libre*, committed against his daughter,[12] doña Josefina, which had not resulted in imprisonment or any other penalty that could be used as punishment for her [María Cofignie] or another of her status.[13] The exponent returns to bring this matter to the attention of Your Honor, so that with respect to it, and the attached documentation, the court will deign to give a hearing to a complaint so strongly grounded it follows that [each piece of] evidence can be checked one against the other. He states this without presuming to instruct the court.[14]

I request that Your Honor mete out justice according to what I ask, [and] I hope to receive favor from what Your Honor decides. New Orleans, May 21, 1795.

[Signed] Pedro Favrot.

[Margin note in Carondelet's handwriting: New Orleans, June 8, 1795. The judge advocate (auditor de guerra) *passed by [and] brought to my attention that there is no jail for women at this time.[15] Signed El Barón de Carondelet.]*

Court clerk Carlos Ximénez states that Favrot's petition and the document that accompanies it have been translated by don Juan Josef Duforest with the customary formalities. With the assistance of the interpreter, he has also confirmed the signatures of the persons whose names appear on the document. These statements are made known to Governor Carondelet in New Orleans, June 8, 1795, and are as follows:

21.2 Statement Made by Rosalía Carlota Barré

As translated from French to Spanish by Juan Josef Duforest:

I have signed Rosalía Carlota Barré, widow of Mr. Dutisne, by reason of the verbal suit of Mr. Favrot, captain of the regiment of Louisiana, who has required that I give a statement and a detailed report of what I may have heard of the impertinences that have been directed at doña Josefina, his daughter. I declare that, [while I was] in the doorway of my house, [located] almost opposite [to Favrot's house],[16] between six and seven in the afternoon, there were several children playing on the sidewalk[17] of Mr. Favrot's house. I saw a small *mulato* [18] throwing dirt in the face of the young woman [doña Josefina], who repeatedly asked him to stop it and leave them alone. They [doña Josefina and her friends] ran after the small *mulato*, who was always falling over them. He escaped and ran to his mother, called María Cofignie, *mulata libre*, who lives next to my house.[19] She left in a fury and approached the young Miss Favrot and addressed her as the daughter of a whore (*hija de puta*), saying "you can f . . . yourself, señorita" (*usted se f . . . de usted señorita*).[20] "I am free like you are. I well know that you want to hit my son or threaten him. Those bloody, beastly[21] Frenchmen,[22] because they are white, believe that we are made to be scorned and spurned. I am free and I am as worthy as you are; I have not earned my liberty on my back."[23] I [Barré] declare that this *mulata*, María Cofignie, has pronounced the most vile atrocities that were as outrageous to me as those that have caused a revolution.[24] I had a very strong feeling that [as] [doña Josefina's] father and mother were absent from their house at that moment, [it] prevented an escalation [of the argument] and checked Cofignie's scandalous behavior; the parents' absence and the child's vulnerability proved sufficient to curb the excessive insolence that this rogue of a *mulata* had demonstrated. She had spoken of the whites in general with disdain and with the greatest contempt. In addition, Madame Grenot, who lives with me, could say that she had heard everything that I have just declared as she was also at the doorway of the house. Mr. Favrot's servants, who went out to quiet her [Cofignie] down, could also very well state that they had heard all of these abominations. All of which I swear to be the truth and to which I take an oath. This matter occurred on Tuesday, the second of the current [month and year] in the afternoon, and I sign this day in New Orleans, May 15, 1795. Mr. Beaupre has written this statement [and signs as a witness].

21.3 Statement Made by Doña Vitoria Amarante Bossie, [Wife of Grenot]

On this same day and year there appeared Madame Manuel Grenot, who lives in the house of the person giving evidence [Barré]. She affirms that the statement [made by Barré] is the same that she had heard from María Cofignie and that there was still more than what was declared if it was necessary to go into an even more substantial account. She has signed with us [the clerk and interpreter].

Clerk Carlos Ximénez certifies that this translation was made well and faithfully by the interpreter according to his trustworthy knowledge and understanding, without grievance by any of the parties, and he signs in front of me [Ximénez].

21.4 Verification of Earlier Statements by Barré and Bossie

In New Orleans, June 17, 1795, I, the clerk, assisted by the interpreter, don Juan José Duforest, went by the residence of doña Rosalía Carlota Barré, the widow Dutisne, who, by means of the interpreter, received the oath sworn before God and the cross according to the law, and was charged with pledging to tell the truth concerning whatever she was questioned. She was asked if she recognized her signature stamped on the first leaf of the document presented by Captain don Pedro Favrot, and she replied that everything was as it was supposed to be and by the letter [of the law], as construed and recognized as such. She is certain of the contents of the document written by Mr. Beaupre, and of which she, the declarant, was informed of its particularities. She responds that what she has said and declared is the truth as charged by her oath. She is fifty-five years old and signs the statement with the interpreter.

In New Orleans on the same day, I, the clerk, by means of the interpreter, received the oath of doña Vitoria Amarante Bossie, [wife of] Grenot, sworn before God and the cross according to the law. She was charged with promising to tell the truth when questioned and to state whether it was her signature stamped on the first leaf of the document presented by Favrot. She states that it is in her hand-writing and style and because of that she recognizes it. She is twenty-two years old and signs with the interpreter.

On the same day, I, the clerk, by means of the interpreter, disclosed the two signatures stamped on the first leaf of the document to don Lorenzo Beaupre, who stated that he served as witness for the certification of the two women, the widow Dutisne and Bossie Grenot, whose statements the declarant [Beaupre] took, as was his responsibility. He translated what they told him, without knowing any-thing about the stories that they related. He recognizes their signatures, and with respect states that this is the truth as charged by his oath as ratified by law. He is seventy-four years old and signs with the interpreter.

21.5 Governor Carondelet's Edict

In view of these proceedings, and attentive to what will result from them against the free *mulata* María Cofignie, because of the excess that she committed against doña Josefina Favrot,[25] proffering slander[26] and insults, I order that she be placed under house arrest[27] until a new order can be issued, due to the fact that there has been no appropriate, proportionate space for women in the Royal Jail since it was destroyed by the fire that occurred in December of last year [1794]. Serve a summons on Cofignie for what she is accused and take her prisoner. And ver-ify the expressed proceeding, as well as provide a translation to Captain don Pe-dro Favrot, so that he can exercise his rights and ask what is suitable to him.

Decree certified by the clerk, Carlos Ximénez, in New Orleans, July 2, 1795. On July 7, 1795, by means of the public interpreter, don Juan Josef Duforest, Ximénez made known to María Cofignie, *parda libre*, the contents of the preced-ing judicial decree. So informed, she expressed to the clerk that she would respect the arrest intended for her, even though there was no motive for her being bur-dened with the punishment given her. Ximénez made known the translation of the decree to don Pedro Favrot on July 13, 1795.

21.6 Statement Given by María Cofignie

María Cofignie, *parda libre*, *vecina* (resident, citizen) of this city, in the criminal proceedings that don Pedro Favrot, captain of the infantry regiment of this plaza, pursues against me concerning slander that he says I proffered against his wife and daughter, and to which I say:

It has been more than fifteen days since I suffered the distressing arrest that Your Honor imposed on me in the ruling made the second of this month; and in view of the fact that I am a miserable poor person[28] burdened with a family of four children, without having the wherewithal to provide for my pressing needs, except for what I can personally acquire with my own labor, I humbly plead with Your Honor that you order, as an act of charity, which in this case has been lack-ing, that you do not believe that I should be required to serve any more of the sentence of house arrest than what I have already suffered. I naturally protest any succeeding amendment of the sentence [for a longer duration]. And I request that you reduce the house arrest, releasing me[29] for the benefit of my poor family, because even though matters have been made known to don Pedro Favrot, he has not done or said anything about the decree up to the present. Presented for the party [Cofignie] and signed, Antonio de los Rios, her legal representative.

Statement taken by the clerk Carlos Ximénez in the court of Governor Carondelet, New Orleans, July 28, 1795.

21.7 Don Pedro Favrot's Response

In New Orleans on this day, month, and year [July 28, 1795] I, the clerk [Ximénez], made known to don Pedro Favrot, captain of the fixed infantry regiment of this plaza, the statement of Cofignie and the decree that was ordered. And Favrot asked that I put as his response that his intention was not to enter into a judicial contest with the *mulata*, for one because his position in the royal service did not permit it, and for another because of the complete poverty of the *mulata*. For that, he agrees that the house arrest should be relaxed, provided that in front of the tribunal the *mulata* give a complete apology to his wife to her satisfaction. Favrot signs.

Ximénez provided a translation of the above to María Cofignie, and made it known to the governor.

21.8 Cofignie Returns Again

María Cofignie, *parda libre*, in the criminal proceedings that don Pedro Favrot, captain of the infantry regiment of this plaza, pursues against me, attributing me with having proffered slanderous words to his wife and daughter, and about which I state:

That I have been presented with the translated response given by don Pedro in which he will relax or loosen my arrest provided that I will satisfy his wife. Desiring to calm my soul[30] and secure my freedom so that I can seek the daily nourishment of my poor family, I agree to pass by his house and leave him satisfied, even though my intention never has been to offend the señora, knowing her character and the circumstances, all in all. I beg that you order the judicial costs be adjudicated fairly as necessary. Presented for the party [Cofignie] and signed, Marcos Rivera, her legal representative.

This document was provided to the governor in New Orleans on August 8, 1795. Ximénez also made its contents known to don Pedro Favrot on the same day.

21.9 Governor Carondelet's Final Ruling

In view of and with respect to finding that María Cofignie has given the wife of Captain don Pedro Favrot the apology that he solicited, as verified by the present notary, who drew up the corresponding proceedings so that it is on record, this petition concludes, preparing María Cofignie to get ready to pay in the future the court costs associated with the case at a fair, just appraisal, with two pesos for the adviser's fee. Signed by the governor, El Barón de Carondelet, and the lieutenant governor, Nicolás María Vidal. Attested to by the clerk, Ximénez, and dated August 13, 1795 in New Orleans.

21.10 Ximénez Makes Sure Justice Is Carried Out

In New Orleans on August 17, 1795, Court Clerk Ximénez, in fulfillment of the previous decree and assisted by the public interpreter, don Juan Josef Duforest, passed by the house of Captain don Pedro Favrot. While there he made known to Favrot's wife the previous decree and that María Cofignie, *mulata libre*, having appeared in court on her own recognizance, had asked to be pardoned and stated that she had made the necessary complete apology to the wife of Captain don Pedro Favrot. In completing this case, Ximénez has confirmation from the interpreter. He concludes the proceeding and signs that it was made faithfully.

There were no court costs adjudicated, due to [Cofignie's] insolvency.[31]

NOTES

ACKNOWLEDGMENTS   I would like to thank the following institutions for their help in funding this research: the American Philosophical Society, the Oklahoma Humanities Council (formerly the Oklahoma Foundation for the Humanities), and the University of Tulsa Faculty Development Summer Fellowship Program and Faculty Research Program.

1. A phrase commonly associated with New Orleans because of its carefree attitude.
2. I use the inclusive somatic terms "free black," "free person of color," and *"libre"* to encompass anyone of African descent, that is, any free nonwhite person whether he or she be pure African, part white, or part Native American. The exclusive terms *pardo* (light-skinned) and *moreno* (dark-skinned)—preferred by contemporary free blacks over *mulato* and *negro*—are used to distinguish elements within the nonwhite population. Occasional references delineate further between *grifo* (offspring of a *pardo[a]* and a *morena[o]*, and in some cases of a *pardo[a]* and an *india[o]*), *cuarterón* (offspring of a white and a *pardo[a]*), and *mestizo* (usually the offspring of a white and an *indio[a]*, but in New Orleans sometimes meaning the offspring of a *pardo[a]* or *moreno[a]* and an *india[o]*).
3. For an elaboration of Louisiana's and New Orleans's early history, see John G. Clark, *New Orleans, 1718–1812: An Economic History* (Baton Rouge, La.: Louisiana State University Press, 1970); Gilbert C. Din and John E. Harkins, *The New Orleans Cabildo: Colonial Louisiana's First City Government, 1769–1803* (Baton Rouge, La.: Louisiana State University Press, 1996); and Daniel H. Usner Jr., *Indians, Settlers, and Slaves in a Frontier Exchange Economy: The Lower Mississippi Valley before 1783* (Chapel Hill, N.C.: University of North Carolina Press for the Institute of Early American History and Culture, 1992).
4. This occurred only after an experiment allowing Louisianians to continue under French law and custom had failed. When in 1768 a group of French adminstrators, merchants, planters, and farmers ousted the first Spanish governor, famed scientist Antonio de Ulloa, the Spanish Crown toughened its stance and ordered General Alejandro O'Reilly to take troops from Cuba and restore order in Louisiana in 1769. He firmly but fairly implemented a Spanish colonial system (Din and Harkins, *New Orleans Cabildo*, pp. 38–55).
5. An ecclesiastical tribunal presided over by the vicar general decided disputes pertaining to issues of "morality" and the sacraments, particularly marriage, or those in which a person protected by the ecclesiastical *fuero* was involved.

6. For further information on the judicial system in colonial Louisiana and location of documents, refer to Henry Putney Beers, *French and Spanish Records of Louisiana: A Bibliographical Guide to Archive and Manuscript Sources* (Baton Rouge, La.: Louisiana State University Press, 1989) and Henry P. Dart, "Courts and Law in Colonial Louisiana," *Louisiana Bar Association Reports* 22 (1921): 17–63.
7. "Criminales Seguidos por don Pedro Fabrot contra María Cofinie, parda libre, sobre palabras injuriosas." Spanish Judicial Records, 8 June 1795, Louisiana State Museum Historical Center. Consistent spelling was not a priority in the eighteenth century, and in Louisiana Spanish scribes found creative ways to spell the French names that predominated. In this translation I have regularized the spelling of personal names, selecting the most common usage found in the document (Cofignie, Favrot, and Grenot, rather than their variants Cofinie, Coffiny; Fabrot; Greneux, Grenaux).
8. I have omitted some of the routine certifications that are repetitive and add nothing to the text, such as the translator accepting his appointment and certifying that he would provide a true and accurate translation.
9. "Promovido por María Cofiny Parda Libre sobre que se estime su hermano Antonio Esclavo de doña Francisca Monget para su Libertad," Spanish Judicial Records, 23 June 1795, Louisiana State Museum Historical Center.
10. Nonwhite Baptisms, books 3a, 4a, 5a, 6a, 7a, 8a, and 9a, 1785–1806, Archives of the Archdiocese of New Orleans.
11. Kimberly S. Hanger, *Bounded Lives, Bounded Places: Free Black Society in Colonial New Orleans, 1769–1803* (Durham, N.C.: Duke University Press, 1997), pp. 136–62, and "Conflicting Loyalties: The French Revolution and Free People of Color in Spanish New Orleans" *Louisiana History* 34:1 (winter 1993): 5–33.
12. This is how I have translated "pidiendo sustiese del exceso que tubo María Cofinie, mulata libre con la niña del suplicante," which could also be more literally translated "requesting justice for the excess [behavior] that María Cofignie, *mulata libre*, had with the daughter of the suplicant."
13. "A otro de su esfera" translates literally as "another of her sphere or place."
14. The original states "sin castigo," conveying the sense of "without presuming to instruct the court." I would like to thank the editors for their helpful suggestions on this and other questionable translations.
15. Two large fires swept New Orleans in the eighteenth century, one in March 1788 and another in December 1794. Although the 1788 "Great Conflagration" covered more acreage, the 1794 fire destroyed more valuable property. One of these properties was the women's prison.
16. According to the 1791 census of New Orleans, the widow Dutisne lived on Conti Street with one other white female and an older male slave. María Cofignie also resided on Conti Street with three *mulato* male children and an elderly free *mulata*; she had no slaves. On the same street was the household of don Pedro Favrot, made up of Favrot, his wife, Josefina, two male sons, and eight male and five female slaves (Census of the City of New Orleans, 6 November 1791, New Orleans Public Library, Louisiana Division).
17. The word given here is *la banqueta*, the Spanish rendition of *la banquette*, the French term for footway and used in New Orleans even to today to refer to sidewalks. Especially in the French Quarter, the banquettes serve as social spaces where young and old interact in between the busy streets and the house fronts that sit almost directly on the streets.
18. This *pequeño mulato* was either Juan Isidoro, who in 1795 was nine years old and who died in 1812 at the age of twenty-six, or Pedro, then five and a half years old. Court documents never state the name of Cofignie's son (Nonwhite Baptisms, book 3a, 20 July 1786, and book 4a, 19 March 1790; Nonwhite Burials, [book 5], 1 October 1812, Archives of the Archdiocese of New Orleans).
19. As the 1778, 1791, and 1795 house-by-house censuses of New Orleans reveal, there was little residential segregation in the city, either by race or by class, with white and black, slave and free, rich and poor living next to or in the same households with one another. There was a slight tendency, however, for the wealthier, more substantial houses to be located closer to the river and around the central plaza.
20. The text does not indicate what "f . . ." represents, but it most likely translates as "screw" or "fuck." In some parts where a witness is quoting a statement made by another person, the missing or underlined word is in French (such as with "fichu" below), but I have been

unable to match "f . . ." with any word in French or Spanish. However, while the form of the letter most closely approximates an "f," the clerk may have intended to write a "j." If so, the missing word was likely a conjugated form of the Spanish verb "joder," which means "to screw" or "to fuck." Note that even when swearing at the young white woman, Cofignie refers to her as a señorita and uses the address "usted," both terms of respect. Perhaps, though, she said both with a tone of sarcasm.

21. Text provides the word *fichu*, an underlined French adjective meaning blooming, beastly, rotten. It is a curse word equivalent to the English "bloody" or the American "damn."
22. "Pieles franceses," literally, French skins.
23. "Sobre las espaldas," i.e., as a prostitute.
24. The revolution to which Barré referred was the Haitian Revolution, which broke out in 1791 and resulted in the brutal killing of many whites, free blacks, and slaves. The slaves, however, eventually triumphed and declared Haiti independent in 1804. For its effects on Louisiana, see Hanger, "Conflicting Loyalties," pp. 5–33.
25. "Por el exceso que tuvo con doña Josefina" could also be translated more literally and possibly with a greater sense of neutrality as "for the excess that she had with doña Josefina."
26. "Palabras injuriosas," or insulting, offensive words.
27. "Procedase al arresto de su persona, el que guardará en su casa."
28. "soy una pobre miserable"; *miserable* in this context means wretched, pitiful.
29. "Poniédoseme en libertad" or putting me in liberty.
30. "Tranquilizar mi espíritu."
31. "No hay costas, por insolvencia"; that is, Cofignie was broke, as she had warned the court she would be if left under house arrest without any means to seek gainful employment.

DOCUMENT THEMES

African/Afro-Latin American Peoples; Crime; Cultural Contact/Ethnogenesis/ Resistance; European-Mestizo Peoples; Family; Gender; Honor; Insults; Popular Culture; Race; Town Life; Women.

SUGGESTIONS FOR FURTHER READING

Beers 1989.
Din and Harkins 1996.
Hall 1992.
Hanger 1993.
Hanger 1996.
Hanger 1997.
Hanger 1998.
Usner 1992.

CHAPTER
22

Urban Slavery in Salvador, Bahia, Brazil: The Wills of Captain Joaquim Félix de Santana, Colonel Manoel Pereira da Silva, and Rosa Maria da Conceição
(1809, 1814, 1843)

Hendrik Kraay

INTRODUCTION

Wills offer a unique and often surprisingly personal perspective on peoples' lives. The following three, from early nineteenth-century Salvador, capital of the Portuguese colony (and after 1822 Brazilian province) of Bahia, allow us to glimpse some social relations of an urban slave society. The city, commonly also referred to as Bahia, at that time had a population of about fifty thousand.[1] Nearly half (40 percent) of its residents were slaves, mostly Africans, and the remainder were about equally divided between Portuguese and Brazilian-born whites, and free-born and freed blacks and mulattos, along with a small number of freed Africans. The city was a bustling commercial center focused on the slave trade and sugar exports and an important military base with a large contingent of regular and militia troops (the latter segregated by race). The city's residents practiced a rich baroque Catholicism, reflecting both African and European cultural influences.

Wills followed the principles of Brazilian inheritance law and thus, like all legal documents, took a standard form.[2] Those principles, most importantly, consisted of the following: that couples held property jointly unless specified otherwise in a contract drawn up before marriage, and that property automatically passed to what were sometimes called "forced heirs." This meant that on the death of a spouse, the surviving spouse retained half of the couple's joint property, while the other half (the deceased's share) was divided equally between children of the marriage. Writing a will, however, allowed testators to bequeath one-third of their half of the estate (that is, one-sixth of the total joint property) to whatever person or institution they might choose. Property of widows and widowers was automatically distributed to children, but again, up to one-third of it could be disposed of by testamentary provisions. In the absence of children (or grandchildren), property passed to ascendants, parents and grandparents. Men and women without any forced heirs—a common situation among the African population wrenched away from their kin in the slave trade—enjoyed full freedom to dispose of their property in wills.

Luso-Brazilian law distinguished between three classes of children: legitimate (those born of married parents), natural (those born of unmarried parents who, at the time of their relationship, were legally able to marry), and spurious (those born of parents who could not legally marry because one or both were already married or because of other impediments). By law, natural children enjoyed equal rights with their legitimate half-siblings and, to leave no doubt as to the status of their natural children, testators often mentioned them in their wills. Spurious children, in contrast, had no legal claim on their parents' property, although testators could favor them with bequests.

The third will, that of Rosa Maria da Conceição, includes an inventory, a court-supervised assessment of the estate that would have been used in the formal distribution of assets according to inheritance law. On their death, the wills of Joaquim Félix de Santana and Colonel Manoel Pereira da Silva (22.1 and 22.2) were opened in the presence of a notary—we know of their existence because they were recorded in notarial registers—and a similar inventory was begun. But these two inventories, unfortunately, have not survived.

Despite the rules and the other legal formalities in these documents, we can hear the testators' own voices as they dictated their final testaments and spoke of the things that were most important to them. Although the religious invocations and the naming of ancestors and spouses frequently follow standard formulae, they nevertheless allowed the testators to situate themselves within both the sacred and secular worlds. References to other people in these wills, whether the testator's spouse or children, debtors or creditors, friends or enemies, slaves or former masters, are essential sources that historians use to map the social relationships that these people maintained. Testators' casual comments hint at the quality of these relationships.

Two of these testators—Joaquim and Rosa Maria—were freedpeople, while Colonel Manoel held the highest government post available to a black man in Brazil, command of the segregated black militia regiment. Although his military rank was important to him, Colonel Manoel's will is a largely personal document and its main purpose is to recognize his natural daughter.

Manumission—the freeing of slaves—was relatively common in Brazil, as masters like Colonel Manoel freed favored slaves, sometimes gratuitously, other times requiring the slaves to pay for their liberty. Buying one's freedom, as Joaquim did, was relatively common; in a sample of 1577 manumissions registered in Salvador between 1808 and 1842, historian Mieko Nishida identified no less than 520 self-purchases, about one-third of the total.[3] While these 520 fortunate men and women represented a tiny minority of the tens of thousands of slaves who lived and worked in the city, their success indicates the determination with which Africans and Afro-Brazilians struggled to better their lives. The urban economy offered opportunities to slaves, whose masters often required them to work independently in return for paying a fixed daily or weekly sum. By custom, the skilled and the lucky who earned more than their quota could usually keep the difference and, perhaps, buy their freedom. Joaquim, a barber and musician, probably earned his freedom in this way, and apparently allowed some of his own slaves to do so as well. Numerous visitors to nineteenth-century Brazil remarked that African and Afro-Brazilian women dominated petty food-selling, an occupation that allowed some women to acquire property. None of these little freedoms, however, detracted from the overall power structures of slavery; if anything, they reinforced them. Masters well knew that such incentives would motivate slaves to work harder. Manumission was never assured, for masters were under no obligation to accept a slave's offer of his or her value.[4] Both Colonel Manoel and Joaquim imposed conditions on manumissions; failure to fulfill these terms would result in the slaves' remaining in captivity.

Joaquim's detailed description of his property and Rosa Maria's bitter account of the swindle that cost her most of her goods indicate the importance of material wealth and the security that it represented to people who had known deprivation during much of their lives. Needless to say, Joaquim and Rosa Maria were the lucky few. For every dapperly dressed freedman like Joaquim, a slave-owner, impresario, and moneylender, there were countless others who suffered and toiled, never attaining freedom, let alone modest prosperity. Premature death from disease and overwork was their most likely fate; Joaquim's description of the death of Josefa, one of his wife's slaves who "suddenly and immediately" passed away, can stand for the experience of the majority of Brazil's slaves.

THE DOCUMENTS

22.1 Will of Captain Joaquim Félix de Santana, October 30, 1809 (Deceased December 25, 1814)[5]

1. In the name of the Most Holy Trinity, Father, Son, and Holy Spirit, three distinct persons in one sole true God.

2. Be it known to all who see this public instrument of testament that in the year of our Lord Jesus Christ 1809, on October 30, in this city of Bahia de Todos os Santos,

3. I, Joaquim Félix de Santana, being in perfect health, and with my clear sense and understanding which the Lord our God was pleased to give me, and fearful of death, desiring to put my soul on the path of salvation, for I do not know how nor when I will be called to the supreme tribunal of the most highest to give a strict and rigorous account of my life, order this my last will and testament in the following form and manner:

4. First, I commend my soul to the Holy Trinity that created it, and I beseech the Eternal Father through the passion and death of his only begotten son that he will receive it, just as he received his when he expired on the tree of the holy cross. And [I commend my soul] to my Lord Jesus Christ, purified by his divine wounds, [who] already in this life did me the grace of giving his precious blood and will redeem me through grace in the future and eternal life in which we hope to give praise forever because we were all made for this purpose. I beseech the glorious blessed ever Virgin Mary, Mother of God and our Lady, and her hus-

band, the patriarch Lord Saint Joseph; [I beseech] my guardian angels; the saints of my name; and all the other saints and angel spirits, inhabitants of the celestial city, that they may intercede [on my behalf]; and I beseech God, now and at the hour of my death, because as a true and faithful Christian, I solemnly affirm to live and die in the law and faith of Jesus Christ, for I have faith in all that he believes, and in his Holy Roman Catholic Church. And in this same faith I aspire to save my soul not because of my merits but by the merits of the passion and death of the Son of God.

5. I beseech in the first place my wife, Joaquina de Melo, and in second place senhor Captain Manoel Justiniano Ferreira de Andrade, and in third place senhor Inácio José da Silva, whom I beseech for the service of God to be my executors, taking care of all of my goods; receiving, paying, [and] collecting all that pertains to me, fulfilling and satisfying all my dispositions and legacies that I determine in this my will.

6. I declare that I am a *crioulo*, native of this city, the son of Mariana de São José ([of the] nation from the Mina Coast); and that we were slaves of Alexandre Marques da Silva; and that on his death I passed to his son, Captain Felipe Binício; and from him I passed to a friar of the Order of Saint Benedict, brother Manoel Joaquim; and from him I finally became slave of Captain Félix da Costa Lisboa; and from him I gained freedom, giving for myself the sum of 135$000.[6]

7. I declare that on my death, I desire to be shrouded in a white sheet and taken in a casket to the chapel of Our Lady of the Rosary on João Pereira Street, where I have thrice served as judge and twelve years as counselor without owing the same brotherhood anything at all. And [I desire] that my reverend vicar [and] his sacristan[7] accompany me, and be given the customary donation and the one-pound candle,[8] and that another twenty clergymen accompany me, to whom shall be given the customary donation and the half-pound candle.

8. I declare that on the day of my death, my executor order a requiem mass *praesente cadavere*[9] be said for my soul, and in the same manner have said twelve requiems of the $320 donation, and if it becomes impossible to do the services on the day of my death, they will be said on the third day.

9. And in the same way my executor will have three *capelas* of masses celebrated for my soul (each of the $320 donation); twelve masses for the soul of my late mother Mariana de São José; five for the soul of my late father Tomás Pereira de Carvalho; six for the soul of my late mistress who raised me, Feliciana da Trindade; twelve for the soul of my first wife, Josefa de São José; four for the souls of the captives who are in purgatory; two for the souls of my friends and enemies; two for the souls of the good and evil-doers; and five to my guardian angel; and all of these masses [will be] of the *pataca* donation.

10. I declare that I am a member of the brotherhoods of Our Lady of the Rosary of Vitória [parish] of which I was judge and that, during my year [in office], I arranged the procession of Saint Anthony Catagerona;[10] of Our Lord of Martyrs in Barroquinha [church], of which I have been president; of Jesus Mary Joseph in Carmo [church], whom my executor will advise to accompany my body to the grave and to say the prayers for my soul which they are obliged to do.

11. I declare that I was first married to Josefa de São José, *crioula*, freedwoman, daughter of Maria da Silva, of which matrimony we had no children whatsoever,

and after my wife passed away from this present life, I buried her with all that was necessary at my own expense, without receiving anything at all from my mother-in-law for the burial of my wife; rather, my mother-in-law kept in her possession some money of mine, which would have been about 90$000 or so.

12. I declare that, on the death of my wife, I left the house of my mother-in-law where I had been [living], with only that with which I entered, namely a slave by the name of João of the Mina nation, still young, and the rest of the furnishings of my house, with nothing at all that belonged to my mother-in-law.

13. I declare that my mother-in-law, Maria da Silva, had me sell one of her *parda* slaves by the name of Apolinária, which slave I in fact sold to the gypsy, Antônio José de Moura Rolim, for the price of 125$000. And after having bought her, he brought her back to me, not wanting her any longer, both because she was pregnant and because she was in poor health. And on the request of the late Major Caetano Maurício Machado, I took back the slave and returned to the same gypsies the 125$000 out of my own pocket. And [after I had] taken the slave into my power, that slave left my company for the house and possession of my mother-in-law after two months had passed, [document torn] result[ing] in a lawsuit by me against my mother-in-law for that same slave. And this lawsuit lasted two years and, because I had right on my side, I won it, but I did not have the sentence carried out, for she did not have the means to pay me the [court] costs. And, [as is recorded] in the transcript of the same case, I gave a letter of manumission to the slave, Apolinária, for the sum of 160$000 which I received in the office of the notary, Agostinho Barbosa de Oliveira.

14. I declare that I married for a second time and am married to Joaquina de Melo, of the nation from the Mina Coast, and from this matrimony we have no children at all.

15. I declare that my second wife brought [into our marriage] as her [property]: 150$000 in money; three slaves by the names of Maria; Josefa ([I declare] that this one suddenly and immediately died); and Luiza, who was bought before we married with our money, and whom I sold immediately after getting married because [she was] a scoundrel and prone to run away. And I bought others for the price of 60$000 [for which I sold Luiza] by the names of Ana and Francisca Mina; the additional 85$000 [came] out of my own money.[11]

16. Of those same slaves that my wife brought, of necessity I sold one by the name of Maria . . .[12] for the price of one 140$000, which she was not worth, and I bought another in place of her, for 176$000, the difference [of 35$000 coming out of my pocket]. . . . [Later] I freed this slave for 200$000 and received her value in cash, and in her place I bought another, who is presently [for sale] for 120$000. I spent the difference [between 120$000 and] the 200$000 because I could do so.

17. I declare that my wife also brought a pound of gold jewelry, which at the time of [writing] this [will] is intact, in the same form in which she brought it, without me having used it for any purpose whatsoever. She also brought twelve *oitavos* of silver, in the [form of] shoe buckles, and others to hold up stockings [garters]. She also brought a wooden image of [our] Lady Saint Anne, less than one palm in length, with her Holy Child with the silver halo of one *oitavo* in weight; [and] one wooden child Lord Jesus. She also brought five old leather-backed chairs, a small table [made of] jacaranda wood, an old jacaranda bed with

a wooden and leather box spring; she also brought six picture frames with their paper pictures, all very old; she also brought an old mahogany box for her own use.

18. I declare that of the 150$000 that she handed over to me in money, I took 50$000 and 100$000 remained. I further collected some debts of my wife that came to 100$000. With the 100$000 that she brought, these made 200$000. With 350$000 of mine, it came to 550$000 with which I bought this house in which we are living, which a friend of mine sold me by [the terms of a] written contract, and the deed is in my possession.

19. The goods thus declared were those that my wife brought when she married me.[13]

20. I declare that the goods acquired by me are the following: A complete oratory[14] with the following images: a holy image of our Lord Jesus Christ completely outfitted in silver, with its large rays, title, stitches, border, [and] halo, and I mention its purple stone; another holy image of the Lord in marble, without silver fittings, and only on its jacaranda cross; an image of Saint Joachim with its silver halo; two images of Lord Saint Joseph, one wooden and the other marble, without silver fittings; one image of Our Lady of Conception; an image of [Our] Lady Saint Anne; an image of Our Lady of the Rosary with its silver crown; two images of Saint Anthony; a jacaranda bed, with no bedding; a half-sized commode; a desk; a large table with old turreted legs; another small table; another leather table; a mahogany chest; another smaller chest; six leather-backed chairs; two leather and mahogany chairs; three mahogany footstools and two of leather; a large bench with drawers; two wicker chairs; two plates, one of Saint Anthony and another of Saint Francis; a round glass plate that is in the oratory; two copper basins, one large one to wash feet and another small one to wash hands; a copper cauldron; a tin basin and spout; two mortar-and-pestles, one of metal and another of marble; twelve bronze basins for shaving; three lamps, two small and one old large one [made of] fine brass; a fine brass chocolate pot; two copper kettle drums; two big drums, one wooden and the other of tin plate; two [document torn] to play; four pairs of [document torn], namely three old and one new; two sets of bugles; two sets of wind clarinets; six rebecks;[15] one big rebeck that is in its own case; various instruments of my own use that will all be found, including new and old, already used, and all of them complete; a large tub for taking baths; a set of teacups with their fittings; three dozen plates, namely, some old ones of porcelain and others of clay, with some Indian soup bowls; four cups; six flasks; a dozen bottles, and two more, which makes fourteen; sixteen sheets; one printed cotton blanket; four large African blankets for bedding, two of superior quality and two of lesser [quality]; one white cotton blanket; twenty pairs of white socks; two pairs of silk [socks], one in pearl-white color and striped, the other black and also striped; six pillowcases [document torn]; four linen pillowcases, large and small; two more of cambric,[16] one large and the other small; a dozen and a half French Breton linen shirts; twelve napkins, six of *guimarães*[17] and six of linen; three tablecloths, two large ones for banquet table, and one new thin cotton one; three pairs of shoe buckles, namely one of gold, another of stone, and another large pair of engraved silver; four pairs of belt buckles, namely two silver pairs, one large and another small, one pair of stone belt buckles, and another

of gold; two *espadons*,[18] one of gold, and the other of silver; one gold crucifix with four loops of chain; two silver candlesticks; two silver trays without legs, one larger and the other smaller; twelve silver spoons, six large and six smaller; six large forks, and two small, which makes eight; one table knife with a silver handle; two pocket watches, namely one with a gold chain and a worked gold and topaz link and the other with a steel chain; a pair of gold cuff links; a gold cross that is inside the gold cross studded with stones; two lace [table]cloths; thirteen linen towels for shaving; my three coats; one blue suit; four pairs of pants, one of black cashmere; another of black velvet; another of Moorish cashmere; and another of blue knit; three silk jackets, namely one of embroidered white silk; . . . and another of black silk with a worn lining.

21. I declare that I also own the following slaves: Dionísio, Joaquim, Amaro, Adriano, Alberto, Domingos, Alexandre, Isidoro, Rosa, Fabiana, Ifigénia, and Ana Francisca.

22. I declare further that I have freed the slaves listed below by name, namely: Mariana; Felisarda; Maria do Rosário, her son Antônio Joaquim; Agostinho; Benedito; João; André; and Cipriana, *crioulinha*, whom I freed of my own will, and that of my wife, without payment; and from the above-mentioned I received the value of their freedom, as is recorded in the letters [of manumission], that I granted them on the condition that after my death each of these freedmen have a *capela* of [requiem] masses of the one *pataca* donation said for my soul, being understood that after having had the *capela* of masses celebrated for my soul, as will be stated in the receipt issued by the reverend priest, this [receipt] will be duly notarized. Then they will receive their letters [of manumission], which are in the possession of the persons mentioned below, who will free them to enjoy their liberty after my death.

23. I declare that the *crioulinha*, Agostinha, was freed on her baptism by the payment of 20$000, which I received from the hand of her godfather, as is stated in the letter [of manumission]. Even though she was baptized as freed, I gave her a letter of manumission, which is with the others; the same goes for the *crioulinho*, Antônio Joaquim.

24. I declare that I have in my possession three tables, namely one large one of painted mahogany and two more small [ones]; six leather field chairs and one old cot, which belong to a *parda senhora* by the name of Custódia. When she faced the confiscation of these goods for nonpayment of a debt of 7$000, I paid the debt and now hold them as collateral.

25. I declare that I further possess another two-story stone house between where I live and Quitanda Velha Street, on land leased from the Benedictine friars, and seven and a half *patacas* rent has been paid on it yearly.

26. I declare that I received from Manoel Salgado, who was then conducting business for the reverend canon of São Tomé,[19] Matias so-and-so, four Angolan slaves to teach the trades of barber and playing [musical instruments]. On the death of Manoel Salgado, they passed to his next representative, José Mendes, who sold one of the slaves, called André; another one by the name of Claudino died and two remained who are still alive, one by the name of Ananias, and another [by the name of] Malaquias, who are at this time in my possession, and now belong to the executor of the canon, Hipólito so-and-so, resident of Angola, against whom I have

Figure 15 Black (and possibly slave) musicians, like those owned by Joaquim, salute a procession of the Host in Rio de Janeiro (Debret 1834–1839).

filed a lawsuit that is recorded in the notarial office that belonged to Capelo. This [action] is for 212$000 to settle the account with the said Manuel Salgado: namely 200$000 for the training and clothing that I gave to the [slaves]; and now [the suit is against] the said Hipólito Joaquim de Andrade, as [the canon's] trustee.

27. I declare that the letters of manumission for the slaves that I leave free are in the convent of Our Lady of Mercy, in the possession of the illustrious ladies, mothers Bernardina de Sena and dona Ana de Salvador, and in the absence of these illustrious ladies, they will pass to whoever may then be the illustrious and most reverend Mother Superior. I beseech them for the love of God that, after my death, when any one of the freedmen present a notarized receipt for having had a *capela* of masses celebrated, each one will be given his letter. Each one will go with my executor, who will receive from the illustrious ladies the payment in full on his account,[20] for which I request and beseech that there be no delay.

28. I declare that I leave as a bequest to the *crioulinho* Agostinho, my *cria*,[21] 50$000 which will be given to him in money and in the same way I leave him all my clothes, both new and old, and I leave him further a pair of large silver buckles and another pair of silver ones for socks. All this will be given to him if he is able to receive [inheritances];[22] if not it will be given to his mother, the *preta* Felisarda.

29. I declare that I further leave as a bequest to the *crioulo* Miguel, son of a *preta* woman by the name of Agostinha, both slaves of Matias Fernandes, resident in this city, 50$000 that my executor will give him in money and, in the absence of Miguel, it will be given to his mother.

30. I leave to my master's wife (*minha senhora*) Veríssima de Torres, 2$000.

31. I declare that to the female slaves I have freed, I set the period of one year during which they must account for the *capela* of masses; to the male slaves

also freed, I grant the period of six months to each one of them to account for the said *capela* of masses to which they are also obliged. Be it understood that if those [male] slaves are unable to give account of the said *capela* of masses in six months, I grant them three more months, and be the same understood for the females that I grant them another three months.

32. I declare that before being married for the first and second times, I had a *crioula* daughter by the name of Maria do Carmo who was slave of my late master, Félix da Costa Lisboa, and today is slave of his wife and *minha senhora*, Verissima de Torres. At the time of writing, this daughter is alive; thus, this my daughter living in captivity [will receive] the inheritance of my goods. Her mother, Ana da Costa, will [receive the inheritance] and free my said daughter and, after freeing [her], have her marry, giving her all the rest that belongs [to her] because this is my will.

free daughter

33. I declare that, in the event that Ana da Costa is not alive, or for any reason cannot take care of the inheritance of my daughter, in that case I beseech that whoever may be the illustrious lady Mother Superior of the convent of Our Lady of Mercy, for the love of God by the most holy heart of Jesus, take care of the inheritance that belongs to my daughter and have her in her possession to free her, and afterwards set her up in the best way possible, marrying her to someone capable and, in payment for this task, I leave her 10$000.

34. I declare that after having satisfied all my dispositions and legacies that I have declared in this my testament, I institute as heir of all my remaining property my daughter, Maria do Carmo, for this is my last and final desire.

35. I declare that I leave in recompense to whichever of my executors who does me the favor of accepting this my executorship 50$000, and I grant him the time of two years to take care of this my testament.

36. I declare that I do not remember owing signed debts to anyone, and in case I owe any, demonstrated by true notes, they will be paid, without legal wrangling; in the same way the debts that I am owed will be collected, in the same manner; and there will be suits only against those people who are remiss in paying me if they have the goods to do so and do not.

37. Finally, having concluded and finished this my last will and testament, I again beseech and request my wife, Joaquina de Melo, and senhores Captain Manoel Justiniano Ferreira de Andrade and Inácio José da Silva that, for the service of God and me, they do me the grace of accepting this executorship, to whom and to each one individually I concede all my powers, which by right I can do, and I institute them as my full agents, with full dominion over my property to act in my benefit [and carry out] all that is contained in this [document]. If for [this will] to be fully valid, there are missing some clause, words, or clauses, I hereby consider them expressed as if fully written and declared so that all of this be expressed and for this I beseech the justices of His Royal Majesty, whom God keep, in this and other jurisdictions, to thus carry it out and protect it in the way that it is written and, to establish that this is true, I requested Captain José Rodrigues Carneiro to write this for me and sign as a witness, for I have had him read this my will and, finding it to my satisfaction, I consider it approved in Bahia.

Witnesses: Ubaldo da Rocha Torres, Vicente Francicso Ferreira da Mata, Feliciano Pereira, Antônio Alvares de Araujo Mendes, Floréncio Pereira Pimentel.[23]

Figure 16 Soldier and officer in Salvador's black militia regiment, which Colonel Manoel Pereira da Silva commanded, and in which Captain Joaquim Félix de Santana served (Vilhena 1922).

22.2 Will of Colonel Manoel Pereira da Silva, March 9, 1814 (Deceased: June 2, 1815)[24]

In the name of the Lord, Amen.

1. Be it known to all who see this my testament that in the year of our Lord Jesus Christ 1814, on March 9, I, Manoel Pereira da Silva, Roman Catholic, colonel of the third militia regiment of this city of Bahia, baptized in the parish of San-

tana do Sacramento, natural son of the late Faustino Pereira da Silva, being sound of mind and body, prepared this will to discharge my conscience in the following form and manner:

2. I name as my executors, first, Anastácia Pereira da Silva; second, Laurência Pereira da Silva (my granddaughter); third, Antônio de Cristo; and I beseech each that they do me this favor of accepting the executorship.

3. I declare that I was married to Teresa Pereira de Paiva according to the rites of the Holy Mother Church, from which matrimony I have no children, and after she died I carried out her testamentary dispositions and, therefore, my goods are free . . . [of encumbrances].[25]

4. I declare that my first executor, besides being my natural child, was my slave, acquired through purchase from Nicolau de Azevedo on April 25, 1777. I bought her in order to free her because she is my daughter, which freedom I confer upon her just as I have already conferred it by the letter of manumission that I bestowed upon her on April 25, 1796. Having no children or grandchildren from my marriage, my goods will belong to my daughter Anastácia Pereira da Silva, and for this reason, I name my daughter and executrix Anastácia Pereira da Silva as the sole heir of all of my property. Because she is constant, faithful, and God-fearing, I am satisfied that my funeral and suffrages be left to her discretion; because of her capacity, I will be content with what she does.

5. I declare and determine that my slave, Antônia, be assessed at 100$000, which she will give to my heir and executrix, and to pay it I grant her the period of one year. At the end of this time, if she has not given the stipulated money, she will remain captive and the favor that I bestow in this article will be of no value to her.

6. I declare that my said slave, Antônia, has a child by the name of Henrique Pereira da Silva whom, for the love that I have for him from having raised him, I grant freedom as if born of a free womb. This article will be the title of his liberty.

7. My third executor, on the day of my death, will do me the favor of reporting it to my regiment and the major of the said regiment in the report that he makes to the superior [i.e., the governor of the colony] will tell him that I beseech His Excellency the favor of sending no soldiers to accompany my cadaver because I do not want to have with me this accompaniment.[26]

8. Having thus completed this my testament with which I revoke all others and codicils that I have made because I want only this one to be valid and be carried out properly and correctly in all ways; subjecting me fully and in all ways to the laws of his Royal Highness, and the justice of the Lord, I beseech that they carry out and protect all that is written here for this is my final wish. I asked Pedro Alexandrino Machado de Barros to write this for me, witness it, and sign it, it being also signed by me.

[Signed] Manoel Pereira da Silva

As the witness who wrote this: Pedro Alexandrino Machado de Barros
Witnesses: Cipriano Alvarez Rigaud, José Severiano da Silva, José Antônio Pereira Santiago, Ubaldo da Rocha Torres, Maurício Fernandes Santiago.

22.3 Will and Inventory of Rosa Maria da Conceição[27]

The year 1843, Santana parish. Rosa Maria da Conceição passed away, leaving [her] will, on February 1, 1836.

Second District Civil Court [of Bahia?]. Inventory of the goods of the late Rosa Maria da Conceição, continued by her executor, Maria Eugênia Coelho. Notary Domingos José do Amorim.

In the year of our Lord Jesus Christ 1843, on March 28, in this Loyal and Valorous city of São Salvador [da] Bahia de Todos os Santos, in the office of the undersigned notary, I registered the petition, certification, and will that follows, in witness whereof I began this document. I, Luiz José Gomes de Almeida, sworn-in scribe, write this. I, Domingos José de Amorim, notary, undersign this.

Will:

1. I, Rosa Maria da Conceição, native of the coast of Africa, freedwoman, and widow of Caetano de Couto, also of the same nation, formerly slave of the late Clemente Luiz, a *pardo* man, sound of mind, and desiring to bequeath my property, order my will to be made as follows:

2. I declare that I had no children, neither while I was single, nor while I was married, nor while I was a widow, and for that reason I have no obligatory heirs, descendants who prevent me from bequeathing to whomever I desire.

3. My executors will be, in the first place, Maria Eugênia Coelho, African *preta* freedwoman; in the second, her son, José Maria, *cabra*; and in the third, her daughter named Maria Margarida, *cabra*. I beseech them to do this favor for me, and for God, accepting this executorship, fulfilling the following dispositions:

4. I declare that on June 11 of this year, on the request of Manoel de Almeida, I prepared another will, which was written by José Elias Xavier da Conceição, a friend of that Manoel de Almeida, who had already conspired together. This will was written with fraudulent intent not only because the said Elias declared his friend, Almeida, as my heir, but also because it did not declare my jewelry, gold coins, and silver, which Almeida took away in a basket on the pretext of storing it—he kept all of it—and finally because this will did not leave any bequests at all to relatives of my late patron. I was completely deceived but discovered this plot when I ordered the will opened and found all of these falsehoods; therefore, it will not have the least effect, and by this [article] I declare it to be revoked in its entirety.

5. I declare that I will be buried in the Saint Francis Monastery, accompanied by my reverend parish priest, sacristan, its priests (to whom will be given the customary fees [and] the half-pound candle), and the brotherhoods of Saint Benedict and Our Lady of the Rosary of Shoemakers' Hollow. I will be shrouded in the Franciscan habit, and fifty requiem masses *praesente cadavere*[28] of the *pataca* alm will be recited in the said monastery, in *piedade* (convent), and in my parish [church].

6. Furthermore, 2$000 will be given in alms to the poor that accompany [my funeral] at forty *réis* each, and fifty more masses of the same donation will be said for the soul of my husband, three for the souls in purgatory, and three more, one

to the purity of our Lady, one to my guardian angel, and one to the saint of my name, all at forty *réis* each.

7. I declare that the property that I presently possess, because the said Manoel de Almeida carried off my valuables, is a little residence on Genipap Street, from which value (whether or not it is auctioned off after being assessed) my dispositions will be carried out, including the sum of 4$000, which I leave to any heir of my late patron who appears [to claim] it. Of the balance [of my estate] I institute as my universal heir my first executor Maria Eugênia Coelho; and, in the event of her death, her daughter, [my] third executor; and, in the event of the death of both, her son, my second executor.

8. I declare that I do not owe anything, nor do I have any debts to collect.

Having therefore concluded my sole and final testament, annulling forever the other one, I request that His Imperial Majesty's justice see that it is executed, and kept in the present form. Knowing neither how to read, nor write, I requested that this testament be prepared and, on my request, signed by the undersigned in Bahia on June 30, 1835.

Written on the request of the testator, Rosa Maria da Conceição,

[signed] João Francisco da Rocha

Swearing in and Inventory:

[March 29, 1843. The formal swearing-in of the executor, Maria Eugênia Coelho, who reported that Rosa Maria da Conceição had died on October 1, 1836 [sic], and the assessors, Master Carpenter Simão Moreira do Nascimento, and Master Mason José Moura Patatiba.]

House:

One one-story house on Genipap Street, sixteen palms (*palmos*) wide on the front, with a door and a window, with a two-story false front, with an open [and] tiled living room, two bedrooms, and kitchen, with independent side walls on stakes, with a single adobe brick and tile front wall, with a small free-standing mud-and-wattle building in the yard. The house has a yard with a wall that does not belong to it and is fenced on the other side. The house is forty palms deep, built on its own property and, because it is damaged, by common consent it is assessed for 500$000.

[Followed by the formal closing of the inventory and the signatures of the assessors, notary, and judge.]

NOTES

ACKNOWLEDGMENTS Renato Soares dos Santos transcribed Joaquim's will while Teresa dos Reis Lima transcribed Manoel's will. I thank João José Reis for assistance with points of translation.

1. While Salvador and Bahia were the two most common ways to refer to the city, longer versions of the name highlighted its location at the mouth of the vast Bay of All Saints: in Rosa

Maria's will, for example, the scribe refers to the "Loyal and Valorous City of the Holy Saviour of the Bay of All Saints." "Loyal and Valorous" was a title granted to the city after independence; the city was dedicated to the Saviour ("Salvador" in Portuguese); and it was located on the Bay ("Bahia" in Portuguese) of All Saints. Salvador was also known more simply as the City of the Bay (Bahia), after its geographical location, and the wills that follow demonstrate the variety of nomenclature for the city still known as either Salvador or Bahia.

2. The following discussion is limited to legal provisions relevant to these three documents. For fuller treatments of Brazilian family and inheritance law, see Linda Lewin, "Natural and Spurious Children in Brazilian Inheritance Law from Colony to Empire: A Methodological Essay," *The Americas* 48:3 (January 1992), 351–96; Kátia M. de Queirós Mattoso, "A família e o direito no Brasil no século XIX: subsídios jurídicos para os estudos em história social," *Anais do Arquivo Público do Estado da Bahia* 44 (1979), 217–44; and Maria Beatriz Nizza da Silva, "Family and Property in Colonial Brazil," *Portuguese Studies* 7 (1991), 61–77.

3. Mieko Nishida, "Manumission and Ethnicity in Urban Slavery: Salvador, Brazil, 1808-1888," *Hispanic American Historical Review* 73:3 (August 1993), 380–81.

4. Manuela Carneiro da Cunha, "Silences of the Law: Customary Law and Positive Law on the Manumission of Slaves in 19th-Century Brazil," *History and Anthropology* 1:2 (1985), 427–43.

5. Arquivo Público do Estado da Bahia, Seção Judiciária, Livro de Registro de Testamentos, vol. 7, fols. 30v–41r.

6. That is 135,000 *réis* in this standard way of denoting Brazilian monetary sums. See *real* in the glossary. For clarity, sums of less than 100 *réis* will be spelled out as, for example, forty *réis*.

7. "Vicar" (*vigário*) refers to a parish priest, while "sacristan" (*sacristão*) refers to a layman charged with the care of church ornaments and religious implements.

8. Candle wax functioned as a currency for the payment of church services.

9. By requesting that these requiem masses be said *de corpo presente* (in Catholic church jargon, *praesente cadavere*), Joaquim wishes them to be said before he is buried.

10. A black saint of particular devotion to Afro-Brazilians.

11. The passage is unclear. The purchase price of Ana and Francisca Mina cannot have been 60$000, for then there would have been no need to add 85$000. If 60$000 is the sale price of Luiza, then Ana and Francisca Mina cost 145$000.

12. The text includes the words "and one," referring apparently to another slave but it is probably a slip of the scribe's pen, for the rest of the passage is in singular tense and Joaquim has already accounted for his wife's three slaves.

13. By specifying his wife's property in Articles 15 to 19 and listing his own separately in the next articles, Joaquim appears to be establishing that he and his wife held their property seperately as a way of avoiding the community property provisions of Brazilian inheritance law (see introduction). He does not mention a marriage contract, however, and has treated his wife's property as his own (see previous note). Because no record of the disposition of his goods has survived, it is impossible to know whether this couple drew one up before their marriage.

14. Oratories are small private chapels or devotional niches often containing, as in Joaquim's case, crucifixes, and images of Jesus and other saints. They were common in eighteenth- and early nineteenth-century Brazilian households. Oratory images tended to be small and portable (see the description of his wife's image of Saint Anne in Article 17). The quality of the ornaments depended on the wealth of the household, and Joaquim's vary significantly in value, suggesting that he was in the process of accumulating additional pieces or improving the ones that he had. The marble image of the Holy Lord may have been awaiting a silver trim. Today, elaborate oratories can be seen in many Brazilian historical museums.

15. A stringed instument resembling a violin.

16. Fine white linen or cotton.

17. Cloth produced in the Portuguese town of Guimarães.

18. The reference is ambiguous: these are either large old Portuguese coins (*espadins*) or large swords (*espadões*). The former is suggested by the description of gold and silver; the latter by Joaquim's military rank.

19. A Portuguese island off the coast of Africa.

20. Ever business-like, Joaquim here refers to the handing over of the letters of liberty as payment in full on the slaves' account.
21. A poor free person raised in a wealthier family's household. The child may be the son of Felisarda, declared to have been freed in Article 25 (above), in which case *cria's* other meaning—a slave child still nursing—may indicate both Agostinho's young age and his background as the son of a former slave. He is probably not a slave, on which point see note below.
22. That is, if he has reached the age of majority. The passage may also indicate Agostinho's slave status, for slaves were legally—though not always in practice—barred from inheriting. On this point, compare Articles 32 and 34.
23. This document is a certified copy of an original and there is no indication that Joaquim had signed it. Possibly he was too ill to do so.
24. Arquivo Público do Estado da Bahia, Seção Judiciária, Livros de Registro de Testamentos, vol. 5, fols. 51v–53v.
25. The original Portuguese, "e não tem dados," is unclear, but Manoel's intent—to declare that he is free to dispose of his goods—is clear.
26. Colonel Manoel's refusal of military honors is unusual; deceased officers' families usually insisted that a platoon of soldiers be sent to accompany funeral processions. At least three speculative explanations exist for this article. First, possibly Manoel wanted to spare the part-time militia soldiers in his regiment the trouble of performing this task. Second, as Manoel might have been badly treated by the inspector-general—who wanted to get rid of black officers and have the segregated militia commanded by white men—he may not have wanted his funeral to be dominated by military ceremony. Third, the refusal of military honors may have combined with the fact that he requested that his daughter take care of his funeral without making any requests for masses (Article 4). In contrast to Joaquim and Rosa Maria, this may indicate that he has privately instructed his daughter to arrange for illegal Afro-Brazilian funeral rites. This is only speculation; he may simply have been a less-than-devout Catholic.
27. Arquivo Público do Estado da Bahia, Seção Judiciária, Inventários e Testamentos, 05/2956/2428/06, fols. 3r–5v, 8r.
28. See note 9 (above).

Document Themes

African/Afro-Latin American peoples; Economy and Work; Family; Inheritance; Manumission; Religion; Slavery; Town Life.

Suggestions for Further Reading

Dias 1995.
Hünefeldt 1994.
Karasch 1987.
Kraay 1998.
Mattoso 1986.
Reis 1993.
Reis 1996.
Reis forthcoming.
Russell-Wood 1982.
Schwartz 1985.
Schwartz 1992.

CHAPTER
23

Meltdown in New Spain:
Viceroy Apodaca's Account
of the State of the Rebellion
(Mexico, 1816)

Christon I. Archer and Alex Taylor del Cid

INTRODUCTION

When Viceroy Juan Ruíz de Apodaca arrived in New Spain in 1816 he found himself in an entrenched and fragmented guerrilla war that showed few signs of ending. While the enormous forces unleashed in 1810 by Father Miguel Hidalgo were no longer active, insurgency and banditry pressed the available capacities of the royalist forces. Efforts to garrison troops in every town and region left few units to form operational armies that could attack the plethora of rebel fortifications. To root out so many strongholds established in rugged mountainous regions, on islands in lakes, and in isolated places such as Mezcala, Coporo, Cerro Colorado, and Silacayuapan, would have required mobilizing expensive siege forces. This was not exactly the situation described by Apodaca's predecessor, Viceroy Félix Calleja, who viewed himself as the commander who had brought the rebels of New Spain to their knees. Indeed, even the Mexican historian Lucas Alamán stated that if the Independence War had not been rekindled, Calleja would have been recognized as a new Hernando Cortés, the reconqueror of New Spain.

But Alamán was wrong. From the moment that Apodaca arrived at Veracruz, he knew that the revolution was by no means concluded. First, like any new administrator he needed to learn about the complex geography, the population, and the near-Byzantine administrative structure of New Spain. Then he had to move beyond his briefings to try to understand the nature of the Independence War and of the personalities and issues on both sides of it. As this document illustrates, he recognized immediately the growing level of exhaustion among royalist commanders and he joined their chorus demanding new transfers of expeditionary regiments from Spain—fresh blood to be consumed in a bitter conflict between insurgents and counterinsurgents. This was a war that would resonate with many similar struggles through the twentieth century.

In New Spain, Apodaca had to learn quickly which officers were capable, where the main trouble spots were, and how to continue funding a war that had severely damaged or even destroyed the economy. He had to balance the needs of counterinsurgency that required expensive military dispositions and the mobilization of the populace with the equally pressing need to restore the devastated mining districts, ruined agriculture, and interdicted commerce. Even to move silver bullion from the interior of New Spain to the port of Acapulco for shipment on the Manila galleon, or to move bullion to the strategic port of Veracruz on the Gulf Coast, required the organization of powerful convoys guarded by army units. Well back from the roads where the convoys moved, other royalist commanders were ordered to deploy their troops so as to prevent any coalescence of rebel bands. Indeed, the fear that the disunited rebels might somehow once again form great assemblies was sufficient to make Apodaca's blood run cold. His plan was to offer a carrot-and-stick approach: amnesty and reincorporation to those insurgents who would seek royal pardon, and suffocating military pressure to root out the *gavillas* (implacable rebel gangs) from their rugged hideaways who rejected pardon. Finally, Viceroy Apodaca had to concern himself with rumors of invasion forces from the United States and contraband traders from New Orleans and other ports who carried arms and munitions for sale to the rebels of New Spain. Being viceroy in ordinary times was a post that exhausted many incumbents. One can only wonder how Apodaca managed that office during the insurgency war when the pressures of a broad spectrum of executive, administrative, and military responsibilities were intensified tenfold.

This interesting document illustrates the full range of complexities relating to the independence movements in Spanish America. Students will note that Apodaca had to fight an entire panoply of enemies and that often there were few if any references to noble causes such as justice, republicanism, and even independence. The war was a chronic and bitter struggle based in the regions and districts where local factors blended with broader concepts such as independence or home rule. In New Spain, the war developed different levels of intensity, burned out for a time, then again suddenly flared up, but few were somnolent and willing to turn the clock back to the epoch of the eighteenth-century colony. As Viceroy Apodaca would learn, colonial powers—even those with apparent military predominance—seldom achieve success in wars of the people.

THE DOCUMENT[1]

Confidential
To: The Marqués de Campo Sagrado
Excelentísimo Señor:

23.1 Valladolid

A few days after taking command of this kingdom, Lieutenant Colonel don Felipe Castañón informed me that he had occupied the small Island of Xanicho in

Lake Pátzcuaro, in the province of Valladolid, where the rebels had fortified them-selves. He compelled them to throw into the water eight pieces of artillery that they had assembled with the corresponding munitions.

Nevertheless, this has not contributed toward improving the fortunes of that region where with the exception of its capital [Valladolid or today Morelia], and the towns of Zamora and La Piedad, it is completely occupied by seditious ele-ments. In Uruapan, several *gavillas* led by Dr. [José María] Cos, [Manuel] Muñiz, Sánchez, and other *cabecillas* (ringleaders) operate under the protection of the fortress that they constructed a long time ago at Jaujilla.[2] Despite the efforts of the royalist troops dispatched to crush them, from this stronghold they have continued the insurrection of the province. Given this situation, I ordered the *comandante* of Valladolid province, Lieutenant Colonel don Antonio Linares, to leave an adequate garrison to protect the city of Valladolid and to set out with the rest of his forces in an active pursuit against the enemy. He is to take advan-tage of any opportunity that presents itself to expel the enemy from Juajilla and in case he cannot accomplish this goal by a sudden surprise attack, he will orga-nize a tight blockade of that position assisted by troops from neighboring Nueva Galicia. The *comandante general* of that province, Field Marshall don José de la Cruz, has been given the corresponding orders to assist this plan.

23.2 Guanajuato

During the past two months the rebels of the province of Guanajuato have con-structed two forts, one next to the town of León and the other near the town of Pénjamo. At León, the rebels repelled the detachment commanded by Lieutenant Colonel don Pedro Monzalve with the loss of soldiers and some officers. After careful reconnaissance at Pénjamo, Colonel don Francisco de Orrantia reported an enemy fortification that because of the difficult nature of the terrain and the strong defensive works will require a formal siege. Due to the shortage of troops and pressure of duties that employ them, it will not be possible for now to un-dertake this enterprise.

The *gavillas* of that country, strengthened by numbers and daring because of the resources that support their ferocity and wealth, have won advantages over some of our troop detachments. In addition, they have ruined agriculture, de-stroyed commercial traffic, burned haciendas and towns, and left royalist gar-risons under a restricted blockade so that they can scarcely breathe. They suffer shortages, misery, and the depopulation of their districts. These ills have weak-ened the *real* of Guanajuato,[3] where due to a lack of essential goods most mines are abandoned and flooded. Some are being worked only in the upper levels.

To speed the remedy of these evils, I have advised the provincial *comandante* that he must pursue the rebels constantly, maintain open communications be-tween the *pueblos organizados* (towns with militias and fortifications), and guard the transit of frequent convoys to Guanajuato. He must restore that mining cen-ter, and ensure that it is provided with the necessary products. I am considering the appointment to command in that province of Colonel don Cristoval Ordóñez, who will relieve don Francisco Orrantia, who in his entreaties has made it clear to me that he does not find himself capable of discharging these duties. Without flattering myself, notwithstanding the very rooted nature of the insurrection, these measures and others that I will be taking to suit the circumstances, will soon pacify that region.

23.3 San Luis and Zacatecas

The provinces of San Luis and Zacatecas continue in a good state, except for the fact that the *gavillas* of Guanajuato, penetrate them to commit their accustomed robberies and atrocities. When this occurs, they are pursued and punished wherever they are found.

23.4 Nueva Galicia

Nueva Galicia is not as pacified because in addition to the incursions made by the *gavillas* of Valladolid and Guanajuato, the rebel assembly on the Island of Mezcala [in Lake Chapala] continues. From time to time, insurgents depart this den to cause misfortunes among our troops and in the *pueblos organizados*. In his recent reports, *comandante general* don José de la Cruz has indicated that his forces are winning advantages over the rebels.

23.5 The Northern Frontier

I have no news that any new developments have occurred in the *provincias de occidente* (western internal provinces), that since 1812 have continued to enjoy a state of tranquillity obtained with the imprisonment and punishment of the first *cabecillas* (leaders) of the rebellion. In regard to the *provincias de oriente* (eastern internal provinces), I have received the instructions that Your Excellency gave me in *reales ordenes* (Royal Orders) of June 1st and 4th this year. I replied in separate letters to the news that came by way of the governor of the Island of Cuba referring to His Majesty's chargé d'affaires in the United States, don Luis de Onís. I have learned recently that an expedition of eighteen to twenty vessels has been prepared in New York and Baltimore to carry two thousand men and two hundred officers. Their objective is to strike at the heart of the Mexican Gulf Coast and to establish a port at Boquilla de Piedras [north of Veracruz] or some other point on the coast. This information forced me to forewarn the *comandante general* of the *provincias internas*, Brigadier don Joaquín de Arredondo, that he must assemble the troops under his command and be ready for operations. The expeditionary *Regimiento de infantería de Extremadura* (Infantry Regiment of Extremadura)[4] now on garrison duty in San Luis Potosí will march immediately to Tampico. There, the commander of this unit, Colonel Benito Armiñán will organize a provisional *distrito militar* (military district) that will include the defensive forces of Tuxpan and Huejutla. The objective is to unite the army units and resources of the country under one hand to oppose the designs of these enemies. Armiñán's force will

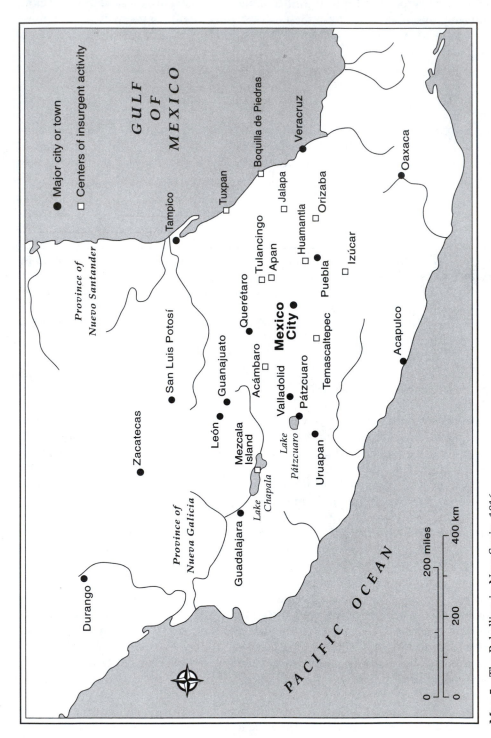

Map 5 The Rebellion in New Spain, 1816

defeat and pursue them, preventing them from heading inland where they might join the *gavillas* that operate in the interior.

Two months have passed since the above-mentioned expedition [from New York and Baltimore] must have left its ports and there has been no news whatsoever of sightings on our coasts. I have therefore informed Armiñán that in the district of his command north to Tampico, he must assemble reliable information on the points where the enemy might disembark. If the landing takes place at the Bay of Espíritu Santo, or elsewhere in Texas, he will march to that province in order to secure and to rectify the situation. I have also ordered Brigadier Arredondo to communicate with Armiñán using the utmost diligence regarding the warnings and news about the designs and strength of the rebel forces. With this goal in mind, he will send loyal scouts and spies to the frontier and ports of Texas. In case the enemy has not disembarked at any coastal point, or if it is not possible to confirm that such a landing will take place shortly, Armiñán will head to Boquilla de Piedras and other rebel positions between Tuxpan and Veracruz. He will attack and expel them, making certain that the necessary garrisons are left behind, before his forces march to pursue the bands that exist in proximity to the coasts.

23.6 The Near North: From Mexico City to Querétaro

The territory between Querétaro and the capital has enjoyed great tranquillity for some time so that convoys with rich cargoes of silver and merchandise travel with small escorts. However, I have ordered these guards reinforced in order to prevent robberies and to give the towns and haciendas along the routes confidence to provide abundant grain and livestock. A *gavilla* formed at the beginning of last month in the Sierra Gorda region situated to the north of these territories. Although these insurgents have caused some damages, this situation is not a reason for great concern since they are being prosecuted with great energy by the troops of the Tula and Querétaro garrisons.

23.7 West of Mexico City

To the south of both jurisdictions and to the west of this capital, the *partidos* (military patrols) from Toluca and Ixtlahuacan, find themselves in pacified country that enjoys a regular state of agriculture and commercial traffic. However, on some occasions small rebel *gavillas* penetrate to execute robberies and exact taxes. Lieutenant Colonel don Matías Martín y Aguirre, who covers the second of those jurisdictions, makes frequent expeditions against Cerro de Coporo, where the Rayones (the Rayón clan) fortified themselves. While royalist forces have chased and harassed them with some results and curtailed their means of subsistence, to expel them from that advantageous position will require a formal siege involving at least three-thousand men. I do not have this number available right now and while it is better to economize possible losses, I cannot risk fate in a bloody assault.

23.8 The Mining Zone North and Northwest of Mexico City

The *minerales* (mines in a mining district) of Temascaltepec, Sultepec, Aganguío, Tlalpujahua, Zitácuaro, and others of the sierra that runs to the south of Ixtlahuacan, Maravatío, and Acámbaro, find themselves still frequented by the rebels, and their mines are almost all abandoned. My intention is that after the infantry regiments of Puebla and Mexico arrive here from Havana[5] and are built up again, I will dispatch one of them with a section of cavalry to the first of those *minerales* mentioned above in order to commence the reorganization of the others. By this measure, I will give more encouragement to the important field of mining that in general finds itself in great decadence.

23.9 The Acapulco Coast

The coast of Acapulco and the road between that port and this capital [Mexico City], covered by the detachment of Colonel don José Gabriel de Armijo, is without large rebel gatherings. But there is no shortage of *gavillas* that at times gain the advantage against our patrols. Royalist units cannot always be as strong as is necessary due to the great extension of the country, and the many fortified points occupied by our troops. To the left of the above-mentioned road is the town of Tlapa from the direction of which come frequent enemy incursions. These are more dangerous because they are sustained by the *gavilla* fortified for two years at Silacayuapan, and by other bands that operate between the limits of Armijo's jurisdiction and the province of Oaxaca.

　　This officer has my orders to move when the rivers rise with the forces that he can assemble to pursue rebel assemblies in coordination with the troops of Izúcar and of Huajuapan until they achieve the pacification of the region. To this end, I have also directed corresponding dispositions to the *comandante general del sur* (Commandant General of the South), who has jurisdiction over these places. Nevertheless, I do not promise myself that complete tranquillity will be achieved in that territory while our enemies remain in control of Silacayuapan. Given the failure of previous attempts to throw them out of that fortification, this operation will require a formal siege.

　　Tomorrow a convoy will leave this capital for Acapulco carrying 1,280,948 pesos in silver coin that must be shipped aboard the frigate *Victoria*, which is ready to set sail for Manila. With the goal of avoiding any surprise directed against this rich shipment, I have taken the dispositions for its security that seemed to me as most opportune.

23.10 East of Mexico City

The *llanos* (plains) of Apan reduced by Colonel don Manuel de la Concha continue in a good state, but this country very much resents the misery in which the rebels left it with its agriculture and commerce destroyed, and the majority of the towns and haciendas burned. Only in the production of *pulque* were the rebels not completely successful in annihilating the entire economy. It is one area that produces some profits to private investors and to the treasury, but so little until now that in this current month it was necessary to assist those troops with almost 30,000 pesos provided by this treasury [of Mexico City] and from the revenues of Pachuca.

Colonel don Joaquín Márquez Donallo, in combination with Concha, has smashed the *gavillas* that escaped from the Apan region. He has pacified and garrisoned the towns of Huamantla, Nopalucan, San Juan de los Llanos and other points throughout the province of Puebla with a force from the *Ejército del sur* (Army of the South). In accordance with the orders that I gave him for that region just as for the *llanos* (plains), Tulancingo and Pachuca, that are encompassed within the demarcation of [Apan], a considerable number of individuals, many with arms and horses have presented themselves for royal amnesty, and are now serving with utility united to our troops. They are supported with *contribuciones* [taxes] imposed on *pulque* production and other municipal *arbitrios* (taxes), that the treasury would not be able to find if those resources were not available.

23.11 The Huasteca Region

To the northeast of Tulancingo one finds the jurisdiction of Huejutla in the Huasteca, where since the middle of this year a *gavilla* of rebels has formed headed by José Joaquín Aguilar. He reunited rebels dispersed from Zacatlan and Huachinango, who have committed robberies, the destruction of towns, and other hostilities in that demarcation and in Tampico. At this time, the *comandante* of Tuxpan, Lieutenant Colonel don Carlos María Llorente is on the march to track them down. He has orders not to return to his base until he has succeeded in exterminating or reducing these rebels, and clearing the road from the *puertos de barlovento* [ports to the windward of Veracruz] that have been obstructed by the enemy. These rebels maintain relations with the insurgents of Misantla, Boquilla de Piedras and other points along the coast through which they receive arms, munitions, and other assistance. According to Llorente, he lacks the people he needs to do the job, which is the general complaint of all the *comandantes*.

23.12 Mexico City and Its Vicinity

This capital and its vicinity are to be found in complete tranquillity, provisioned with food, livestock, and consumer goods that are introduced freely from all directions following the destruction of the *gavillas* that existed previously. The detachments and patrols from military posts situated in this extensive valley pursue the *pequeñas caudrillas de ladrones* (small bands of thieves) that have remained. Most of the jurisdiction of Chalco and the Puebla road through Río Frío are in the same state of pacification under the shelter of two small forts constructed to guard the road and by a detachment of the *Ejército del sur* that provides cover under the command of Colonel don Francisco de Hevia. Although the two small forts have not been completed and lack artillery, the troops of their garrisons are sufficient for now. I have commanded that the defensive works under way shall be completed with 1,500 pesos made available by the *consulado* (the Merchant Guild of Mexico City) in addition to 5,000 pesos given previously.

Up to this point, I have spoken to Your Excellency about the state in which one finds the provinces and military districts situated to the west, north, and south of this capital, and of the eastern parts that encompass the region of Apan, with its borders with Huamantla and San Juan de los Llanos. I will do the same with regard to the provinces of Puebla, Oaxaca, and Veracruz that are located to the east and the southeast.

23.13 Puebla, Oaxaca, Veracruz

Although great concentrations of rebels do not exist in the first two provinces that comprise the demarcation of the *Ejército del sur* under the command of Brigadier Ciriaco del Llano, there are some more or less numerous *gavillas* that if coalesced would form a rebel mass of some consideration. Moreover, they maintain their military position at Cerro Colorado in the province of Puebla, and those of Silacayuapan, Santa Lucía, and Teotitlán del Camino in Oaxaca. From these positions, they harass the *pueblos organizados* and obstruct the roads that cannot be traveled without competent forces. They maintain under their control extensive and fertile territories that our troops cannot cover properly. The rebels enjoy the production and profits of these regions. Although they are pursued incessantly by our troops and in general we cause them to suffer losses and setbacks, they recover with facility with the resources offered by the country, and with the exactions and levies that they impose at their capricious desire.

The district that lies between Puebla and the towns of Orizaba and Córdoba through the valley of San Andrés finds itself still at the mercy of the rebels. Because we need to make frequent expeditions to conduct tobacco from that factory to the one in Puebla,[6] and since communications between Veracruz and the towns are completely intercepted, I have decided that these districts must be separated from the government of the port city. Instead they will be attached as they were before to the province of Puebla and the demarcation of the *Ejército del sur*. In cases of necessity, they will receive more and quicker aid. At Monteblanco near Orizaba over the past few months, the *cabecilla* Guadalupe Victoria has built a great fortification. I do not know why it was not impeded, nor why Colonel don José Ruíz could not take it since he has a respectable force available in that territory,

The *cabecillas* of the Terán clan who dominate Cerro Colorado, Tehuacán, and other positions of the provinces of Puebla and Oaxaca, have suffered two defeats in the latter jurisdiction caused by royalist troops and the military detachments of the *costa de sotavento* [the Leeward coast of Veracruz] under *teniente de navío* (Warship Lieutenant) don Juan Bautista Topete, whom I returned to the command of the coast to the south of Veracruz. He had renounced this post due to quarrels, but his outstanding services have made him worthy of general appreciation. I just received detailed dispatches from this officer that have not yet been inserted in the *Gazeta*. I ordered Brigadier Llano, and the commander of Oaxaca, Lieutenant Colonel don Nicolas del Obeso, to be relentless in pursuit of enemy forces in all directions so that they do not have time to unite or to fix their attentions upon a specific point.

Despite its own resources and the number of troops that cover its territory, the province of Veracruz is far from pacified. Indeed, it is inundated with *gavillas* that occupy the territory to the left and right of the road from Jalapa to the city of Veracruz. The military posts along the road from one point to another were established by Brigadier Fernando Miyares with a great deal of effort and expenditure. During my passage through the region, I ordered the situation rectified and improved. Also, I ordered the capture of Boquilla de Piedras with complete details kept on all corresponding matters concerning the campaign. The rebels are masters of La Campaña and they have cut communications. They have taken the above-mentioned coastal point of Boquilla de Piedras and others that they have fortified between Tuxpan and Veracruz. From these positions they communicate directly with the pirates and subversives of Louisiana that provide them with arms, munitions, people, and every type of assistance.

Guadalupe Victoria, who leads the rebel *reuniones* (gatherings) of that direction, attacked Jalapa three weeks ago with the objective of distracting the garrison there while he situated his forces, as has been verified, at the Cerro de El Iquimite that borders the town. There he has constructed parapets, partially blockaded this locality, and further limited the blocked communications with Veracruz. This event, and the disagreements that erupted between the *ayuntamiento* (municipal government) of Jalapa and the *comandante militar* Lieutenant Colonel don Vicente Patiño, forced me to turn over that command to Brigadier don Joaquín del Castillo y Bustamante. He had already held this post on a previous occasion and was in the town at the time.

The 15th of this month a convoy destined for Veracruz from the capital [Mexico City] commenced its march with 3,520,396 pesos in minted coin, and it arrived without incident at Puebla. The convoy will continue to its destination when the mules sent to the towns of Córdoba and Orizaba return to the city with tobacco needed to fill shortages in these factories. In the meantime, funds to be remitted from Puebla should amount to something like half a million pesos.

With the objective of assuring the march of the convoy, I have ordered that Colonel Márquez will depart with a strong military detachment to clear the road of *gavillas* that have congregated to attack it. He will flatten any obstacles that he encounters. Then three or four days later the convoy will depart escorted by the *Regimiento expedicionario de infantería* of Zamora that accompanied it from this capital under the command of Colonel don Rafael Bracho, with a competent cavalry force. At the same time from the left and right of the Veracruz road, two units of troops under colonels don José Morán and don Manuel de la Concha will protect the transit of the convoy until the heights of Perote or Jalapa where they will leave it secure for the last leg of the trip. From this last point, it will be protected by the military posts and Colonel Márquez will employ all available forces to avoid any surprises against that valuable shipment. It would cause us incalculable evils if this convoy fell to the enemy.

To attend as soon as possible to the bad state in which one finds the province of Veracruz, I have ordered Colonel Márquez, with the *Regimiento expedicionario*

Figure 17 During the fight for independence, a Mexican creole on horseback faces the line of fire and lassoes a royalist officer (Linati [1828] 1956, plate 21).

de infantería de Lovera under his command, to remain there after the convoy returns from the port city to Jalapa. The objective will be to guard the posts of the *vía militar* (military road), and to destroy the rebel *reuniones* that infest the country. In case Colonel Armiñán receives news from the *provincias de oriente* that he must head for Texas in the shortest time possible, Márquez will dispatch a competent number of troops to expel the enemy from Boquilla de Piedras. He will be assisted from the sea by the governor of Veracruz with whatever forces that he can spare, and by land with forces made available from the *comandante* of Tuxpan.

The *regimiento* of Zamora will remain in the *Ejército del sur*, relieving the *regimiento* of Lovera, so that it can assist Veracruz from bases in Perote and the towns of Jalapa, Córdoba, and Orizaba. In this capital [Mexico City], we will assemble the companies of the *Regimiento de ordenes militares*.[7] Three companies of this Spanish expeditionary unit escorted me to Mexico City with the remainder of the *batallón* of Ferdinand VII and two hundred men from the *Regimiento provincial de tres villas*. I took these last soldiers from the detachment of Tula, replacing them there with *Realistas de caballería* (cavalry militiamen) to provide garrison duty. I should point out that these steps were motivated by my desire to deploy the only available *tropa de linea* (regular army line forces from Spain).

The fortress city of Veracruz requires an active chief, who is resolute and experienced enough so that he can unite land and sea forces under his command. He must be motivated by great zeal so that he can take rapid and efficient decisions in the difficult events that can occur. I recommend that a *capitán de navío* (naval warship captain), or a *brigadier de marina* (a senior naval officer who commanded a division of a fleet) be appointed *gobernador político y militar* (the political-military governor of Veracruz). I propose that there should be a *brigadier* or a *general de ejército* (an army brigadier or a general) who will serve as *comandante general* and *intendente* (Commander General and Intendant) for military operations of the province who will reside in Jalapa. At least while the revolution endures, these changes will bring great advantages for the royal service since one of the ills suffered by the province of Veracruz is the lack of communication between its chief and this *gobierno superior* (the viceregal government in Mexico City).

In regard to naval forces to cruise Veracruz and its coasts, I have ordered the corvette *Diana* that carried me from Havana to remain in these waters with the brigantine *Saeta* and the schooner *Prosperina*. These vessels will be sufficient for now to provide convoy escort for the coastal traffic along the coasts to the north and south of Veracruz, Also, because they always say in the Veracruz treasury that there is a lack of money that causes difficulty to provide maintenance for these ships. When I am informed about the income produced by customs revenues and other branches of taxation at Veracruz, I will be able to take other measures that may be sufficient to allow us to cruise against the enemy in the Gulf of Mexico.

23.14 Apodaca Characterizes the Rebels

Because of the news and reports that I have received up to the present, I observe that at this time the great masses of rebels assembled at the beginning of the insurrection, and the mobs of Indians that formed the majority of those gatherings no longer exist today. Also, it is certain that not all the *cabecillas* are in agreement among themselves about waging war and how to work together against our troops. Although their system of devouring everything that they encounter is the same everywhere, sometimes they even fight against each other, and snatch stolen property from one another. However, the *gavillas* that are disseminated throughout the kingdom generally are composed of the most perverse and audacious of the rebels, of army deserters, and of lost and abandoned peoples. Because of these evil qualities that they have lived with for a very long time, they are not attracted to any other occupation than robber, assassin, and libertine. The long time that they have carried on the rebellion has hardened them to the military campaign, and provided them with sufficient skill in the use of arms—especially regarding cavalry. With the help of some officers of our forces who have deserted to their ranks, and others who came from the United States, they have learned the art of making war and the means of fortifying advantageous positions.

The insurgent military positions of Isla de Mezcala, Coporo, Cerro Colorado, Silacayuapan, and others where more than once they have shattered our forces are an undeniable proof of this truth. From those *madrigueras* (rebel dens), they issue forth frequently and in a manner reminiscent of a cloud of locusts they burn the country, rob, and lay waste to whatever they encounter. The defenseless towns and haciendas give them all they have in order to free themselves of their atrocities. It is not possible that the royalist troops cover all the points in the immense territorial extension where they are distributed. Even though our forces pursue the rebels constantly and almost always with results, as the *Gazetas* that I am sending to Your Excellency separately will illustrate, the rebels easily repair their losses, and prepare themselves to undertake new incursions.

In general the towns and the people of the countryside where the rebels dominate are scourged by the atrocities that they commit, by the exactions that they demand, and by the disorder that they must endure. They long for the troops of the king and they are glad to defend themselves and to equip themselves for their own defense. But because royalist troops cannot be in all places at all times, these good dispositions remain without effect.

Through the manifestations that I have made, Your Excellency will know of the need to send to this kingdom the troops requested by my predecessor with officers of dragoons and cavalry for the instruction and expansion of this military branch that is absolutely necessary, and six to eight thousand muskets with their bayonets. The increase of forces will cause great hardships for this government to provide them with subsistence during the first months, and even to maintain communications. However, once the mines are reorganized, and agriculture and commercial traffic are restarted, these branches of the economy will produce what they are capable of, and the treasury will receive the funds that now it lacks.

Regarding the question of income, I have issued many executive orders to subordinates commanding them to send exact records of income and expenditures and of the branches of the economy that produce them. The enormous amount of more than 30 million pesos that the Royal Treasury of Mexico owes to corporations[8] and private individuals, and more than 50 million pesos to other treasuries and establishments of His Majesty, means that we cannot collect today for the most urgent expenses and for the payment of interest on capital. The situation is such that one cannot doubt the embarrassment in which I find myself for any disposition that occurs requiring funding to put it in practice, be it military or political.

For now this is as much as I can tell Your Excellency without many details due to the short period of a month and a half that I have been in charge of this command. Although my predecessor [Calleja] advised Your Excellency in letter no. 11, of September 6th last year, and he also told me that he would instruct me regarding the state in which he would deliver this kingdom to me, his preoccupation with organizing his departure that he has accomplished with the convoy to Veracruz, has not permitted him to do so up to the present. All that I have manifested to Your Excellency, you can decide to inform the king our lord, deigning to assure His Majesty that I will not overlook any means or sacrifice even though it may be that of my own life to improve the state of this precious portion of his dominions, pacifying it, and conserving it in the state of obedience owed to the best of sovereigns.

May God guide Your Excellency,
Mexico, October 31, 1816.

Most Excellent Sir, Minister of War

NOTES

1. The present document comes from Mexico's Archivo General de la Nación, Historia, vol. 152, ff. 111–16.
2. Juajilla was one of many fortifications built by the rebels through the course of the decade of war. Situated on a small island in Laguna de Zacapu near Valladolid (Morelia), the fort was surrounded by water and swamplands joined by a narrow tongue of land to the shore. The rebels first fortified this excellent natural site in 1812 and continued to use it as a base for regional rebel bands that supported a governing junta at Juajilla. Note, then, that fortified places were concentrations of "political" as well as "military" activity. In 1818, the *comandante general* of Michoacán, Matías de Aguirre, besieged the fort and captured it after the rebels surrendered in exchange for amnesties.

   During the war, the lightly armed insurgents often sought to situate themselves in strongholds located in rugged mountainous regions and on islands in lakes or swamps that had the potential to resist the better armed and disciplined royalist forces. The theory was that the royalists would exhaust themselves, lose morale, and suffer diseases in lengthy sieges that tied down their forces. The idea was good, but the rebels lacked the staying power to withstand long sieges. Nevertheless, the strategy did in fact weaken the royalist armies and caused them to divide and subdivide their forces into hundreds of garrisons. At Isla de Mezcala in Lake Chapala for example, a relatively small insurgent garrison withstood royalist attacks from 1813 to 1816. The insurgents forced José de la Cruz, *comandante general* of Nueva Galicia, to mobilize large forces and to build a fleet of rowed gunboats and an artillery platform manned by naval officers and rowed by prisoners of war. (See Christon I. Archer, "The Indian Insurgents of Mezcala Island on the Lake Chapala Front, 1812–1816," in Susan Schroeder, ed., *Native Resistance and the Pax Colonial in New Spain* [Lincoln and London: University of Nebraska Press, 1998], pp. 84–128, 158–165.) In addition, Cruz had to introduce a brutal counterinsurgency program, a scorched earth policy, and a plan to resettle the populace from the littoral of the lake into guarded villages. Some other famous rebel forts were Monteblanco, Palmillas, and Coyoxquihui in Veracruz province, Cóporo in Michoacán, Cerro del Sombrero and San Gregorio in Guanajuato, and Tepeji and Teotitlán in Tehuacán.
3. The term *real* refers to a mining jurisdiction where there are silver mines. Guanajuato was one of the leading silver-producing districts administered from the city of the same name.
4. It is important to stress that these units were expeditionary forces dispatched to New Spain from the metropolitan Spanish army. Beginning in 1812 even before the complete expulsion of French invaders from Spain, the imperial government sent battalions and sometimes full regiments to help crush rebellion in the Americas. With the restoration of Ferdinand VII in 1814 and the total defeat of Napoleon, Spain was able to send expeditionary forces to New Spain, New Granada, and Peru. Often, these forces were dispatched under strength with the idea of recruiting additional soldiers from the populations of the Americas. The second tier of units—infantry, dragoons, and cavalry—belonged to the army of New Spain that predated the outbreak of the independence epoch in 1810. The third tier were provincial militia regiments of infantry, dragoons, and cavalry recruited for part-time service in the defense of New Spain. After a few years of mobilized service during the war, and often away from their home provinces, these units became almost indistinguishable from regular forces. The fourth tier were local urban and rural militia forces raised to defend their home jurisdictions and often paid by local taxes imposed upon the population.
5. The *regimientos de infantería* of Puebla and Mexico had been transferred to Havana during the wartime crises of the 1790s. While each viceroy demanded the return of these units, the Cap-

tains General of Cuba refused to do so under the argument that they could not afford to weaken the Havana garrison. In addition, these Mexican troops served in Florida, Louisiana, Santo Domingo, and as marines aboard Spanish warships in the Caribbean and Gulf of Mexico. As might be expected, yellow fever, malaria, and other diseases depleted these units. When ordered to send replacements, the army of New Spain dispatched men from the regular infantry regiments who were delinquents, gamblers, murderers, deserters, mentally and physically unfit for duty—or the scum of the army.

6. The tobacco factory refers to one in the growing region that sent tobacco from the valley of San Andrés to another factory in Puebla. At the first factory, the tobacco was dried and prepared, and at the Puebla factory it was made into *cigarros* (cigarettes).

7. *Ordenes militares* refers to the ancient Spanish military crusading orders of Santiago, Calatrava, Alcántara. Other military orders such as the Order of Carlos III and Isabel la Católica allowed the nations to recognize and to give special privileges to noteworthy soldiers.

8. Corporation here refers to groups of people—merchant guilds (*consulados*), Mining Tribunal, army, church, and artisan groupings—with a legal identity as defined in charters granted by the Crown specifying their rights and privileges as members of a given corporate group.

DOCUMENT THEMES

Governance, Colonial; Military/Rebellion.

SUGGESTIONS FOR FURTHER READING

Anna 1978.
Archer 1977.
Archer 1989.
Archer 1994.
Guardino 1996.
Hamnett 1986.
Rodríguez O. 1998.
Tutino 1986.
Van Young 1986.
Van Young 1988.
Van Young 1993.

Glossary

abogado: lawyer.

advenedizo -za: Indian newcomer to a town. Also known as a newly arrived *forastero*.

aguardiente: a potent liquor made from cane sugar, often with anise.

ah cuch cab: a leader or *principal* in Maya communities, sometimes without a formal position, sometimes equivalent to a *cabildo* member (Yucatec).

albacea: executor [of an estate].

albardero: saddler.

alcabala (pl: **alcabalas**): sales tax.

alcahuete: go-between, intermediary between lovers, pimp, procurer; often used to insulting effect. See also *Celestina, tercera persona.*

alcaide: sheriff or bailiff.

alcalde mayor: Spanish official who was governor of a district. See also *corregidor.*

alcalde ordinario: member of a town council who was elected for a term as judge of first instance. Sometimes referred to simply as *alcalde.*

alcalde: a judicial and governing office in the *cabildo* or town council.

alférez: (1) standard bearer and sponsor of a church festival. Generally the most expensive and highest ranking office in a confraternity (lay religious brotherhood); an annually rotating office. See as well *mayordomo*. Alférez was also an annually elected member of a municipal council (see *cabildo*); he had the honor of carrying a banner on behalf of the council on ceremonial occasions. (2) a commissioned officer at the rank of ensign or lieutenant.

alguacil: bailiff or constable. He assisted a judge or prosecutor by making arrests, seizing property, collecting evidence, and maintaining order in the courtroom.

alqueire: a measure of volume (such as a bushel) for grains or liquid that varied from place to place. Also a measure of land that varied regionally (Brazil).

altepetl: Nahua provincial state.

altiplano: high plain that stretches north from what is now central Bolivia to encompass the Titicaca Basin.

anejo: literally annex. These were towns with their own church, festivals, and town council. They were under the jurisdiction of a *cabecera*, or "head town."

arbitrios: municipal taxes

arbitrista: analyst of social, political and economic themes concerning the Spanish empire.

arroba: a measure of weight equal to about 15 kilograms.

asesor: a lawyer sitting as an advisor to a judge (who often was not a lawyer) to give expert legal advice on the application of the law.

audiencia: a high court, court of appeals, and advisory council to the viceroy or governor of a district; the district itself. Sometimes, a hearing.

auditor de guerra: judge advocate.

auto de inventário: all the documents, including the inventory and will, if there was one, produced by the probatelike process of settling an estate under Portuguese law.

auto: a judge's decree, finding, or order issued in the name of the court in civil and criminal trials. In the plural *autos* refers to a legal proceeding as a whole.

ayllo (ayllu): an Andean social group whose members controlled specific lands and/or resources and who considered themselves descended from a common mythical ancestor and a particular origin place (Aymara and Quechua).

Aymara: language spoken by people living in the south-central Andes, especially on the *altiplano*.

ayudante: assistant priest.

ayuntamiento: municipal council.

azo (acsu/aqsu): woman's skirt (Quechua).

balanzario: accountant.

barrio: neighborhood in a town or city.

bastón: also known as a *vara*, the staff of office carried by town officials.

batab (pl: batabob): governor of a Maya community. The office carried over from preconquest times and was recognized by Spanish authorities, who referred to the holder as *gobernador* or *cacique* (Yucatec).

batallón: an infantry unit composed of eight or ten companies commanded by captains with a lieutenant, sublieutenant, non-commissioned officers—sergeants and corporals—and common soldiers.

beata: a religious laywoman who wore a habit, but had not professed solemn vows of religion and who generally lived an uncloistered life

bebedizo: a beverage adulterated with poison or substances of witchcraft.

braça: measurement of length, equivalent to about 2 meters (Brazil).

brigadier: an army officer one rank higher than a colonel.

brigadier de marina: a senior naval officer who commanded a division within a fleet. Fleets and squadrons were not of any particular size in the Spanish navy and thus this rank does not correspond exactly to the equivalent rank in the British or American fleets.

caballero principal: expression signifying high social standing but not a synonym for "noble."

caballo: horse.

cabecera: principal town of a district and site of local government.

cabecilla: a negative term for a rebel chief and band leader.

cabildo: municipal council. Later in the colonial period any official meeting and sometimes referred to as a *consejo*.

cabra: dark mulatto (Brazil).

cacique: an Arawakian (Taino) term used for leaders in the Caribbean islands. The Spanish generalized this term to all indigenous hereditary lords, regardless of the language of the local people.

cah (pl: **cahob**): self-governing Maya community (Yucatec).

calidad: a term that summarized a person's 'quality' or overall reputation with reference to race, wealth, social connections, and character.

capela de missas: 50 masses.

capitán: a minor Indian leader and official ranking below the *cacique*.

capítulo (pl: **capítulos**): in general "chapter" or "article." With reference to Spanish judicial practice *capitulos* refer to the set of questions drawn up at the beginning of an investigation and asked to each witness.

cárcel de corte: prison within the jurisdiction of a viceregal capital.

careamento: from *carear*, to face. A face-to-face meeting in which a complainant and defendant confront one another. The process was often used in marriage disputes to allow young women and men to express their will free from parental interference and intimidation. In criminal cases a *careamento* forced defendants to confront their accuser(s) in order that a judge could question them together about conflicting/contradictory testimony.

carta de favor: an official document granting certain rights or privileges.

casta (pl: **castas**): a term used in Spanish America to signify persons of racially mixed ancestry (for example *castizos*, *mestizos*, or *mulatos*) and arranged hierarchically as a 'system' called a *régimen de castas*. In colonial society *castas* were always considered inferior to Spaniards, but some categories within *casta* groupings ranked higher than others.

castizo -za: offspring of a Spaniard and a *mestizo*.

cebo: animal feed; bait.

Celestina: equivalent to *alcahuete*; derived from the go-between/procuress and adept-at-love-magic heroine portrayed by Fernando de Rojas in his celebrated novel *La Celestina* (1499).

celogía: grate, usually of latticework wood, placed in windows for privacy.

chácara: field or farm (Quechua).

chapetón (pl: **chapetones**): a pejorative term used for recently arrived peninsular Spaniards.

Chibcha: language spoken by Muisca people of New Granada (present-day Colombia). See Muisca.

chicozapote: a type of fruit tree native to the Americas and the fruit that the tree produces. The latter, also referred to as *zapote*, has white flesh and is very sweet.

china: a *mestiza*, but in New Spain also a cultural type, somewhat idealized as the *poblana* or *china poblana*. A *china* was a plebeian woman but one who refused to be subservient. She lived in comfort supported by her husband, lover, or by her own industry. She was also known for her attractive appearance, her beauty, and for her provocative dress and manner. The masculine form, **chino**, only has the racial connotations of mixed Spanish and Indian heritage. *La China* can also mean the Philippines.

chocho (pl: **chochos**): white beans still highly prized in Ecuadorian cuisine.

cholo -la: person of mixed cultural heritage. When used by Andeans against others it was a defiant taunt that pushed those so-named into a marginal category, neither Spanish nor Andean.

chontal (pl: **chontales**): term used by Spaniards in New Granada to characterize an Indian who spoke no Spanish and had not adopted Spanish attire or customs (chapter 5), as opposed to one who was acculturated (*ladino*).

ciudad: city.

coartación: a customary and legal procedure whereby a slave purchased his or her freedom at the "just price" set by a court. With the price fixed and some of it paid, the owner's claims to the slave's person were increasingly "restricted," or *coartado*. A *coartado* was not yet a free person but became increasingly freer while living and working independently and making payments until the price was fully paid.

colegio de niñas: a residential girls' school much like a convent.

comandante: the army commander of a post, district, or province.

comandante general: a senior army commander in charge of a province, territory, or high military-administrative post.

comendador: friar in charge of particular responsibilities within a monastery.

común (pl: **comunes**): assembly (assemblies) of common people; community; the commons (plural).

comunidad (pl: **comunidades**): community; see also *pueblo*.

confesión: declaration of an accused person, whether to admit or deny guilt, after a formal complaint and preliminary statements had been heard by a court. Taking a *confesión* marked a kind of transition to a trial proper in which further evidence was collected, ratified, and evaluated.

conquistador (pl: **conquistadores**): person who participated in the early military subjugations of native states and chiefdoms.

contador: comptroller and accountant; also auditor.

contaduría mayor: the chief auditing and accountancy office for the Crown, attached to the Council of Indies.

contribuciones: in the military context these were special taxes levied on consumption to support local urban and rural militia forces. Also *contribuciones militares*.

corregidor (pl: **corregidores**): Spanish official entrusted with tribute collection, labor recruitment, and local justice in an administrative district called a *corregimiento*.

corregimiento: a judicial and administrative district corresponding to a province, presided over by the Spanish official known as the *corregidor*.

costa de barlovento: the windward coast of Veracruz, that is the coast to the north of the city including Antigua and other coastal points.

costa de sotavento: the leeward coast of Veracruz, that is, the coastline to the south including Alvarado and other coastal points. The port city is the dividing line.

criollo -lla: an American-born Spaniard; a hispanized native Andean living in a city, as in "indio criollo" (see chapter 10), or more generally, with reference to a place of origin, "native to" or "born in," as in descriptions of slaves petitioning to marry (see chapter 19).

crioulinho -ha: little creole (Brazil).

crioulo -la: Brazilian-born black; creole.

cristianos viejos: literally Old Christians; a term used for lineages that claimed to be free from Islamic or Jewish ancestors.

cuca (pl: **cucas**): Indian shrine (Muisca).

cundaval: word of African derivation of unknown meaning.

cura: a pastor in charge of a parish.

curaca (kuraka): Quechua term used interchangeably with *cacique*. Refers to governing hereditary native lords.

curador: court-appointed guardian and defender to help a defendant in a law suit. *Curadores*, sometimes referred to as *defensores*, were provided for minors, for people deemed to be ignorant, and for anyone unable to defend themselves.

curato: parish (or curacy) administered by a member of the secular clergy, that is a priest under the jurisdiction of a bishop.

curtidor: tanner.

dalmática: a vestment worn by deacons, clerics a rank below priests, in the Roman Catholic Church.

defensor: court-appointed defender of persons in a law suit, often with reference to their goods (in cases where property was in dispute) and often with reference to people unable to defend their interests in person.

depósito: temporary legal custody of a woman in a *recogimiento* (secular institution), convent, hospital or an honorable home, to keep her under surveillance and protect her against violence or other forms of retribution. She was to remain enclosed until the legal dispute to which she was party was completed, a process that sometimes lasted more than a year.

doctrina: an Indian parish (usually an outlying village) administered by a missionary friar whose task was to "indoctrinate" indigenous people until they were ready to be ministered to by the secular clergy. Isolated *doctrinas* had no friar in residence but were visited by a friar on circuit and thus were sometimes referred to as *visitas*.

dom/dona: honorific in Portuguese equivalent to don/doña in Spanish.

don/doña: honorific in medieval Spain reserved for kings and the royal family. At the end of the Middle Ages it had come to include important nobles, especially the titled nobility. In Spain and the Spanish colonies, the term was dramatically debased from the sixteenth to the eighteenth century as it increasingly became an informal term granted to or claimed by a continually wider social spectrum.

doncella: virgin or maiden.

Ejército del Sur: Army of the South. This force had its headquarters in Puebla.

ejido: common pasturelands.

embustero: cheat, con artist, deceiver, fraud, swindler, trickster.

encomendero: holder of an *encomienda*. In theory the encomendero provided protection to his (and sometimes her) Indian charges and ensured that they received proper spiritual supervision.

encomienda: a grant in tribute and labor of people subject to one or more indigenous rulers.

escribano: clerk, scribe, or notary. An older spelling variant is *escrivano*.

estancia: ranch or farm; in the Andes could also refer to a hamlet.

fábrica: mill, factory, business, sumptuous building; can refer both to a physical structure and to its upkeep or operation.

familiar: unpaid but officially-appointed lay auxiliary of the Inquisition. Also, can mean member of a household, relative, or person of trust.

fazenda: a large farm or ranch (Brazil).

firma: signature.

fiscal: prosecutor.

fiscal: Nahua official responsible for religious affairs.

forastero -ra: a person who had abandoned his/her community of origin. His/her descendants were also called *forasteros*.

fuero: set of privileges accorded to corporate groups, including judicial favors, pensions, and rights to wear certain clothing.

gavilla: a derogatory royalist term for an insurgent band or gang, in general a gathering of people of a low sort.

Gazeta: a reference to the *Gazeta de México* which was the royalist news organ that published battlefield reports submitted by the regime.

generales de la ley: qualities of witnesses—for example, that they were minors, friends (or enemies), relatives, or interested parties to the outcome of the case—that would disqualify testimony as partial.

gobernador político y militar: a provincial or city governor who also commanded the armed forces under his jurisdiction.

gobernador: a Spanish-appointed Indian official whose most important duties were to assist in the collection of tribute and in the requisitioning of Indian labor. The highest Nahua official of an *altepetl*.

grana: cochineal, a scarlet dye derived from a Mexican insect.

grifo -fa: offspring of black and mulatto parents.

hacienda: a large estate, ranch, or plantation.

halach uinic: supreme Maya political officer or territorial ruler of a province in pre-conquest times; in the colonial period referred to the Spanish governor (Yucatec).

hampi: medicine (Aymara and Quechua).

hechizero -ra: sorcerer, sorceress, or witch.

hechizo: spell.

hechizos: elements of witchcraft, substances of sorcery with magical powers.

herrador: blacksmith.

hidalgo/hidalguía: lowest rank of the Castilian hierarchy of nobility and a basic social ideal. Hidalguía was understood first of all as noble birth (*hidalguía de sangre*) and derived from the descent of at least two generations of nobles, that is of noble parents and grandparents. Nobility could derive also from a royal privilege (*hidalguía de privilegio*), but like *nouveau riche*, persons newly named to the status enjoyed—at least in the first two generations—less esteem. Social reputation was always an important characteristic and even a basis of a person's noble status (as expressed by the term *hidalguía notoria*).

higo: fig tree.

huipil: traditional embroidered tunic worn by indigenous women in Guatemala.

indio -a: Indian.

Indios originarios: literally original Indians, a category in the Spanish tribute-paying system. Those so designated were theoretically natives of that particular town, and generally owned more land and paid higher tribute than those not assigned that category.

Intendente: governor of a province, so termed in the eighteenth century.

jeque: priest or guardian of a shrine (Muisca).

jícara: chocolate cup; small bowl made out of a gourd.

jornal: a daily wage. Also a self-hire system for slaves.

joyante: silk of fine texture and high lustre.

jubetero: maker of short, tight-fitting jackets or doublets, sometimes mail-covered (*jubetes*).

juez: judge.

juez comisario: a judge "commissioned" to act on behalf of a higher court or more senior judge, usually in an outlying jurisdiction. Sometimes spelled *jues comisario*.

juez de residencia: judge commissioned to review the performance of an outgoing colonial official.

juez receptor: scribe to a judge on assignment. Also *receptor*.

justicia mayor: chief justice of a jurisdiction.

justicia: general term for judicial officials in a town or village.

kuluinicil (pl: kuluinicob): "principal man," often with reference to a governor or *batab* in preconquest and colonial Maya communities; the plural, "principal men," referred to leaders or community notables (Yucatec).

labrador: farmer, usually of his own small property.

ladino -na: Spanish-speaking, hispanized Indians or African slaves.

lanço: a word used in describing in rough terms the size of a house; a row of rooms. A house with two *lanços* had two rooms on the front followed by two rows of rooms behind (Brazil).

libre: a free nonwhite.

licenciado: an honorific reserved for the holders of a university licentiate degree.

limpieza de sangre: purity of blood, a Spanish sociocultural concept that meant old Christian ancestry, that is, without any Muslim or Jewish ancestry. In Spanish America this concept, also known as *limpieza de toda mala raza*, excluded any Indian and black ancestry.

lliquilla (lliclla/lliklla): woman's shawl (Quechua).

madama (pl: madamas): from the French *madame* and equivalent to señora but with overtones of elegance and flattery associated with the court and nobility.

madrigueras: in general hidden or secluded place where bad people congregate. The term also refers to a rabbit warren. In the context of the insurgency, it meant isolated and clandestine rebel nests, dens, or bases.

maese de campo: military field officer.

maestro: a Spanish-imposed position in Maya communities whose duties included those of schoolmaster and choirmaster. More generally *maestro* means "master" or teacher, or signifies that one is fully qualified in a craft (as opposed to being under another's supervision).

maleficio: spell or curse; general term for sorcery.

mão: a measure used in the sale of corn (Brazil).

maravedí: the smallest Spanish coin and a standard unit for accounting. There were 272 maravedís in a *peso de ocho* (a peso, worth eight *reales*; was also referred to as a "piece of eight").

Marica: an affectionate and familiar form of María.

Marquesdo del Valle: vast *encomienda* granted to Hernando Cortés.

mayordomo de la ciudad: A steward employed by the town council.

mayordomo: a secondary office, which rotated annually in a confraternity (see *alférez*); a steward who served the local church, or who acted as an administrator or foreman in a ranch, hacienda, or business.

mecatl: land measure (Nahua).

médico: physician.

membrillo: quince tree.

mercader: in the eighteenth century merchants with businesses limited to regional or interregional retail trade. With their own retail shops (*tiendas*); these storekeepers were also called *mercaderes de tienda abierta*. The social status of *mercaderes* was considered lower than that of the *comerciantes*, wholesale merchants, who engaged in overseas trade and who normally did not have shops but storerooms (*almacenes*) closed to the public. In the sixteenth and seventeenth centuries *mercader* connoted wholesale and long distance traders.

merced: literally a "favor," "grace," or grant (chapter 1). The reference in chapter 14 refers to a neighborhood in Veracruz that had as its patroness our Lady of Mercy (*Nuestra Señora de la Merced*).

mestizo -za: person of mixed European and Indian descent.

Mina Coast: The West African coast around the slave-trading port of El Mina, stretching roughly from modern-day Ghana to Nigeria; by extension, a generic ethnic label for people from any one of several ethnic groups exported to Brazil from this region.

minerales: mining districts.

mita: from Quechua, "turn." Used in both preconquest and colonial times for state mandated draft labor system.

mitanis: people who carried out rotational labor service (*mita*).

moça (moza): young, unmarried woman. A masculine form, **mozo**, is also common.

montañés: *mestizo* of a higher social standing and supposedly a higher purity of blood than ordinary *mestizos*.

morador: a property-owning resident.

muchacho: a boy; one who lacks the experience, knowledge, and possibly physical development of an adult.

Muisca: indigenous Chibcha-speaking peoples who inhabited the Eastern Highlands of Colombia. The Muisca never referred to themselves collectively by a single term, for the region they occupied was divided into provinces and valleys, with each valley governed by a different *cacique*. By the end of the sixteenth century, however, chroniclers were referring to all the Indians from the provinces of Santa Fe and Tunja as Muisca. The term comes from the Chibcha word *muexca*, meaning "man" or "person."

mulato -ta: a person of mixed African and Spanish, or African and Indian, descent.

Nahuatl: language spoken by the Nahuas of central Mexico.

natural: native (of a certain place), as in *natural de* . . . ; indigenous.

naturaleza: place of origin in the sense of place of birth and/or race/lineage/descent.

negrita: literally a "little black girl," but "little" in a patronizing, rather than a literal or endearing, sense although some of the latter might be inferred in some contexts. The *negritas* mentioned in chapter 15, whether slave or free, were clearly viewed as servile types. A masculine form, *negrito*, would also be possible.

negro -ra: person of complete or almost complete African ancestry; term used by the Portuguese for Indians (*negro da terra*, negro of this land) or Africans (*negro tapanhum*, foreign negro).

oidor (pl: **oidores**): high court judge, that is judge of an *audiencia*.

oitavo: one-eighth of an ounce; 3.56 grams.

padre: father, either in reference to the male parent of a child or to a priest.

padrino: godparent, or best man at a wedding.

palabras injuriosas: slander; insulting, offensive words.

palla: noblewoman, elegant woman (Quechua).

palmo: measurement of length, equivalent either to the distance from the tip of the thumb to the tip of the little finger, roughly eight or nine inches (chapter 11), or to the width spanned by four fingers held together.

pardo -da: in Brazil, mulatto, brown-skinned; in New Orleans, a nonwhite person of light coloring, a term preferred by *libres* over *mulato/a*.

pataca: silver coin worth 320 *réis* (Brazil).

patrimonio: land (or other property) acquired through inheritance which was closely associated with an individual household and could be sold (in contrast to *tributario*).

peça de serviço: used by the Paulistas to label their Indian laborers/servants. Though Indians were legally free, the phrase exemplifies the ambiguity of their status since *peça* was a word used for slaves.

pecado nefando: literally, the abominable (or unmentionable) sin; referred to intimate relations between members of the same sex; often modified by the terms *contra natura* (against nature) and *de sodomia* (of sodomy).

peso: Spanish coin worth eight *reales*.

pongo: a house servant. From the Quechua *puncu* meaning door.

preto -ta: black, usually African-born (Brazil).

principal (pl: **principales**): denotes a leadership role within indigenous communities. It was generally used to describe someone who held a formal office within the town government. It also carries a general sense of "leading citizen." Holding public office, however, was key to the status.

procurador de los naturales: attorney appointed to represent native Andeans.

promotor fiscal: see *fiscal*.

protector de los naturales: official charged with helping the indigenous peoples in his jurisdiction, in theory by settling disputes, providing legal counsel, and guaranteeing that they were paid for their labor and well treated.

protomedicato: a medical regulatory board composed of physicians.

provincial: the friar-superior of all convents and houses pertaining to a religious order in a province.

Provincias de Occidente: The western *provincias internas*, or internal provinces, on the northern frontier of New Spain.

Provincias de Oriente: The eastern *provincias internas* on the northern frontier of New Spain.

provisor: Chief ecclesiastical judge in a bishopric (see *vicario*), often encharged with additional administrative duties.

pueblo: literally a "people" but also a town or village. In chapter 5, for example, *pueblo* refers to both the inhabitants and the physical settlement of Iguaque.

pueblos organizados: royalist towns that had been militarized or organized with local militias called *realistas* and with taxes imposed locally to support these forces.

puertos de barlovento: ports on the windward coast of Veracruz.

Pukina: a language spoken by people living in the Titicaca Basin; now extinct.

pulque: an alcoholic drink made by fermenting the sap of the maguey cactus.

puna: high, cold, arid plateau.

punche: punch, presumably made with *aguardiente*, probably with rum.

puto: man suspected of the *pecado nefando*; an insult derived from *puta*, female whore.

Quechua: official language of the Inka state; spoken throughout the Andean region in the colonial period.

ramo: branch or section as in the 'grants section' of Mexico's national archive.

real (pl: **réis**): monetary unit in colonial Brazil. One thousand *réis*, written 1$000, was worth U.S.$1 in the 1810s and $ .50 in the 1840s.

real: a Spanish coin (plural *reales*); eight *reales* equalled one peso.

Reales Ordenes: Royal Orders issued by the crown.

realistas de caballería: royalist cavalry militias.

recogimiento: women's house of penitence and safekeeping that in some contexts could amount to virtual penal incarceration (for example, as threatened in chapter 12).

reducción: resettlement town in the Andes; the process of resettlement. Andeans were forcibly moved into *reducciones* to facilitate control, conversion to Christianity, and the extraction of labor and tribute. Referred to as *congregación* in New Spain.

regidor: councilman in a Spanish or native municipal council. (See *cabildo*).

regimiento: regiment; a military fighting unit of infantry composed of two or three battalions. The regiment was commanded by a colonel, and seconded by a lieutenant colonel who commanded the individual battalions if they were separated. The third in command was the "sargento mayor" or major who was the regimental administrative officer responsible for day to day book keeping and operations. There were several adjutants, a surgeon, a priest, fifers, drummers, and other specialists in the staff called the *plano mayor*.

réis: see *real*.

rentas: income.

repartimiento: a grant of indigenous tribute and labor; in the Andes the term was used interchangeably with *encomienda*. *Repartimiento* also referred to the corresponding administrative district assessed the labor quotas. In New Spain, a forced labor draft.

reuniones: the coalescence of rebel bands to create large forces (chapter 23).

rocote: a hot pepper.

sacristán: lay assistant to a priest entrusted with the care, cleaning, and safekeeping of a parish church's property, including the vestments, vessels, and ornaments kept in the sacristy.

santuario: religious shrine; sacred place. In present-day Venezuela and Colombia can mean or imply native idol and/or buried treasure.

secretario: chief scribe of an *audiencia* or advisory council.

sertão: wilderness, backlands, bush, or hinterland (Brazil).

taipa de mão: thick walls made of parallel supports of posts or wicker filled with mud and then allowed to dry in the sun (Brazil).

taipa de pilão: walls built like *taipa de mão*, but even stronger because the mud is mixed with stones (Brazil).

taita (tayta): papa, an affectionate address often given a biological "father." It can also be used by family members—even a wife—to address the patriarch, or head of the household (Quechua).

tambo: supply station and inn for travelers. *Tambos* were important sites on the Inka road system, later utilized in the colonial period (Quechua).

tejuelo: a small, flat piece of gold, perhaps used as an amulet or talisman.

teniente: lieutenant or deputy, usually to a *corregidor* or *alcalde mayor*.

teniente de navío: lieutenant on a warship.

teopixqui: Nahuatl term for priest or member of a religious order.

tequitlalli: Nahuatl term for tribute land.

tercera persona: "third person" or go-between; actions akin to sense of English verb "to beard"; equivalent to *alcahuete*. See *Celestina*.

tlalcohualli: land acquired through purchase (literally "purchased land") which could be sold (in contrast to *tributario*) (Nahuatl).

tlalquahuitl: Nahua land measurement.

tlaxilacalli: Nahuatl term for subdistrict of *altepetl*.

tómin: Spanish coin worth one-eighth of a peso. See *real*.

tonoci: reference to an "ordinary" grade of silk, possibly from the Otomí pueblo of Pahuatlan (in the mountainous district near Puebla) whose silk worm was known as *tonoci*.

tostão: Portuguese coin worth 100 *réis*.

tributario: land on which indigenous communities assessed tribute that individual households worked but could not sell (in contrast to *patrimonio* or *tlalco-*

hualli). A *tributario* could also be a person liable to pay an annual tribute to a lord as a vassal or to the Crown as a subject.

tropas de linea: regular line infantry. In chapter 23 the viceroy Apodaca referred to troops of the Spanish expeditionary regiments sent to crush revolt in New Spain as *tropas de linea*.

tunjo (pl: tunjos): a type of idol, often wrapped in cloth (Muisca).

vale: from Latin, farewell. Commonly used at the close of letters in the medieval period.

vara: measurement of length equivalent to 1.10 meters.

vecino -na: citizen or permanent resident of a town or city, often established by property ownership and the carrying out of religious duties in a local parish. The usage of the term varied regionally and temporally; it might refer to a status exlusively held by prominent (largely European) citizens, or it might refer more inclusively to all permanent residents, including the indigenous and Afro-Latin American population.

vía militar: a military road protected by posts, patrols, and communications.

vicario: in the Catholic Church a cleric given the power and authority of a priest or prelate to carry out duties in his name. Also the term for an ecclesiastical judge of first instance, who was sometimes referred to as the *ordinario* or *vicario del obispo* when the jurisdiction was the diocese.

villa: small Spanish town or municipality. Larger and more important than a *pueblo*.

visita: administrative or ecclesiastical tour of inspection or inquiry; specific investigation into malfeasance or corruption; in New Spain *visita* could also signify the district subject to inspection, as in chapter 3.

visitador-general: a special appointee commissioned to inspect or investigate. He had authority to summon witnesses and possibly use torture (see chapter 5) to obtain information. In carrying out his mandate he had supreme authority over local officials.

visitador: a person with a special commission from the Crown, usually a judge, sent to investigate malfeasance or corruption within a jurisdiction.

visitador: ecclesiastical delegate or a secular authority who led a tour of inspection in a particular area.

yanacona: term used in the Andes for a personal retainer (from Quechua).

Yucatec: Maya language spoken in the Yucatán.

yum: father or lord (Yucatec).

zacate: hay; grass; animal fodder.

zambo -ba: a person of Indian and African descent.

Bibliography

Abercrombie, Thomas A. *Pathways of Memory and Power: Ethnography and History Among an Andean People*. Madison: University of Wisconsin Press, 1998.

———. "Tributes to Bad Conscience: Charity, Restitution and Inheritance in Cacique and Encomendero Testaments of Sixteenth-Century Charcas." In *Dead Giveaways: Indigenous Testaments of Colonial Mesoamerica and the Andes*, edited by Susan Kellogg and Matthew Restall, 249–289. Salt Lake City: University of Utah Press, 1998.

Alchon, Suzanne. *Native Society and Disease in Colonial Ecuador*. Cambridge: Cambridge University Press, 1991.

Anna, Timothy E. *The Fall of the Royal Government in Mexico City*. Lincoln: University of Nebraska Press, 1978.

Archer, Christon I. *The Army in Bourbon Mexico, 1760–1810*. Albuquerque: University of New Mexico Press, 1977.

———. "La Causa Buena: The Counterinsurgency Army of New Spain and the Ten Years' War." In *The Independence of Mexico and the Creation of the New Nation*, edited by Jaime E. Rodríguez O., 85–108. Los Angeles: Institute of Latin American Studies, 1989.

———. "Insurrection-Reaction-Fragmentation: Reconstructing the Choreography of Meltdown in New Spain during the Independence Era." *Mexican Studies/Estudios Mexicanos* 10, no. 1 (1994): 63–98.

Archivo General de la Nación. *El libro de las tasaciones de pueblos de la Nueva España, Siglo XVI*. Mexico City: Archivo General de la Nación, 1952.

Archivo Municipal de Quito. *Libro Segundo de Cabildos de Quito*. Quito: Archivo Municipal de Quito, 1934.

Argondoña y Pasten, Pedro Miguel de. *Constituciones Sinodales del Arzobispado de La Plata*. Cuernavaca, 1971.

Arquivo do Estado de São Paulo. *Inventários e Testamentos: Papéis que pertenceram ao 1 Cartorio de Orfãos da Capital*. 44 vols. São Paulo: Arquivo do Estado de São Paulo, 1922–1977.

Arriaga, Pablo Jose de. *The Extirpation of Idolatry in Peru*. Edited and translated by L. Clark Keating. Lexington: University of Kentucky Press, [1621] 1968.

Beers, Henry Putney. *French and Spanish Records of Louisiana: A Bibliographical Guide to Archive and Manuscript Sources*. Baton Rouge: Louisiana State University Press, 1989.

Behar, Ruth. "Sex, Sin, Witchcraft, and the Devil in Late-Colonial Mexico." *American Ethnologist* 14 no. 1 (1987): 34–54.

———. "Sexual Witchcraft, Colonialism, and Women's Powers: Views from the Mexican Inquisition." In *Sexuality and Marriage in Colonial Latin America*, edited by Asunción Lavrin, 178–206. Lincoln: University of Nebraska Press, 1989.

Berthelot, Jean. "Une Région Minière des Andes Péruviennes: Carbaya Inca et Espagnole (1480–1630)." Thèse pour le doctorate de 3e cycle, Ecole des Hautes Etudes en Sciences Sociales, Université de Paris X-Nanterre, 1977.

Bertonio, Ludovico. *Vocabvlario de la Lengva Aymara*. Cochabamba: Centro de Estudios de la Realidad Económica y Social, [1612]1984.

Betanzos, Juan de. *Narrative of the Incas*. Translated by Roland Hamilton and Dana Buchanan. Austin: University of Texas Press, 1996.

Bilinkoff, Jodi. "A Spanish Prophetess and Her Patrons: The Case of María de Santo Domingo." *Sixteenth-Century Journal* 23, no. 1 (1992): 21–34.

Borah, Woodrow. *Silk Raising in Colonial Mexico*. Vol. 20, *Ibero-Americana*. Berkeley and Los Angeles: University of California Press, 1943.

———. *Justice by Insurance: The General Indian Court of Colonial Mexico and the Legal Aides of the Half-Real*. Berkeley: University of California Press, 1983.

Bowser, Frederick P. *The African Slave in Colonial Peru 1524–1650*. Stanford: Stanford University Press, 1974.

Boyer, Richard. "Women, *La Mala Vida*, and the Politics of Marriage." In *Sexuality and Marriage in Colonial Latin America*, edited by Asuncion Lavrin, 252–86. Lincoln: University of Nebraska Press, 1989.

———. "The Inquisitor, the Witness, and the Historian: The Document as Dialogue." *Revista Canadiense de Estudios Hispánicos* 18, no. 3 (1994): 393–403.

———. *Lives of the Bigamists: Marriage, Family, and Community in Colonial Mexico*. Albuquerque: University of New Mexico Press, 1995.

———. "Honor Among Plebeians: *Mala Sangre* and Social Reputation." In *The Faces of Honor: Sex, Shame, and Violence in Colonial Latin America*, edited by Lyman Johnson and Sonya Lipsett-Rivera, 152–78. Albuquerque: University of New Mexico Press, 1998.

Brading, David A. *The First America*. Cambridge: Cambridge University Press, 1991.

Bradley, Peter T. *The Lure of Peru: Maritime Intrusion into the South Sea, 1598–1701*. Basingstoke & London: The MacMillan Press, 1989.

Brandes, Stanley. *Metaphors of Masculinity: Sex and Status in Andalusian Folklore*. Philadelphia: University of Pennsylvania Press, 1980.

Brundage, James A. "The Politics of Sodomy: Rex V. Pons Hugh De Ampurias (1311)." In *Sex in the Middle Ages: A Book of Essays*, edited by Joyce E. Salisbury, 239–46. New York: Garland, 1991.

Burkhart, Louise. *The Slippery Earth: Nahua-Christian Moral Dialogue in Sixteenth-Century Mexico*. Tucson: University of Arizona Press, 1989.

Burkholder, Mark A., and Lyman L. Johnson. *Colonial Latin America*. Third ed. New York & Oxford: Oxford University Press, 1998.

Büschges, Christian. "Nobleza y Estructura Estamental Entre Concepto y Realidad Social: El Caso de la Ciudad de Quito y su Región (1765–1810)." *Jahrbuch für Geschichte von Staat, Wirtschaft und Gesellschaft Lateinamerikas* 33 (1996): 165–86.

Cahill, David. "*Curas* and Social Conflict in the *Doctrinas* of Cuzco, 1780–1814." *Journal of Latin American Studies* 16, no. 2 (1984): 241–76.

Caro Baroja, Julio. "Honour and Shame: A Historical Account of Several Conflicts." In *Honour and Shame: The Values of Mediterranean Society*, edited by John G. Peristiany, 79–137. Chicago: University of Chicago Press, 1966.

Carrasco, Rafael. *Inquisición y represión sexual en Valencia: Historia de los sodomitas (1565–1785)*. Barcelona: Laertes, 1985.

Castañeda Delgado, Paulino, and Pilar Hernández Aparicio. *La Inquisición de Lima*. Vol. 1. Madrid: Editorial Deimos, 1989.

Chandler, D. S. "The Montepíos and Regulation of Marriage in the Mexican Bureaucracy, 1770–1821." *The Americas* 43, no. 1 (1986): 47–68.

Chinchilla Aguilar, Ernesto. *La Inquisición en Guatemala*. Guatemala, 1953.

Chuchiak, John. "The Indian Inquisition and the Extirpation of Idolatry: The Process of Punishment in the Ecclesiastical Courts of the Provisorato de Indios in Yucatán, 1563–1812." Ph.D. dissertation, Tulane University, 1999.

Ciamitti, Luisa. "One Saint Less: The Story of Angela Mellini, a Bolognese Seamstress." In *Sex and Gender in Historical Perspective*, edited by Edwin Muir and Guido Ruggiero, 141–76. Baltimore: Johns Hopkins University Press, 1990.

Clark, John G. *New Orleans, 1718–1812: An Economic History*. Baton Rouge: Louisiana State University Press, 1970.

Clendinnen, Inga. *Ambivalent Conquests: Maya and Spaniard in Yucatan, 1517–1570*. Cambridge: University of Cambridge Press, 1987.

Cline, S.L. *Colonial Culhuacan, 1580–1600: A Social History of an Aztec Town*. Albuquerque: University of New Mexico Press, 1984.

Códice Sierra. Edited by Nicolás León. Mexico: Museo Nacional de Arqueología, Historia y Etnografía, 1933.

Concolorcorvo. *El Lazarillo, a Guide for Inexperienced Travelers Between Buenos Aires and Lima*. Bloomington: Indiana University Press, 1965.

Cook, Noble David, and Alexandra Parma Cook. *Good Faith and Truthful Ignorance: A Case of Transatlantic Bigamy*. Durham: Duke University Press, 1991.

Cope, R. Douglas. *The Limits of Racial Domination: Plebeian Society in Colonial Mexico City, 1660–1720*. Madison: University of Wisconsin Press, 1994.

Covarrubias, Sebastián de. *Tesoro de la Lengua Castellana o Española*. Barcelona: S.A. Horta, [1611]1943.

Crosby, Alfred. *The Columbian Exchange: Biological and Cultural Consequences of 1492*. Westport, Conn.: Greenwood Press, 1972.

Cunha, Manuela Carneiro da. "Silences of the Law: Customary Law and Positive Law on the Manumission of Slaves in 19th-Century Brazil." *History and Anthropology* 1, no. 2 (1985): 427–43.

Curcio-Nagy, Linda. "Rosa de Escalante's Private Party: Popular Female Religiosity in Colonial Mexico City." In *Women in the Inquisition: Spain and the New World*, edited by Mary Giles, 254–69. Baltimore: Johns Hopkins University Press, 1999.

Cutter, Charles. *The Legal Culture of Northern New Spain, 1700–1810*. Albuquerque: University of New Mexico Press, 1995.

Dart, Henry P. "Courts and Law in Colonial Louisiana." *Louisiana Bar Association Reports* 22 (1921): 17–63.

Davis, Natalie Zemon. *Fiction in the Archives: Pardon Tales and Their Tellers in Sixteenth-Century France*. Stanford: Stanford University Press, 1987.

Dean, Warren. *With Broadaxe and Firebrand: The Destruction of the Brazilian Atlantic Coastal Forest*. Berkeley: University of California Press, 1995.

Dias, Maria Odila Leite da Silva. *Power and Everyday Life: The Lives of Working Women in Nineteenth-Century Brazil*. Translated by Ann Frost. Cambridge: Polity Press, 1995.

Din, Gilbert C. and John E. Harkins. *The New Orleans Cabildo: Colonial Louisiana's First City Government*. Baton Rouge: Louisiana State University Press, 1996.

Erauso, Catalina de. *Lieutenant Nun: Memoir of a Basque Transvestite in the New World*. Translated by Michele Stepto and Gabriel Stepto. Boston: Beacon Press, 1996.

Farriss, Nancy M. *Maya Society Under Colonial Rule: The Collective Enterprise of Survival*. Princeton: Princeton University Press, 1984.

Few, Martha. "Women, Religion, and Power: Gender and Resistance in Daily Life in Late-Seventeenth-Century Santiago de Guatemala." *Ethnohistory* 42, no. 4 (1995): 627–37.

———. "*Mujeres de Mal Vivir*: Gender, Religion, and the Politics of Power in Colonial Guatemala, 1650–1750." Ph.D. dissertation, University of Arizona, 1997.

———. "Illness Accusations and the Cultural Politics of Power in Colonial Santiago de Guatemala, 1650–1720." Working Paper, International Seminar on the History of the Atlantic World, Harvard University, 1998.

Fisher, Lillian Estelle. *The Last Inca Revolt, 1780–1782*. Norman: University of Oklahoma Press, 1966.

Flores Galindo, Alberto. "In Search of an Inca." In *Resistance, Rebellion, and Consciousness in the Andean Peasant World, 18th to 20th Centuries*, edited by Steve J. Stern, 193–210. Madison: University of Wisconsin Press, 1987.

Flores Galindo, Alberto, and Magdalena Chocano Mena. "Las Cargas del Sacramento." *Revista Andina* 2, no. 2 (1984): 403–34.

Francis, J. Michael. "The Muisca Indians Under Spanish Rule, 1537–1636." Ph.D. dissertation, Cambridge University, 1998.

Fraser, Valerie. *The Architecture of Conquest: Building in the Viceroyalty of Peru, 1535–1625*. Cambridge: Cambridge University Press, 1990.

Gerhard, Peter. *A Guide to the Historical Geography of New Spain*. Cambridge: Cambridge University Press, 1972.

Gilmore, David D., ed. *Honor and Shame and the Unity of the Mediterranean*. Washington, D.C.: American Anthropological Association, 1987.

González Casanova, Pablo. *La Literatura Perseguida en la Crisis de la Colonia*. Mexico: SEP, 1986.

González Echevarría, Roberto. *Myth and Archive: A Theory of Latin American Narrative*. Cambridge: Cambridge University Press, 1990.

González Holguín, Diego. *Vocabvlario de la Lengva General de Todo el Perv Llamada Lengua Qquichua o del Inca*. Lima: Imprenta Santa María, [1608] 1952.

Gosner, Kevin. *Soldiers of the Virgin: The Moral Economy of a Colonial Maya Rebellion*. Tucson: University of Arizona Press, 1992.

Greenleaf, Richard. *The Mexican Inquisition of the Sixteenth Century*. Albuquerque: University of New Mexico Press, 1969.

Griffin, Patricia C. *Mullet on the Beach: The Minorcans of Florida, 1768–1788*. Jacksonville: University of North Florida Press, 1991.

Griffiths, Nicholas. *The Cross and the Serpent: Religious Repression and Resurgence in Colonial Peru*. Norman and London: University of Oklahoma Press, 1996.

Gruzinski, Serge. "Las cenizas del deseo: Homosexuales novohispanos a mediados del siglo XVII." In *De La Santidad a La Perversión: O de porqué no se cumplía la ley de Dios en la sociedad novohispana*, edited by Sergio Ortega, 255–81. México, D.F.: Editorial Grijalbo, S.A., 1986.

Guaman Poma de Ayala, Felipe. *El Primer Nueva Corónica y Buen Gobierno*. Edited by John V. Murra and Rolena Adorna. Quechua text translated by Jorge L. Urioste. 3 vols. México: Siglo Veintiuno, [1615] 1980.

Guardino, Peter. *Peasants, Politics, and the Formation of Mexico's National State: Guerrero, 1800-1885*. Stanford: Stanford University Press, 1996.

Guha, Ranajit. "Chandra's Death." In *Subaltern Studies V: Writings on South Asian History and Society*, edited by Ranajit Guha, 135–65. New York and Oxford: Oxford University Press, 1987.

Gutiérrez, Ramón. *When Jesus Came, the Corn Mothers Went Away: Marriage, Sexuality, and Power in New Mexico, 1500–1846*. Stanford: Stanford University Press, 1991.

Haliczer, Stephen [ed. and tr.]. *Inquisition and Society in Early Modern Europe*. London and Sydney: Croon Helm, 1987.

Hall, Gwendolyn Midlo. *Africans in Colonial Louisiana: The Development of Afro-Creole Culture in the Eighteenth Century*. Baton Rouge: Louisiana State University Press, 1992.

Hamnett, Brian R. *Roots of Insurgency: Mexican Regions, 1750–1824*. Cambridge: Cambridge University Press, 1986.

Hanger, Kimberly S. "Conflicting Loyalties: The French Revolution and Free People of Color in Spanish New Orleans." *Louisiana History* 34, no. 1 (1993): 5–33.

———. "'The Fortunes of Women in America': Spanish New Orleans's Free Women of African Descent and Their Relations with Slave Women." In *Discovering the Women in Slavery: Emancipating Perspectives on the American Past*, edited by Patricia Morton, 153–78. Athens: University of Georgia Press, 1996.

———. *Bounded Lives, Bounded Places: Free Black Society in Colonial New Orleans, 1769–1803*. Durham: Duke University Press, 1997.

———. "'Desiring Total Tranquility' and Not Getting It: Conflict Involving Free Black Women in Spanish New Orleans." *The Americas* 54, no. 4 (1998): 541–56.

Hanke, Lewis, and Jane M. Rausch, eds. *People and Issues in Latin American History. The Colonial Experience—Sources and Interpretations*. New York: M. Wiener, 1993.

Haskett, Robert. *Indigenous Rulers: An Ethnohistory of Town Government in Colonial Cuernavaca*. Albuquerque: University of New Mexico Press, 1991.

———. "'Not a Pastor, But a Wolf': Indigenous-Clergy Relations in Early Cuernavaca and Taxco." *The Americas* 50, no. 3 (1994): 293–336.

Hemming, John. *Red Gold: The Conquest of the Brazilian Indians*. Cambridge: Harvard University Press, 1978.

———. "Indians and the Frontier." In *Colonial Brazil*, edited by Leslie Bethell. New York: Cambridge University Press, 1987.

Holler, Jacqueline. "I, Elena de la Cruz: Heresy and Gender in Mexico City, 1568." *Journal of the Canadian Historical Association* N.S. 4 (1993): 143–60.

———. "More Sins than the Queen of England: Marina de San Miguel before the Mexican Inquisition." In *Women in the Inquisition: Spain and the New World*, edited by Mary Giles, 209–28. Baltimore: Johns Hopkins University Press, 1998.

Horn, Rebecca. *Postconquest Coyoacan: Nahua-Spanish Relations in Central Mexico, 1519–1650*. Stanford: Stanford University Press, 1997.

———. "Testaments and Trade: Interethnic Ties among Petty Traders in Central Mexico (Coyoacan, 1550–1620)." In *Dead Giveaways: Indigenous Testaments of Colonial Mesoamerica and the Andes*, edited by Susan Kellogg and Matthew Restall, 59–83. Salt Lake City: University of Utah Press, 1998.

Hünefeldt, Christine. *Paying the Price of Freedom: Family and Labor Among Lima's Slaves, 1800–1854*. Translated by Alexandra Minna Stern. Berkeley: University of California Press, 1994.

Jaramillo Uribe, Jaime. "Mestizaje y Diferenciación Social en el Nuevo Reino de Granada en la Segunda Mitad del Siglo XVIII." *Anuario Colombiano de Historia Social y de la Cultura* 3, no. 2 (1965): 21–48.

Johnson, Lyman, and Sonya Lipsett-Rivera, eds. *The Faces of Honor: Sex, Shame, and Violence in Colonial Latin America*. Albuquerque: University of New Mexico Press, 1998.

Jurado Noboa, Fernando. *Los Descendientes de Benalcazar en la formación social ecuatoriana, siglos XVI a XX*. Quito: Amigos de la Genealogía, 1984.

Karasch, Mary C. *Slave Life in Rio de Janeiro, 1808–1850*. Princeton: Princeton University Press, 1987.

Karttunen, Frances. "Nahuatl Literacy." In *The Inca and Aztec States, 1400–1800: Anthropology and History*, edited by George A. Collier, Renato I. Rosaldo and John D. Wirth, 395–417. New York: Academic Press, 1982.

Keen, Benjamin, ed. *Latin American Civilization*. Third ed. 2 vols. Boston: Houghton Mifflin, 1974.

Kellogg, Susan. *Law and the Transformation of Aztec Culture, 1500–1700*. Norman, Okla.: University of Oklahoma Press, 1995.

Konetzke, Richard. "La Formación de la Nobleza en Indias." *Anuario de Estudios Americanos* 3, no. 10 (1951): 329–57.

Kraay, Hendrik. "The Politics of Race in Independence-Era Bahia: The Black Militia Officers of Salvador, 1790–1840." In *Afro-Brazilian Culture and Politics: Bahia, 1790s–1990s*, edited by Hendrik Kraay, 30–56. Armonk, N.Y.: M. E. Sharpe, 1998.

Ladd, Doris M. *The Mexican Nobility at Independence, 1780–1826*. Austin: University of Texas Press, 1976.

Landers, Jane G. "Francisco Xavier Sánchez, *Floridano* Planter." In *Spanish Pathways in Florida*, edited by Ann L. Henderson and Gary R Mormino, 168–87. Sarasota: Pineapple Press, 1991.

————. *Black Society in Spanish Florida*. Urbana and Chicago: University of Illinois Press, 1999.

————, ed. *Against the Odds: Free Blacks in the Slave Societies of the Americas*. London: Frank Cass, Inc., 1996.

Larson, Brooke. "Caciques, Class Structure and the Colonial State in Bolivia." *Nova Americana* 2 (1979): 197–235.

————. *Cochabamba, 1550–1900: Colonialism and Agrarian Transformation in Bolivia*. Second ed. Durham: Duke University Press, 1998.

Lavallé, Bernard. "Divorcio y Nulidad de Matrimonio en Lima (1650–1700) (La Desavenencia Conyugal Como Indicator Social)." *Revista Andina* 4, no. 2 (1986): 427–64.

Lavrin, Asunción. "Sexuality in Colonial Mexico: A Church Dilemma." In *Sexuality and Marriage in Colonial Latin America*, edited by Asunción Lavrin, 47–95. Lincoln: University of Nebraska Press, 1989.

Lavrin, Asunción, ed. *Sexuality and Marriage in Colonial Latin America*. Lincoln: University of Nebraska Press, 1989.

Leonard, Irving. *Books of the Brave*. Berkeley: University of California Press, 1992.

Lewin, Boleslao. *Tupac Amaru el Rebelde: Su época, sus Luchas y su Influencia en el Continente*. Buenos Aires, 1943.

Lewin, Linda. "Natural and Spurious Children in Brazilian Inheritance Law from Colony to Empire: A Methodological Essay." *The Americas* 48, no. 3 (1992): 351–396.

Lipsett-Rivera, Sonya. "*De Obra y Palabra*: Patterns of Insults in Mexico, 1750–1856." *The Americas* 54, no. 4 (1998): 511–39.

————. "A Slap in the Face of Honor: Social Transgression and Women in Late-Colonial Mexico." In *The Faces of Honor: Sex, Shame, and Violence in Colonial Latin America*, edited by Lyman Johnson and Sonya Lipsett-Rivera, 179–200. Albuquerque: University of New Mexico Press, 1998.

Lockhart, James. *Spanish Peru, 1532–1560: A Colonial Society*. Madison: University of Wisconsin Press, 1968.

————. *The Nahuas After the Conquest: A Social and Cultural History of the Indians of Central Mexico, Sixteenth through Eighteenth Centuries*. Stanford: Stanford University Press, 1992.

Lohmann Villena, Guillermo. *Los Americanos en las Ordenes Nobilarias (1529–1900)*. 2 vols. Madrid: CSIC, 1947.

López, Adalberto. *The Revolt of the Comuneros*. Cambridge: Cambridge University Press, 1976.

Lovell, W. George, and Christopher H. Lutz, eds. *Demography and Empire: A Guide to the Population History of Spanish Central America, 1500–1821*. Boulder and San Francisco: Westview Press, 1995.

Lunenfeld, Marvin, ed. *1492: Discovery, Invasion, Encounter—Sources and Interpretations*. Lexington, Mass.: D.C. Heath and Company, 1991.

Lutz, Christopher. *Santiago de Guatemala, 1541–1773: City, Caste, and the Colonial Experience*. Norman: University of Oklahoma Press, 1994.

MacCormack, Sabine. "From the Sun of the Incas to the Virgin of Copacabana." *Representations* 8 (1984): 30–60.

Maravall, José Antonio. *Poder, Honor y Elites en el Siglo XVII*. 3rd ed. Madrid: Siglo XXI Editores, 1979.

Martin, Cheryl. "Popular Speech and Social Order in Northern New Mexico, 1650–1830." *Comparative Studies in Society and History* 32, no. 2 (1990): 305–24.

Martínez-Alier, Verena. "Elopement and seduction in nineteenth-century Cuba." *Past and Present* 55 (1972): 91–129.

Mattoso, Kátia M. de Queirós. "A família e o direito no Brasil no século XIX: subsídios jurídicos para os estudos em história social." *Anais do Arquivo Público do Estado da Bahia* 44 (1979): 217–44.

———. *To Be a Slave in Brazil, 1550–1888*. Translated by Arthur Goldhammer. New Brunswick: Rutgers University Press, 1986.

McBrien, Richard P., ed. *The Harper Collins Encyclopedia of Catholicism*. New York: Harper Collins Publishers, Inc., 1995.

McCaa, Robert. "Marriage, Migration and Settling Down: Parral, Nueva Vizcaya, 1770–1778." In *Migration in Colonial Spanish America*, edited by David J. Robinson, 212–37. Cambridge: Cambridge University Press, 1990.

McKnight, Kathryn Joy. "Blasphemy as Resistance: An African Slave Woman before the Mexican Inquisition." In *Women in the Inquisition: Spain and the New World*, edited by Mary Giles, 229–53. Baltimore: Johns Hopkins University Press, 1999.

Melville, Elinor. *A Plague of Sheep: The Environmental Consequences of the Conquest of Mexico*. Cambridge: Cambridge University Press, 1994.

Mendoza, Gunnar. "Guía de Fuentes Inéditas en el Archivo Nacional de Bolivia para el Estudio de la Administración Virreinal en el Distrito de la Audiencia de Charcas, Años 1537–1700." In *Guía de Las Fuentes en Hispanoamérica para el Estudio de la Administración Virreinal Española en México y en el Perú, 1535–1700*, edited by Lewis Hanke and Gunnar Mendoza, 46–255. Washington, D.C.: Organization of American States, 1980.

Metcalf, Alida. "Fathers and Sons: The Politics of Inheritance in a Colonial Brazilian Township." *Hispanic American Historical Review* 66, no. 3 (1986): 455–84.

———. *Family and Frontier in Colonial Brazil: Santana de Parnaíba, 1580–1822*. Berkeley: University of California Press, 1992.

Miller, Gary M. "Bourbon Social Engineering: Women and Conditions of Marriage in Eighteenth-Century Venezuela." *The Americas* 46, no. 3 (1990): 261–90.

Mills, Kenneth. *Idolatry and its Enemies: Colonial Andean Religion and Extirpation, 1640–1750*. Princeton: Princeton University Press, 1997.

Mills, Kenneth, and William B. Taylor, eds. *Colonial Spanish America: A Documentary History*. Wilmington, Del.: Scholarly Resources, 1998.

Moliner, María. *Diccionario de uso del español*. 2 vols. Madrid: Editorial Gredos, 1984.

Monteiro, John. "From Indian to Slave: Forced Native Labour and Colonial Society in São Paulo during the Seventeenth Century." *Slavery and Abolition* 9, no. 2 (1988): 105–27.

Monter, William. "Women and the Italian Inquisitions." In *Women in the Middle Ages and the Renaissance: Literary and Historical Perspectives*, edited by Mary Beth Rose. Syracuse, 1986.

Morse, Richard. *The Bandeirantes: The Historical Role of the Brazilian Pathfinders*. New York: Knopf, 1965.

Motolinía, Fray Toribio de. *Memoriales de Fray Toribio de Motolinía, manuscrito de la colección del Señor Don Joaquin García Icazbalceta. Publícalo por primera vez su hijo Luis García Pimental*. Mexico City, Paris, and Madrid, 1903.

Murra, John V. "An Aymara Kingdom in 1567." *Ethnohistory* 15, no. 2 (1968): 115–51.

———. "Andean Societies Before 1532." In *Cambridge History of Latin America*, edited by Leslie Bethell, 59–90. Cambridge: Cambridge University Press, 1984.

Murray, Jacqueline, and Konrad Eisenbichler, eds. *Desire and Discipline: Sex and Sexuality in the Premodern West*. Toronto: University of Toronto Press, 1996.

Myers, Kathleen. "Testimony for Canonization or Proof of Blasphemy? The New Spanish Inquisition and the Hagiographic Biography of Catarina de San Juan." In *Women in the Inquisition: Spain and the New World*, edited by Mary Giles, 270–96. Baltimore: Johns Hopkins University Press, 1999.

Nader, Helen. *Liberty in Absolutist Spain: The Hapsburg Sale of Towns, 1516–1700*. Baltimore: Johns Hopkins University Press, 1990.

Nazzari, Muriel. "Parents and Daughters: Change in the Practice of Dowry in São Paulo, 1600–1770." *Hispanic American Historical Review* 70, no. 4 (1990): 639–65.

———. *Disappearance of the Dowry: Women, Families, and Social Change in São Paulo, Brazil (1600–1900)*. Stanford: Stanford University Press, 1991.

———. "Transition Toward Slavery: Changing Legal Practice Regarding Indians in Seventeenth-Century São Paulo." *The Americas* 49, no. 2 (October) (1992): 131–55.

Newson, Linda. *Life and Death in Early Colonial Ecuador*. Norman: University of Oklahoma Press, 1995.

Nishida, Mieko. "Manumission and Ethnicity in Urban Slavery: Salvador, Brazil, 1808–1888." *Hispanic American Historical Review* 73, no. 3 (1993): 361–91.

O'Phelan-Godoy, Scarlett. "Rebellions and Revolt in Eighteenth Century Perú and Upper Perú." *Latinamerikanische Forschungen* 14 (1985).

Pardo, J. Joaquin, Pedro Zamora Castellanos, and Luis Lujan Muñoz. *Guía de Antigua Guatemala*. Second ed. Guatemala, 1968.

Parry, John H., and Robert G. Keith, eds. *New Iberian World: A Documentary History of the Discovery and Settlement of Latin America to the Early 17th Century*. 5 volumes. New York: Times Book, 1984.

Penyak, Lee Michael. "Criminal Sexuality in Central Mexico, 1750–1850." Ph.D. dissertation, University of Connecticut, 1993.

Pérez-Marchand, Monalisa Lina. *Dos Etapas Ideológicas del Siglo XVIII en México a Través de los Papeles de la Inquisición*. México: UNAM, 1945.

Peristiany, John G., and Pitt-Rivers, Julian, eds. *Honor and Grace in Anthropology*. Cambridge: Cambridge University Press, 1992.

Perry, Mary Elizabeth. "Beatas and the Inquisition in Early Modern Seville." In *Inquisition and Society in Early Modern Europe*, edited by Stephen Haliczer, 147–67. London: Croom Helm, 1987.

———. *Gender and Disorder in Early Modern Seville*. Princeton: Princeton University Press, 1990.

Perry, Mary Elizabeth, and Anne J. Cruz, eds. *Cultural Encounters: The Impact of the Inquisition in Spain and the New World*. Berkeley and Los Angeles: University of California Press, 1991.

Pitt-Rivers, Julian. "Honour and Social Status." In *Honour and Shame: The Values of Mediterranean Society*, edited by John G. Peristiany, 19–77. Chicago: The University of Chicago Press, 1966.

Platt, Tristan. "Liberalism and Ethnocide in the Southern Andes." *History Workshop Journal* 17 (1984): 3–18.

———. "The Andean Experience of Bolivian Liberalism, 1825–1900: Roots of Rebellion in 19th-Century Chayanta (Potosí)." In *Resistance, Rebellion, and Consciousness in the Andean Peasant World, 18th to 20th Centuries*, edited by Steve J. Stern, 280–323. Madison: University of Wisconsin Press, 1987.

Poole, Deborah A. "A One-Eyed Gaze: Gender in 19th Century Illustration of Peru." *Dialectical Anthropology* 13 (1988): 333–64.

Poole, Stafford. *Pedro Moya de Contreras: Catholic Reform and Royal Power in New Spain, 1571–1591*. Berkeley: University of California Press, 1987.

Powers, Karen Vieira. *Andean Journeys: Migration, Ethnogenesis and the State in Colonial Quito*. Albuquerque: University of New Mexico Press, 1995.

Ramos, Donald. "Marriage and the Family in Colonial Vila Rica." *Hispanic American Historical Review* 55, no. 2 (1975): 200–25.

Rappaport, Joanne. *The Politics of Memory: Native Historical Interpretation in the Colombian Andes*. Cambridge: Cambridge University Press, 1990.

Rasnake, Roger. *Domination and Cultural Resistance: Authority and Power Among an Andean People*. Durham: Duke University Press, 1988.

Real Academia Española. *Diccionario de Autoridades*. 3 vols. Madrid: Editorial Gredos, [1726–1739] 1979.

Reichel-Dolmatoff, Gerardo. *Colombia*. London: Thames and Hudson, 1965.

Reis, João José. *Slave Rebellion in Brazil: The Muslim Uprising of 1835 in Bahia*. Translated by Arthur Brakel. Baltimore: Johns Hopkins University Press, 1993.

———. "'Death to the Cemetery': Funerary Reform and Rebellion in Salvador, Brazil, 1836." In *Riots in the Cities: Popular Politics and the Urban Poor in Latin America*, edited by Silvia M. Arrom and Servando Ortoll, 97–113. Wilmington, Del.: Scholarly Resources, 1996.

———. *Death is a Festival*. Translated by Sabrina Gledhill. Chapel Hill: University of North Carolina Press, forthcoming.

Restall, Matthew. "'He Wished It in Vain': Subordination and Resistance among Maya Women in Post-Conquest Yucatan." *Ethnohistory* 42, no. 4 (1995): 577–94.

———. *The Maya World: Yucatec Culture and Society, 1550–1850*. Stanford: Stanford University Press, 1997.

———. *Maya Conquistador*. Boston: Beacon Press, 1998.

Ricard, Robert. *The Spiritual Conquest of Mexico. An Essay on the Apostolate and the Evangelizing Methods of the Mendicant Orders in New Spain, 1523–1572*. Edited and translated by Lesley Byrd Simpson. Berkeley: University of California Press, 1966.

Rípodaz Ardanaz, Daisy. *El Matrimonio en Indias: Realidad Social y Regulación Jurídica*. Buenos Aires: Fundación para la Educación, la Ciencia y la Cultura, 1977.

Rivera Ayala, Sergio. "Lewd Songs and Dances from the Streets of Eighteenth-Century New Spain." In *Rituals of Rule, Rituals of Resistance: Public Celebrations and Popular Culture in Mexico*, edited by William H. Beezley, Cheryl Martin, and William French, 27–46. Wilmington, Delaware: Scholarly Resources Press, 1994.

Rocke, Michael. *Forbidden Friendships: Homosexuality and Male Culture in Renaissance Florence*. New York and Oxford: Oxford University Press, 1996.

Rodríguez Freyle, Juan. *El Carnero*. Caracas: Biblioteca Ayacucho, 1979.

Rodríguez O., Jaime E. *The Independence of Spanish America*. Cambridge: Cambridge University Press, 1998.

Rowe, John. "El Movimiento Nacional Inca." In *Tupac Amaru II-1780*, edited by Alberto Flores Galindo. Lima, 1976.

Ruggiero, Guido. *The Boundaries of Eros: Sex Crime and Sexuality in Renaissance Venice*. New York and Oxford: Oxford University Press, 1985.

———. *Binding Passions: Tales of Magic, Marriage, and Power at the End of the Renaissance*. New York and Oxford: Oxford University Press, 1993.

Russell-Wood, A. J. R. *The Black Man in Freedom and Slavery in Colonial Brazil*. London: MacMillan, 1982.

Saldivar, Gabriel. *Historia de la Música en México*. Toluca, Mexico: Gobierno del Estado de México, 1980.

Salomon, Frank. *Native Lords of Quito in the Age of the Inca: The Political Economy of North Andean Chiefdoms*. Cambridge: Cambridge University Press, 1986.

Santamaría, Francisco J. *Diccionario de mejicanismos*. Mexico City: Editorial Porrúa, 1959.

Schwaller, John Frederick. *The Church and Clergy in Sixteenth-Century Mexico*. Albuquerque: University of New Mexico Press, 1987.

Schwartz, Stuart B. *Sugar Plantations in the Formation of Brazilian Society: Bahia, 1550–1835*. Cambridge: Cambridge University Press, 1985.

———. *Slaves, Peasants, and Rebels: Reconsidering Brazilian Slavery*. Urbana: University of Illinois Press, 1992.

Seed, Patricia. *To Love, Honor, and Obey in Colonial Mexico: Conflicts over Marriage Choice, 1574–1821*. Stanford: Stanford University Press, 1988.

Serulnikov, Sergio. "Disputed Images of Colonialism: Spanish Rule and Indian Subversion in Northern Potosí, 1777–1780." *Hispanic American Historical Review* 76, no. 2 (1996): 189–226.

Silva, Maria Beatriz Nizza da. "Family and Property in Colonial Brazil." *Portuguese Studies* 7 (1991): 61–77.

Silverblatt, Irene. *Moon, Sun, and Witches: Gender Ideologies and Class in Inca and Colonial Peru*. Princeton: Princeton University Press, 1987.

Socolow, Susan M. "Acceptable Partners: Marriage Choice in Colonial Argentina, 1778–1810." In *Sexuality and Marriage in Colonial Latin America*, edited by Asunción Lavrin, 209–51. Lincoln: University of Nebraska Press, 1989.

Spalding, Karen. "Social Climbers: Changing Patterns of Mobility Among the Indians of Colonial Peru." *Hispanic American Historical Review* 53 (1970): 645–64.

———. *Huarochirí: An Andean Society Under Inca and Spanish Rule*. Stanford: Stanford University Press, 1984.

Bibliography

Spurling, Geoffrey. "Honor, Sexuality, and the Colonial Church: The Sins of Dr. González, Cathedral Canon." In *The Faces of Honor: Sex, Shame, and Violence in Colonial Latin America*, edited by Lyman Johnson and Sonya Lipsett-Rivera, 45–67. Albuquerque: University of New Mexico Press, 1998.

Stavig, Ward. "Ethnic Conflict, Moral Economy, and Population in Rural Cuzco on the Eve of the Thupa Amaro II Rebellion." *Hispanic American Historical Review* 68, no. 4 (1988): 737–70.

———. "'Living in Offense of Our Lord': Indigenous Sexual Values and Marital Life in the Colonial Crucible." *Hispanic American Historical Review* 74, no. 4 (1995): 597–622.

———. *The World of Túpac Amaru: Conflict, Community, and Identity in Colonial Peru*. Lincoln: University of Nebraska Press, 1999.

Stern, Steve J., ed. *Resistance, Rebellion, and Consciousness in the Andean Peasant World, 18th to 20th Centuries*. Madison: University of Wisconsin Press, 1987.

Stern, Steve J. *The Secret History of Gender: Women, Men, and Power in Late Colonial Mexico*. Chapel Hill: University of North Carolina Press, 1995.

Stewart, Frank H. *Honor*. Chicago: The University of Chicago Press, 1994.

Stroud, Matthew D. *Fatal Union: A Pluralistic Approach to the Spanish Wife-Murder Comedias*. Lewisburg, Penn.: Bucknell University Press, 1990.

Taylor, William B. *Drinking, Homicide, and Rebellion in Colonial Mexican Villages*. Stanford: Stanford University Press, 1979.

———. *Magistrates of the Sacred: Parish Priests and Indian Parishioners in Eighteenth-Century Mexico*. Stanford: Stanford University Press, 1996.

Thomson, Sinclair. "Colonial Crisis, Community, and Andean Self-Rule: Aymara Politics in the Age of Insurgency (Eighteenth-Century La Paz)." Ph.D. dissertation, University of Wisconsin, 1996.

Toledo, Francisco de. *Disposiciones Gubernativas Para El Virreinato del Perú, 1569–1574*. Transcribed by María Justina Sarabia Viejo. 2 vols. Sevilla: Escuela de Estudios Hispano-Americanos, 1986.

Traslosheros H., Jorge E. "Los motivos de una monja: Sor Feliciana de San Francisco. Valladolid de Michoacán, 1632–1655." *Historia Mexicana* 47, no. 4 (1998):735–64.

Trexler, Richard C. *Sex and Conquest: Gendered Violence, Political Order, and the European Conquest of the Americas*. Ithaca: Cornell University Press, 1995.

Tutino, John. *From Insurrection to Revolution in Mexico: Social Bases of Agrarian Violence, 1750–1940*. Princeton: Princeton University Press, 1986.

Twinam, Ann. "Honor, Sexuality, and Illegitimacy in Colonial Spanish America." In *Sexuality and Marriage Colonial Latin America*, edited by Asunción Lavrín, 118–55. Lincoln and London: University of Nebraska Press, 1989.

———. *Public Lives, Private Secrets: Gender, Honor, Sexuality, and Illegitimacy in Colonial Spanish America*. Stanford: Stanford University Press, 1999.

Usner, Daniel H., Jr. *Indians, Settlers, and Slaves in a Frontier Exchange Economy: The Lower Mississippi Valley before 1783*. Chapel Hill: University of North Carolina Press (for the Institute of Early American History and Culture), 1992.

van Deusen, Nancy E. "Determining the Boundaries of Virtue: The Discourse of *Recogimiento* among Women in Seventeenth-Century Lima." *The Journal of Family History* 22, no. 4 (1997): 373–89.

Van Young, Eric. "The Mad Messiah of Durango and Popular Rebellion in Mexico, 1800–1815." *Comparative Studies in Society and History* 21 (1986): 386–413.

———. "Islands in the Storm: Quiet Cities and Violent Countrysides in the Mexican Independence Era." *Past & Present* 118 (1988): 130–55.

———. "The Cuautla Lazarus: Double Subjectivities in Reading Texts on Popular Collective Action." *Colonial Latin American Review* 2 (1993): 55–79.

Villamarín, Juan A., and Judith E. Villamarín. "The Concept of Nobility in Colonial Santa Fe de Bogotá." In *Essays in the Political, Economic, and Social History of Colonial Latin America*, edited by Karen Spalding, 125–53. Newark: University of Delaware Press, 1982.

Viqueira Albán, Pedro. *¿Relajados o Reprimidos? Diversiones Públicas y Vida Social en la Ciudad de México Durante el Siglo de las Luces*. Mexico: Fondo de Cultura Económica, 1987.

Warren, Kay. "Interpreting *La Violencia* in Guatemala: Shapes of Maya Silence and Resistance." In *The Violence Within: Cultural and Political Opposition in Divided Nations*, edited by Kay B. Warren. Boulder and San Francisco: Westview Press, 1993.

Windler, Christian. *Elites Locales, Señores, Reformistas: Redes Clientelares y Monarquía Hacia Finales del Antiguo Régimen*. Seville: Universidad de Córdoba & Universidad de Sevilla, 1997.

Sources and Credits for Illustrations

Maps 2 and 4: The approximate boundaries of viceroyalty, captaincy, and *audiencia* districts are adapted from Cathryn L. Lombardi, John V. Lombardi, and K. Lynn Stoner, *Latin American History: A Teaching Atlas* (Madison: University of Wisconsin Press, 1983).

Figures 1, 8, 9, and 17: Linati, Claudio. *Trajes Civiles, Militares, y Religiosos de México (1828)*. Translated by Justino Fernández. Mexico City: Imprenta Universitaria, Universidad Nacional Autónoma de México, [1828] 1956. Courtesy of the Instituto de Investigaciones Estéticas, Universidad Nacional Autónoma de México.

Figures 2, 3, 4, and 7: Guaman Poma de Ayala, Felipe. *El primer nueva corónica y buen gobierno*. Edited by John V. Murra and Rolena Adorno. 3 vols. México: Siglo Veintiuno, [1615] 1980. Courtesy of Siglo Veintiuno Editores.

Figures 5 and 10: Martínez Compañón, D. Baltasar Jaime. *Trujillo del Perú a fines del Siglo XVIII*. Madrid, [1790] 1936.

Figure 6: Courtesy of The Bancroft Library.

Figures 11 and 12: Courtesy of the Archivo Histórico del Banco Central, Quito.

Figure 13: Courtesy of Ken Barrett, Jr. (Copyright © 1998, Ken Barrett, Jr.)

Figure 14: Courtesy of the Florida State Archives.

Figure 15: Debret, Jean Baptiste. *Voyage pittoresque et historique au Brésil, ou séjour d'un artiste français au Brésil, depuis 1816 jusqu'en 1831 inclusivement, époques de l'avénement et de l'abdication de S.M. D. Pedro Ier. fondateur de l'empire brésilien*. 3 vols. Paris: Firmin Didot Frères, 1834–1839.

Figure 16: Vilhena, Luiz dos Santos. *Recopilação de noticias soteropolitanas e brasilicas*. 2 vols. Edited by Braz do Amaral. Salvador: Imprensa Official do Estado, 1922.

Contributors

THOMAS A. ABERCROMBIE is Associate Professor of Anthropology at New York University. He received his Ph.D. in social anthropology in 1986 from the University of Chicago. Recent publications include: *Pathways of Memory and Power: Ethnography and History Among an Andean People* (Madison, 1998); "Tributes to Bad Conscience: Charity, Restitution, and Inheritance in Cacique and Encomendero Testaments of Sixteenth-Century Charcas," in Susan Kellogg and Matthew Restall, eds., *Dead Giveaways* (Salt Lake City, 1998); "Q'aqchas and the Plebe in Rebellion: Carnival vs. Lent in 18th-Century Potosi," *Journal of Latin American Anthropology*, 1996; "El carnaval postcolonial de Oruro: Clase, etnicidad, y nacionalismo en la danza folklórica," *Revista Andina*, 1992.

CHRISTON I. ARCHER (Ph.D. in Latin American History, State University of New York at Stony Brook, 1971), is Professor of History at the University of Calgary. He has written extensively on the army of New Spain and on the insurgency. His works include *The Army in Bourbon Mexico* (Albuquerque, 1971), which won the Bolton Prize and the Pacific Coast Branch, American Historical Association Prize. He is currently working on the royalist army in New Spain during the struggle for independence and on Spanish marine history in the eighteenth century.

WOODROW BORAH, Professor Emeritus of History at the University of California, Berkeley, has been producing scholarly works of fundamental importance in the field of Latin American history for more than 50 years. He has written on population history, trade and commerce, colonial governance, social welfare, the seventeenth-century depression, urbanization, and price history. He received the Bolton Prize for his *Justice by Insurance: The General Indian Court of Colonial Mexico and the Legal Aides of the Half-Real* (Berkeley and Los Angeles, 1983).

RICHARD BOYER, Professor of History at Simon Fraser University, received a Ph.D. in Latin American history from the University of Connecticut. In recent years he has been working mainly with Inquisition records in an effort to better understand the "small people" of colonial Mexico. His *Lives of the Bigamists: Marriage, Family, and Community in Colonial Mexico* (Albuquerque, 1995) was awarded the Wallace K. Ferguson Prize by the Canadian Historical Association.

CHRISTIAN BÜSCHGES received his Ph.D. in colonial social history at the University of Cologne. He is the author of *Familie, Ehre und Macht. Konzept und soziale Wirklichkeit des Adels in der Stadt Quito (Ecuador) während der späten Kolonialzeit (1765–1822)* (Stuttgart, 1996) and has published several articles, including most recently "Urban Public Festivals as Representations and Elements of Social Order in Colonial Ecuador," in *Observation and Communication: The Construction of Realities in the Hispanic World*, edited by Tamar Herzog and Johannes-Michael Scholz (Frankfurt/Main, 1997), and "Eugenio Espejo, la Ilustración y las Elites," in *Jahrbuch für Geschichte von Staat, Wirtschaft und Gesellschaft Lateinamerikas*, 1997. He is currently researching the sociopolitical history of the Spanish empire in the first half of the seventeenth century under a scholarship from the Deutsche Forschungs-gemeinschaft.

MARTHA FEW is Assistant Professor of Colonial Latin American History at the University of Miami. She received her Ph.D. from the University of Arizona in 1997 and is currently completing a book that analyzes the connections between gender, religion, and power in colonial Guatemala.

J. MICHAEL FRANCIS is Assistant Professor of History at the University of North Florida. He received his Ph.D. from the University of Cambridge in 1998 where, under the supervision of D. A. Brading, he wrote a dissertation that focused on the indigenous peoples of Colombia's eastern highlands in the sixteenth and seventeenth centuries. In 1998 he participated in the BBC production *The Lost World of El Dorado*, and now has another proposal dealing with pirates under review by the BBC and The Discovery Channel. He is currently preparing a book manuscript on the Muisca Indians under Spanish rule.

KIMBERLY S. HANGER was Associate Professor of History at the University of Tulsa. She received her doctorate in colonial Latin American history from the University of Florida. Her book *Bounded Lives, Bounded Places: Free Black Society in Colonial New Orleans, 1769–1803* (Durham, 1997) won the Kemper and Leila Williams Prize for the best book in Louisiana history published in that year. She also wrote *A Medley of Cultures: Louisiana History at the Cabildo* (Louisiana Museum Foundation, 1996), as well as numerous articles and essays. Kimberly S. Hanger died after a brief illness in March 1999.

JACQUELINE HOLLER received her Ph.D. from Emory University in 1998. She is currently a Social Sciences and Humanities Research Council Postdoctoral Fellow at Simon Fraser University. She has published articles in the *Journal of the Canadian Historical Association* and in Mary Giles, ed., *Women in the Inquisition: Spain and the New World* (Baltimore, 1998), and is currently revising her dissertation, "'Escogidas Plantas': Nuns and Beatas in Mexico City, 1531–1601," for publication.

REBECCA HORN is Associate Professor of History at the University of Utah. Her book, *Postconquest Coyoacan: Nahua-Spanish Relations in Central Mexico, 1519–1650*, studies Nahuas and Spaniards in the central Mexican jurisdiction of Coyoacan from the Spanish conquest until 1650, crafting a multidimensional portrait of their relations in both institutional and informal settings. She is Associate Editor of the Nahuatl Studies Series, a publication that presents the transcription, translation, and analysis of Nahuatl documents to students and scholars. She has research interests in colonial Mexico as well as comparative colonialism in the Americas.

HENDRIK KRAAY is Assistant Professor of History and Political Science at the University of Calgary, Calgary, Alberta, Canada. He received his Ph.D. from the University of Texas at Austin in 1995 and has most recently edited *Afro-Brazilian Culture and Politics: Bahia, 1790s–1990s* (M. E. Sharpe, 1998). He is now completing a book-length social history of Brazilian military institutions from the 1790s to the 1840s.

JANE LANDERS is Associate Professor of History at Vanderbilt University. She completed her Ph.D. at the University of Florida in Latin American History. Her newest publication is *Black Society in Spanish Florida* (Urbana, 1999). She has also edited *Against the Odds: Free Blacks in the Slave Societies of the Americas* (London, 1996) and co-edited *The African American Heritage of Florida* (Gainesville, 1995); her articles have appeared in *American Historical Review*, *Slavery and Abolition*, *The Americas*, *The New West Indian Guide*, and the *Colonial Latin American Historical Review*.

SONYA LIPSETT-RIVERA is Associate Professor in the History Department of Carleton University. She received her doctorate from Tulane University in 1988. Along with Lyman Johnson, she co-edited *The Faces of Honor: Sex, Shame, and Violence in Colonial Latin America* (Albuquerque: University of New Mexico Press, 1998). Her most recent articles are "*De Obra y Palabra*: Patterns of Insults in Mexico, 1750–1856" and "The Intersection of Rape and Marriage in Late-Colonial and Early Nineteenth-Century Mexico," which received honorable mention from the Conference on Latin American History in their article prize. Her book, *To Defend Our Water with the Blood of our Veins: The Struggle for Resources in Colonial Puebla*, is forthcoming with the University of New Mexico Press in 1999.

MURIEL NAZZARI received her Ph.D. from Yale University in 1986 and is now Associate Professor Emerita of History at Indiana University. Her publications include *Disappearance of the Dowry: Women, Family, and Social Change in São Paulo, Brazil (1600–1900)* (Stanford, 1991), "Concubinage in Colonial Brazil: The Inequalities of Race, Class, and Gender," in *Journal of Family History*, 1996, and "Widows as Obstacles to Business: British Objections to Brazilian Marriage and Inheritance Laws" in *Comparative Studies in Society and History*, 1995.

S. ELIZABETH PENRY is Assistant Professor of History at Fordham University. She earned her Ph.D. in Latin American History at the University of Miami in 1996. Currently she is engaged in research on the intellectual origins of indigenous political discourse as a National Endowment for the Humanities Fellow at the John Carter Brown Library (1998–99).

KAREN VIEIRA POWERS received her Ph.D. from New York University and is currently Associate Professor of Comparative Colonization in the Department of History at Northern Arizona University. She has written extensively on the Andean region. Her book, *Andean Journeys: Migration, Ethnogenesis, and the State in Colonial Quito* (Albuquerque, 1995), was awarded the Howard Francis Cline Memorial Prize by the Conference on Latin American History.

MATTHEW RESTALL was educated at Oxford University and UCLA, where he received his Ph.D. He is currently Associate Professor of Colonial Latin American History and Women's Studies at the Pennsylvania State University. He has published a number of articles and four books, including *The Maya World: Yucatec Culture and Society, 1550–1850* (Stanford, 1997) and *Maya Conquistador* (Boston, 1998).

SERGIO RIVERA AYALA is an Instructor at the Universidad Nacional Autónoma de México's School of Extension in Canada. He received his Ph.D. in Latin American Literature from Syracuse University (1998). His research focuses on the strategies of power in Colonial Mexican literature. He is currently working on a series of articles about the conceptions of colonial urban landscape and preparing his dissertation, "Space, Body and Power: Strategies of Colonial Discourse in Some Texts of New Spain," for publication.

JOHN F. SCHWALLER is the Associate Provost, Associate Vice President for Academic Affairs, and Professor of History at The University of Montana. He holds the Ph.D. in colonial Latin American history from Indiana University. He has written extensively on the history of the Church in early colonial Mexico, based on research in the Archive of the Cathedral of Mexico, the Archivo General de la Nación, and the Archivo General de Indias, among other repositories. He has also written about the Aztec language, Nahuatl.

SUSAN MIGDEN SOCOLOW, Dobbs Professor of Latin American History at Emory University and the current president of the Conference on Latin American History (CLAH), has worked extensively in the history of colonial Rio de la Plata. A graduate of Columbia University, Professor Socolow is the author of *The Merchants of Buenos Aires, 1778–1810:*

Family and Commerce and *The Bureaucrats of Buenos Aires, 1769–1810: Amor al real servicio.* She has also coedited *Cities and Society in Colonial Latin America* and *The Countryside in Colonial Latin America* and edited *The Atlantic Staple Trade.*

GEOFFREY SPURLING, Assistant Professor in the Latin American Studies Program at Simon Fraser University, completed his Ph.D. in anthropology at Cornell University. He has written on Andean social history and ethnohistory and is currently researching sexuality and politics in the early colonial period.

ALEX TAYLOR DEL CID is completing his doctoral degree on modern Argentina at the University of Calgary. He has a master's degree from the University of Saskatchewan and has extensive experience in the field of Central American history. He has published a number of articles in the field.

ANN TWINAM is Professor of History at the University of Cincinnati. She received her Ph.D. from Yale University (1976) and is the author of numerous articles as well as *Miners, Merchants and Farmers in Colonial Colombia* (Austin, 1982) and *Public Lives, Private Secrets: Gender, Honor, Sexuality and Illegitimacy in Colonial Spanish America* (Stanford, 1999).

NANCY VAN DEUSEN received her Ph.D. from the University of Illinois, Urbana-Champaign. She is Assistant Professor in History at Western Washington University. Her book manuscript, "Between the Sacred and the Worldly: *Recogimiento* for Women in Colonial Lima," is complete, and she recently published an article in the *Colonial Latin American Historical Review* on seventeenth-century lay pious houses for women.

Index

Note: Page numbers in *italics* indicate illustrations. Page numbers followed by "g" indicate a glossary entry.

Index

Index

Index